Feminist Critical Policy A

Education Policy Perspectives

General Editor: Ivor Goodson, Professor of Education, Warner Graduate School, University of Rochester, USA; Chair in Education, University of East Anglia, UK

Education policy analysis has long been a neglected area in the UK and, to an extent, in the USA and Australia. The result has been a profound gap between the study of education and the formulation of education policy. For practitioners, such a lack of analysis of new policy initiatives has worrying implications, particularly at a time of such policy flux and change. Education policy has, in recent years, been a matter for intense political debate – the political and public interest in the working of the system has come at the same time as the breaking of the consensus on education policy by the New Right. As never before, political parties and pressure groups differ in their articulated policies and prescriptions for the education sector. Critical thinking about these developments is clearly imperative.

All those working within the system also need information on policy-making, policy implementation and effective day-to-day operation. Pressure on schools from government, education authorities and parents has generated an enormous need for knowledge among those on the receiving end of educational policies.

This Falmer Press series aims to fill the academic gap, to reflect the politicalization of education, and to provide the practitioners with the analysis for informed implementation of policies that they will need. It offers studies in broad areas of policy studies, with a particular focus on the following areas: school organization and improvement; critical social analysis; policy studies and evaluation; and education and training.

Feminist Critical Policy Analysis I:
A Perspective from Primary and Secondary Schooling

Edited by

Catherine Marshall

 The Falmer Press

(A member of the Taylor & Francis Group)
London • Washington, D.C.

UK   Falmer Press, 1 Gunpowder Square, London, EC4A 3DE
USA   Falmer Press, Taylor & Francis Inc., 1900 Frost Road, Suite 101,
        Bristol, PA 19007

First published in 1997

**A catalogue record for this book is available from the British
Library**

ISBN 0 7507 0634 1 cased
ISBN 0 7507 0635 x paper

**Library of Congress Cataloging-in-Publication Data are
available on request**

Jacket design by Caroline Archer

Typeset in 10/12 pt, Times by
Graphicraft Typesetters Ltd., Hong Kong.

*Printed in Great Britain by Biddles Ltd., Guildford and King's Lynn on
paper which has a specified pH value on final paper manufacture of
not less than 7.5 and is therefore 'acid free'.*

Contents

Contents

Acknowledgments

The Editor and Publishers wish to thank the following for permission to reproduce articles:

Lois Weis, 'Gender and the reports: The case of the missing piece', in Ginzberg, R. and Plank, D., *Commissions, Reports, Reforms and Educational Policy*, pp. 173–92. Reprinted with permission of Greenwood Publishing Group, Inc., Westport, CT (1996).

Sandra Hollingsworth, 'Feminist praxis as the basis for teacher education: A critical challenge'. Portions were previously published as 'The problem of gender in teacher education', *Mid-Western Educational Researcher*, **8**(2), pp. 3–12 (1995). Reprinted with permission.

Dedication

To the thousands I've taught over decades, like Tammy and Beth, eighth-grade students in the 1970s. Beth earned good grades and wanted to be an astronaut; Tammy was in the low track and had learned to get by being seductive and sweet. I've wondered whether my teaching them US History, with asides on women's suffrage and Rosa Parks as a symbol in the Civil Rights movement, and projects documenting the portrayal of women on television and advertising, made any difference. This book intends to make a bigger difference.

Preface

Can the chair of the Senate Education Committee fathom the critical theorist's lecture on schooling and democratic practice? Will the board selecting the new chancellor understand the implications of the feminist critique of bureaucracy and leadership? Will the new Chancellor work with the senator who has raised those critiques to change the curriculum for training and certifying teachers and administrators so educators will work more for social justice? Will commissions making recommendations to support women in science and math find ways to understand the experience of women students and faculty? What kinds of analyses will gain policy attention for the non-participants – those who have received messages that they do not belong, that the education system does not really want their kind? Will those conducting the study of teacher incentive systems or funding for extracurricular activities include insights focusing on effects on women and girls? The purpose of *Feminist Critical Policy Analysis I: A Perspective from Primary and Secondary Schooling* is to move us closer to being able to say 'yes'.

Policy researchers and analysis have gained and retained legitimacy by focusing on the problems and methods identified by powerful people. Those with a different focus are silenced, declared irrelevant, postponed, coopted, 'put on the back burner', assigned responsibilities with no training, budget, personnel or time, or otherwise ignored. Policies – authoritative agreements among powerful people about how things should be – have been made without a feminist critical glance. These two volumes focus on those areas of silence, on the policy issues at the fringe and on the kinds of policy analysis methods, findings and recommendations that will disrupt but will also open possibilities. The two volumes identify theories and tools for dismantling and replacing the politics, theories and modes of policy analysis that built 'the master's house'. The individual chapters illustrate how and why to expand policy questions and policy analysis methods to incorporate critical and feminist lenses, demonstrating the promise of politics, analyses and policymaking that thoughtfully and thoroughly works to uncover any source of oppression, domination or marginalization and to create policies to meet the lived realities, needs, aspirations and values of women and girls and others kept on the margin.

The volumes name and develop a new field: Feminist Critical Policy Analysis. The promise of this field lies in its incorporation of perspectives that 'write against the grain': the feminist critical stance with policy analysis that includes methods for focusing on the cultural values bases of policies; deconstruction of policy documents; analysis of a policy intention and its potential effects (for example, affirmative action and, Title IX); studies of the micropolitical (for example, the dynamics of a school board task force on sexual harassment, a tenure system's effect on women academics, or the role of girls' access to computers in the implementation of computer policies); and analyses of policies, programs and political stances that *do* focus on neglected needs in schooling.

Policymakers and analysts need to pause in order to recognize how issues of gender, the needs of particular groups like the urban poor, women and non-dominant nationalities are left out of education policy analyses. In order to connect effectively, women need to take a hard look at the structures and arenas of policy. By presenting literatures, methods and examples, these books name the field: feminist critical policy analysis leaps at the challenge.

The challenge emerged from a cavernous silence at the American Educational Research Association. Background: I was asked, several years ago, to write a chapter on 'The future: Challenging theories and methods' for the *Politics of Education Yearbook*. In the crowded AERA symposium celebrating and presenting the *Yearbook*, the symbolic silence of the discussant and the audience reaction to our presentation 'Rethinking the public and private spheres: Feminist and cultural studies perspectives on the politics of education' (Marshall and Anderson, 1995) helped me see how unfamiliar and scary the feminist agenda must be to politics of education and public administration professors, policy analysts and political scientists. We were challenging not only their views of literatures, policy arenas and issues, and modes of analysis, but also their power to dominate a field, their work environments and perhaps their personal relationships!

Similarly, as I wandered through and beyond familiar liberal texts (including my own) on ways to make education systems more equitable, studies of women's and girls' experiences in education and feminist literatures, I saw a need to connect, to weave those understandings with the realities of power and politics. 'We must always think political when we think educational' (Apple, 1994: 350).

'Critical feminist consultant – that's an oxymoron', Gary Anderson and I concluded; we had drawn a blank trying to figure out which directors, deans, school boards, or legislators would hire us to tell them how they were being oppressive. We also had fun trying to figure out what critical feminist consultants would wear. Although these volumes provide examples of what the feminist critical policy analyst can do, they may not provide a fashion guide.

The world of the legislators, lobbyists and analysts that I met in state capitals – their days, their careers, and their agendas – are foreign to feminists concerned with widening the canon, with feminist pedagogy, with women's feeling undervalued on university faculties, with girls' turning away from math and science. In turn, the world and words of critical theorists, women's studies scholars, feminist poststructuralists, are foreign, and often offensive (in all senses of the word) to those who fit well into the policy world, those who think of bottom lines and tangible outcomes, and those whose careers depend upon their managing to garner support from voters and powerful groups. Policy analysis *can* be the communication device between the worlds of policymakers and those of critical and feminist scholars.

My tasks, conceptualizing and creating these volumes, were supported by an international network, enabling me to include analyses from six different countries, from all levels of education systems, from new as well as experienced scholars, with chapters ranging from the microinteractions of identity politics to the macro-arena analyses of major education reform documents. Special thanks to Sandra Acker, Yvonna Lincoln, Sheila Slaughter, Carmen Luke and Estela Bensimon for providing insights and connections for the postsecondary world, and to the Queensland University of Technology in Brisbane for the fellowship that cemented my connections to gender equity policy analysis internationally. A range of individuals provided assistance in finding good authors: thanks to Gaby Weiner, Lynda Stone, Jean Patterson, Cindy Gerstl-Pepin, Kerstin Carlson-LeFloch, Linda Grant and John Schopler, for insights, reactions, edits and connections.

Finally, taking off from Lorde's provocative statement, 'The master's tools will never dismantle the master's house', (1984: 112), these two volumes analyze what goes on in the master's house (Part I, The Legitimatized Formal Arenas of Policy) and how the master's tools keep women's needs silent and off-agenda (Part II, The Politics of Silence and Ambiguity). The volumes also contribute to fashioning new tools (Part III, New Politics, New Policy) by presenting cases where women's values and needs were heard amid discussions of feminist, postpositivist and critical policy analysis.

References

APPLE, M. (1994) 'Texts and contexts: The state and gender in educational policy', *Curriculum Inquiry*, **24**(3), pp. 349–59.
LORDE, A. (1984) *Sister Outsider: Freedom*, GA, Crossing Press.
MARSHALL, C. and ANDERSON, G. (1995) 'Rethinking the private and public spheres: Feminist and cultural studies perspectives on the politics of education', in SCRIBNER, J. and LAYTON, D. (Eds) *The Study of Educational Politics*, London, Falmer Press.

Catherine Marshall
Chapel Hill, NC
August 1996

Chapter 1

Dismantling and Reconstructing Policy Analysis

Catherine Marshall

Dismantling Policy Analysis[1]

'It's really an indictment on us and on our society when 12- and 13-year-olds don't see their future beyond having a baby', said Dr Henry Foster, President Clinton's advisor on teen pregnancy (Paik, 1995). Yet, it seems impossible to connect such statements to a focus on education policies for girls. And what about others at the margin in schools – boys who are not on sports teams, kids who do not wear the right shoes, whose families do not speak the right language. Policymakers focus on the guns-and-knives school violence but do not include sexual harassment as a school violence issue. Can our policy literatures change this? Can critical and feminist theory reframe the policy world?

Do policymakers pay more attention to the outcomes-focused analyses reporting numbers of girls-in-math per dollar spent for special programs or to the story of the 14-year-old skipping class, embarrassed and confused about her algebra teacher's exuberant compliments on her figure? What goes on in shaping training, certification, selection and promotion of educational administrators that ensures white male dominance and leaders oriented toward bureaucratic maintenance? These are feminist and critical policy questions, often neglected. This chapter dismantles policy analysis in order to open, widen and reframe policy questions and methods.[2] It introduces the perspectives and literatures that underpin feminist critical policy analysis, perspectives illustrated in the ensuing chapters, focusing on policy agendas and arenas for elementary and secondary schooling.[3]

How can we publish and use analyses of teachers' status and work lives which blithely skip over the significance of the fact that most teachers are white women (as in Rowan, 1994). How can we *not notice* that Oakes' (1985) book on tracking focuses on race and class inequities and makes no connection to gender? How can we cooperate with education systems that support the persistent underrepresentation of women and minorities in administrative and policy positions in education (Bell and Chase, 1993; Ortiz and Marshall, 1988), defining it as an issue of competency and/or access. How can school leaders countenance reforms that sweep past, or under the rug, concerns about persistent race, class and gender inequities? Why should schools continue informal curriculum practices that reinforce definitions of femininity and masculinity, ignoring how social constructions of gender limit and constrain human possibility? Why have reforms of schooling failed to challenge 'the "male-as-norm" conceptions of educational purpose, of students, of teachers, of curricula, of pedagogy, and of the profession of education' (Leach and Davies, 1990: 322).[4] Feminist critical policy analysis raises such questions.

We need theories and methods that integrate gender issues with the realities of power and politics. The master's tools must be cast aside, by bringing into question all things that were common sense, structured and assumed, from male–female difference to male norms of leadership and power. Integrating feminist and critical theory into policy analysis will add critical issues and ways of framing questions about power, justice and the state. All that is needed is the political choice to do so. Politics of education scholars can take the lead in this dismantling and reframing. Feminist critical policy analysis is research that conducts analyses *for* women while focusing on policy and politics. This perspective asks an often neglected question of every policy or political action: how is it affected by gender roles?

Curriculum theorists, education philosophers and researchers of teaching careers and classroom dynamics have made important contributions but few scholars in politics and policy have engaged with gender issues or reframed with feminist and critical perspectives. Feminist critical policy analysis is new and rare; it begins with the assumptions that gender inequity results from purposeful (if subconscious) choices to serve some in-group's ideology and purpose. It is research identifying how the political agenda benefitting white males is embedded in school structures and practices.

There is room for decades of policy research which asks first, how does this policy or structure exclude certain publics (subordinate nationalities, religions, women, the urban poor, the working class, homosexuals), then asks, what political arrangements support policies and structures that devalue alternative perspectives, that reinforce gender, ethnic/race and class inequities, and asks, who benefits from these arrangements, and finally, what are possible ways to restructure power dynamics and political arrangements to address issues of social justice? Also, scholars of politics of education can test their mettle on the array of related policy issues. What happens, for example, when we include gender issues, using models, concepts and methods developed from more mainstream policy issues like choice, desegregation, decentralization, inclusion, school finance or testing? Do the models and methods work? How are the issues redefined?

Such feminist and critical theory-driven questioning will not only inform gender equity issues, it will expand our models and methods. Looking at the more subtle and micropolitical, what happens when we ask deep questions about girls' and boys' negotiating identities in the mix of cultural messages about career choices: such feminist theory-driven questioning will reframe important findings about education policy.

Feminist critical policy analysis is ideological, centers on gender, states a clear values base, and identifies the formal and informal processes of power and policy that affect women's and men's advancement and full development. Feminist analysis assumes that where policy apparatus creates and maintains male-normed systems, gender issues, by definition, come to the policy system as a challenge, to be resisted. Thus, traditional policy analysis assumptions and methods will not suffice for examining areas of silence, taboo topics, hidden injuries, non-events, and non-decisions. This chapter argues the need to dismantle conventional and limiting definitions of policy analysis, offering the literatures for viewing policy culturally, for expanding methodologies for policy analysis, for incorporating feminist and critical theories. It demonstrates openings for a rich and democratizing agenda for education policy analysts to embrace.

What Needs Dismantling?

'For the master's tools will never dismantle the master's house' (Lorde, 1984: 112).

Knowledge, laws, traditions which developed in a public discourse dominated and peopled by white males has left us with constrained methods of policy analysis and 'partial and perverse understandings' (Harding, 1986: 26) from limited theoretical and political frameworks – greatly in need of dismantling. Critical and feminist education scholars, policy analysts and political scientists provide rationales for the dismantling by describing the limits of traditional, mainstream conceptions and methods and demanding a widened view of policy arenas, policy, policy discourse, politics and policy agendas. Traditional policy analysis is 'grounded in a narrow, falsely objective, overly instrumental view of rationality that masks its latent biases and allows policy elites and technocrats to present analyses and plans as neutral and objective when they are actually tied to prevailing relations of power' (Schram's 1995 review of Forester's stance: 375).

The appeal of traditional policy analysis.   Traditional policy analysis tries to identify and calculate effects of policies with apolitical, objective, neutral methods. Seeing social problems as diseases which have real causes and need real and/or symbolic solutions, they endeavor to assist and they assess the merits and efficacy of solution-implementations (Scheurich, 1994). This is appealing and fits with a dominant liberal optimism of educators and policymakers – an assumption that there will be decisionmakers who will assess, formulate and fund policies and programs that hold clear promise to promote a clearly defined and agreed-upon purpose.

   To be employed, to earn contracts, policy analysts must conduct studies that inform the policy debates raised in arenas of power. Thus, dominant values shape problem definitions and determine which are the relevant, significant questions, issues and answers (Scheurich, 1994). The questions and frameworks and the modes of analysis raised by feminist critical theory are excluded. Bias, power, and values *drive* the identification and legitimation of a problem and the methods seen as useful for studying and solving it. Whether its a cost–benefit analysis of university athletic programs or an analysis of women's studies programs, the questions, methods and policy-relevant recommendations will be those judged appropriate by dominant interests. Thus, traditional assumptions about value-free, neutral, objective

Catherine Marshall

research and analyses become devices that *guarantee* that dominant ways of thinking will be reinforced by the research and analyses. Further, power, bias and values
are embedded in institutions, such as legislatures, family and schools in ways that
affect what we do and do not *see* as problems; some become 'areas of silence'
(Anderson, 1993). By focusing on measurable, tangible facts that are part of public
arena discourse, policy issues are made logical/rational, fixable and free of issues
of power differentials.

For less partial analyses, political activism by the oppressed and silenced must
be exercised, in order to raise different questions. This book lays out literatures to
move to a widened view of policy.

Interconnections of politics and policy in education.   Politics and policy surround
educators. This chapter presents literatures that widen our definitions to encompass
the day-to-day politics and policies we live. When I teach my Politics of Education
class, I start with the formal arenas (Congress, state agencies, local boards), with
models and systems analysis and the policy issues in the *Education Week* headlines; students dutifully take notes. Their engagement deepens when we uncover
symbolic politics in studies of discrepancies between rhetoric, action and outcomes.
Then we get to micropolitics; they *know* those politics of interaction; they have felt
the politics of silencing; they have observed the politics of inattention and symbols-
manipulation. The next day I teach a different class on feminist issues in education,
where students read about the federal government's enforcement of Title IX and
about the politics of identity negotiation for adolescents in the context of schools'
informal curriculum. Down the hall are classes called Curriculum Theory, Program
Evaluation, Philosophy of Education. On the bulletin board, the job announcements
all have their affirmative action statements. Outside the front office, there's a sign
saying, 'If the Dean ain't happy, ain't NOBODY happy!', a notice of legislators'
latest budget slash, and someone from housekeeping (with a staff that is 95 per cent
African American) empties the trash bins. All of these are teaching about politics
of education; all are about policy arenas.

Cultural approaches in political science, feminist, cultural studies, critical and
postpositivist turns in education policy literature lead the critique and promising
new direction for policy analysis, broadening the arenas for analyses of power,
politics and policy.

Cultural Approaches to Political Arenas

By looking culturally, we can see values bubbling in a 'policy primeval soup'
cauldron (Kingdon, 1984) and focus on the power-driven social constructions that
shape education policy.

Defining politics.   The straightforward, traditional definition of politics: 'who gets
what when and how' (Lasswell, 1936) is rendered more complex by Easton's definition: 'the authoritative allocation of values'. But C. Wright Mills' definition: 'turning

4

personal troubles into public issues' – recognizes that human agents decide, based on their values, what should be part of the authority-based (policy arena) agenda and thus, what should be a public issue (Mitchell *et al.*, 1995). This definition turns attention to *which* or *whose* troubles get positive public attention and helpful resources (corporate farmers, school sports) and whose troubles do not garner such attention (child care, prevention of sexual harassment in schools, arts education) or negative controlling attention (welfare mothers, teacher quality).[5] Some issues are not part of policy debates – women coping with an abusive boss or husband, girls who remain passive and quiet in classroom discussions, women teachers who don't aspire to be superintendents. By defining these as private choices, they are ignored in policy arenas.

Cultural values and choices in policy arenas. Cultural values create the power that drives choices.[6] In the policy primeval soup, ideas are constantly floating around. Some policy ideas are not even acknowledged, much less considered viable options, if they do not coincide with prevailing ideology and culture. Value acceptability, or how a given idea fits with national culture or ideology, affects how these values enter into policy decisions. 'Policy windows' (Kingdon, 1984) open to these acceptable values because of a change in the political stream (a change of administration, a shift in Congress or national mood), or because a new problem captures the attention of policymakers.[7] Thus, Sputnik opened policy windows for math and science curriculum policy but no such window opened for government-supported curricula for prevention of violence toward women.

Policy communities, assumptive worlds, and logical frames. Policymakers are political creatures (a fact that too many policy analysts forget) in political communities where language, ideas and information are the medium of exchange. A policy community is a loose network of policy professionals and advocates who cluster around a specific area of governmental action – agencies, politicians, political parties, interest groups and their leaders and staff, policy advocates, and experts. Policy communities function within norms like 'keep it in the family', roles of the main members and the exchange–relationships and tensions among them (Campbell *et al.*, 1989) and the 'assumptive worlds' of policy actors – their understandings about how to act and talk, about who initiates action, and what are the limits on policy options (Marshall, Mitchell and Wirt, 1989). 'Logics', 'models' or 'frameworks' are important units of analysis in public policy for probing policymakers' thoughts (Anderson, 1978; Rein, 1983). They are the basis for policy formulation as well as 'standards of how to judge and criticize policymaking performance' and have the power to offer different definitions of what is real and important. Thus, policy analyses can identify how, for example, legislators attend to a gender policy for girls in math but declare inappropriate any policy discussion of power/sexuality dynamics in sex education curricula.[8]

The public sphere, agenda-setting, and masternarratives. Where is the policy arena, where does public policy take place? How does an elite dictate what is right and good, relegating other people and other agendas to the margin, and what happens among subaltern counterpublics 'members of subordinated groups [who] invent and circulate counterdiscourse to formulate opposition interpretation of their identities, interests, and needs' (Fraser, 1994: 123)? Those who decide the agenda in the public sphere arrange 'the . . . hegemonic mode of domination' (Fraser, 1994: 117).[9] Thus, the arrangements and boundaries for public, dominant, legitimate discourse matter. As discourse in the public sphere helped to institutionalize a more bureaucratic elite form rather than a participatory–democratic form of government then counterpublics resist that oppressive nature.[10] Traditions and state apparatuses structured around the economic market and patriarchal traditions affect policy agendas, determining whether or not a problem is on the public agenda, part of public discourse and possible state intervention, or whether it's marginal or belonging to the private – the world of the individual or the domestic and emotional (do governments interfere with industrial pollution; with teenagers' decisions to get abortions; do governments shape girls' career choices by influencing school curricula?). Fraser also urges us to distinguish among the logics of the marketplace, the political apparatus, and the public sphere, to avoid being limited to the logics of those spheres and, instead, viewing the public sphere as 'a theater for debating and deliberating' (Fraser, 1989: 111). These widened definitions of public sphere and explications of counterpublics offer hope for alternative transformational discourse, defying domination and control ideologies and apparatuses. Alternative counterpublics invent and circulate counterdiscourses to formulate oppositional interpretations of their identities, interests and needs (seen in home-schooling, the women's movement creating the language and labels for double shift, in ecology and consumer groups, and in separatist antigovernment groups).

Alternate views of power.   We get expanded views of power from seeing power embedded in institutions: legislatures, courts, education systems, the professions (psychiatry, law, medicine, education) that categorize humans with labels and make them submissive subjects, collaborating with those who control and manage them (Ball, 1993; Foucault, 1977). Power is revealed through its backlash and resistance. Active *resistance* might be the child who yells obscenities at the vice principal; passive, silent resistance to power might be the woman who drops out of a male-dominated leadership program.

A traditional view of power defined as power-over, in competitive, controlling, commanding, dominating terms (see Max Weber, 1947) has been expanded to incorporate the ability to change behavior. Often a political elite gets what it wants through managing the discourse in the policy process by public agenda-setting and policy preference outcomes, preventing disruptive change from being legitimized, and getting people to *believe* in and value what the powerful elite want.

Power resides in knowledge that has legitimacy (Foucault, 1981). Debates over education policy are power conflicts over which knowledge is the *truth*. Power is enacted by control of knowledge. Those who control the discourse discredit or marginalize other truths. Thus, debates over required curriculum, the canon, the requirements for professional credentials – are power/knowledge struggles.

Language, access to the discourse, the policy community. How does an idea gain the momentum, legitimacy and support to become dominant enough to get an audience in a policy system, and then, perhaps, to become a law, a program, a budget priority, a mission statement, a curriculum component (and how others are silenced)? Focusing on language shows how ideas, preferences and values attain the stature of statute. Ball evokes the controlling power by saying, 'we do not speak the discourse. The discourse speaks us' (1990: 18) by constructing only limited possibilities for thought. People use speech as a power tool – to create power, to effect a desire or goal, and to block, resist and create opposing strategies (Foucault, 1981; Ball, 1990). Privileged speakers' truths (and policy analyses) prevail; a 'discourse of derision' can be used to displace or debunk alternative truths (Ball, 1990). Gaining access to the public discourse is essential power: 'Language is power . . . those who suffer most from injustice are the least able to articulate their suffering; and that the silent majority, if released into language, would not be content with a perpetuation of the conditions which have betrayed them' (Rich, 1979: 67).

Micropolitics. Politics of education occurs in 'a conglomeration of sites and agencies concerned with the regulations of the education system' (Ball, 1990: 20). Looking at those sites and agencies micropolitically reveals that they function from ideologically-based decisions, sub-rosa, privatized conflict, continuous negotiations over boundaries and turf, interest groups (Marshall and Scribner, 1991). Therefore, a micropolitical lens is needed to study, analyze, work within and change schools, and to reveal the less visible, the silences, the non-events like the ways schools silence voices (Fine, 1991), filter out administrators who raise uncomfortable questions (Marshall and Mitchell, 1991), and 'funnel student diversity and idiosyncrasy into a narrow range of school-approved behavior' (Anderson and Herr, 1993). Micropolitical lenses focus on internal negotiations, as affected by schools' messages, as in students' identity work (Wexler, 1988), the acquisition of acquiescence (Malen, 1995); and schools as sites of resistance.

Policy implementation. As policies are implemented through a conglomeration of sites and agencies, educators' abilities to alter, resist, translate, opportunistically adopt and remake policy are well-documented (Berman and McLaughlin, 1978; Sproull, 1981; Weatherly and Lipsky, 1977; Weick, 1976). Not only do communications get distorted in loosely coupled systems, but also, 'nothing gets done which is unacceptable to dominant or influential political groups, which may be defined to include the "bureaucratic leadership group"' (Minogue, 1983: 73). Policies are managed and translated to fit the values and meanings systems of powerful decisionmakers with ongoing district and site needs and constraints. Analyses of policy formulation, then, must ask whether appropriate incentives, resources, time, expertise, supports, accountability and evaluation are built in to enforce and reinforce policy intent. Analyses of policy implementation must look for policy slippage and symbolic policy compliance, and recognize that policies will create arenas of struggle – sometimes just over resources and turf, but more often over ideology, over what is and is not valuable and useful.

Purposeful policy studies. Once we see that policy systems, schools and know-ledge are the work benches for power tools, our social science pretenses of value neutrality are abandoned. Analysts must identify a purpose, a stance. Kahne calls for policy analysis that reconnects education systems with the creation of demo-cratic community, starting with 'the miniature community created within the school classroom' (1994: 239). Giroux calls for critical educators to have a radical politics of democracy in order 'to work with other cultural workers in various movements to develop and advance a broader discourse of political and collective struggle' (1992: 42). He urges a move beyond theoretical postmodern and feminist discourse to 'a project in which a politics of difference can emerge within a shared discourse of democratic public life' (p. 42).

New views of policy analysis, then, emerge from such cultural lenses – where policy arenas are wide and deep and with analyses that include those that recognize value-driven agendas and those that identify the dominant narratives driving policy and the ways they become dominant. *This* is where we connect the world of pol-itics, policy analysis and feminist and critical theory, framing analyses that aim to uncover how policies and politics (in the formal arena and in the politics of silence and ambiguity) continue to disadvantage girls and women in education systems *and* conduct analyses with the purpose of upsetting such systems of dominance. We can then create schools that could actually *practice* inclusion, that could be locations for self-development and that would be freed from embedded practices that create divisions and inequities. *This* can be the basis for policy analysis framed for demo-cratic and socially just education.

Emerging Methods for Policy Analysis

What is a policy analyst to do, with positivism abandoned, with the recognition that the policy system is not a mechanical structure, that policymaking is *not* rational deliberation in the formal arena, with reality as socially constructed; with theory, research and policy stances culturally and historically determined (Kelly and Maynard-Moony, 1993; Lindblom, 1990) given power brokers' biases and shifts in policymakers' assumptive worlds? Should policy analysis actually take a posi-tion, a values stance?

Interpretive and Narrative Policy Analysis

If policymaking is embedded with values conflicts and ethical and philosoph-ical debates,[11] we need policy analysis that identifies interpretations, that clarifies values stances and the modes of access and action in policy communities (Callahan and Jennings, 1983; De Haven-Smith, 1988; Kahne, 1994). Analysts must recog-nize that: 1) behind every policy issue lurks a contest over conflicting, though often equally plausible conceptions of the same abstract goal; 2) languages of sym-bols and numbers are used to promote their value interpretation; 3) stakeholders' problem definitions have their own definitions of causes, array of interests, and preferred decision; and 4) each policy choice has connected mechanisms for getting change, such as incentives, new structures and these mechanisms are *also* arenas of conflict (Stone, 1988). Defining something as a problem (teacher accountability, double shift, school choice) is making a judgment. A policy problem is 'a political condition that does not meet some standard . . . It is a conscious contrivance, reflecting human purposiveness' (Anderson, 1978: 19–20).[12]

The communicative acts that create and maintain social relations – in staff rooms, classrooms, boards and legislatures – need to be part of policy analysis. Focusing on 'the dimensions in which we act communicatively: those of making and testing claims about states of affairs in the world, about appropriate and legitimate social relationships, about personal and social identities, and about ways of framing issues at hand' (Forester, 1993: 12). Communications include talk but also threatening, criticizing, explaining, insulting, forgiving and recommending (recall the acquisition of acquiescence and the discourse of derision discussed earlier).

Interpretive and narrative policy analysis use stories, scenarios and tales to *explore and elicit* when 'the issues' empirical, bureaucratic, legal, and political merits are unknown, not agreed upon, or both' (Roe, 1989: 251). Analysts seek out the stories of all stakeholders. Such policy analysis includes systematic ways of eliciting such storytelling, especially 'when the storytelling at issue has arisen in order to articulate those recognizably complex and uncertain issues that otherwise continue to defy adequate specification . . . [by] microeconomics, statistics, organizational analysis and the law' (Roe, 1989: 253). Further, analysts recognize asymmetries, power differentials among the stakeholders. As stakeholders' stories are competing, some stakeholders have easier access to economic and political power; for any group, their articulated stories are the tool, the method for gaining access to power (Roe, 1989). The job of interpretive and narrative policy analysis then, is eliciting the stories, portraying the dynamics among stakeholders, especially where policy issues are so uncertain and complex that one cannot identify which arguments are good, bad, strong or weak.[13]

Critical Policy Analysis

Critical theorists place at the center of analysis the power, policies and structures that restrict access; their work often demonstrates how privilege is maintained and the disempowered and silenced are kept that way, raising 'serious questions about the role of schools in the social and cultural reproduction of social classes, gender roles, and racial and ethnic prejudice' (Anderson, 1989: 251). Such is the basis for critical policy analysis, focusing on the battle between those who would restrict access to knowledge and power to elites and those who seek a more equal and participatory society (Weiler, 1993). Critical policy analysis is not value-neutral. Prunty describes the stance as:

> anchored in the vision of a moral order in which justice, equality and individual freedom are uncompromised by the avarice of a few. The critical

analyst would endorse political, social, and economic arrangements where persons are never treated as a means to an end, but treated as ends in their own right (1985: 136).

Such an analyst must be adept in the political world to be effective and to provide methods for the oppressed to gain power, while viewing school policy critically to expose oppressive structures, including ways that oppressed unknowingly cooperate with their oppressors.

Critical policy analysis, then, is a search for improvement of the human condition, an emancipatory social science; analysts must assist in identifying more radical alternatives. Policy analysis, then, must consider whether a policy will empower and democratize, whether it will dispense goods to the have-nots as much as they consider traditional questions such as whether a policy is efficient. Dryzek and Brobow (1987) envision policy analysis aimed toward wholesale reconstruction of political institutions and public life.

Guides to Reconstructed Policy Analysis

Policy analysts would have to pay attention to the policy deliberations, 'including such processes as how decision premises are covertly built into decision structures are the ways in which non-decisions can preshape political agendas' (Fisher, 1989: 950) and the interests and values of the stakeholders 'so that we can examine particularly ways that citizens are (or are not) able to speak and act politically, to question facts, rules, or stereotypical identities' (DeLeon, 1988; Forester, 1993: 130).[14] Insiders in policy debates are creating the master narrative, so the analyst (an outsider) must identify the value-laden and various interpretations of those insiders, studying politics from the inside, uncovering evaluative presumptions and 'policy makers' theoretical premises and actions' (DeHaven-Smith, 1988). Their 'manifest rationales' and the 'normative standards and framework of reasoning of practitioners' (Anderson, 1978).

To move beyond the master narratives, to be critical, the analyst must *do* something, must report, act to enfranchise and to disrupt and dismantle oppressive policy directions. But decisionmakers and power brokers seldom employ or enjoy analysts and evaluators who criticize policies they created (Ryan, 1988; Scheurich, 1994). The astute analyst can provide reports and can act in and around the public arena to provide information for critical reflection on any policy actions, calling attention to 'the cultural embeddedness of policies' (Kelly and Maynard-Moody, 1993: 138) and creating a forum for multiple truths. The policy analyst then becomes a facilitator of deliberation bringing together multiple perspectives to explore alternative courses of action and to help people see the limits of their current perspectives in policy debates. The analysts' report incorporates the perspectives of key stakeholders and it incorporates the multiple, conflicting and negotiated subjective perspectives of people who lay meaning on policies. Such an approach requires qualitative methodology by a politically astute analyst with a moral purpose. This may not eliminate oppressive structures, but the analysis can help groups raise fundamental questions or get the oppressed to see, label and articulate their stories, increasing their power in policy agenda setting (Friere, 1985; Ryan, 1988).

Now, with an expanded sort of policy analysis, including a cultural view of policy arenas and expanded methodologies, feminist and critical theoretical perspectives not only *fit* within policy analysis, they are essential!

Feminist and Critical Theory and the Policy Arena

Critical and feminist theories point to new arenas of political contestation and provide the lenses and tools for discovering and disrupting modes of oppression and reweaving, recreating relationships. Feminist and critical theories offer lenses for looking at schools and understanding these as policy issues:

- the social construction of gender as limiting human possibilities, including ways race/ethnicity, class, and classifications according to confining constructions of masculinity and femininity;
- white male dominance embedded in institutional life through control of identity formation, language, legitimized knowledge, definitions of competence, access to societal benefits or agenda setting;
- gender and sexuality as mechanisms for control – as in gendered hierarchies in the workplace – and how race, class and gender intertwine;
- differences between the values, moral orientations, life experiences, and work/life styles of men and women, with white males' ability to define their own as the legitimate ways through their power in the major institutions; but also how women's lives, values and behaviors redefine and reconstruct our institutions;
- the embedded structures of politically supported institutions (schools, welfare agencies) that reify definitions of 'women's issues' as needy-dependent and suspect and women's place as subordinate and service/care-providing;
- ways people resist domination.

They use methods to deconstruct text, discourse, knowledge, metanarratives, policy agendas, institutionalized assumptions and revise and reconstruct, from the standpoint of the range of women's realities and incorporating voices from the counterpublics, the silenced, the non-events, the meaning-making from the popular culture.

The next sections describe the particulars of feminist theoretical contributions prior to a section discussing how feminist, critical and postmodern theoretical strands blend to be foundations for feminist critical policy analysis.

Feminisms Evolving

'The cat is out of the bag, and it is a tom', said Virginia Woolf (quoted in Franzway, Court and Connell, 1989: 145) Feminist theory 'brings to consciousness facets of our experience as women that have . . . contradicted predominant theoretical accounts of human life' (Keohane, Rosaldo and Gelpi, 1982: vii). Current feminist analyses have a theoretical pragmatism, incorporating what is useful from feminisms, critical, poststructural and postmodern, experimenting with both theory and methodologies.

Feminist scholarship puts women at the center, (not just in comparison to men), uncovers cultural and institutional sources and forces of oppression (rather than the blame-the-victim compensatory approach), thus moving beyond descriptions of women's status and barriers to females' equal access to educational opportunity. It demands examination of intimate relationships as well as national policies. Feminist theory, when connected with cultural analyses of politics and policy, helps explain the inability of government to connect policy analyses for schooling with what happens to girls in school.

Feminisms have evolved to include a range of complementary perspectives (Eisenstein, 1993; Tong, 1989; Weiler, 1988) useful for examining education policy. *Liberal feminism* is the basis for policies like affirmative action, the Equal Rights Amendment and comparable worth – laws that assume that simply eliminating barriers and placing women in positions will change institutional and cultural values. This fits well in liberal democracies' assertions of individual rights, (Hawksworth, 1994; Marshall, 1996) supporting research and policy that aims to uncover barriers and deficiencies, make a correction and open access to females. What is missing from Liberal feminist perspectives is the realization that the people with power in political, institutional and professional cultures that *created* sexist and differential access are being relied on to create new power and access processes. Liberal reform proposals depend upon men in power to give up their privilege and willingly and thoughtfully change the gender, class and the power dynamics of the systems that give them power (see Weiler, 1988; Stromquist, Chapter 3, this volume; and Marshall, 1996, for more on this critique).

Women's Ways feminisms demonstrate that women have different socialization, different orientations to moral decisionmaking, ways of knowing, and ethics (Belenkey, Clinchy, Golberger, McVicker and Tarule, 1986; Chodorow, 1978; Gilligan, 1980; Noddings, 1984). They name and value women's subjective experience. They offer hopeful new visions: of relationship- and community-building, of networks of caring and nurturance; they challenge men and women to value the emotions and tasks usually designated as women's work for the private sphere (child rearing, caretaking). Promising alternatives are generated from Women's Ways: the possibility of facilitative, non-hierarchical leadership – power-with rather than power-over; coalitions built from women's commonalities, like the women's movement to save their children from war and ecological disasters (Elshtain, 1982). However, Women's Ways, pursued without recognizing how these are devalued and relegated to the private sphere, leave women vulnerable and segregated, with all the caring and community duties and no recognition of the political forces defining their worth. The danger also comes from essentializing women and endowing them exclusively with these perspectives, leaving men free of relationship and caring responsibilities.

Power and Politics feminisms[15] identify the institutional, economic purposes and the political and cultural processes that create and maintain exclusion of females, focusing on:

- how men keep the power to control, hurt and take advantage of women, through family structures, sex, violence and even the burdens of mothering;
- how the power of capitalism and patriarchy combine to oppress women;[16]
- the myths and stereotypes created to maintain women in the place of *other* – with men in control of myth-creation and maintenance and men deciding women's feminine identity;
- how all structures are social constructions, created for some political purpose, often hurting women; femininity *and* masculinity are problematic categories with constant and tense negotiating among multiple, personal, public and politically evolving identities.

For example, conventions for behavior and discourse, norms for leaders, for professionals, for demonstrating competence are artifices; when they exclude women from leadership or when they instruct boys that art, emotion, teaching careers are only for women – this is sexual politics.

This Power and Politics theoretical strand recognizes that simply gaining power in the context of existing power structures will not suffice.[17] Instead, MacKinnon says, 'feminism revolutionizes politics' (1982: 3). Patriarchy, the gender regime, and the gender order are phrases that evoke the power of the state to regulate women's lives. Authors such as Connell (1987), Eisenstein (1990), Franzway *et al.*, (1989) and Watson (1990) build a basis for a theory of the state that incorporates explanations of state-imposed oppression of women, in welfare, medical, education and other state regulated systems; a feminist theory of the state is emerging from this foundation. 'The state as patriarch' frames detailed analyses of bureaucratic, legal and governmental politics affecting women's status across the world (Franzway *et al.*, 1989: 29).[18]

Power and Politics feminisms identify the gender regime and hegemony; the grounding for their research, policy and action is the political choices and power-driven ideologies and embedded forces that categorize, oppress and exclude. They identify the ways political systems can be societally constructed to institutionalize (in schools, legal precedents, job classifications) the inequities of gender, race or class and can solidify social injustices. As Apple says,

> Gender and its regulation is not just an afterthought in state policy. Rather, it is a constitutive part of it. Nearly all of the state's activity is involved in it. One need only think of the following areas of state policy – family, population, housing, the regulation of sexuality, child care, taxation and income redistribution, the military, and what concerns us the most here, education – to see the role of the state in gender politics even when it is not overtly discussed in official documents. (Apple, 1994: 356)

presaging a rich agenda of theory building based on extensive analyses of gender-related policies.

Feminisms Applied

The feminist critique of science has revealed androcentric biases in theory and inspired important reframing (Harding, 1986; Keller, 1983; Lather, 1991; Smith, 1981). For example:

- in political science, Elshtain (1982, in Keohane *et al.*) calls for political language that 'does not silence particular persons or groups, nor proscribe particular topics and spheres of life from discourse' (p. 144), and Ferguson (1984) demonstrates how the structures, rules, language and patterns of dominance in bureaucracies serve to keep women controlled, contributing their work while suppressing (under the guise of good and rational management) their alternative ways of talking, valuing and living their lives;
- in legal studies, MacKinnon demonstrates ways in which governance, social welfare, justice and legal systems are structured to promote the interests of white males, using such examples as rape, incest, abortion, birth control, sexual harassment, lesbianism, domestic battery, prostitution and pornography (MacKinnon, 1989: 7). 'Sexuality, then, is a form of power . . . [which] institutionalizes male sexual dominance and female sexual submission [in] pervasive powerlessness to men' (p. 21);
- in economics, Waring (1988), in *If Women Counted*, demonstrates how the world economy would be altered if women's work in the home and in service, volunteer, nurturing and teaching the young were valued.

Feminist scholarship also demands that research methodologies build relationships and contribute to social betterment. So action research, collaborative research, co-creation of life histories replace the dispassionate experimental manipulation of research subjects.

Feminist Education Scholarship

'Ask these questions, with an eye to gender, as critique of any science: Does the nature of the sample match the nature of the conclusions? Who is missing from this picture? and Why?' (Goodnow, 1985: 30).

From early research on sex role socialization, to Madeleine Arnot's coining the term *sociology of women's education* (Middleton, 1993: 38) emerged feminist research and theory for education, benefitting from an interdisciplinary and action-oriented stance. Liberal feminist frameworks have championed the long term agenda focusing on sex role stereotyping in curriculum, counseling and school policies and have entered the political arena to promote equal access agendas, working within the extant political system to support women leaders' access, to enforce Title IX, and to gender-neutralize vocational education (see for example, Wilson's (1991) compilation on the status of girls' education in the European Community, Klein's *Handbook for Sex Equity* (1985) and others (Marshall, 1981; Ortiz, 1982; Sadker, Sadker and Klein, 1986; Schmuck, Charters and Carlson, 1981; Shakeshaft, 1986) who pioneer by calling attention to gender inequity).

Gilligan (1980) and Noddings (1988) exemplify Women's Ways education feminist scholarship that challenges educators to see that female modes of managing moral dilemmas emphasize caring and relationships; Belenkey *et al.* (1986) demonstrate the complexities in women's response to the dispensed curriculum. Descriptions of women's work as teachers and administrators (see Acker, 1989, 1995; Biklen, 1980; Casey and Apple, 1989; Foster, 1993; Grumet, 1988) include both the Women's Ways stance and a political stance of valuing women's perspectives, contributions and the rhythms of women's lives. Some researchers' agendas expand to examine how class, sexuality, ethnic and cultural difference interact with gender issues (see Borman, Mueninghoff and Piazza, 1989; Holland and Eisenhart, 1988; Lutrell, 1993;, McKellar, 1989; Valli, 1988; Zambrana, 1988).

Connecting a political analysis with feminism is essential. A number of examples (especially those in this volume) show how Power and Politics feminisms reveal important insights for education policy. Analyses of national policies for gender equity demonstrates the low priority given to gender. In the US 'gender is not a relevant category in the analysis of excellence in schools' (Fishel and Pottker, 1977; Tetrault and Schmuck, 1985: 63) and is a 'national blind spot' (Sadker, Sadker and Steinham, 1989: 46). Wolpe's (1978) analysis of British government papers demonstrates how governments channel girls' choices for work and unpaid homemaking. Middleton's (1993) personal/political account of the intersections between New Zealand's education policy developments and the development of education feminists explain how the personal is political. Evans' (1993) policy implementation analysis is an example of asking a traditional policy question (what happens during implementation?) but asking about gender effects. Kenway's policy analysis demonstrates the need to ask feminist questions about the ideology driving gender equity curricular reforms that assume girls' access to traditionally boys' spheres is the desideratum.

The Power and Politics feminisms assume that schooling and class and capitalism are interconnected, that patriarchy and capitalism are mutually reinforcing systems. Therefore, race, sexuality, class and gender questions must be analyzed with the purpose of uncovering how schools reproduce assumptions that an elite's needs should prevail, that men should rule, and schools should help to classify people to serve patriarchal and capitalist ends (Weiler, 1988). Research on women seeking to exercise power and reframe education, leadership and policy practices, are particularly useful for highlighting embedded power (see especially Blackmore, in press; Deem and Ozga, Chapter 2, Volume II, and Mawhinney, Chapter 12, this volume; Ortiz and Ortiz, 1993; Weiler, 1988). Deeper analysis demonstrates how the culture of the formal policy arena and the micropolitics of organizational and professional

Catherine Marshall

cultures blunt gender equity policies in Australia and Great Britain (see Blackmore, Kenway, Willis and Rennie, 1993; Connell, 1987; Yeatman, 1993). Yates' analysis of Australian gender policy usefully examines embedded assumptions and blind spots in the early policy discourse framed by liberal education theory by focusing the problem on the domestic labor and reproduction issues for girls, leaving out the boys, and viewing women and girls as one category, with Aboriginals, rural, migrant categories as add-on issues (see Chapter 2, this Volume).

Seeing the state as an agent in sexual politics raises important new angles for analysis, focusing how sexual dynamics affect power arrangements, silencing and categorizing women, allowing men (mostly) in the public sphere the power to dominate and regulate.[19] Franzway *et al.* (1989) and Watson (1990) provide a model for studying gender politics, studying Australian 'femocrats', feminists who have attained high positions in bureaucracies and juggle between needing to work with the extant political system while doing so undermines their credibility with grass roots feminists.

Power and Politics feminisms apply usefully to informal institutional and inter-personal politics. Such analyses identify the political decisions establishing the managerial model for school leadership (Tyack and Hansot, 1983) and a coincid-ing gender hierarchy, reified and perpetuated by sponsorship and by the fact that, by controlling the definitions of good leadership and policy, white male elites can squelch challengers. Thus 'dominance is maintained, and the actions of the powerful are seen as virtuous, valued actions' (Ortiz and Marshall, 1988: 136). Such analyses combine cultural and power analysis. Micropolitical approaches show, for example, how gender joking in the staff room undercuts women teachers' status (Cunnison, 1989). Power is demonstrated, too, as women and girls collude with and/or resist these dynamics, as when women school administrators deny and cover feelings of difference and exclusion, thus easing gender anxieties (Marshall, 1985; 1993).

These early Power and Politics studies created the agenda for research on policymaking affecting gender. But often this has been a dangerous, unfunded and marginalized agenda for feminist scholars and an unacknowledged agenda for politics of education scholars. For the most part, governments do not generate research agendas or set up centers to study the connection between political choices and females' opportunity.[20] (Sponsorship of programs for girls in math and science is an important exception.) Indeed, 'feminist historians of education have shown that through the development of state education, there has been a commitment (often explicit) to the principle of maintaining gender differentiation' (Arnot and Weiner, 1987: 17).

In sum, politics and power become the focal point for analysis, not the women and girls. Further, the problem is re-focused – it is not longer about women's dif-ferences (often seen as deficiencies) and it is no longer about simplistically iden-tifying barriers that make women victims. Such grounded analyses were important beginnings for developing a feminist theory of the state, with separate philosophies, arenas, actors and strategies. Feminist approaches to politics and policy analysis have created useful theoretical tools for dismantling traditional and gendered assumptions in policy and for including women in the analyses.

Integrating Critical, Feminist, Postmodern[21]

Critical theory is primarily concerned with issues of social justice and problematizes the institutions and structures of society and education that operate powerfully to maintain unequal and unjust social and political relations. It focuses on the methods and meanings of domination, including the historical evolution of ideologies that buttress power to reveal the politicization of knowledge and language (Giroux, 1983).[22]

Both critical theory and feminist theory share concerns about the relationship between the individual subject and an oppressive social structure. Critical and feminist theories also subscribe to the view that social structures and knowledge, as well as our experience and selves are socially constructed, and are therefore open to contestation and change. Feminists (while attacking their failure to speak in accessible language and to encompass gender) have used critical theoretical perspectives.

Most critical feminists recognize 'the whiteness of theory' (hooks, 1990; Simmonds, 1992: 53), with emerging recognition that black and white women 'occupy different positions even in relation to men' (Simmonds, 1992: 53). They also reject the notion that gender is the only axis of domination and emphasize the importance of understanding the multifaceted nature of domination and its intersection along the lines of sex, race, sexuality and class.[23] Critical race theory focuses on systemic, cultural and structural inequalities, working to end racial oppression, challenging the color-blindedness, meritocratic 'ideology of equal opportunity' (Matsuda, Delgado, Lawrence and Crenshaw, 1993: 6) as ahistorical and simplistic. 'Working-class feminism' (Connell, 1987: 265) more often takes the forms of 1) structuring of work – in the labor force and the household; 2) power issues in family and in treatment of female workers; and 3) control of one's own sexuality – in the family and in the workplace.

Postmodernism rejects grand theory as grand narratives of privileged discourse used to explain social phenomena in terms of predictable, patterned interrelationships. Viewing humans as full of disarray and contradiction, inscribed by multiple and contested discourses, it embraces differences and rejects essentializing (Lather, 1991).[24] Feminism politicizes postmodernism, rejects abstract discourse as an intellectual exercise for white male academic elites (Yeatman, 1994). Postmodern feminists recognize the importance of grounding narratives within the contexts of the lives of individuals in order to connect public discourse on policy issues to their ever-evolving complexities, viewing, for example, women and girls as active participants in the construction of meaning and identity, not simply passive recipients of these processes (Martusewicz and Reynolds, 1994). It also reflects Women's Ways feminism by intrinsically valuing the subjectivities of women heretofore excluded from analysis (Alcoff, 1988; Belenky, et al., 1986). Weiler's *Women Teaching for Change* (1988) and several chapters in these Volumes (especially Chapters 7, 8, and 9 in this volume and Chapters 6, 7 and 8 in Volume II), are examples, focusing on the struggle as gender is socially constructed within the institutional and ideological power arrangements of schools.

Similarly, feminists and postmoderns correct the overdeterminism of critical theory by rediscovering human agency. While economic and political systems create institutions that reproduce elite privilege, humans resist and humans negotiate their identities. Meaning is always contested, temporal, emergent, elusive and partial, as meanings of words are embedded in language use (Lather, 1991). Words and our understanding of them create our understanding. Culture and the self or subject are viewed as *texts*, a complex interweaving of metaphor, signs, interpretations and practices.[25] Language contributes to the construction of reality rather than simply reflecting reality (Agger, 1991; Martusewicz and Reynolds, 1994).[26][27]

Feminist critical policy analysis draws upon all these theoretical advances, focusing on policy and politics, with a recognition that political and institutional practices function to maintain white male power and privilege. It has the particular goal of identifying ways to make our policy system more inclusive and equitable and, thus, democratic and socially just. Policy analysis for a field such as education should be embracing such responsibilities, such stances.

Feminist Critical Policy Analysis: Expanding Policy Questions[28][29]

Scholars and practitioners of politics of education, political science, policy analysis, politics and administration, by combining critical perspectives with feminist theories, need to look behind the political foreground at the ideological background in discourse (Ball, 1990; Hargreaves, 1983). Feminist theory-driven questioning will not only inform gender equity issues, it will expand our questions, models and methods. Feminist critical policy analysis seeks ways to make our policy system more just, democratic and equitable, demanding that the following expanded issues be included in all policy analysis:

Gender, the Public Sphere and Masternarratives

Now we know to avoid being limited to the domination and control ideologies and apparatuses of the public arena. Widened definitions of public sphere and explications of counterpublics offer hope for alternative transformational discourse. We recognize the policy issues in people's everyday, lived, personal realities.[30]

Policy analysis and feminism intersect over questions about what is public and what is private and who decides: Thus, analyses of women administrators' negotiations to fit their identities into male-structured leadership norms (see Blackmore, 1996; Marshall, 1985), feelings of exclusion and frustration over being unappreciated for nurturing, counseling and relationship work are no longer private emotional women's problems but matters for analysis of public policy affecting women's place in education (see especially Chapter 7, this Volume, and the chapters by Acker and Feuerverger, Chapter 7; Glazer, Chapter 4; Stage, Chapter 6; and Walker, Chapter 3 in Volume II) and critiques of masculinist legitimized science (e.g., Parker, Chapter 10, this Volume) then become education policy analysis. Such critiques promise expansions that can break through limited, mechanistic, dehumanizing assumptions.[31]

Counterpublics' Policy Issues

Can there be policy analyses for non-dominants, for silenced issues, for marginalized populations?[32] Or is feminist critical policy consultant an oxymoron? What happens among subaltern counterpublics? What are the parallel discourses and counterdiscourses and opposing interpretations (Fraser, 1994: 123) that exist beyond the discourse in the public sphere?[33] What are the arrangements for setting up boundaries for public, dominant, legitimate discourse? These questions speak to basic questions about democracy; they can also help policy analysts ask about students who drop out, girls who get pregnant, educators who only pretend to comply with policy directives from above, and parents who are cynical about participatory decisionmaking.

State Intervention

For social justice, what is the role of the state? Can the state be relied upon for analyses of inequities?[34] What are the related issues that surface when gender is the policy issue? Examples of such issues are 1) the debate over how much the state should intervene in family and private affairs 2) whether government should be satisfied with addressing (but not redressing) an equity issue, and 3) whether policy recommendations for small add-on fixes and identifying victims' deficiencies and providing compensatory supports are enough. Chapters 2 through 5 in this Volume explore these questions in analyses of several countries' policies for gender equity in schooling; Chapters 2 through 5 in Volume II analyze postsecondary policy arenas to assess the likelihood of substantive equity policy formulation. Because policymakers represent a ruling class, contested lines of exclusion, vision and meaning are not part of the discourse. When you go to the state, you reaffirm the state's power to fix the problem, giving it further right to dominate you. Thus, girls are those to be done to, fixed. This silences the discourse about the economic and political systems' effects on women and the discourse about male gender roles as being problematic. It focuses on the problem of women's poor choices that get them in economic trouble and pushes aside information about inequities in the workplace.

So, feminist policy analysts worry over going to the formal, centralized state for redress.[35] Ferguson (1984) worries about being silenced by bureaucratic processes; Australian analysts have worried that the femocrats in their bureaucracies lost their radical determination when coopted by being put in high positions. Sometimes local and regional politics have thwarted feminist advances (the US Equal Rights Amendment) but other times, state and local politics made up for national rescissions involving child care and battered women's shelters (Boneparth and Stoper, 1988). Sometimes working the political system (lobbying, forming coalitions, attaining political leadership) and court cases have helped women, but Boneparth and Stoper wonder whether this solidifies opposition and Faludi (1991) documents such backlash. (Also, Chapter 12, this Volume, shows the difficulty of using the courts for women's equity).

'Outing' Symbolic Policy

If language is the power tool of politics, analysts can focus on words and ask whether the words in policy speeches and documents match with real outcomes. Feminist critical policy analyses see through symbolic inaction,[36] suspicious of policy actors' rhetoric and policies with no enforcement. In this volume, Chapter 3 by Stromquist and Chapter 4 by Weis (and Chapter 4 by Glazer in Volume II) reveal how symbolic policy can be harmful, like the placebo that gives only the pretense of treatment. Chapter 9, by Hollingsworth, unpacks the realities of policy implementation, where program rhetoric announces goals for teacher education for sex equity but programs just never quite fit it in. After reading Laible's account of sexual harassment policy formulation in Chapter 11, one wonders how useful the policy will be when key players are not sure there's a problem, or view it as individual women's problems, not connected to ideal of equity and democracy.

'Your laws are ineffective', Wen declared. 'Why? Because no system of control will work as long as most of those administering the law against an evil have more than a finger dipped into it themselves' Han Suyin (Scutt, 1985: 138).

Cautions about Simplistic Remedies

Recognizing the embedded power relations in our institutions like courts, schools and school boards requires a caution: traditional policy recommendations for remedies will not be applied in vacuums, free of the power relations of race, class or gender (Ball, 1990). Therefore, typical recommendations and remedies (give scholarships, create add-on programs, threaten penalties) will often be inappropriate at least, and even damaging (by allowing symbolic policy to seem adequate or by leaving the burden of enforcement on the individual). For example, policies with gender-neutral goals fail by ignoring the accumulation of advantage by males from extant cultural practices and institutions. Pateman and Gross (1987) spell this out, noting that liberal individualism embedded in law gives us gender-neutral, equal opportunity policies and language that 'result in absurdities, or work against women' (p. 8), for example, in placing a woman or minority person in a token position left to flounder, in divorce or maternity benefits which leave intact the race and gender patterns that exclude.* Stage's Chapter 6 in Volume II demonstrates how easily our analyses slip into well-intentioned recommendations that leave women dangling.

Further, policy analysis cannot ignore the intertwining of 'isms'. Analysis of teacher policy must include recognition of occupational segregation (that most teachers are women), that gender does affect status. Analyses must also explore the meaning of low minority representations in the profession, must ask what is lost when men are boosted out of teaching into administration, must ask policy questions about the adequacies of school curricula and counseling for disabled children,

---

* In 1996, California started using affirmative action policy to assert the need to hire more white male typists – an ironic twist of policy originally aimed at helping women and minorities.

children from immigrant families, and girls negotiating identities, like Karen in Chapter 8 (this Volume).

The Historical and Comparative Perspective and the Effects of Political/Economic Shifts

Overly focused and decontextualized policy analyses often miss historical, economic or cultural contexts that situate the political aspects of classroom dynamics, limit girls' access to computer terminals in third grade, and when legislators refuse to raise teacher pay.[37] Analyses, for example, for teacher recruitment policy issues, can benefit from Michelle Foster's (1993) life histories of black women teachers before desegregation for deeper understanding of policy effects. Analysts benefit by looking beyond education, for example, at Ferguson (1984) and Cockburn (1991) on organizational life, for a cross-organizational comparison of how opportunity structures and bureaucratic processes affect women's opportunity. For example, in Chapter 7, this volume, the pregnant teen who is 'lost' shows how policies and programs formulated in disconnected agencies, with inappropriate categories, labels and mechanisms, effectively drop out the clients they intend to help. Boneparth and Stoper's (1988), Goodnow and Pateman's (1985), Pateman and Gross's (1987) and Watson's (1990) collections of analyses of gender in a range of bureaucracies, trades and professions and of women's status in different political systems and as clients and categories in social welfare systems have tremendous use for identifying the political and economic influences, moving analysis beyond simplistic focus.

Moving Beyond Essentialing Labels

Statisticians are fond of neat categories: by sex, age, socio-economic status (SES), and so on. Critical feminist analysis insists upon recognition of complexity – that the categories are mixed, have many elements that make up whole beings, and are not static but evolve. Analyses and recommendations, therefore, cannot simply aim at some universal target to fix *the* woman thing. Thus, labels like Latina, postmenopausal, high achiever, lesbian, single mother and so on do not describe the complex and dynamic issues in women's lives and identities. Chapter 8 in this volume is a case study by Adams of a student rebelling against categories and Chapter 8 by Bensimon in Volume II, 'Lesbian existence . . .'; both chapters illustrate the need for policy formulations to incorporate complexity. Further, policy issues are expanded by studying women in their own right, not just as 'other', to include perspectives and experiences heretofore on the margin.

Critiquing Bureaucracy, Leadership, Power and Community

Schools constructed to build support and facilities for nurturing self-development, for relationship- and community-building around an ethic of care, with leaders working toward such purposes, build from the feminist critique (Foster, 1986; Laible, this volume; Marshall, 1995; Marshall, Rogers, Steele and Patterson, 1996; Noddings, 1988). Theorizing collaborative, shared, power-with (Arendt, 1972; Ball, 1993; Habermas, 1986) fits well for examining power exercised in diffuse, fragmented societies and power exercised as community- and relationship-building, with an ethic of care and feminist perspectives, with a belief that cooperation creates shared power that gets things done (Stone, 1989), and the possibility that a social justice ethic could be incorporated into the notion of power to view power as a force for good. In-depth case studies, for example, urban principals (Dillard, 1995; Marshall *et al.*, 1996) or women teachers (Acker, 1995) allow exploration of expanded views of educators' work: their work is about creating opportunities to teach and about relationships and community, so models about traditional bureaucratic leadership and teaching skills have poor explanatory power. Think about the possibilities for reframing policy for teacher and administrator preparation and evaluations!

Searching for Belonging, for Meaningful Citizenship, and Altered Priorities

Once the questions are widened to delve into making democracy and community real, *and* the master's tools/master's house critique is surfaced, what organizations and politics are still viable, once the status of women question has status? What could communities, schools, other organizations and policymaking be like once we acknowledge the need for struggling politically, in identifying oppressions in the current systems, and in creating new knowledges, and organizing counterpublics and articulating counternarratives? In these volumes, Part III entitled 'New Politics, New Policies', looks, for example, at how women scholars could explore their authority and power (Chapter 12, Volume II, by Luke) how a feminist teacher can make the classroom a place for honest exploration of racism and sexism (Chapter 10, Volume II) – although 'Women's Work in Academe' (Chapter 7, Volume II) and Chapter 11, 'A Feminist in a PE Classroom' demonstrate that the institutional structures are not always in place to support such exploration. Chapters on the feminist struggle to expand the canon, like 'A Model for Gender-Inclusive School Science' (Chapter 10, this volume) and Chapter 5, Volume II on women's studies, demonstrate the value of the work in expanding knowledge to include women. Finally, although the struggle to use the policy process to end sexual harassment described in this volume in Chapter 11 (Laible) and the legal battle of Canadian women teachers described in Chapter 12 (Mawhinney) are carried on in resistant legal and political systems, they do give hints on how to manage gradual rebuilding toward education supportive of women, and thus supportive of community and democracy.

But traditional policy analysis assumptions and methods will not suffice. As Evers said, until we have a different approach to complexity, 'we prosper by confronting complexity with reliable simple falsehoods' (Evers, 1988: 232).

Expanding Research Methodologies

Widening theoretical frameworks opens unexplored methodologies for policy analysis. Cost benefit analyses give way to the microanalytic, sociolinguistic, ethnographic.
Policy analysis, then, includes political, critical and administrative ethnography. Systematic research on the cultures of public bureaucracy, can focus on 'patterns of
speech, written language, internal interaction . . . architectural settings, office accou-
terment, personal life styles . . . organizational stories, ceremonial rites of passage,
logos and nomenclatures, and models of heros and villains' (Goodsell, 1990: 496).
Policy analysis, then, includes life histories and discourse analysis, and sociolinguistic methods elicit narratives, frameworks of reasoning and values. It includes
deconstruction to uncover values and interests suppressed far beneath the surface
of the text (Agger, 1991; Lather, 1991; Martin, 1990).

The methodological approaches useful for asking feminist critical theory-driven
questions include:

1   personal narratives and oral histories that interrupt imperialist gender re-
    gime theories and metanarratives;
2   narratives for the stories/values of all stakeholders;
3   deconstruction of policy texts;
4   journals and life histories as data bases uncovering how policies affect
    self-identity negotiations.

Analysts' stance toward their endeavor can embrace precepts of interpretive,
post-positivist, feminist thinking to create new policy analysis traditions, include
these challenges:

*   to construct research that creates a relationship with individuals and respects
    their meaning-making;
*   to be openly ideological and activist – write and work against the grain;
*   to challenge metanarratives;
*   in every policy analysis and evaluation, in every policy formulation; ask
    who benefits, who loses, and how do those usually silenced and marginalized
    fare?

Research agendas can include:

*   identifying policy agenda setting and its exclusionary effects;
*   backward mapping, to identify the gaps and policy slippage due to sym-
    bolic and simplistic policy formulation; and to actively seek how policies
    affect individuals' negotiations with identity, policies' effects on social
    justice goals;
*   power as domination, but also resistance to power;
*   research on borderlands, the areas of silence and non-events, the counter-
    narratives and counterpublics;

- intersection of talk and the structures of power – talk is power; management of knowledge and language is an important site of political struggle;
- subjectivity and identity negotiation, identity construction;
- critiquing policy assumptions that embed private–public inconsistencies like welfare, abortion; policies' abilities to empower and support self-development; policies' abilities to support community and relationship-building and democratic ethos; recognizing the genderedness of organizations and careers and the power differentials and benefit/outcomes differences with attention to ethnicity, gender, race, national origin and disability.

As a beginning example, ask gender questions about how power and privilege get reinforced and how people get silenced and disempowered. Some beginning questions about any policy proposed to create gender equity could include: How forceful is it? Which feminisms? Does it: See sexism affecting males too? Assume all women as one unit of analysis? Incorporate ethnicity? Focus on school environment? Recognize schools' interconnections with other institutions? Demand constant critical assessment and timelines? Demand monitoring and reporting? Deal with self-esteem? Deal with women's ways of knowing and moral reasoning? Deal with needs for relationship, collaboration? Deal with incorporating the private sphere? Focus on only the high achievers? How all-encompassing is it? What mechanisms does it include for reaching curriculum, program definition, training, finance, governance, buildings and facilities?[38] Does it acknowledge resistance to change and economic and political and historical contexts? Who is the target audience? Who carries the burden of implementation and are they capable?

Such methodologies, used as policy analysis, hold great promise and a long-missing agenda for education, asking widened questions with policy issues generated inclusively.

Shaping the Future: Strengths, Limitations, Warnings[39]

'great are the penalties of those who dare resist the behests of the tyrant Custom' (Elizabeth Cady Stanton, *Eighty Years and More*, 1898)[40].

Feminist and critical theorists challenge elite male-stream theory; in doing so, they are vulnerable. Pursuing feminist research and interventions in academia is full of 'crazy-making' punishments and contradictions (Luke and Gore, 1992). Still, the scholarly literature amasses, energized in large part by women's uncovering of the dense layers of phallocentric knowledge and discourse and demonstrating the need for counterhegemonic theory and practice.

In shaping these agendas, several cautions should be mentioned. First, the feminist project to end patriarchal domination has internal debates ranging from theoretical and ideological to personal. The struggle of any oppressed group to write against the grain combines with feminisms' problems with elitism, blindness to class and race, middle-class, heterosexual bias. But the challenge is too big and too important to expend energy on infighting. In an appeal for unity, bell hooks says, 'We must understand that patriarchal domination shares an ideological foundation with racism and other forms of group oppression, that there is no hope that it can be eradicated while these systems remain intact' (hooks, 1989: 22).

Next, resist the tendency to essentialize, to accept analyses and policies that look at women as one unified category. Categorizing is an act of power right out of the masters' tool box. Relatedly, resist othering – the tendency to adhere to one correct stance, in theoretical, professional, personal, career, fashion, politics or sexuality – and denigrate or undermine others. For example, endless debates about which feminism is correct undermine the strength of feminist critical policy analysis (but will be supported by dominant discourse, such as in stories of the decline of feminism). Exacerbating this tension is the power of dominant discourse which *accept as legitimate* the liberal feminist stances and undercuts radical, lesbian, black, anarchist and other such labels of feminisms (Eisenstein, 1981).[41]

Still, some discriminations are important: a caution about being coopted: new political and theoretical arrangements that leave intact the liberal view that separates the private and public spheres are emerging. Lather (1984: 52) warns against 'the neo-marxists [who are] rather ominously polite to the women's movement' without revising their theories. Luke (1992) cautions that liberal and critical theory allows women into the public sphere but still leaves women with all the duties of the private sphere (it is fine if you want to be president as long as you can manage your family's needs for nurturance and support too.) A related question: would men's entry into feminist scholarship ruin it for women, in this social and political environment where men's voices are lent automatic power and legitimacy?[42] Yet, claiming female epistemological privilege, assuming that a woman's experience of marginality provides her automatically with different scientific insights, can be a trap (Acker, 1994; Haste, 1994)[43].

Feminist analysis often heats up gender tensions.[44] It disturbs 'to argue that sexual domination is central to, though unacknowledged in, modern social and political theory, is to touch on some emotions, interests, and privileges very different from those disturbed by arguments about class' (Goodnow, 1987: 2). No one likes to be called as 'an oppressor, the enemy, collaborator, or bystander (however innocent) in discrimination or disadvantage' (Goodnow, 1985: 31) and no one likes a complainer.[44] Men are uncomfortable with the thought that their advantages were not necessarily earned but rather bestowed by institutions and professions structured to support them. Still, men need to have a role, for 'no single oppressed group can possibly win significant structural change on its own, nor can any be trusted to look out for the interests of the others. Moreover, social transformation requires struggle in the sense of engagement with one's opponents. In academic arenas this means challenging ideological distortions built into mainstream perspectives and, insofar as possible, compelling their adherents to respond' (Fraser, 1989: 13).

Resist backsliding: it is easy to grab the master's tools when feminist tools and women's ways are denigrated and we gain legitimacy only when we use the master's discourse, the 'appropriate' methods. Ellsworth's (1992) suspicion of the male discourse of critical pedagogy points to the need to keep feminist and critical as separate. Theory and research *for* women must be held apart. Similarly, it is too easy to slip in the implication that 'girls should be more like boys if they want to get on' (Kenway and Modra, 1992) whether in the curriculum, in scholarship, or in politics.[45]

Next, it is easy to want to get sidetracked and diffused by token changes. For example, Goldring and Chen (1993) show how the tremendous rise in the number of female principals in Israel is *not* a signal that women's leadership capacities are preferred but rather a trend connected with centralization of power and lower status and pay for principals.

Similarly, we must watch for the gender effects of the array of reforms for schooling. For example, from feminist analysis we can inspect how choice and privatization arguments (see, for example *Gender Justice*, Kirp, 1985) and arguments for family values' inculcation have embedded agendas for controlling females' choices. Yet it is easy to forget. Excited and inspiring exhortations by policymakers who have discovered empowerment language and even critical theorists who want to democratize education lay a burden on teachers to make change without addressing the impossibility of carrying that burden in entrenched patriarchal systems (Gore, 1992). We can see how governments' failure to document women's underrepresentation in educational leadership is legitimizing and reinforcing an area of silence. But sometimes it is difficult to see areas of silence and neglect. Also, it is easy to forget gender equity when more appealing (politically salient and funded) issues attract attention.[46] Recall that, in the height of attention given to Oakes' (1985) important documentation of tracking's processes and effects on race and ethnic minorities, we easily overlooked her blindness to gender tracking.

Next, the agenda for action is crucial and the demands to develop grand theory may distract. A recurrent question, does feminism need a theory of the state? continues (Evans, 1986; Kenway, 1992) but, meantime, women's interests are contorted – in supposedly gender-neutral divorce laws which result in feminization of poverty; in government rulings that fail to see escaping genital mutilation as a rationale for political asylum for a woman; and in the Georgia school district refusing responsibility for protecting an elementary schoolgirl from five months of sexual harassment from a peer (Update, 1996). Abstracted theorizing should not divert us from research and action for those at-risk females when policymakers cannot yet see the risks and waste of girls' possibilities.

Then there's the challenge of action competing with analysis for the feminist critical policy analyst: can one manage the politics of legitimacy for programs and maybe the politics of Title IX class action suits *and* be conducting scholarly work too? Yet can one be credible in feminist critical policy analysis *without* taking political action?

Such strong cautions would indicate that feminist critical policy analysis needs a safe place and sponsorship in education, a protected space, perhaps in the development of a feminist theory of the state, theory that guides political awareness of gender as a stand-alone and separate issue, independent of critical theory, cultural studies and mainstream politics.

Moving Toward New Agendas

Feminist critical policy analysis asks: how does this analysis illuminate the conditions of disenfranchised and marginalized people, represent multiple and differing voices? Does it incorporate a conception of women that recognizes women's full humanity? It begins with assumptions that inequities result from culturally framed choices to serve some in-group's ideology and purpose. It is research identifying how the political agenda benefitting elites is embedded in school structures and practices. There is room for decades of feminist critical research on such political arrangements.

Rich, earthy, bountiful agendas and exploratory methodologies beckon; they explore possibilities for education as a democratic, community- and relationship-based institution for self-development.

Notes

1 In these volumes, *policy analysis* is used as an umbrella term, encompassing the work of scholars who study politics of education, who conduct policy studies, who carry out evaluations of school programs, and those more conventional analysts, whose policy analyses are projections of the costs and benefits of particular focused policy proposals. The volumes are an argument that the term policy analysis must encompass this range and that conventional analysis is constrained and limited.

2 Audre Lorde, saying 'for the master's tools will never dismantle the master's house' (1984: 112) calls to attention the need to rethink theory, methods and practices, but also to examine the institutions and system within which they were created.

3 In Volume II, the Chapter 1 by Bensimon and Marshall provides an introduction with a particular focus on postsecondary education.

4 I focus on gender in this book, intentionally, so most examples and applications are derived from gender issues and feminist theory. However, gender issues are intertwined with race, class, heterosexism, ethnicity issues and feminist theory, research and pragmatic politics increasingly incorporate that realization. Further, once we accept that identities, labels and definitions of problems are socially constructed, the feminist critique of knowledge and politics demands an investigation into all the isms, asks, for example, by what process did the US discourse emerge to focus policy attention on teenage dropout moms on welfare (ignoring the racist assumptions and the facts that most of these young women are impregnated by older men with power over them, that young women's search for meaning and sense of self is often unsupported in school – and other systems). My hope is that this book will provide the kind of connections between politics, policy analysis and gender issues that critical and critical race theory has provided for class and race issues.

5 Steinam (1978) has made this point on lecture tours humorosly by tellingly, saying, 'if men got periods, tampons would be tax deductible.'

6 Viewing policy variables as choices: of scope (of public vs. private responsibilities), of policy instruments (what structures and tools?), of distribution (who gets what?), and choices of how to proceed (Heidenheimer, Heclo and Adams, 1990).

7 'If one of the three elements is missing – if a solution is not available, a problem cannot

be found or is not sufficiently compelling, or support is not forthcoming from the political stream – then the subject's place on the decision agenda is fleeting' (Kingdon, 1984, 187).

8   Feminist theorists notice the value-bases of policy actors: policymakers debate on and on about, abortion for example, without acknowledging that women are the only ones who have abortions. Feminists notice the assumptions about women (women's bodies, women's intuition, women's deficiencies, symbolic representations of women – as evil, as witchily powerful, as irrational –) are used to buttress societal, institutional and political domination – as in women need to be controlled, to be helped, to be protected. Feminists notice the artificial separation of the spheres: public (political rights, citizenship, reasoned debate, contracts – the rational world and the proper concern for social and political theory) and private (emotion, love, partiality and particularity – the proper concern for the family, the domestic, the non-rational) spheres. *And* notice how that separation can be used to assert that women cannot be leaders, cannot attend prestigious military schools, that women need men in Senates to decide on definitions of sexual harassment and whether they need permission to have abortions).

9   Political theory maintains deep assumptions about women's place. The Greek polis was based upon the existence of a private sphere where women and slaves took care of life's necessities (Stivers, 1990). Thenceforth political theory, economies, institutions, professions and nations depended upon a separation between public and private life, women's and men's spheres, with the public sphere constructed on masculine lines.

10 Fraser's definition of public sphere goes beyond government and includes anywhere where 'political participation is enacted through the medium of talk' (Fraser, 1994: 111) – so it is not the economy, not just the legislature, it is a 'theater for debating and deliberating' (Fraser, 1994: 111) – a place where participatory democracy can take place, but the ideal has degenerated because the public sphere has oppressive structures and unequal power relations within it.

11 As Ball (1990) notes, classical political analysis assumed that there is a neutral government adjudicating, when necessary, between participants who themselves are generating much of the policy.

12 Hence, the policy analyst must be explicit about normative orientations, so 'a subtle and sympathetic appraisal of the intentions and self-understandings of the agents involved is crucial . . . the interpretive reconstruction of practical reasoning also seems to be closer to the kinds of political, psychological, and sociological judgments that policymakers and most experienced policy analysts actually make' (Jennings, 1983).

13 Examples of policy analysis attuned to political dynamics include: Roe's (1989) narrative analysis of the medfly controversy; Kelly and Maynard-Mooney's (1993) effort to apply post-positivist thought to a policy analysis of the Economic Development District.

14 Forester provides several examples of how critical policy analysis (of toxic waste, budget reductions, and local health services) gives the issues of interests 'a multidimensional cast – so that we can examine how systemic rationalizing of commodifying forces obliterate or dominate popular voice' (1993: 130).

15 These include the cultural reproduction theorists, the radical critique, Marxist, socialist, existentialist, poststructuralist and postmodern strands of feminism.

16 'Capitalism needs patriarchy in order to operate efficiently' (Franzway *et al.*, 1989: 16).

17 De Beauvoir and others (see Mackinnon, 1982) caution against simplistically seeking representation in political spheres and power to create the world from one's own point of view pointing out that these are the political strategies of men, combining legitimation with force.

18 Dietz urges feminists to develop a 'comprehensive theory of citizenship before they can arrive at an alternative to the non-democratic liberal theory' (1992: 78)

19 As seen in Eisenstein's (1979) analysis of President Carter's support of the Equal Rights Amendment and her (1993) recounting of the politics of affirmative action in New South Wales demonstrating the male–female dynamics (when the Minister was hurt when feminists did not stroke his ego for his support of affirmative action, saying 'Why should we be concerned about his ego?' (p. 7).

20 In the US gender equity has been a political non-issue; the few policies and programs were formulated without effective implementation strategies, funds or monitoring (Stromquist, Chapter 3, this volume).

21 Although feminist theory does incorporate critical theory, postmodernism and post-structuralism, this section's purpose is to identify their particular emphases and contributions to feminist theory and especially to show how these theoretical strands are interwoven yet serve as critiques to each other. For example, critical theory helps move feminisms toward a critique of the economic, class and power issues and feminisms move critical and postmodern theorists to look for grounding in real life and to make their work more accessible – or at least construct shorter sentences with shorter words.

22 It ridicules logical positivism, the modern promise of Enlightenment rationality to liberate the world through science, promising a new basis for social theory and political action (Agger, 1991; Giroux, 1983).

23 bell hooks (1989, 1990) critiqued postmodernism as a discursive practice dominated by white male intellectuals and academic elites who speak to and about one another with coded familiarity in a language grounded in the master narratives it claimed to challenge. hooks questions how well *understanding* can disrupt prevailing power relations, as understanding slips, Giroux says, 'into a theoretically harmless and politically deracinated notion of pastiche' (1992: 68). bell hooks asserts that political agendas should drive intellectual and cultural work contesting patriarchy (Giroux, 64). She called for constructing a feminism that is self-consciously political.

24 It is in contrast to humanism's subject who is an autonomous being capable of full consciousness and endowed with a stable self constituted by a set of static characteristics such as race, gender, class, disability and sexual orientation. Thus, social constructions of man and woman are 'at once empty and overflowing categories. Empty because they have no ultimate, transcendent meaning. Overflowing because even when they appear to be fixed, they still contain within them alternative, denied, or suppressed definitions' (Scott, 1986: 1074).

25 For several decades the notion that the personal is political has been central to feminist theory, implying a complex relationship between social practices and the construction of subjectivity through the use of language (Agger, 1992; Alcoff, 1988; Giroux, 1992).

26 As such, women are texts inscribed with the sentiments and interests of men. Popular culture in text and screens is viewed as an arena of political contestation (Agger, 1991) and powerful transactions of messages defining women.

27 Such frameworks can ground exploration of how women become constructions of men and male culture, uncovering the male texts that claim to speak for or about women, as the weaker or secondary sex, as sex objects and as having primary responsibility for domestic activities, child rearing and caregiving.

28 See Bensimon and Marshall's Chapter 1 in Volume II for a presentation focused directly on feminist analysis.

29 In critical policy analysis, one asks: how does power and privilege get reinforced through political (and educational) institutions? By what processes do the silenced and

disempowered get kept in their place? *Feminist* critical policy analysis focuses on women, adds postmodern to reinvent human agency, and recognizes that people can resist structures and that people negotiate their identities and choices while living with political and institutional forces.

30 Dorothy Smith seeing everyday life as problematic and political (1981) and Jean-Bethke Elshtain bringing the mothers searching for sons lost to terrorists (1982) as a focus for political scientists are examples of this redefinition of what constitutes a political analysis.

31 For example, exploration of women's critique of assumptions of educational leadership – the career, the theory, and the practice – a counternarrative – holds promise for a reconceptualizing free of outdated male and managerial norms (benefitting men and women and children), as explicated in Marshall, 1995.

32 Policy choices reflect shifts in public values and the shifts (from valuing efficiency to valuing choice, equity and quality exemplified in the work of Callahan, 1962; Clark and Astuto, 1986; Garms, Guthrie and Pierce, 1978; Marshall, Mitchell and Wirt, 1989). However, by focusing on the dominant values recognized as winners in values conflicts, we assist in the exclusion of alternative values. When analysts of politics and policy focus on the policies that have the most support, they miss the values emerging in counterpublic arenas – voices that pose alternative views, whether the alternative values are posed by philosophers like Maxine Greene, Jane Roland Martin, or Nell Noddings (who reintroduce caring, connection, relationship, emotion, the personal and the issues usually relegated to the private sphere) or by educators/citizens/parents/children.

33 Fraser's (1994) definition of public sphere goes beyond government and includes anywhere where 'political participation is enacted through the medium of talk' (p. 111) – so it is not the economy, not just the legislature, it is a 'theater for debating and deliberating' (p. 111) – a place where participatory democracy can take place, but the ideal has degenerated because the public sphere has oppressive structures and unequal power relations within it.

34 The US Senate had to deal with two highly visible cases regarding sexual harassment: first, when many women gave evidence of Senator Packwood's misdeeds; and second, when Anita Hill's sexual harassment complaint against the then-nominee for Supreme Court, Clarence Thomas, became the focus of his confirmation hearings. Watching the US Senate protect Senator Packwood for so long and grill Anita Hill makes one cynical about the will and capacity of government to upset itself over a 'woman's issue'.

35 Yates (1993) shows how the language of feminist politics is taken up but transformed and contained when it is made policy.

36 In her study of Canada's Royal Commission on the Status of Women, Trimble concluded, 'When faced with demands for policy changes that fundamentally challenge the prevailing conception of gender roles, the federal government will conduct research and invoke non-coercive policy instruments' (Trimble, 1990: 41).

37 They are particularly useful analyses played out in the midst of 'the realignment of politics following the success of neo-conservative forces in the 1980s' (p. 210) and the 'rapid growth of world wide corporate capitalist economic system.' Where, she says, we cannot predict 'what sort of politics will emerge to mobilize groups around a progressive agenda' (Arnot: 210). Weiler and Arnot's (1993) analyses of education policy in settings ranged from Maori women to women academics in Britain and Black American women teachers. A huge policy agenda beckons, for comparisons of education systems, within the context of political and economic systems and their effects on women.

38 Such questioning, derived from a taxonomy of education policy mechanisms (Marshall

et al., 1989) used at the state level, can be useful in calling to mind a wide spectrum of ways to influence what happens in school. For example, policymakers often forget to think about changing buildings and facilities, yet some pedagogical strategies such as group work, single sex classes, would require it, or policymakers may mandate a governance change without contemplating the funding or training needed to get the change in place.

39 In this section I focus a great deal on cautions for women working the feminist agenda since our positions in academia and policy arenas are so easily toppled. As Jean O'Barr notes in Volume II (Chapter 5), one must try to separate the discriminations that are sexism from those that are just resistance to change. But the dismantler who is female is particularly vulnerable.

40 Quoted in McPhee and FitzGerald (1979) *Feminist Quotations: Voices of Rebels, Reformers and Visionaries.*

41 We need more case studies, self-reflective analyses, empirical research, not internal critique and debates about whether critical, feminist, postmodern and/or some sub strand of each is more correct. As Middleton says, feminists can be 'theoretically promiscuous' (1993: 42) a stance which will facilitate vital cross-pollination,

42 Connell (1987) has taken leadership; he lays out his feminist credentials as he introduces *Gender and Power*, and the Australian gender equity project's success may be attributed in part to its focus on the social construction of gender, thus including males' needs.

43 Acker notes that the feminist researcher's work cannot always be purely feminist and that we should avoid checklists for feminist credibility. She also cautions, 'I believe some standards have to be set beyond personal validation of data' (1987: 431). Exploratory case studies can pull forth and name phenomena but 'it is still necessary to know under what conditions such findings will and will not obtain, if oppression is to be fought most effectively' (1987: 431).

44 As Florence Nightingale learned, by being nicknamed 'the great complainer', in her work for improved medical treatment.

45 This is not to say – anything goes. Indeed, there will be long debates over evolving standards and credibility and validity (Lather, 1991).

46 For example, citing the glaring statistics about schools' failures and the need for role models, special academies or African American males; only the National Organization for Women noted and fought against the denigrating message to African American girls (Alston, 1993).

References

ACKER, S. (Ed) (1989) *Teachers, Gender and Career*, London, Falmer Press.

ACKER, S. (Ed) (1994) *Gendered Education: Sociological Reflections of Women. Teaching and Feminism*, Buckingham, Open University Press.

ACKER, S. (1995) 'Carry on caring: The work of women teachers', *British Journal of Sociology of Education*, **16**(1), pp. 21–36.

AGGER, B. (1991) *A Critical Theory of Public Life: Knowledge, Discourse and Politics in an Age of Decline*, London, Falmer Press.

AGGER, B. (1992) *Cultural Studies as Critical Theory*, London, Falmer Press.

ALCOFF, L. (1988) 'Cultural feminism versus poststructuralism: The identity crisis in feminist theory', *Signs: Journal of Women in Culture and Society*, **13**(3), pp. 405–36.

ALSTON, K. (1993) 'Community politics and the education of African American males: Whose life is it anyway?', in MARSHALL, C. (Ed) *The New Politics of Race and Gender*, London, Falmer Press, pp. 117–27.

ANDERSON, C.W. (1978) 'The logic of public problems: Evaluations in comparative policy research', in ASHFORD, D.E. (Ed) *Comparing Public Policies: New Concepts and Methods*, Beverly Hills, CA, Sage.

ANDERSON, G.L. (1989) 'Critical ethnography in education: Origins, current status, and new directions', *Review of Educational Research*, **59**(3), pp. 249–70.

ANDERSON, G.L. (1990) 'Toward a critical constructivist approach to school administration: Invisibility, legitimation, and the study of non-events', *Educational Administration Quarterly*, **26**(1), pp. 38–59.

ANDERSON, G.L. and HERR, K. (1993) 'The micro-politics of student voices: Moving from diversity of voices in schools', in MARSHALL, C. (Ed) *The New Politics of Race and Gender*, Washington, DC, Falmer Press, pp. 58–68.

ANYON, J. (1983) 'Intersections of gender and class: Accommodations and resistance by working-class and affluent females to contradictory sex-role ideologies', in WALKER, S. and BARTON, L. (Eds) *Gender, Class and Education*, Lewes, Falmer Press.

APPLE, M. (1994) 'Texts and contexts: The state and gender in educational policy', *Curriculum Inquiry*, **24**(3), pp. 349–59.

ARENDT, H. (1972) 'On violence', in *Crisis of the Republic*, New York, Harcourt, Brace, Jovanovitch.

ARNOT, M. and WEILER, K. (Eds) (1993) *Feminism and Social Justice in Education: International Perspectives*, London, Falmer Press.

ARNOT, M. and WEINER, G. (1987) 'Introduction', in ARNOT, M. and WEINER, G., *Gender and the Politics of Schooling*, London, Unwin Hyman.

BALL, S. (1987) *The Micro-politics of the School: Towards a Theory of School Organization*, London, Methuen Press.

BALL, S. (1990) *Politics and Policymaking in Education: Explorations in Policy Sociology*, London, Routledge.

BALL, T. (1993) 'New faces of power', in WARTENBERG, T. (Ed) *Rethinking Power*, Albany, NY, State University of New York Press.

DE BEAUVOIR, S. (1970) *The Second Sex*, (edited and translated by H.M. PASHLEY), New York, Alfred A. Knopf.

BELENKY, M.F., CLINCHY, B., GOLDBERGER, N.R. and TARULE, J.M. (1986) *Women's Ways of Knowing: The Development of Self, Voice and Mind*, New York, Basic Books.

BELL, C. and CHASE, S. (1993) 'The underrepresentation of women in school leadership', in MARSHALL, C. (Ed) *The New Politics of Race and Gender*, London, Falmer Press, pp. 141–54.

BERMAN, P. and MCLAUGHLIN, M. (1978) *Federal Programs Supporting Educational Changes, Vol. VIII: Implementing and Sustaining Innovation*, Santa Monica, CA, Rand Corporation.

BIKLEN, S. (1980) 'Introduction: Barriers to equity – Women, educational leadership, and social change', in BIKLEN, S. and BRANNIGAN, M. (Eds) *Women and Education Leadership*, Lexington, MA, DC Heath, pp. 1–25.

BLACKMORE, J., KENWAY, J., WILLIS, S. and RENNIE, L. (1993) 'What's working for girls?: The reception of gender equity policy in two Australian schools', in MARSHALL, C. (Ed) *The New Politics of Race and Gender*, London, Falmer Press, pp. 183–202.

BLACKMORE, J. (in press) 'Policy as dialogue: Feminist administrators working for educational change', *Gender and Education*.

BONEPARTH, E. (1982) 'A framework for policy analysis', in BONEPARTH, E. (Ed) *Women Power and Policy*, New York, Bergin and Garvey.

BONEPARTH, E. and STOPER, E. (1988) *Women, Power and Policy: Toward the Year 2000*, 2nd ed, Elmsford, NY, Pergamon Press.

BORMAN, K.M., MUENINGHOFF, E. and PIAZZA, S. (1988) 'Urban Appalachian girls and young women: Bowing to no one', in WEIS, L. (Ed) *Class, Race and Gender in American Education*, Albany, NY, State University of New York Press, pp. 230–48.

BOWLES, G. and KLEIN, R.D. (1983) 'Introduction: Theories of women's studies and the autonomy/integration debate', in BOWLES, G. and KLEIN, R.D. (Eds) *Theories of Women's Studies*, London, Routledge and Kegan Paul, pp. 1–26.

CALLAHAN, R.E. (1962) *Education and the Cult of Efficiency: A Study of the Social Forces that have Shaped the Administration of Public Schools*, Chicago, IL, University of Chicago Press.

CALLAHAN, D. and JENNINGS, B. (Eds) (1983) *Ethics, the Social Sciences and Policy Analysis*, New York, Plenum Press.

CAMPBELL, J.C., BASKIN, M.A., BAUMGARTNER, F.R. and HALPERN, N.P. (1989) 'Afterword on policy communities: A framework for comparative research', *Governance: An International Journal of Policy and Administration*, **2**(1).

CASEY, K. and APPLE, M.W. (1989) 'Gender and the conditions of teachers' work: The development of understanding in America', in ACKER, S. (Ed) *Teachers, Gender and Careers*, Basingstoke, Falmer Press, pp. 171–96.

CHODOROW, N. (1978) *The Reproduction of Mothering: Psychoanalysis and the Socialization of Gender*, Berkeley, CA, University of California Press.

CLARK, D.C. and ASTUTO, T.A. (1986) 'The significance and permanence of changes in federal education policy', *Educational Researcher*, **15**, 8, pp. 4–13.

CLARK, D.L. and TERRY, A. (1986) 'The significance and permanence of changes in federal education policy', *Educational Researcher*, October, pp. 4–13.

CLARRICOATES, K. (1987) 'Dinosaurs in the classrooms: The hidden curriculum in primary schools', in ARNOT, M. and WEINER, G. (Eds) *Gender and the Politics of Schooling*, London, Unwin Hyman, pp. 155–65.

COCKBURN, C. (1991) *In the Way of Women: Men's Resistance to Sex Equality in Organizations*, Basingstoke, MacMillan.

CONNELL, R.W. (1987) *Gender and Power*, Cambridge, England, Polity Press.

CUNNISON, S. (1989) 'Gender joking in the staff room', in ACKER, S. (Ed) *Teachers, Gender and Careers*, Basingstoke, Falmer Press, pp. 151–67.

DEEM, R. (1978) *Women and Schooling*, London, Routledge and Kegan Paul.

DE HAVEN-SMITH, L. (1988) *Philosophical Critiques of Policy Analysis: Lindblom, Habermas, and the Great Society*, Gainesville, FL, University of Florida Press.

DELAURENTIS, T. (Ed) (1986) *Feminist Studies/Critical Studies: Issues, Terms, Contexts*, Bloomington, IN, Indiana University Press.

DELEON, P. (1988) *Advice and Consent: The Development of the Policy Sciences*, New York, Russell Sage.

DIETZ, M. (1992) 'Feminism and theories, of citizenship', in MOUFFE, C. (Ed) *Dimensions of Radical Democracy: Pluralism, Citizenship, Democracy*, London, Verso, pp. 63–85.

DILLARD, C.B. (1995) 'Leading with her life: An African American feminist (re)interpretation of leadership for an urban high school principal', *Educational Administration Quarterly*, **31**(4), pp. 539–63.

DRYZEK, J.S. and BOBROW, D.B. (1987) *Policy Analysis by Design*, Pittsburgh, PA, University of Pittsburgh Press.

EISENSTEIN, Z.R. (1979) *Capitalist Patriarchy and the Case for Socialist Feminism*, New York, Monthly Review Press.

EISENSTEIN, Z. (1981) 'Reform and/or revolution: Towards a unified women's movement', in SARGENT, L. (Ed) *Women and Revolution: A Discussion of the Unhappy Marriage of Marxism and Feminism*, Boston, MA, Southend Press, pp. 339–62.

EISENSTEIN, H. (1990) 'Femocrats, official feminism and the uses of power', in WATSON, S. (Ed) *Playing the State: Australian Feminist Intervention*, London, Verso.

EISENSTEIN, H. (1993) 'A telling tale from the field', in BLACKMORE, J. and KENWAY, J., *Gender Matters in Educational Administration and Policy*, London, Falmer Press, pp. 1–8.

ELLSWORTH, E. (1989) 'Why doesn't this feel empowering: Working through the repressive myths of critical pedagogy', *Harvard Educational Review*, **59**(3), pp. 297–324.

ELSHTAIN, J.B. (1982) 'Feminist discourse and its discontents: Language, power and meaning', in KEOHANE, N., ROSALDO, M.Z. and GELPI, B.C. (Eds) *Feminist Theory: A Critique of Ideology*, Chicago, IL, University of Chicago Press.

EVANS, J. (1986) 'Feminism and political theory', in *Feminism and Political Theory*, Beverly Hills, CA, SAGE Publications, pp. 1–16.

EVANS, T. (1993) 'Equal opportunity, integration and parental participation: A gender-critical case study of educational policy implementation between two schools', in BLACKMORE, J. and KENWAY, J., *Gender Matters in Educational Administration and Policy*, London, Falmer Press, pp. 125–36.

EVERS, C.W. (1988) 'Policy analysis, values, and complexity', *Education Policy*, **3**(3), pp. 223–33.

FALUDI, S. (1991) *Backlash: The Undeclared War against American Women*, New York, Crown Press.

FERGUSON, K.E. (1984) *The Feminist Case against Bureaucracy*, Philadelphia, PA, Temple University Press.

FINE, M. (1991) *Framing Dropouts: Notes on the Politics of an Urban Public High School*, Albany, NY, SUNY Press.

FISCHER, F. (1989) 'Beyond the Rationality Project: Policy Analysis and the Postpositivist Challenge', *Policy Studies Journal*, **17**, pp. 941–51.

FISHEL, A. and POTTKER, J. (1977) 'Performance of women principals: A review of behavioral and attitudinal studies', in POTTKER, J. and FISHEL, A. (Eds) *Sex Bias in the Schools*, Cranbury, NJ, Associated University Press.

FORESTER, J. (1993) *Critical Theory, Public Policy and Planning Practice: Toward a Critical Pragmatism*, Albany, NY, State University of New York Press.

FOSTER, M. (1993) 'Othermothers: Exploring the educational philosophy of black American women teachers', in ARNOT, M. and WEILER, K. (Eds) *Feminism and Social Justice in Education: International Perspectives*, London, Falmer Press, pp. 101–23.

FOSTER, W. (1986) *Paradigms and Promises: New Approaches to Educational Administration*, Buffalo, NY, Prometheus Books.

FOUCAULT, M. (1977) *Discipline and Punish*, New York, NY, Vintage.

FOUCAULT, M. (1981) 'The order of discourse', in YOUNG, R. (Ed) *Untying the Text*, London, Routledge and Kegan Paul.

FRANZWAY, S., COURT, D. and CONNELL, R.W. (1989) *Staking a Claim: Feminism, Bureaucracy and the State*, Cambridge, England, Polity Press.

FRASER, N. (1989) *Unruly Practices: Power, Discourse and Gender in Contemporary Society*, Minneapolis, MN, University of Minnesota Press.

FRASER, N. (1994) 'Rethinking the public sphere: A contribution to the critique of actually existing democracy', in CALHOUN, C. (Ed) *Habermas and the Public Sphere*, Cambridge, MA, The MIT Press, pp. 109–42.

FREIRE, P. (1985) *The Politics of Education*, South Hadley, MA, Bergin and Garvey.

GARMS, W., GUTHRIE, J. and PIERCE, L. (1978) *School Finance: The Economics and Politics of Education*, Englewood Cliffs, NJ, Prentice-Hall.

GILLIGAN, C. (1980) *In a Different Voice*, Harvard, MA, Harvard University Press.

GIROUX, H.A. (1983) 'Introduction', in GIROUX, H. (Ed) *Critical Theory and Educational Practice*, Victoria, Australia, Deakin University.

GIROUX, H. (1992) *Border Crossings: Cultural Workers and the Politics of Education*, New York, NY, Routledge.

GOLDRING, E. and CHEN, M. (1993) 'The feminization of the principalship in Israel: The trade-off between political power and cooperative leadership', in MARSHALL, C. (Ed) *The New Politics of Race and Gender*, London, The Falmer Press, pp. 175–82.

GOODNOW, E. (1987) 'Topics, methods, and models: Feminist challenges in social science', in PATEMAN, C. and GROSS, E. (Eds) *Feminist Challenges: Social and Political Theory*, Boston, Northeastern University Press, pp. 1–31.

GOODNOW, E. and PATEMAN, C. (1985) (Eds) *Women, Social Science and Public Policy*, Wincester, MA, Allen and Unwin, Inc., pp. ix–xvi.

GOODSELL, C.T. (1990) 'Emerging issues in public administration', in LYNN, N.B. and WILDAVSKY, A. (Eds) *Public Administration: The State of the Discipline*, Chatham, NJ, Chatham House Publishers, p. 496.

GORE, J. (1992) 'What can we do for you! What *can* "we" do for "you"?: Struggling over empowerment in critical and feminist pedagogy', in LUKE, C. and GORE, J. (Eds) *Feminisms and Critical Pedagogy*, New York, Routledge, pp. 54–73.

GRUMET, M. (1988) *Bitter Milk: Women and Teaching*, Amherst, MA, University of Massachusetts Press.

HABERMAS, J. (1986) 'Hannah Arendt's communications concept of power', in LUKES, S. (Ed) *Power*, New York, New York University Press.

HARDING, S. (1986) *The Science Question in Feminism*, Ithaca, NY, Cornell University Press.

HARGREAVES, A. (1983) 'The politics of administrative convenience', in AHIER, J. and FLUDE, M. (Eds) *Contemporary Education Policy*, Beckenham, Croom Helm.

HASTE, H. (1994) *The Sexual Metaphor*, Cambridge, MA, Harvard University Press.

HAWKESWORTH, M. (1994) 'Policy studies within a feminist frame', *Policy Sciences*, **27**, pp. 97–118.

HEIDENHEIMER, A.J., HECLO, H. and ADAMS, C.T. (1990) *Comparative Public Policy*, New York, St. Martin's Press.

HOLLAND, D.C. and EISENHART, M.A. (1988) 'Women's ways of going to school: Cultural reproduction of women's identities as workers', in WEIS, L. (Ed) *Class, Race and Gender in American Education*, Albany, NY, State University of New York Press, pp. 266–301.

hooks, b. (1989) *Talking Back*, Boston, MA, South End Press.

hooks, b. (1990) *Yearning: Race, Gender and Cultural Politics*, Boston, MA, South End Press.

JENNINGS, B. (1983) 'Interpretive social science and policy analysis', in CALLAHAN, D. and JENNINGS, B. (Eds) *Ethics, the Social Sciences and Policy Analysis*, New York, Plenum Press.

KAHNE, J. (1994) 'Democratic communities, equity and excellence: A Deweyan Reframing of Educational Policy Analysis', *Educational Evaluation and Policy Analysis*, **16**(3), pp. 233–48.

KELLER, E.F. (1983) 'Gender and science', in HARDING, S. and HINTINKKA, M.B., *Discovering Reality*, Dordrecht Holland, D. Reidel.

KELLY, M. and MAYNARD-MOODY, S. (1993) 'Policy analysis in the post-positivist era: Engaging stakeholders in evaluating the economic development districts program', *Public Administration Review*, **53**(2), pp. 135–42.

KENWAY, J. (1992) 'Feminist theories of the state: To be or not to be?', in MUETZELFELDT, M. (Ed) *Society, State and Politics in Australia*, Leichhart, Australia, Pluto Press, pp. 108–44.

KENWAY, J. and MODRA, H. (1992) 'Feminist pedagogy and emancipatory possibilities', in LUKE, C. and GORE, J. (Eds) *Feminisms and Critical Pedagogy*, New York, Routledge, pp. 138–66.

KEOHANE, N., ROSALDO, M.Z. and GELPI, B.C. (Eds) (1982) *Feminist Theory: A Critique of Ideology*, Chicago, IL, University of Chicago Press.

KINGDON, J.W. (1984) *Agendas, Alternatives and Public Policies*, New York, HarperCollins Publishers.

KLEIN, S.S. (1985) *Handbook for Achieving Sex Equity through Education*, Baltimore, MD, Johns Hopkins University Press.

KLEIN, S.S. (1988) 'Using sex equity research to improve education policies', *Theory into Practice*, **27**(2), pp. 152–60.

KIRP, D. (1985) *Gender Justice*, Chicago, IL, University of Chicago Press.

LASSWELL, H.D. (1936) *Politics: Who Gets What, When and How*, New York, McGraw Hill.

LATHER, P. (1984) 'Critical theory, curricular transformation and feminist mainstreaming', *Journal of Education*, **166**(1), pp. 457–72.

LATHER, P. (1991) *Getting Smart: Feminist Research and Pedagogy*, New York, NY, Routledge.

LEACH, M. and DAVIES, B. (1990) 'Crossing boundaries: Educational thought and gender equity', *Educational Theory*, **40**(3), pp. 321–32.

LINDBLOM, C. (1990) *Inquiry and Change: The Trouble Attempt to Understand and Shape Society*, New Haven, CT, Yale University Press.

LORDE, A. (1984) *Sister Outsider*, Freedom, GA, Crossing Press.

LUKE, C. (1992) 'Feminist politics in radical pedagogy', in LUKE, C. and GORE, J. (Eds) *Feminisms and Radical Pedagogy*, New York, Routledge, pp. 25–53.

LUKE, C. and GORE, J. (1992) 'Women in the academy: Strategy, struggle and survival', in LUKE, C. and GORE, J. (Eds) *Feminisms and Critical Pedagogy*, New York, Routledge, pp. 192–210.

LUTRELL, W. (1993) '"The teachers, they all had their pets": Concepts of gender, knowledge, and power', *Signs*, Spring, pp. 505–45.

MACKINNON, C.A. (1982) 'Feminism, marxism, method and the state', in KEOHANE *et al.* (Eds) (1982) *Feminist Theory: A Critique of Ideology*, Chicago, IL, University of Chicago Press, pp. 1–30.

MACKINNON, C.A. (1989) *Toward a Feminist Theory of the State*, Cambridge, MA, Harvard University Press.

MCCARTHY, M., KUH, G. and IACONA, C. (1988) *Under Scrutiny: The Educational Administration Professoriate*, Tempe, AZ, University Council for Educational Administration.

MCKELLAR, B. (1989) 'Only the fittest of the fittest will survive: Black women and education', in ACKER, S., *Teachers, Gender and Careers*, Washington, DC, Taylor and Francis, pp. 69–85.

MCROBBIE, A. (1978) 'Working class girls and the culture of femininity', in WOMEN'S STUDY GROUP, CENTER FOR CONTEMPORARY CULTURAL STUDIES, *Women Take Issue*, London, Hutchinson, pp. 96–108.

MCPHEE, C. and FITZGERALD, A. (Eds) (1979) *Feminist Quotations: Voices of Rebels, Reformers and Visionaries*, New York, Crowell, p. 135.

MALEN, B. (1995) 'The micropolitics of education: Mapping the multiple dimensions of power relations in school polities', in SCRIBNER, J.D. and D.H. (Eds) *The Study of Educational Politics*, London, Falmer Press, pp. 147–68.

MARSHALL, C. (1981) 'Organizational policy and women's socialization in administration', *Urban Education*, **16**, pp. 205–31.

MARSHALL, C. (1985) 'The stigmatized woman: The professional woman in a male sex-typed career', *Journal of Educational Administration*, **23**(2), pp. 132–52.

MARSHALL, C. (1993) 'The politics of denial: Gender and race issues in administration', in MARSHALL, C. (Ed) *The New Politics of Race and Gender*, London, Falmer Press, pp. 168–74.

MARSHALL, C. (1995) 'Imagining leadership', *Educational Administration Quarterly*, **31**(3), pp. 484–92

MARSHALL, C. (1996) 'Undomesticated gender policy', in BANKS, B.J. and HALL, P.M. (Ed) *Gender Equity, and Schooling*, New York, Garland Publishing Co.

MARSHALL, C. and MITCHELL, B. (1991) 'The assumptive worlds of fledgling administrators', *Education and Urban Society*, **23**(4), pp. 396–415.

MARSHALL, C. and SCRIBNER, J.D. (1991) ' "It's all political": Inquiry into the micropolitics of education', *Education and Urban Society*, **23**(4), pp. 347–55.

MARSHALL, C., MITCHELL, D. and WIRT, F. (1989) *Culture and Education Policy in the American States*, London, Falmer Press.

MARSHALL, C., ROGERS, D., Steele, J. and PATTERSON, J. (1996) 'Caring as career: An alternative model for educational administration', *Educational Administration Quarterly*, **32**(2), pp. 271–94.

MARTIN, J. (1990) 'Deconstructing organizational taboos: The suppression of gender conflict in organizations', *Organizational Science*, **1**(4), pp. 339–59.

MARTUSEWICZ, R.A. and REYNOLDS, W.M. (1994) 'Introduction', in MARTUSEWICZ, R.A. and REYNOLDS, W.M. (Eds) *Inside/out: Contemporary Critical Perspectives in Education*, New York, St. Martin's Press, pp. 1–20.

MATSUDA, M.J., DELGADO, R., LAWRENCE, C.R. and CRENSHAW, K.W. (1993) *Words that Wound: Critical Race Theory, Assault Speech, and the First Amendment*, Westview.

MIDDLETON, S. (1993) *Educating Feminists: Life Histories and Pedagogies*, New York, Teachers College Press.

MINOGUE, M. (1983) 'Theory and practice in public policy and administration', *Policy and Politics*, **11**(1), pp. 63–85.

MITCHELL, D.E., BOYD, W., COOPER, B., MALEN, B. and MARSHALL, C. (1995) 'Taxonomy and Overview', in *Educational Administration: The UCEA Document Base: Domain V: Policy and Political Studies*, Princeton, NJ, McGraw-Hill, Inc.

NODDINGS, N. (1984) *Caring: A Feminine Approach to Ethics and Moral Education*, New York, Teachers College Press.

NODDINGS, N. (1988) 'An ethic of caring and its implications for American education', *American Journal of Education*, **96**(2), pp. 215–30.

OAKES, J. (1985) *Keeping Track: How Schools Structure Inequality*, New Haven, CT, Yale University Press.

ORTIZ, F.I. (1982) *Career Patterns in Education: Women, Men and Minorities in School Administration*, New York, Praeger.

ORTIZ, F.I. and MARSHALL, C. (1988) 'Women in educational administration', in BOYAN, N.J. (Ed) *Handbook of Research on Educational Administration*, New York, Longman, pp. 123–42.

ORTIZ, F.I. and ORTIZ, D.J. (1993) 'Politicizing executive action: The case of Hispanic female superintendents', in MARSHALL, C. (Ed) *The New Politics of Race and Gender*, London, Falmer Press, pp. 155–67.

PAIK, A. (1995) 'Teen pregnancy expert touts education', *The News and Observer*, June 20, 1B and 8B.

PATEMAN, C. (1985) 'Introduction', in GOODNOW, J. and PATEMAN, C. (Eds) *Women, Social Science and Public Policy*, Winchester, MA, Allen and Unwin, Inc., pp. ix–xvi.

PATEMAN, C. and GROSS, E. (Eds) (1987) *Feminist Challenges: Social and Political Theory*, Boston, MA, Northeastern University Press.

PRUNTY, J. (1985) 'Signposts for a critical education policy analysis', *Australian Journal of Education*, **29**(2), pp. 133–40.

REIN, M. (1983) 'Value-critical policy analysis', in CALLAHAN, D. and JENNINGS, B. (Ed) *Ethics, the Social Sciences and Policy Analysis*, New York, Plenum Press.

RICH, A. (1979) *On Lies, Secrets and Silence*, New York, NY, W.W. Norton.

ROE, E.M. (1989) 'Narrative analysis for the policy analyst: A case study of the 1980–1982 medfly controversy in California', *Journal of Policy Analysis and Management*, **8**(2), pp. 251–73.

ROWAN, B. (1994) 'Comparing teachers' work with work in other occupations: Notes on the professional status of teaching', *Educational Researcher*, **23**(6), pp. 4–17.

RYAN, A.G. (1988) 'Program evaluation within the paradigms', *Knowledge: Creation, Diffusion and Utilization*, **10**, pp. 25–47.

SADKER, M., SADKER, D. and KLEIN, S. (1986) 'Abolishing misperceptions about sex equity in education', *Theory Into Practice*, **225**(4), pp. 219–26.

SADKER, M., SADKER, D. and STEINDAM, S. (1989) 'Gender equity and educational reform', *Educational Leadership*, **46**(6), pp. 44–47.

SARASON, S. (1982) *The Culture of the School and the Problem of Change*, (2nd ed.) Boston, MA, Allyn & Bacon.

SCHEURICH, J.J. (1994) 'Policy archeology: A new policy studies methodology', *Education Policy*, **9**(4), pp. 297–316.

SCHMUCK, P., CHARTERS, R. and CARLSON, R. (Eds) (1981) *Educational Policy and Management: Sex Differentials*, New York, NY, Academic Press.

SCHRAM, S.F. (1995) 'Against policy analysis: Critical reason and poststructural resistance', *Policy Sciences*, **28**(4), pp. 375–84.

SCUTT, J.A. (1985) 'In pusuit of equality: Women and legal thought 1788–1984', in GOODNOW, J. and PATEMAN, C. (Eds) *Women, Social Science and Public Policy*, Winchester, MA, Allen and Unwin, Inc., pp. 116–39.

SHAKESHAFT, C. (1986) 'A gender at risk', *Phi Delta Kappan*, **67**(7), pp. 449–503.

SIMMONDS, F.N. (1992) 'Difference, power, and knowledge: black women in academia', in HINDS, H., PHOENIX, A. and STACEY, J. (Eds) *Working Out: New Directions for Women's Studies*, Washington, DC, The Falmer Press, pp. 51–60.

SMITH, D. (1981) *The Experienced World as Problematic: A Feminist Method*, Saskatoon Saskatchewan, University of Saskatchewan.

SPROULL, L.S. (1981) 'Response to regulation: An organizational process framework', *Administration and Society*, **12**(4), pp. 447–70.

STEINEM, G. (October 1978) 'If men could menstruate', *Outrageous Acts and Everyday Rebellions: MS Magazine*, New York, Holt Rinehart and Winston, pp. 337–40.

STIVERS, C. (1991) 'Toward a feminist perspective in public administration theory', *Women and Politics*, **10**, 4, pp. 49–65.

STONE, D. (1988) *Policy Paradox and Political Reason*, Glenview, IL, Scott, Foresman and Co.

TETRAULT, M. and SCHMUCK, P. (1985) 'Equity, educational reform and gender', *Issues in Education*, **3**, p. 64.

TONG, R. (1989) *Feminist Thought: A Comprehensive Introduction*, San Francisco, CA, Westview Press.

TRIMBLE, L. (1990) 'Towards transformation: Women, politics and public policy in Canada'. Text for Political Science 350, Department of Political Science, University of Alberta.

TYACK, D. and HANSOT, E. (1982) *Managers of Virtue: Public School Leadersip in America, 1890–1980*, New York, Basic Books.

UPDATE (1996) *National Women's Law Center*, (**9**)1, p. 2.

VALLI, L. (1988) 'Gender identity and the technology of office education', in WEISS, L. (Ed) *Class, Race and Gender in American Education*, Albany, NY, SUNY Press, pp. 87–105.

WALKERDINE, V. (1994) 'Femininity as performance', in STONE, L. (Ed) *The Education Feminism Reader*, New York, Routledge, pp. 57–69.

WARING, M. (1988) *If Women Counted: A New Feminist Economics*, San Francisco, CA, Harper and Row.

WATSON, S. (1990) 'The state of play: An introduction', in WATSON, S., *Playing the State: Australian Feminist Interventions*, London, Verso, pp. 1–20.

WEATHERLY, R. and LIPSKY, M. (1977) 'Street level bureaucrats and institutional innovation: Implementing special education reform', *Harvard Educational Review*, **47**(2), pp. 171–97.

WEBER, M. (1947) *The Theory of Social and Economic Organization*, (HENDERSON, A.M. and PARSONS, T. Trans.) Glencoe, Il, Free Press (first published in 1924).

WEICK, K.E. (1976) 'Educational organizations as loosely coupled systems', *Administrative Science Quarterly*, **21**, pp. 1–18.

WEILER, K. (1988) *Women Teaching for Change: Gender, Class and Power*, South Hadley, MA, Bergin and Garvey.

WEILER, K. (1993) 'Feminism and the struggle for a democratic education: A view from the states', in ARNOT, M. and WEILER, K. (Eds) *Feminism and Social Justice in Education: International Perspectives*, London, Falmer Press.

WEIS, L. (1988) 'High school girls in a de-industrializing economy', in WEIS, L. (Ed) *Class, Race, and Gender in American Education*, Albany NY, SUNY Press, pp. 183–208.

WEXLER, P. (1988) 'Symbolic economy of identity and denial of labor: Studies in high school number 1', in WEIS, L. (Ed) *Class, Race and Gender in American Education*, Albany, NY, State University of New York Press, pp. 302–16.

WILSON, M. (Ed) (1991) *Girls and Young Women in Education: A European Perspective*, Oxford, England, Pergamon.

WOLPE, A. (1978) 'The official ideology of education for girls', in MCDONALD, M., DALE, R., ESLAND, G. and FERGUSSON, R. (Eds) *Politics, Patriarchy and Practice*, Lewes, Sussex, Falmer Press.

YATES, L. (1993) 'What happens when feminism is an agenda of the state? Feminist theory and the case of education policy in Australia', *Discourse: The Australian Journal of Educational Studies*, **14**(1), pp. 17–29.

YEATMAN, A. (1993) 'Contemporary issues for feminism: The politics of the state', in BLACKMORE, J. and KENWAY, J. (Eds) *Gender in Educational Administration and Policy*, London, Falmer Press, pp. 137–45.

YEATMAN, A. (1994) *Postmodern Revisionings of the Political*, New York, Routledge.

ZAMBRANA, R.E. (1988) 'Toward understanding the education trajectory and socialization of Latina American women', in MCKENNA, T. and ORTIZ, F.I. (Eds) *The Broken Web: The Educational Experience of Hispanic American Women*, Claremont, CA, Tomas Rivera Center, pp. 61–78.

Part I

The Legitimized Formal Arenas of Policy

The feminist critique of politics and policy is summarized concisely by Dorothy Smith (1978):

Because men have power, they have power to keep it.

Journalists focus our attention on the visible, authorized, formal, legitimized arenas and positions given power to decide priorities and regulations for schools: school boards, official task forces, deans, professional associations, certification standards boards, lawmakers, reform commissions, code books. Front-of-the-scenes actions set directions for numbers of minutes devoted to national history, for sex education, for minimum standards for schools' computer capacities and wheelchair accessibility. They decide whether single sex schools are valuable. They decide how schools should address the needs of immigrant children. On first glance, their deliberations appear as orderly, rules-driven, decisionmaking informed by estimates, evaluations and technical analyses provided by experts.

A deeper look at the language, the body positioning, the audience and the agenda (what and who is there and not there) reveals some patterns of power and policy in the formal arenas. Theoretical insights, such as critiques of instrumental rationality as destructive of the 'congenial, spontaneous, egalitarian human activity, as antidemocratic and repressive' (Dryzek, 1990: 4) lead the activist and the scholar on a search to uncover and undo oppressive patterns. Feminist and critical theory, such as how the personal is political in the sexual politics of everyday life in education lead the concerned educator, scholar and parent to realign agendas in those formal deliberations.

The ensuing chapters in Part I serve as demonstrations of the need for a feminist analysis of education policy reform. What have governments done to make schools equitable, to respond to research about sex role stereotyping and access to sports, to counsel and support girls aspiring to non-traditional career choices? What philosophies and what resources were embedded in government directives? Readers can compare policy assumptions and actions in the United States, in Stromquist's and Weis' critical reviews, with those in Australia (Yates) and Great Britain (David, Weiner and Arnot). These analysts use government documents, evaluations, and program evaluations to demonstrate that, even in intense efforts to reform education systems, the deeper equity issues are missed. 'Nothing gets done which is unacceptable to dominant or influential political groups, which may be defined to include the "bureaucratic leadership group"' (Minogue, 1983: 73).

References

DRYZEK, J. (1990) *Discursive Democracy: Politics, Policy and Political Science*, New York, Cambridge University Press.

MINOGUE, M. (1983) 'Theory and practice in public policy and administration', *Policy and Politics*, **11**, 1, pp. 63–85.

Chapter 2

Gender, Ethnicity and the Inclusive Curriculum: An Episode in the Policy Framing of Australian Education

Lyn Yates

Typologies of policy research often set up dichotomous options for the policy researcher: the stance of an outside reporter or critic who writes *about* policy; or the stance of an advocate who writes *for* or *to* policy (Codd, 1983; Cunningham, 1992). However, what is perhaps most distinctive about recent feminist policy research in Australia is that it is often positioned in ways that make such a dichotomy inappropriate (see Blackmore and Kenway, 1993; Eisenstein, 1991; Franzway, Court and Connell, 1989; Yeatman, 1990).

Over the past two decades, some aspects of feminist concerns have claimed notable space on Australian policymaking agendas, especially in education. Feminist academics have been employed or consulted as part of the policy process, and (whether employed or not) their research is likely to be read by those formulating policies concerned with girls and women (and, equally, not read by those formulating many areas of general educational policy). In this situation, feminist policy research has a complex task. It must continue to engage in critique and continue to examine and illuminate ways in which policies are framed and enacted, using the broader feminist literature as a source of such critique. But feminist policy research must also consider the effects of its own participation in the policy process and the effects of its own construction of truths (see also Gore, 1993; McLeod, 1995; Weiner, Arnot and David, 1996; Yeatman, 1990).

The approach to feminist policy research that frames this chapter takes an interest in the significance of context and situated theorizing. In the case under discussion here, the context is one in which policy is explicitly concerned with feminist issues. This context locates the work of the feminist policy researcher differently than do contexts where the agenda is untouched by or hostile to such concerns.

I am also interested in how policy as a field (or a discourse or political practice) discursively reshapes agendas (including feminist agendas). The argument I have developed is that state policies reappropriate agendas in particular ways which I have discussed elsewhere at greater length (Yates, 1993b, 1993c). In particular, state policies exclude from their discourse contested meanings, contested line of exclusion and inclusion and contested visions. Also, state policies necessarily function to regulate practice. However, feminist debates whose foundational assumptions about race and ethnicity or postmodern theories challenge such principles also influence substantive reshapings of policy.

The interaction of state policy and feminist policy forms the background for this chapter which discusses one example of Australian education policymaking concerned with gender.[1] It looks at the extent to which and manner in which race and ethnicity have been addressed and reconstructed in successive policy moves concerned with gendered inequality or equal opportunity for girls.[2] It focuses in particular on one stage in these reconstructions, a stage that named attention to ethnicity and difference as a central issue in the education of girls and which named inclusive curriculum as an appropriate way to address ethnicity and difference in the education of girls.

The episode in question focuses on issues which have been highly problematic and much debated. Within feminism, the nature of sexual inequality, the legitimacy or illegitimacy of working with concepts of 'women's ways of knowing', and the significance of difference, ethnocentrism and racism have all been widely debated. In education policy, whether and how inequality is addressed and how curriculum is conceived are core issues, issues that have been subject to marked reformulations throughout the 1980s and 1990s.

Shifts in Australian Policies Concerned with Girls

In 1975, the report of a national committee of inquiry into girls and inequality in Australia, *Girls, School and Society*, declared, 'Sexism in education is a contradiction in terms' (Schools Commission, 1975: 17). This report set out ways in which schooling failed to give girls the same importance and opportunities as boys. It drew attention to the ways in which schooling channelled girls into a very narrow range of jobs and to a lesser share of continuing education. The report also showed that schooling developed girls in ways that did not give them the same confidence and ability to make choices in the world as boys. This report criticized a number of the existing processes of schooling, including the stereotyping of individuals according to their sex, the undermining of girls through the absence of women in the curriculum and the lack of career encouragement to girls, and the failure of the curriculum to teach girls and boys about the realities of work and women's contributions in society.

In brief, the emphasis of this 1975 report was not on what girls lack, it was on how schooling operates to produce poor outcomes for girls. It recommended, as strategies of reform, changes in how schooling was structured (to ensure equal access to all courses), changes in the curriculum (to represent women equally with men), and changes in careers counselling (to pay no attention to gender).

In 1984, a second Commonwealth report, *Girls and Tomorrow: The Challenge for Schools*, found that despite various funding programmes and school-level initiatives, little had actually changed in the outcomes of schooling for girls, and that the initiatives for change had been very patchy. This report led in turn to some further Commonwealth funding of major projects investigating education and girls and, in 1987, to a new *National Policy for the Education of Girls in Australian Schools*.

The 1987 National Policy recommended continued action under four headings: raising awareness of the educational needs of girls; equal access to and participation in appropriate curriculum; supportive school environment and equitable resource allocation. This report was more focused on how girls felt about school and extended into areas not addressed by *Girls, School and Society*, particularly concerning a supportive school environment and resource allocation. In terms of curriculum provision it stressed two themes not prominent in the earlier report: that girls are 'not a homogeneous group' and that curriculum and learning experiences should be 'appropriate' to the group.

Since 1987 the National Policy has been supplemented by annual reports summarizing system initiatives taken each year and by a review and five-year Action Plan for the period 1993–7 (AEC, 1993), which specify further priority areas for action in that period. At time of writing both the policy and the current Action Plan are under revision, a revision particularly sparked by recent public debate about boys as a disadvantaged group.

Where Did Matters of Race and Ethnicity Fit into all This?

A comparison of the 1975 report, *Girls, School and Society*, with the 1987 *National Policy for the Education of Girls in Australian Schools*, shows a marked change in the way ethnicity and race were treated in the analysis of gender, inequality and school reform. In the first report, discussion of 'migrant women and girls' is enclosed in a separate chapter labelled 'Groups with Special Needs'. It is treated as add-on problem of disadvantage, one which might involve special welfare considerations, but which is not part of the mainstream analysis of gender and schooling, or of the curriculum recommendations in relation to the education of girls. Indeed, the emphasis in this report is on providing a 'non-sexist curriculum' to all students:

> There should be no distinction made between girls and boys in school curriculum or organisation, nor any sex-related expectations about behaviour, interests, capacities, personality traits or life patterns (Schools Commission, 1975: 158).

By contrast, the opening chapter in the 1987 Policy is headed 'Being a Girl in an Australian School', and relates anecdotes about many different types of girls, in many different settings. It makes clear that different situations of class, ethnicity and race are part of 'being a girl', and certainly need to be taken into account when building a 'supportive school environment or' reforming curriculum ('to include the contribution of women, from all ethnic backgrounds and social groups'). Its policy framework (that is, the set of principles it labels as such) explicitly and repeatedly includes the need for the recognition of difference (Schools Commission, 1987):

Equality of opportunity and outcomes in education for girls and boys may require differential provision, at least for a period of time.

Strategies to improve the quality of education for girls should be based on an understanding that girls are not a homogeneous group.

To improve schooling for Aboriginal and Torres Strait Islander girls, school authorities will need to take account of the unique culture of Aboriginal and Torres Strait Islander communities.

The effective change and lasting improvements needed in schools will require awareness and understanding of the educational needs of girls on the part of students, parents, teachers and administrators, and institutional support for addressing these needs.

'Inclusive Curriculum'

In Australia, an interest in 'inclusive' curriculum can be seen in discussions, reform projects and policy documents from the early 1980s (Suggett, 1987).[3] In contrast to the USA, where the term 'inclusive' is frequently associated with teaching students with disabilities in mainstream classrooms, the term in Australia has been most commonly associated with the teaching of girls and the teaching of students from different ethnic backgrounds, though policies which use the term may also make some reference to students with disabilities, to rural students, or to students with different class backgrounds. As is evident from its uses in the *National Policy for the Education of Girls*, the concept of inclusive curriculum refers both to curriculum and pedagogy. It embraces the idea that schools and teachers should be sensitive to the backgrounds, values and learning preferences of the students they teach and the idea that students should study subjects that explicitly reflect the contributions of different cultures, not just those of the dominant monoculture.

In the history of recent decades of school reform concerning girls, the agenda of inclusive curriculum represented a particular phase of policy, one which succeeded the rather different earlier emphasis on non-sexist curriculum and preceded the more recent emphasis on construction of gender as the agenda of what teachers should actually be teaching students.[4]

But what does it *mean* to be inclusive of gender and ethnicity (let alone class)? How have these policy developments held up against discussions and debates about ethnicity and race in feminist writings? How have the *policies* functioned in relation to the *practices* of schooling?

Gender, Ethnicity and Feminist Research

At one level, the shifts in policy discussions I have outlined echo a shift that was widely evident in feminist discussions over the same period. Initially, many feminist analyses focused on girls or women as a single category and implicitly took the dominant cultural group as their subject; other cultures and the concerns of other groups within the culture were discussed through an ethnocentric lens. As a result of some fierce debates and movements by women who were not counted in by the mainstream, by the mid-1980s it was becoming more common for feminist researchers to work with a sense of differences and to devote greater attention to them.

Until the 1980s, the Australian academic discussion of ethnicity in education largely remained separate from the discussion of gender in education. For example, a review of research on ethnicity published in 1987 (Smolicz, 1987) has few references in common with a review of research on gender published in the same year (Yates, 1987). The 1975 policy reports treatment of girls as a single group, to which 'girls from non-English speaking backgrounds' (NESB) were appended as a 'group with special needs', reflected a practice widely common within feminist writing and public debate at the time. At this time, NESB women with an active concern about girls and education were more commonly working within the 'multicultural' policy fields rather than as a visible voice of the field defined as 'feminist or girls' policy.

By the early 1980s, debates about racism within feminism had become a more public issue.[5] Feminist research on gender, ethnicity and schooling in Australia now began to develop some differing analyses of this area, analyses with different emphases and different programmatic implications for policy.[6] I will briefly outline three influential writings by feminist education researchers that were receiving attention in Australia around the time 'inclusive curriculum' was becoming a recommendation of policy. The approaches share some overlapping values and analyses, but also suggest some rather different directions for an 'inclusive curriculum' practice – differences which are not adequately described by traditional political typologies of conservative/liberal/radical. The frameworks (or at least the apparent implications of these frameworks) differ regarding whether and to what extent curriculum can simply use existing ethnic and gender formation as the basis for educational practice. What they hold in common is an understanding that 'ethnicity' and 'gender' are not discrete and additive categories, and a concern that frameworks should not treat ethnic students as having a different and less complex subjectivity than those of English-speaking background.[7]

In one feminist research formulation (Stintzos, 1984) the focus was on ways in which girls of Greek background experienced some cultural tensions in negotiating their schooling. Strintzos argued that the girls, through their families, experienced a culture which actively valued separate spheres for men and women, accepted heavy domestic responsibilities for girls, and included a concept of family honour which heavily restricted the social life of the girls and promoted strong double standards for them as compared with male members of their family. On the other hand, they encountered a school culture that valued individual achievement and career orientation and a peer culture that valued unguarded interaction. Strintzos identified a range of responses by Greek girls to this situation, responses heavily mediated by the social class composition of their schooling. She showed that some girls incorporated career orientation and school achievement goals, but maintained the 'good girl' responsibilities of virtue, extreme femininity of appearance and responsibility for domestic labour and general care of men. She showed that other girls made a move towards Anglo styles of leisure and behaviour and were thus labelled as 'bad', though they themselves had not rejected the general concepts of femininity and virtue of their families.

Feminist research of this type was not designed primarily to provide guidelines for pedagogy or curriculum; it was concerned with sociological understanding of the subjectivity of schoolgirls. But feminist research of this kind (popular in a host of sociological ethnographic studies in the early 1980s) may be seen as one foundation of the interest in a differentiated vision of being a girl found in the 1987 policy analysis of girls and school. It sets up ways in which the values and expectations of schooling, of curriculum, may be sources of tension, may *exclude* rather than *include* students as the assumed subjects and subject matter of schooling.

On the other hand, this framework does not make explicit what sort of inclusion would more adequately frame the schooling experiences of these girls. It may work to confirm and reinforce teachers' views of this group as disadvantaged, and to explain away failures in what school achieves for these girls as due to factors outside schooling.

Another feminist approach, explicitly cited in the 1987 policy re-working, was designed to consider ethnic difference affirmatively and not through a lens of disadvantage. This work, by Tsolidis (1984, 1986, 1988), was based on school-based research with students of different backgrounds (female and male; Anglo- and NESB). In these studies, Tsolidis portrayed girls of non-English speaking background as knowledgeable, active subjects who choose which practices they will support. For example, in Australia, teachers often are quick to cite the difficulty they have in getting permission for NESB girls to go on school camps as evidence of the restrictiveness of NESB girls' culture and the disadvantages NESB girls face. Tsolidis argued that her research (as a woman of similar background interviewing the students about these issues) indicated that the girls were primarily concerned about getting a good education that would give them access to good careers. In cases where they themselves saw camps and excursions as educationally worthwhile, they would present them as such to parents and would negotiate permission. However they usually saw the camps as 'slack' and as an unnecessary distraction from the educational function of schooling, and used lack of permission as a means of avoiding them.

Tsolidis' work emphasized the additional knowledge possessed by these girls (especially knowledge related to migration and the second language) – knowledge not possessed to the same extent by boys of that background. She argued that by treating the girls as disadvantaged, rather than appreciating and building on their existing knowledge, school was limiting their education. Tsolidis did not deny that issues of virginity, honour, etc., were issues of significance for these girls and their families, and that these differed from mainstream Australian norms. But she disputed the emphasis and salience given these issues by teachers and policymakers who saw ethnic identity only in terms of deficits and disadvantages. The identity formation of these girls, Tsolidis argued, gave them additional knowledge and certain potential advantages in their education, but their strengths were not being seen and built on.

In relation to 'inclusive curriculum' then, this feminist work was arguing that the schooling aspirations and the specific experiences of these girls should not be interpreted as disadvantages requiring compensatory treatment. These girls should be included, they should be heard, in new and different ways. But the implications of the argument set out in this research for a general policy of inclusive curriculum were less clear. Tsolidis argued that the competence and aspirations for schooling of the NESB girls she studied should be given greater emphasis, while the issues of difference commonly discussed in relation to them (of virtue and honour) should be treated sensitively, but effectively given less emphasis in constructions of curriculum and pedagogy. However, Tsolidis' research also showed that another group of girls, working-class girls of English-speaking background, had low aspirations and learning preferences that worked against their success. Given this, it is apparent that schools cannot build an inclusive curriculum simply by putting in what the students themselves already see as important.

Kalantzis and Cope (1987, 1988) proposed a third way to consider feminism and ethnicity in Australian education. They argued that, given the diversity of cultural and class background, it was not possible to simply build a curriculum on the interests and characteristics of learners, and that many schooling programs that signalled such inclusion of difference were tokenistic and were streaming children towards ethnic activities which disadvantaged them in the mainstream selective processes of schooling and post-school. Kalantzis and Cope were similarly critical of 'naive' programs of 'non-sexist education' which were blind to the cultural specificity of the practices they favoured (for example, in presuming that certain learning styles were the preferences of girls).

In relation to these concerns, Kalantzis and Cope advocated a new common curriculum project (the Social Literacy Project). Here the emphasis was not on having a particular range of experiences represented, but on a structured study of cultures and gender which would have children reflect on how cultures are constructed and on the relation of the individual to their culture and to other individuals.

Kalantzis and Cope's analysis viewed schooling as a system through which material advantages were produced. They argued for sensitivity to cultural differences (such as preferred learning styles) and for attention to the real needs of some groups (help with English for those who have recently arrived in Australia). But Kalantzis and Cope also asserted that ethnicity and gender concerns cannot be simply treated as differences and variety to add together in a curriculum. Rather, an adequate program should have a framework which has an answer to how gender and ethnicity concerns should be represented and how students should learn to analyze them.

Inclusive Curriculum as a Policy Discourse

When the *National Policy for the Education of Girls* (1987) addressed ethnicity as part of its policy principles, it emphasized that 'girls are not a homogeneous group', that students should have access to 'appropriate' curriculum, and that curriculum should 'include the contribution of women, from all ethnic backgrounds and social groups'. These terms of the policy discourse, as Yeatman has noted, are written 'in such a way as to deny the politics of discourse (a politics of contested meaning)' (Yeatman, 1990: 160).

Rhetorically, the National Policy document heeds that part of the debate about feminism and racism that is concerned with acknowledging difference and specificity; what it does not even allude to is that this debate signalled challenges about what constitutes important knowledge: not just whose examples are to illustrate texts, but what issues are to be raised and what directions are to be given to curriculum and pedagogy. (Nor, of course, does it make any gesture to the beginnings of a shift in feminist theory which saw these challenges as ongoing and not appropriately resolved by a fuller and more inclusive theory. See, for example, Hirsch and Fox Keller, 1990; Luke and Gore, 1992; Gunew and Yeatman, 1993; Yeatman, 1994; and the discussion by Martin, 1994.)

'Appropriate' and 'inclusive' sit neatly within the terms of education policies in liberal democratic societies, policies which rhetorically work within tropes of doing increasingly better for all groups of students and which refuse to acknowledge that any groups of students may have their interests harmed by any given developments. Thus, one way to regard the 1987 policy development would be to note that it incorporates and contains challenges about difference, ethnocentrism and racism. The report formally acknowledges these political challenges without imposing substantive redirection on current practices.

This interpretation would gain further support if we go beyond the 1987 policy text and consider both the regulations through which it was enforced as practice and its effects within the wider field of education policies. In the latter case, the injunctions in the 'girls' policy' to be 'inclusive' were not replicated in other curriculum and assessment policies being developed in the early 1980s (Yates, 1988). In the former case, when teacher promotion policies included 'inclusive' teaching as one of the essential criteria, this was given no specification and had no effective force.[8] Indeed the use of the term could encourage a range of the very practices and thinking against which the research on gender and ethnicity had initially been directed: assumptions by teachers that they treated all students as individuals, or interpretation of ethnic sensitivity which effectively constructed students of non-English speaking background in deficit terms and led to modified courses and limited career directions for them.

Of course, texts are only one part of policy as a field (Franzway, 1994; Kenway, Willis, Blackmore and Rennie, 1993). The policy texts discussed here do not constitute a comprehensive story of how this era of policy was practiced, constrained and enacted, just as the feminist texts discussed here do not reveal the lines of association, influence and forms of organization that were an important part of feminist interactions with the policy field. But we can glimpse through these texts ways in which feminist ideas and research contributed new ideas to policy as well as critiqued policy, ways in which policy discourse selectively appropriated and reshaped feminist agendas and ways in which feminist academic work engaged complex questions while avoiding a simple or single formulaic model for reconstructing the complexities of schooling.

Notes

1 Much of this chapter is a revised version of an unpublished paper presented at the 1989 AERA Conference: 'Gender, ethnicity and the "inclusive" curriculum: some contending Australian frameworks of policy and research'. It also draws on some of my subsequent thinking about feminism and policy research (Yates, 1993a, 1993b, 1993c, 1995a, 1995b, 1995c).

2 That is, I am not in this chapter attempting to give a broad overview of policymaking and research concerned with gender and with ethnicity – I am focusing more narrowly on the way in which ethnicity and race have been reconceptualized within policies formally concerned with girls. A more wide-ranging discussion of the developments in both areas can be found in Tsolidis (1993a and 1993b). It should also be noted that in Australia, schooling policy is made both by state governments and at national level. In this chapter I am not able to discuss the complexities of these relationships or the detail of the many policies developed by the different states.

3 This was by no means a uniform emphasis across the country and was seen most explicitly in projects and policies in Victoria and South Australia, and in projects promoted by the national Curriculum Development Centre.

4 I discuss the constructions, values and problems associated with each phase of policy in a previous article (Yates, 1995a).

5 These were prominent at the 1984 fourth national Women and Labour Conference in Australia, and the fierceness of the differences voiced at this conference led to the suspension of these conferences for over a decade – a history that itself might signal that glib references to inclusiveness should be treated with suspicion.

6 The section that follows draws on the AERA paper that I wrote in 1989. It does not pretend to be a full account of feminist work on ethnicity, gender and schooling, but was written when discussions about inclusive curriculum were at their peak, and attempted to draw out work which illustrated the difficulties of enacting such a concept.

7 All the terms here are usefully interrogated in the research I am discussing.

8 From the testimony of people who served on committees, and from some informal unpublished studies, it appears that Promotion Committees had no criteria or concepts by which an applicant's claim to be an inclusive teacher would be judged inadequate, so they effectively disregarded that criterion in their formal deliberations.

References

AUSTRALIAN EDUCATION COUNCIL (AEC) (1993) *National Action Plan for the Education of Girls 1993–97*, Carlton, Curriculum Corporation.

BLACKMORE, J. and KENWAY, J. (Eds) (1993) *Gender Matters in Educational Administration and Policy*, London, Falmer Press.

CODD, J.A. (1983) 'Educational research as political practice', AERA Annual Conference, *Collected Papers*, pp. 91–7.

CUNNINGHAM, S. (1992) *Framing Culture: Criticism and Policy in Australia*, Sydney, Allen & Unwin.

EISENSTEIN, H. (1991) *Gender Shock (How Australian Feminists Make the System Work – and what American Women Can Learn from Them)*, Boston, MA, Beacon Press.

FRANZWAY, S. (1994) 'Education policies and feminist politics: A response to Lyn Yates', *Discourse*, **14**(2), pp. 111–13.

FRANZWAY, S., COURT, D. and CONNELL, R.W. (1989) *Staking a Claim: Feminism, Bureaucracy and the State*, Sydney, Allen & Unwin.

GORE, J.M. (1993) *The Struggle for Pedagogies*, New York, Routledge.

GUNEW, S. and YEATMAN, A. (Ed) (1993) *Feminism and the Politics of Difference*, Sydney, Allen & Unwin.

HIRSCH, M. and FOX KELLER, E. (Eds) (1990) *Conflicts in Feminism*, New York, Routledge.

LUKE, C. and GORE, J. (Eds) (1992) *Feminisms and Critical Pedagogy*, New York, Routledge.

KALANTZIS, M. and COPE, B. (1987) 'Gender differences, cultural differences: Towards inclusive curriculum', *Curriculum Perspectives*, **7**(1), pp. 64–8.

KALANTZIS, M. (1988) 'Aspirations, participation and outcomes: From research to a curriculum project for reform', in FOSTER, V. (Ed) *Including Girls*, Canberra, Curriculum Development Centre.

KENWAY, J., WITH WILLIS, S., BLACKMORE, J. and RENNIE, L. (1993) 'Learning from girls: What girls can teach feminist teachers', in YATES, L. (Ed) *Feminism and Education*, Melbourne Studies in Education 1993, Bundoora, La Trobe University Press, pp. 63–77.

MCLEOD, J.E. (1995) 'Regulating gender: Feminist truths and educational reform in Victoria since 1975', unpublished PhD Thesis, Bundoora, La Trobe University.

MARTIN, J.R. (1994) 'Methodological essentialism, false difference and other dangerous traps', *Signs*, **19**(3), pp. 630–57.

SCHOOLS COMMISSION (1975) *Girls, School and Society*, Report of a Study Group to the Schools Commission, Canberra, Schools Commission.

SCHOOLS COMMISSION (1984) *Girls and Tomorrow: The Challenge for Schools*, Schools Commission Working Party on the Education of Girls, Canberra, Schools Commission.

SCHOOLS COMMISSION (1987) *A National Policy for the Education of Girls in Australian Schools*, Canberra, Schools Commission.

SMOLICZ, J.J. (1987) 'Education for a multicultural society', in KEEVES, J. (Ed) *Australian Education: Review of Recent Research*, Sydney, Allen & Unwin, pp. 316–45.

STRINTZOS, M. (1984) 'To be Greek is to be "good"', in JOHNSON, L. and TYLER, D. (Eds) *Cultural Politics*, Parkville, University of Melbourne.

SUGGETT, D. (1987) 'Inclusive curriculum: A gain or a loss for girls?', *Curriculum Perspectives*, **7**(1), pp. 69–74.

TSOLIDIS, G. (1984) 'Girls of non-English speaking background: Implications for an Australian feminism', in BURNS, R. and SHEEHAN, B., *Women and Education*, Papers of the ANZCIES Annual Conference, Bundoora, La Trobe University, pp. 63–70.

TSOLIDIS, G. (1986) *Educating Voula: A Report on Non-English Speaking Background Girls and Education*, Melbourne, Ministry of Education.

TSOLIDIS, G. (1988) 'Cultural affirmation: Cultural approaches', in FOSTER, V. (Ed) *Including Girls*, Canberra, Curriculum Development Centre.

TSOLIDIS, G. (1993a) 'The equity/difference dilemma in education – a case study related to the schooling of ethnic minority girls and the feminist theorization of social and ethnic difference', unpublished PhD Thesis, Bundoora, La Trobe University.

TSOLIDIS, G. (1993b) 'Difference and identity: A feminist debate indicating directions for the development of a transformative curriculum', in YATES, L. (Ed) *Feminism and Education*, Melbourne Studies in Education, Bundoora, La Trobe University Press, pp. 51–62.

WEINER, G., WITH ARNOT, M. and DAVID, M. (1996) 'Unanticipated equalities: The changing context in the UK of the curriculum and gender', Paper presented to the AERA Annual Conference, New York.

YATES, L. (1987) 'Australian research on gender and education 1975–1985', in KEEVES, J.

(Ed) *Australian Education: Review of Recent Research*, Sydney, Allen & Unwin, pp. 241–68.

YATES, L. (1988) 'Does "all students" include girls? A discussion of recent policy, practice and theory', *Australian Education Researcher*, **15**(1), pp. 41–57.

YATES, L. (1993a) *The Education of Girls: Policy, Research and the Question of Gender*, Melbourne, ACER.

YATES, L. (1993b) 'Feminism and Australian state policy – some questions for the 1990s', in ARNOT, M. and WEILER, K. (Eds) *Feminism and Social Justice in Education*, London, Falmer Press, pp. 167–185.

YATES, L. (1993c) 'What happens when feminism is an agenda of the state? Feminism and the case of education policy in Australia', *Discourse*, **14**(1), pp. 17–29.

YATES, L. (1995a) 'Constructing and deconstructing "girls" as a category of concern in education – reflections on two decades of research and reform', *Lararutbildning och forskning i Umea (Teacher Education and Research in Umea)*, **3–4**, pp. 85–94.

YATES, L. (1995b) 'Not rethinking the grand intellectual' (review of IAN HUNTER, *Rethinking the School*), *Australian Education Researcher*, **22**(1), pp. 119–125.

YATES, L. (1995c) 'Just what sort of endeavour is policy research in education? Some thoughts on feminism, the State, education theories and practices – and the dangers of all-purpose models', Paper presented to the AERA Annual Conference, Hobart.

YEATMAN, A. (1990) *Bureaucrats, Technocrats, Femocrats: Essays on the Contemporary Australian State*, Sydney, Allen & Unwin.

YEATMAN, A. (1994) *Postmodern Revisionings of the Political*, London, Routledge.

Chapter 3

Gender Policies in American Education: Reflections on Federal Legislation and Action

Nelly P. Stromquist

Introduction

The major goals of the feminist movement in this country in the last two decades have been to increase women's access to employment and to improve conditions for women in the labor force. The concern for maternity leave and child care rights that accompanied the movement further emphasized women's role as workers. Formal education, despite its powerful reproductive as well as transformative power, received less attention than it deserved. The creation of equal and unsegregated education was among the objectives of the early feminist movement, but it ranked only sixth on a list of eight.[1] Today's mean political climate, in which the government seeks greater control over women's sexuality, coupled with the government's unwillingness to support the poor, especially women in welfare, has brought new priorities to the women's movement, notably abortion and domestic violence.

The women's movement in the US has been more willing than the women's movement in other countries to accommodate itself to the existing political system; hence its strategies have relied on coalition politics and pragmatic achievements (Gelb, 1989). An important means women have used to improve their condition in general has been legislation, particularly federal legislation. Feminists anticipated that by exerting pressure upon political representatives, laws would be passed whose implementation would decrease gender discrimination in employment, social services, education and other areas of society.

In the area of education, three main federal statutes have been enacted since 1972 to protect or promote women's rights in education. These are: Title IX of the Educational Amendments Act of 1972, the Women's Educational Equity Act (WEEA) passed in 1975, and the Vocational Amendments Act (VEA) of 1976.[2] In addition, 13 states have enacted legislation that parallels Title IX (Kohl, 1987)[3] and 31 states have some legislation prohibiting sex discrimination in primary and secondary education programs (Brown and Reid, 1987).[4]

Title IX essentially prohibits discrimination on the basis of sex in educational programs and activities; it provides for the cutoff of federal funds to educational agencies and institutions that do not comply. Its prohibitions cover the areas of student admissions, recruitment, housing facilities, access to course offerings, financial assistance, employment and athletics. In contrast, WEEA represents the 'carrot' of the law. It provides financial resources and technical assistance to encourage the design, adoption and implementation of new programs that could foster more gender-egalitarian environments in educational institutions.

Since the enactment of these important laws more than 20 years have passed. The purpose of this chapter is to depict the trajectory of these two laws and assess the effectiveness of federal legislation as a means to improve the conditions for women in education. The analyses in this chapter proceed from a feminist perspective, relying on critical theory to link state actions to gender outcomes. While modern societies claim legitimacy by characterizing themselves as democratic, different and often non-democratic rationalities and interests exist in those societies as well. In the case of gender, ideology and material conditions constrain the possibilities of women in society to the advantage of men. Hence, policies addressing the question of gender equality enter a contested terrain where positive outcomes are likely to be few and mild. Analyses of policy impact are methodologically difficult because of the impossibility of establishing a clear causal link between macro-decisions (the law) and micro-consequences (outcomes at the individual level), since numerous other events in society take place simultaneously. Nonetheless, the analytical exercise presented in this chapter enables us to explicate crucial events against the background of important legislative intent.

Analytical Framework

Although the US government refers to both Title IX and WEEA as legislation for gender *equity*, a more correct term would be gender *equality*. Neither of the two laws seeks to provide special consideration to women. To provide *equity* would be to give greater support to women in order to ensure that they ultimately reach a condition of equality with men. Both laws affirm the educational system's obligation to provide *equality of opportunity* in terms of access to resources and services.

We can identify five key elements in the educational system where intervention to address gender equality could take place.

1   *School textbooks and materials* the prime sources of messages and images about gender roles in society. These have an important role in the transmission of ideology; the terms, content and illustrations of textbooks influence students' understandings of what is valued and rewarded in society.
2   *Curriculum content* educational courses and programs represent the concrete manifestation of what is accepted as legitimate knowledge. From a woman's perspective, curriculum is critical to her identity in two ways: it presents knowledge that recognizes her experience as a social actor and offers knowledge that is useful to her in the creation of a society no longer affected by sexual markers.

3 *Provision of pre- and in-service training to teachers* such training would
be intended to modify teachers' differential expectations of and practices
with female and male students.

4 *Guidance in course selection and field of study* this would facilitate girls'
choices of nonconventional fields of study in high school and college.

5 *Presence of women as administrators or professors in educational institutions* this gives women direct access to decisionmaking and enables them
to provide substantive role models for female students.

The Legislation: Intentions and Actual Practices

Title IX

Feminist groups struggled for several years to have federal legislation enacted
against sexual discrimination. Ironically, the most revolutionary educational legislation to date was passed as an unnoticed addendum to a general bill; thus Title IX
of the Education Amendments of 1972 was born. Its main clause reads:

> No person in the United States shall, on the basis of sex, be excluded from
> participation in, be denied the benefits of, or be subjected to discrimination
> under any program or activity receiving Federal financial assistance.

After passage, this objective was perceived by certain groups, particularly those related to intercollegiate sports, to be so threatening that what was then the Department
of Health, Education, and Welfare (HEW) took three years (1972–75) to translate
it into specific regulations and four additional years to produce 'policy interpretations'
dealing with the issues of equity in athletics.

The regulations of Title IX explicitly omitted consideration of anti-discriminatory
practices in texts and even curricular content. Section 86.42 of Title IX regulations
states:

> Nothing in this regulation shall be interpreted as requiring or prohibiting or
> abridging in any way the use of particular textbooks or curricular materials.

Although critics today claim that Title IX introduced affirmative action into education, this legislation is far from being an affirmative action statute as it explicitly
states:

> Nothing contained in [this law] should be interpreted to require any educational institution to grant preferential or disparate treatment to the members of one sex on account of an imbalance that may exist with respect to
> the total number.

An institution, however, is allowed to take affirmative steps to increase participation of students in programs or activities where either girls or boys may have participated only on a limited basis in the past.

The main method for implementation of Title IX involved annual self-evaluations by the educational institutions; each was to assess its own degree of compliance with the legislation. The enforcement of Title IX was not given to a separate agency but was assigned to HEW's Office for Civil Rights (OCR), which was already charged with enforcing nondiscrimination on the basis of race, and which subsequently was given the task of monitoring educational discrimination on the basis of disability (in 1976) and age (in 1978).

Under the Reagan Administration, the courts supported narrow judicial interpretations and decisions which required Congress to clarify the gender equity laws (Flygare, 1982, 1984). Two important legal cases are: a) Grove City College v. Bell (1984), in which the Supreme Court decided that Title IX regulations applied to only those school programs and activities funded directly or indirectly by the government, not to the total institution, and b) the dismissal by a federal court in December 1987 of the Adams order that required the OCR to respond to complaints within 90 days. The first decision effectively nullified Title IX, particularly regarding athletics, since few school athletics departments receive federal funds. It was not until the passing of the Civil Rights Restoration Act of 1987[5] (enacted in March 1988) that Congress reaffirmed its intention to apply anti-discriminatory legislation to 'all operations' of a department or agency of the state, university, local education agency (LEA) or corporation involved in education.

Women's Education Equity Act (WEEA)

Feminist groups lobbied for three years (1971–74) to get this law enacted. It passed as part of the Special Projects Act of 1974 and was extended in 1978, this time as part of the Educational Amendments of 1978. WEEA legislation provided funds for six activities: the development and evaluation of curriculum, textbooks and other educational materials; model pre-service and in-service programs for educational personnel; research and development; guidance and counselling; educational activities to increase opportunities for adult women; and expansion and improvement of educational programs for women in vocational careers, physical education and education administration (US Department of Education, 1992: 1–2). In 1984 WEEA was amended to fund 'comprehensive plans for implementation of equity programs at every educational level' and 'innovative approaches to school-community partnerships'. This amendment reduced its funding for local assistance from $15 million to $6 million. Amendments in 1988 further reduced its funds for local projects from $6 million to $4.5 million; the amendments also eliminated the National Advisory Council on Women's Educational Programs.

Initially the WEEA program had been expected to provide a large amount of financial resources so that school districts and states would be encouraged to explore alternative educational environments to achieve gender equity. Its advocates expected that some $40 million would be available to carry out the program each year. As noted earlier, however, the WEEA Act itself was legislated as part of the Special Projects Act, which was supposed to be funded for $200 million a year.

When President Ford requested only $39 million for the Special Projects Act, the share for the WEEA Program dropped to $6.3 million. WEEA attained its highest level of actual appropriations at $10 million in FY 1981; funding declined to $500,000 in 1992, a figure that was maintained until 1995 and which covered the operating expenses of the WEEA Publishing Center and a few demonstration grants. WEEA was reauthorized in 1994 and its scope expanded to cover assistance to schools in implementing comprehensive gender equity programs but major cuts in the federal budget in 1996 resulted in zero funds for WEEA in 1996, although $4 million has been requested for FY 97.

The initial priorities of WEEA were to help educational institutions to move into Title IX compliance. By 1991, with considerably less funds than expected, its priority had been changed to sponsor the development of innovative educational, training and counseling programs to increase the participation of women in math, science and computer science (US Department of Education, 1992). Competition for WEEA's research and demonstration grants was fierce, with approximately 30 grants funded annually out of over 500 presented. WEEA allocated most of its funds to either universities/research centers or state educational agencies, with local school districts receiving only a minor amount.

WEEA operates on a voluntary basis. This means that to obtain these funds, states and school districts must develop proposals and apply for funding. This also means that funds are limited and not expected to cover all requests. In fact, there is wide consensus that most of the gender-focused activities conducted by the states and by local school districts have been supported not through Title IX or WEEA, but through technical assistance funds provided by Title IV of the Civil Rights Act of 1964 (Brown and Reid, 1987). Title IV of the CRA assigned funding to local school districts and also funded Sex Desegregation Assistance Centers, which provided training workshops, technical assistance to teachers, guidance counselors and administrators and distributed sex-fair materials. State gender-equity initiatives have been hampered by the fact that states must bear a substantial part of the costs themselves. During FY 1982, for instance, the federal government covered only 42 per cent of the average state operating costs in all areas of equity (Brown and Reid, 1987).

The Condition of Women's Education Today

This section traces achievements in the educational areas previously identified as critical to the successful attainment of gender equity in education.

Textbook Materials

As observed earlier, the Title IX guidelines excluded textbooks. Yet the impetus of the feminist movement prompted the creation of textbook review committees in many LEAs to examine the presence of stereotyped messages in school textbooks. Also, several key publishers issued guidelines for the publication of nonsexist materials, a move first started by Scott Foresman in 1972.[6]

Little information is available on the extent to which educational textbooks actually changed at the primary and the secondary level. Important changes in language and illustrations seem to have occurred, but some gender biases and stereotypes are still present. Martinez (1974) observed that while states have enacted legislation requiring that public school texts be purged of sexually defamatory materials and that affirmative materials about the contributions of members of both sexes be added, there has been relatively little implementation or enforcement of the provision. Writing 17 years later, Sleeter and Grant (1991) reported that a review of a large sample of textbooks revealed that whites dominated the story lines in most textbooks and that women and people of color were assigned a much more limited range of roles than white males. In another study, textbooks designed to fit guidelines on gender and race equity for book adoption enacted by California – one of the most progressive states – showed 'subtle language bias, neglect of scholarship on women, omission of women as developers of history and initiators of events, and absence of women from accounts of technological developments' (AAUW, 1992).

We have some evidence from textbooks utilized in teacher training programs. Here a study by Sadker and Sadker (1980) is critical. The authors reviewed 24 of the most popular textbooks used in pre-service teacher training programs during 1973–78, covering the areas of foundations of education, psychology of education and teaching methods in five content areas (reading, language arts, social studies, mathematics and science). Their content analysis of these textbooks revealed that the topic of sexism was given less than 1 per cent of the narrative space, that sex equity tended to be omitted entirely or given incomplete treatment, and that the contributions of women to education were not even mentioned. The authors also found that science and math textbooks – subject areas in which women tend to be considerably less prominent – showed the greatest imbalance in the treatment of boys and girls. The authors discovered, however, that illustrations in the textbooks (in terms of photographs but not drawings) were well balanced by gender, which they took as an indication that the textbook publishers were more sensitive to equity issues than the authors of textbooks. The Sadkers warned that teachers needed to gain an adequate understanding of sexism if they are to alleviate sex bias in the classroom and concluded that 'since it is often difficult for classroom teachers to gain access to educational research, it is crucial that this information be included in teacher–education texts' (1980: 43).

In all, when looking at changes in the area of textbooks, it appears that market forces (i.e., the fear of boycott of certain books by feminist parents), rather than legislation, may have led publishers to modify the gender content of textbooks.

Curriculum Content

Since Title IX excluded textbooks or curricular materials, the modifications that have been made in instructional programs to provide for greater equity have been primarily voluntary. However, WEEA funding has made it possible to introduce new content areas in the classrooms. Between 1974–79 the WEEA Program funded 220 grants totaling over $21 million to develop curriculum and training materials. The most useful products were training materials for administrators and teachers which were designed to familiarize them with the rationale and methodology for implementing Title IX. Less successful appears to have been the design of materials for actual classroom use (Bornstein, 1985). WEEA has produced over 100 educational materials, ranging from texts to videotapes. These materials, however, seem to have had limited circulation, since only three WEEA publications have sold more than 5000 copies and only six more than 3000 copies (Applied Systems Institute, 1985).

Although schools now offer sex education, only 29 states include it as part of their regular curricula and only six make it a required class. There is a wide range of variation in what is covered under the sex education label (Diamond, 1983). It is estimated that between 10 and 55 per cent of the US school districts offer sex education courses. What goes on in these classes? Is sexuality treated in a way that dispels misconceptions about sexual drives and practices and sex stereotypes? A study that observed sex education classes concluded:

> In such classes the content of sex education is so strictly monitored that sensitive subjects such as intercourse, venereal disease, masturbation and homosexuality are usually banned from discussion. In general, sex education does not integrate information about the sex act with other aspects of sexuality such as gender–role stereotyping and values (Rogers and Strover, 1980: 176).

If this is true of most classes, the coverage given by them is far from satisfactory, because women and men need to know not only how to assume reproductive control but also how sexuality structures social relations. Diamond expresses it well: 'We must begin to think of sex education not only as education about the sex organs and intercourse but about the sexual relations between women and men' (1983: 233).

Although Title IX did not incorporate curriculum changes, it did call for schools to allow girls to enter programs previously open only to boys. A major area of contestation in this regard has occurred in sports, where girls have demanded and been given access to athletic activities previously off-limits to them.

Largely because of the prominence of male sports in high school and college extracurricular activities and the revenues they produce, Title IX's provisions related to gender equity in athletics have received the most attention and excited the most controversy. Male-dominated athletic departments fear that opening athletics to women will result in fewer opportunities for boys and lower revenues from intercollegiate sports (particularly football). Athletic scholarships are a major means by which low-income students gain access to higher education, and women have been very poorly represented in the sports for which top scholarships are available. Another reason for the athletics controversy may be that opening more sports to girls contributes to a de-masculinization of these activities thus challenging conceptions of male prowess and skills.

It was therefore in the area of athletics that political support from legislators was the most difficult to obtain (The Editors, 1979). HEW's own assessment has been

Table 3.1: *Educational gains by women in sports as a percentage of total student participation and budget allocation*

Sports and Budget Alloc.	1971–74	1981–82	1994
Girls in interscholastic sports	7%	35%	61%
Girls in intercollegiate athletic programs	15%	30%	56%
Percentage of average college athletic budget assigned to women	2%[a]	13%[b]	26%[c]

Sources: Data for 1971–74 and 1981–82 derive from Hogan, 1982.
Data for 1993 and 1994 from US Congress, 1995.
[a] refers to 1974
[b] refers to 1985
[c] refers to 1993

that athletics is the area in which Title IX faced the strongest resistance to change but also the area in which it has been most successful; HEW cited an increase of over 600 per cent in the number of girls involved in interscholastic sports between 1971 and 1977 (Bornstein, 1981). Although women athletes still do not receive as many benefits as their male counterparts, they certainly receive many more than they did prior to 1972. A female student could by 1982 choose four sports for every seven offered to male students; she could choose only two sports for every seven offered to men in 1974 (Hogan, 1982). In 1972 women represented 2 per cent of the college varsity athletes; they comprised 35 per cent in 1996. In 1972 girls made up 7.4 per cent of the high school athletes; by 1995 they represented 38 per cent (National Women's Law Center, 1996). Special growth has occurred in women's basketball, gymnastics, track and swimming. On the other hand, the budgets for athletics are far from being equitably distributed and opportunities for women coaches at the high school level have *declined* since 1972. The evolution over 20 years in the participation of women and access to funding is presented in Table 3.1; women's share of the athletics budget in college represents a mere 26 per cent. These gains in girls' sports are heavily contested today. Hearings on Title IX conducted by the Federal House of Representatives in 1995 concentrated exclusively on the athletics provision, in response to complaints by sports associations and coaches from several educational institutions that boys' sports were being threatened by the increasing attention to girls' sports (US Congress, 1995).

Teacher Training

Efforts under this rubric were to be covered by WEEA, but its limited funding has allowed only a scant number of training initiatives. Nonetheless, some demonstration projects have been successful in changing intra-district behaviors and attitudes. An important initiative supported by the WEEA program was the development of national models of educational equity at the school district level; five such models were funded. One of these models is the three-year effort in Broward County, Florida, where teachers and administrators underwent various activities to develop gender awareness and adopt educational materials for use in their classroom. The evaluation of this project showed that the LEA gained a good understanding of sex equity education and new practices emerged in several classrooms, but that the project did not succeed in producing an exportable model (Bornstein, 1985). This is not a surprising finding, given the high degree of resistance that confronts efforts to redefine traditional practices and adopt new ones.

Most of the efforts on teacher training have taken place through funds under Title IV of the Civil Rights Act of 1964, which created Sex Desegregation Centers. These funds, as can be surmised, were not sufficient to cover a substantial number of school districts and other educational institutions. Moreover, these funds suffered constant decrease until they became eliminated in the FY 96 budget.

Table 3.2: Women as proportion of total degree holders

Degree Earned	1959–60	1970–71	1980–81	1986–87*
Bachelors degree	35%	43%	50%	52%
Masters degree	34%	40%	50%	51%
Doctorate degree	10%	14%	31%	35%
First professional degree	11%	6%	27%	35%

Source: American Council on Education, 1989.
* Latest available year.

Women's Access to Advanced Educational Programs

In the US, parity between men and women in primary and secondary education has existed for a long time. In 1972, however, there were significant gender disparities in higher education, and the gap widened from the bachelors to the doctorate degree. As Table 3.2 shows, by 1987 women had achieved parity at the bachelors and masters levels. However, comparing these gains with those made between 1960 and 1971 indicates that there was a social trend toward greater levels of education for women even before the gender equity legislation.

Title IX did not establish quotas for student admissions to educational programs, but both Title IX and WEEA introduced requirements for gender counseling that were intended to have a positive impact on the selection of fields and careers by women. Table 3.3 shows seven field of study choices by successful completion at the baccalaureate level. The data show that although women still constitute a small fraction of today's holders of bachelors degrees in civil or mechanical engineering, their representation has increased dramatically as compared to that of 20 years ago. Women have also made steady progress in the fields of mathematics, law and medicine, even though they have not yet reached parity with men. On the other hand, the data also indicate that traditionally feminine fields such as education and foreign languages have continued to be dominated by women.

Table 3.3: Proportion of women attaining bachelors degrees in selected fields

Field	1965–66	1971–72	1979–80	1985–86*
Civil Engineering	0.3%	1%	9%	13%
Mechanical Engineering	0.2%	0.6%	7%	10%
Education	76%	75%	74%	76%
Foreign Languages	73%	75%	75%	72%
Law[a]	4%	7%	30%	40%
Medicine[b]	7%	9%	23%	31%
Mathematics	33%	39%	42%	49%

Source: American Council on Education, 1989.
[a] First professional degree, including bachelors.
[b] MD
* Latest available year.

Women's Presence in Educational Institutions as Faculty and Administrators

The employment clause of Title IX has reportedly been the most difficult to implement, because 'at least eight district courts and three appellate courts have ruled that [the OCR] has no jurisdiction' to apply Title IX to cover staff employment (The Editors, 1979). Moreover, the Supreme Court has refused to review these cases.

Although, as noted above, Title IX did not include a clause for affirmative action, it has become common among the media and politicians to argue that affirmative action has played a role in American education.[7] Some hold that there have been only limited instances of affirmative action. Others believe affirmative action has occurred but has served to benefit white women more than black men and especially black women. The interaction between gender and race variables is an issue of great importance and one that needs much closer examination. The available statistics often do not present simultaneous breakdowns by gender and race, thus preventing analysis of these issues.

Three key indicators of women's presence in important educational leadership positions are the numbers of female school principals, LEA superintendents and university professors. Table 3.4 shows the gains women have made compared to men in the formal educational system as school principals and school district administrators. The changes between 1972 and 1988 have been moderate among principals. Significant shifts occurred within associate superintendent positions, although these statistics include assistant and deputy superintendents, who may not have much authority. The top leadership position, that of superintendent, has registered substantial increase compared to the original baseline data, but the figure is still minuscule.

Regarding women as university faculty members, the data shown in Table 3.5, indicate that their participation has been increasing across all levels. Women represent less than one-sixth of full professors, but growth in this area seems quite

Table 3.4: Women in educational leadership positions as percentage of total employment

Positions	1972	1978	1985	1988*
Principals	15.0%	14.0%	20.4%	24.0%
Superintendents	0.6%	0.7%	2.7%	3.7%
Associate Superintendents[a]	3.0%	8.0%	15.0%	22.0%

Sources: American Association of School Administrators, 1988: 21, 13 and 17. Data on superintendents are based on 39 states.
[a] Includes assistant, deputy, associate and area superintendents.
* Latest available year.

Table 3.5: Women as proportion of full-time university faculty by rank – all institutions

Rank	1972–73	1978–79	1979–80	1982–83	1985–86	1991*
Full professors	9.8	10.1	9.8	10.7	11.9	14.7
Associate professors	16.3	19.1	19.4	22.0	24.3	27.7
Assistant professors	23.8	33.2	33.9	36.1	38.0	39.7
Instructors	39.9	52.1	51.8	51.7	52.0	47.3
All ranks	22.3	26.1	25.9	26.9	28.0	31.7

Sources: Fact Book on Higher Education, 1972–73, 1978–79, 1979–80, 1982–83, and 1989–90 (these years were examined).
* Latest available year, US Department of Education, 1995.

sustained. Women are overrepresented as instructors, positions which are non-tenure track and thus unlikely to lead to professorial appointments.

Accounting for the Outcomes

In observing policy outcomes, a distinction must be made between *gross outcomes* – all observed changes following a given policy, or simply the difference between pre- and post-program values; and *net outcomes* – those that can be reasonably attributed only to the intervention, apart from the effects of any other causes.

The linking of legislative intentions to concrete indicators of women's educational conditions presupposes an intermediary process by which inputs (the various pieces of legislation) are translated into outcomes (improved conditions in women's education). This process unquestionably contains a complex chain of events to which the researcher, using secondary data sources and examining the process after several years have gone by, can have only a crude approximation.

Inputs in Place

The inputs that are made available through legislation are of crucial importance in examining implementation. If resources are promised but not delivered, then it can be concluded that the legislation has no teeth. On the other hand, it is clear that parallel forces such as the women's movement, economic conditions and demographic changes are also at work and are thus also responsible for the observable outcomes.

The federal government responded to feminist pressure by passing legislation that acknowledged women's inferior status in education and the need for immediate improvement. Unfortunately, however, federal actions surrounding the implementation of these laws have presented the following features:

Minimal effort in affecting the core of education. The drafters of Title IX regulations refused to address the content of textbooks or curricular materials (adducing that education is a state's right) and WEEA was not able to provide the massive teacher training that would have been advisable to modify gendered experiences in the schools. Several measures that could have contributed to the equalization of opportunities in higher education, such as providing women with child care programs, special counseling services, and women's social and study centers, were not provided (Bar-Yosef, 1977; Bornstein, 1981).

Limited funding to engage in innovative or corrective efforts within educational institutions. In 1989 federal appropriations for education totaled $9.086 billion; of this, WEEA received close to $3 million, or .03 per cent of the federal budget. In addition, there has been a steady decrease of funds for Title IV of the Civil Rights Act. Under the Reagan Administration, funds for Title IV of the Civil Rights Act were halved (Brown and Reid, 1987). Under the Clinton administration, congressional decisions led to the total elimination of state CRA IV equity grants from the FY 1996 budget. These measures certainly affected the levels of technical assistance and teacher training that could be provided to school districts.

Insufficient enforcement mechanisms. There is wide consensus that OCR has been a poor enforcer of Title IX (Brown and Reid, 1987; Califano, 1981; Flygare, 1984; Gelb and Pauley, 1982; PEER, 1977; Snider, 1989), mostly due to OCR's meager funding compared to the scope of their task. For instance, the OCR's technical assistance budget for FY 1982 was less than one-tenth of the FY 1980 funding level (Brown and Reid, 1987: 11). Some observers argue that given the limited ability of OCR to operate as an effective enforcement agency, 'Title IX will remain largely a rhetorical statement of what women's rights in education should be, rather than a legal statement of the obligations schools and colleges have to their women students and employees' (Fishel and Pottker, 1977: 134).

Extremely limited funds for research on gender issues. In the past some funds were provided by the National Institute of Education and to a lesser extent by OCR. Today neither provides such funding and no other source, public or private, has filled this void (Brown and Reid, 1987: 14). Approximately 95 per cent of the research funds for education distributed by the federal government go to 19 research centers; none of these centers focuses a significant amount of its research effort on issues dealing with gender (cf. US Congress, 1988: 507–24).

Transformations in Educational Organizations

Changes in educational institutions attributable to Title IX may be surmised on the basis of two indicators. The first indicator is the number of litigation cases that have questioned institutional gender practices. The second is the proportion of women who now hold administrative or leadership positions in school districts or teaching positions in higher education; these women might thus be able to inject new perspectives – including gender considerations – in their respective institutions.

The number of sex-related complaints brought against educational institutions has been very small, compared to complaints of other types of discrimination. It is unclear whether the low numbers reflect that conflicts have been resolved internally and thus few complaints were forwarded to OCR or whether women have not felt empowered to use the available legislation. Since 1982 OCR has received an average of about 1400–1800 complaints per year. Title IX has traditionally represented less than 10 per cent of the total OCR complaint loads; most of the complaints have focused on handicap and racial issues. Data for 1993 indicate that 52 per cent of the complaints received by OCR dealt with the handicapped and 25 per cent with race; only 8 per cent of the complaints related to sex. OCR typically reviews only a very small number of these complaints. Of the 101 compliance reviews done in 1993, four addressed the equal opportunity rights of pregnant girls and 21 dealt with discrimination in athletics (US Congress, 1995). It seems, therefore, that Title IX has not been used to incorporate more women into leading educational positions.

As for percentages of women in educational leadership positions, there is still a substantial gender disparity among school principals, associate superintendents and superintendents. The position most resistant to change has been the top administrative job of school superintendent. It would appear that women have felt more confident to seek positions with greater authority, such as principal and assistant or associate superintendent, but have been reluctant to occupy jobs that are still perceived as 'political', 'aggressive', or 'interfering greatly with domestic responsibilities'. It also appears that educational boards – and the communities they represent – have continued to express a belief that the position of superintendents should be limited to men. A third element might be that since the position of superintendent is closely linked to power, white men are most reluctant to share this type of position with competing social groups, such as women or racial minorities. In that case what may be at work is not a lingering reluctance by women to seek office (as the first explanation suggests), but rather the men's active gatekeeping role – a role which, it must be noted, has not been sufficiently challenged by the existing legislation.

The statistics examined in this chapter reveal neither a fast nor steep linear progression. The number of women superintendents seems to be rising, but, as the numbers are so very small, it is not possible to predict whether this trend will continue. As to the presence of women in university positions, the gains are steady, though parity is still distant.

Transformations in Students

The data on the participation of women students by field of study reveal an interesting picture. There have been gains in the participation of women in a number of careers not traditionally seen as feminine. Women have also increased their participation in fields that used to be dominated by men such as law and medicine. On the other hand, women have maintained their position in traditionally feminine fields such as education and foreign languages. The move of women into previously male-dominated fields and the reluctance of men to enter female-dominated fields reflects the low status of the latter fields. Since Title IX and WEEA have had limited impact on the content of textbooks, on teachers' practices in the classroom, and on their expectations toward girls' careers, it would seem inappropriate to attribute the shifts in fields of study to this legislation. Indeed, if the legislation had influenced new career options, we would expect that such fields as education and foreign languages would have experienced an influx of men. The fact that some historical trends, both in the growth of women in university programs and in selected fields of study, preceded the enactment of the legislation also cast doubt on its influence over these outcomes.

What then was at work? Many factors may have been operating simultaneously. The massive and diffuse influence of the women's movement may have affected perceptions of individuals and behaviors of institutions. While the media have continued to portray women in impossible images of youth and beauty, they have also presented women in new roles and responsibilities. The fear of legislative enforcement and a broader popular reading of what these laws can do – i.e., affirmative action – may have prodded institutions into a greater affinity with its anti-discrimination objectives. The growing presence of women's studies in universities, estimated at approximately 500 in 1989, and the large number of postsecondary courses addressing gender issues, approximately 30,000 by 1988, also may have influenced women students.

The State–Gender Link

Reviewing the federal government's performance in the cases of both Title IX and WEEA, it is clear that the government failed to provide to institutions the moral support and financial resources promised by its rhetoric.

A technocratic explanation of state behavior would be that the implementation of complex innovations needs certain preconditions to be successful – especially a clear description of the innovation and, in this case, a large number of personnel trained in gender analysis and project design and implementation. Along these lines, the gender equity legislation failed essentially because the bureaucracy was not prepared to act efficiently and effectively. But the trajectory of Title IX and WEEA suggests that weaknesses lay elsewhere. A more political explanation is that governments support a male-dominated social order and are thus unlikely to strongly support attempts to transform gender relations. Current legislation for women in education has been characterized by weakness in three key areas: the content and scope of the laws, funding levels to enable adequate implementation, and enforcement mechanisms to ensure that educational organizations will comply with the law. Considering the resources in place, those interested in the improvement of women's conditions have reason to suspect that the federal government lacks a strong willingness to alter the status quo in society.

The federal government (or the *state*, in a more abstract sense) plays a role as a key mediating agency between women and social change. In the case of the educational legislation reviewed herein, it seems that the state, being unable to reject outright the concerns of a sizable segment of the American population, passed a series of legislative measures to address gender equity in education. At the same time, it used other means to render the laws largely ineffective. The two pieces of educational legislation examined in this chapter left untouched critical elements that could have contributed to social restructuring. Title IX discouraged sex discrimination but monitoring and enforcement were deficient. It did not address the content of textbooks nor that of courses.

Surprisingly, it is in the area of sports that Title IX seems to have been most effective. The increased presence of women in previously male-dominated terrains is a highly positive development and will result in the effective demolition of many sexual stereotypes – as already reflected in the 1996 Olympics. WEEA expressed in principle the possibility of introducing new content, such as a gender-equitable sexual education program, so that social relations could be redefined. It also provided for the training of teachers. Yet the levels of WEEA funding did not enable large numbers of teachers to undergo training in gender issues; WEEA merely opened up the possibility that the few who asked for help would receive it. WEEA funds also covered a very limited number of new gender-sensitive programs. The Title IX and WEEA policies were designed to have limited impact on the hidden curriculum of schools, so such issues as sexual harassment by teachers and student peers, stereotyped and negative expectations by teachers, and counseling/preparation for nonconventional fields of study were given minimal attention. By design, WEEA relied on voluntary efforts, but voluntary equity programs are unlikely to be very successful in promoting macrosocial change. They encourage, for the most part, only those already inclined to change and provide limited funds for the various needs to be satisfied.

One feminist perspective on the state holds that although the state must be a target for pressure to change, the state acts essentially to support the social relations of male dominance in society. This view contends that the state is not a neutral arbiter of competing interest groups but rather an important means by which patriarchal ideology finds legitimation and support. As Eisenstein reminds us, the subordination of women does not occur because men hate women but rather because men need mothers: 'This involves the caring and love they provide, the children they reproduce, the domestic labor they do, the commodities they consume, the ghet-toized labor force they provide' (1983: 44).

The state should not be viewed as unchanging. Quite the contrary; it should be seen as making many accommodations, particularly those that might increase its legitimacy without setting in motion a restructuring of society. In a country such as the US, where the feminist movement has been one of the strongest in the world, we would expect the state to be responsive in its legislation. In both the Senate and the House there have been amendments to support as well as to restrict gender equity legislation. But we should remember that 'hegemony also accommodates contradiction. It is precisely the illusion of "freedom", "choice", and "opportunity", which remains fundamental to the political management of conflict and resistance' (Coppock, Haydon and Richter, 1995: 183).[8] The strategies for inaction available to the state after passing legislation are numerous. One strategy is to promise change at the rhetorical level and do very little of substance. This is what Edleman has called 'symbolic politics' (1971). Another strategy has been termed 'counterploys'. This refers to actions by which laws are changed, rules contested or modified and a facade of compliance portrayed. The trajectory of Title IX and WEEA clearly indicates the presence of these maneuvers. The funds made available for the efforts were insufficient from the beginning. Today affirmative action is under attack and Title IX is incorrectly seen as part of the problem. In January, 1996 a federal court rejected the 'proportionality principle', which had been established to put more women in certain sports. WEEA was unfunded in 1996.

Against this scenario, politicians commonly take the position that gender equity has already been attained and that no special mechanisms are necessary. This review shows that the legislation did not dramatically affect the schools, that other social influences have been operating, that gender parity in university degrees is being achieved but that the feminization and masculinization of several fields remains uncontested. This review also shows that legislation can be used to call attention to important concerns, but that this legislation can be easily subverted.

Today, gender equity is no longer seen as a priority. In fact, an initiative called the Equal Opportunity Act (which was co-sponsored by the 1996 Republican pre-sidential candidate, then-Senator Bob Dole) would eliminate 'race- and gender-based preferences' (i.e., affirmative action) in federal employment and contracting. In the field of education, the picture is not rosier. A presidential commission in 1995 enacted eight educational goals to be reached by the year 2000. These cover academic performance and completion, literacy, teacher education and professional development, parental participation and the creation of a better school climate. Current evaluations of the nation's move toward accomplishment of these goals (funded at $350 million for 1997) consider gender issues only in regard to goal five, student achievement in math, science and reading (National Education Goals Panel, 1995). In other words, the gender problem in education has been reduced to the academic performance of women in certain disciplines and delinked from contestation of ideological messages sustained by schooling.

The current situation is hostile to gender equality and equity. Yet the legal struggle should continue, because state actions – even when they are negative

Nelly P. Stromquist

– provoke a greater reaction from institutions and individuals than do the actions of private feminist groups. By analyzing these reactions, feminists can identify areas where pressure to change can be more effectively applied. State actions on behalf of women have not been very effective, yet feminists' ability to influence policy and its implementation will be decisive in the advancement of women.

Notes

1 These objectives appeared in the 1967 Bill of Rights of the National Organization for Women (NOW), the largest and most active feminist organization since the 1960s. It should be clarified that while the feminist movement has not zeroed in on formal education with the intensity it merits, the movement has fulfilled intensive and successful educational functions (in the larger sense of the word) through developing feminist critiques of several disciplines, questioning the legitimacy of patriarchal ideologies in society, developing feminist newspapers, magazines, journals and publishing companies, and establishing women's studies programs in numerous universities.
2 Broader laws protecting women's equity are Title VII of the Civil Rights Act of 1974, which includes the prohibition of discrimination by educational institutions against students seeking employment, and Title VII and VIII of the Public Health Service Act of 1971, which prohibit discrimination in admissions to federally funded health programs.
3 These states are Massachusetts, Washington, Connecticut, Hawaii, Illinois, Iowa, Minnesota, Alaska, New Jersey, New York, Oregon, Pennsylvania, and Montana.
4 Reportedly the most progressive states in gender equity are California, New York and Massachusetts (Brown and Reid, 1987).
5 This bill was endorsed by over 200 national organizations, including the Leadership Conference on Civil Rights, the National Association of Independent Colleges and Universities, and numerous religious organizations.
6 This document was entitled *Guidelines for Improving the Image of Women in Textbooks*. Others that followed suit were Houghton Mifflin's guidelines for *Avoiding Stereotypes* (1975) and McGraw-Hill's *Guidelines for Equal Treatment of the Sexes* (1974).
7 Affirmative action plans are weak instruments that merely formalize a university's awareness that it still has a skewed faculty distribution in terms of race and gender; these plans do not commit institutions to rectify specific conditions by a specific period of time.
8 At the global level, interesting similarities regarding gender policy implementation obtain. The documents produced at world conferences on women (Nairobi 1985; Beijing 1995) present careful and complete identification of measures needed to improve the condition of women, yet funds for implementation and the machinery for enforcement are notoriously absent.

References

AMERICAN ASSOCIATION OF SCHOOL ADMINISTRATORS (1988) *Women and Minorities in School Administration, Facts and Figures 1987–1988*, Washington, DC, American Association of School Administrators.
AMERICAN ASSOCIATION OF UNIVERSITY WOMEN (1992) *How Schools Shortchange Girls: A Study of Major Findings on Girls and Education*, Washington, DC, AAUW.

AMERICAN COUNCIL ON EDUCATION (1989) *1989–90 Fact Book on Higher Education*, New York, American Council on Education.

APPLIED SYSTEMS INSTITUTE (1985) *A Descriptive Analysis of the Women's Educational Equity Program*, Washington, DC, ASI.

BAR-YOSEF, R. (1977) 'Equalizing educational opportunity for women', in BAILEY, S. (Ed) *Higher Education in the World Community*, Washington, DC, American Council on Education.

BORNSTEIN, R. (1981) 'Title IX compliance and sex equity: Definitions, distinctions, costs and benefits', New York, Columbia Teachers College, mimeo.

BORNSTEIN, R. (1985) 'Ambiguity as opportunity and constraint: Evaluation of a federal equity program', *Educational Evaluation and Policy Analysis*, **7**(2), pp. 99–114.

BROWN, C. and REID, J. (1987) *Twenty Years On: New Federal and State Roles to Achieve Equity in Education*, Washington, DC, National Center for Policy Alternatives.

CALIFANO, J., JR. (1981) *Governing America*, New York, Simon and Schuster.

COPPOCK, V., HAYDON, D. and RICHTER, I. (1995) *The Illusions of 'Post-Feminism'*, London, Taylor and Francis.

DIAMOND, I. (Ed) (1983) *Families, Politics, and Public Policy. A Feminist Dialogue on Women and the State*, New York, Longman.

EDELMAN, M. (1971) *The Symbolic Uses of Politics*, Urbana, IL, University of Illinois Press.

EISENSTEIN, Z. (1983) 'The state, the patriarchal family, and working mothers', in DIAMOND, I. (Ed) *Families, Politics, and Public Policy*, New York, Longman.

FISHEL, A. and POTTKER, J. (1977) *National Politics and Sex Discrimination in Education*, Lexington, KY, D.C. Heath.

FLYGARE, T. (1982) 'Supreme Court Says Title IX covers employment but raises a serious question about the future impact of the law', *Phi Delta Kappan*, **64**, pp. 134–6.

FLYGARE, T. (1984) 'The Supreme Court's and Title IX decision: Who won?', *Phi Delta Kappan*, **65**, pp. 640–1.

GELB, J. (1989) *Feminism and Politics: A Comparative Perspective*, Berkeley, CA, University of California Press.

GELB, J. and PAULEY, M. (1982) *Women and Public Policies*, Princeton, NJ, Princeton University Press.

HOGAN, C. (1982) 'Revolutionizing school and sports: 10 years of Title IX', *Ms*, **10**, pp. 25–9.

HOUGHTON MIFFLIN (1975) *Avoiding Stereotypes*.

KOHL, J. (1987) 'Women and political action: The sex equity in education act in California', *Contemporary Education*, **58**(4), pp. 211–5.

MARTINEZ, S. (1974) 'Sexism in public education: Litigation issues', *Inequality in Education*, **18**, pp. 5–11.

MCGRAW-HILL (1974) *Guidelines for Equal Treatment of Sexes*.

NATIONAL EDUCATION GOALS PANEL (1995) *The National Education Goals Report*, Washington, DC, NEGP.

NATIONAL WOMEN'S LAW CENTER (1996) *The Battle for Gender Equity in Athletics*, Washington, DC: NWLC, May.

PEER (1977) *Stalled at the Start*, Washington, DC: Author.

ROGERS, E. and STROVER, S. (1980) 'Peer communication and sexuality', in ROBERTS, E. (Ed) *Childhood Sexual Learning. The Unwritten Curriculum*, Cambridge, MA, Ballinger Publishing.

SADKER, M. and SADKER, D. (1980) 'Sexism in teacher-education texts', *Harvard Educational Review*, **50**(1), pp. 36–46.

SCOTT FORESMAN (1972) *Guidelines for Improving the Image of Women in Textbooks*.

SLEETER, C. and GRANT, C. (1991) 'Race, class, gender and disability in current textbooks', in APPLE, M. and CHRISTIAN-SMITH, L. (Eds), *The Politics of the Textbook*, New York, Routledge and Chapman Hall.

SNIDER, W. (1989) 'Civil-rights unit shirks its task, 2 reports charge', *Education Week*, **8**(23), p. 1.

THE EDITORS (1979) 'An interview on Title IX with Shirley Chisholm, Holly Knox, Leslie R. Wolfe, Cynthia G. Brown and Mary Kaaren Jolly', *Harvard Education Review*, **4**(4), pp. 504–26.

US CONGRESS (1988) House, Committee on Appropriations, Departments of Labor, Health and Human Services, Education, and Related Agencies Appropriations for 1989; Hearings Before a Subcommittee of the Committee on Appropriations. 100th Cong., 2nd Sess., Part 6. Washington, DC, US Government Printing Office.

US CONGRESS (1995) Hearing on Title IX of the Education Amendments of 1971. Hearing before the Subcommittee on Postsecondary Education, Training, and Life-long Learning of the Committee on Economic and Educational Opportunities, House of Representatives, 104th Congress, First Session. Washington, DC, US Government Printing Office.

US DEPARTMENT OF EDUCATION (1992) *Women's Educational Equity Act Program: Report of Activities 1988–1992*, Washington, DC, US Department of Education.

US DEPARTMENT OF EDUCATION (1995) *Digest of Education Statistics 1995*, Lanham, MD, National Center for Education Statistics, US Department of Education.

Chapter 4

Gender and the Reports: The Case of the Missing Piece*

Lois Weis

Introduction

Since *A Nation at Risk* (National Commission on Excellence in Education, 1983), there have been a large number of reports on the state of the American educational system. The American school system, it is alleged, is 'soft'; students do not learn enough; teachers are not well trained or motivated; and we are, by and large, falling behind Japan and Germany in a much-touted economic war. We simply are not competitive enough economically, and the educational system surely is to blame. If only we had a better educated citizenry, one more willing to be creative (but not too creative) on the job, one that at least can read training manuals, then we would not be in the deplorable situation we are in. This cry has been in the air for ten years now. It ebbs and flows, of course, but we are looking primarily at the schools as both the cause of our economic woes and our savior if we are to regain our competitive edge.

There are obvious problems with this analysis, but it is not my intention to focus on these at great length here. It must be pointed out, however, that the state of the economy and the increasing lack of highly paid jobs is only partially related to the American school system. The movement of capital *out* of American borders in search of lower-paid workers certainly explains to a greater extent the decreasing number of jobs in the traditional working class than does the form and content of the educational system, for example (Bluestone and Harrison, 1982; Weis, 1990). So, too, the slashing of middle- and upper-level jobs in corporate bureaucracies such as Catherine Newman (1988) examines has more to do with the competitive market economy than with the educational failings of these upper-level corporate managers. The fact is that we are living in a totally different economic age than we did 20 years ago, and that the educational system explains only partially the position of the American worker. Since the economy is too difficult to unpack, however, numerous observers, all of whom think they know everything about school since they attended one, focus on the woes of the educational system to explain

* Weis, L. (1996) 'Gender and the reports: The case of the missing piece', in Ginzberg, R. and Plank, D. *Commissions, Reports, Reforms and Educational Policy*, Reprinted with permission of Greenwood Publishing Group, Inc., Westport, CT, pp. 173–92.

America's position in the global network rather than pay serious attention to the movement of capital and the consequences of both this movement and the internal restructuring of the corporate sector (Reich, 1991).

My purpose here, however, is to direct our attention to another missing component in these reports, that being the question of gender and patriarchy. It is most striking that, although the movement for gender equality has received considerable attention in the last 20 years, the national, state and local reports surrounding education take little note of this. In other words, issues raised by those concerned with gender equality receive virtually no attention in these reports. In point of fact, not one of the leading reports takes seriously issues raised by persons concerned with gender.

A Nation at Risk, for example, highlights the following indicators of risk: 'Over half the population of gifted students do not match their tested ability with comparable achievement in school'; 'Many 17-year-olds do not possess the higher order intellectual skills we should expect of them. Nearly 40 per cent cannot draw inferences from written material; only one-fifth can write a persuasive essay; only one-third can solve a mathematics problem involving several steps' (National Commission on Excellence in Education (1983) 8–9). In line with the report's concern with Japan and Germany, it further draws attention to the supposed fact that 'International comparisons of student achievement, completed a decade ago, reveal that on 19 academic tests American students were never first or second and, in comparison with other industrialized nations, were last seven times' (1983: 9). The crisis, then, is defined as one relating to certain measures of academic achievement, and the relative position of the United States *vis-à-vis* other nations in terms of these measures.

Since the release of this report, there have been numerous others issued at the state and local levels, originating from both the public and private sector (Boyer, 1983; College Board, 1983; Making the Grade, 1983). The sources of these reports were, in fact, diverse; the federal government and its agencies (*A Nation at Risk* and the National Science Foundation reports); state governments and their agencies like the Education Commission of the States; private organizations such as the Carnegie Fund for the Advancement of Teaching and the Twentieth Century Fund; business interests like Dow Chemical Company, AT&T, and the Policy Committee for Economic Development; higher education, such as the two Holmes Group Reports; and individuals such as Theodore Sizer and John Goodlad, who were funded by public and private philanthropic foundations and educational organizations like the Association of Secondary School Principals to study American schools. Despite these diverse sources, all of the reports, according to surveys conducted by both the Education Commission of the States and MDC, an independent evaluation firm, are concerned with five main issues: curricular reform, professional development of teachers and administrators, student evaluation and testing, graduation requirements, and teacher certification and preparation. According to MDC's report, the major initiatives generated by the state-based agencies call for the establishment of the following programs:

1   a variety of new state-developed curricular or curriculum guides, often focusing on basic skills, but also covering many other academic areas;

2 a range of new school accreditation standards designed to address quality, requirements for local district and individual school site-planning, and expanded state review of local instructional programs;

3 numerous broad-based and comprehensive school improvement programs, sometimes specifically including an effective schools program in which the characteristics of the most effective schools are identified and attempts are made to replicate those characteristics in other school settings;

4 many state-initiated dissemination and adoption assistance programs, local capacity-building and problem-solving initiatives, and a wide array of new technical assistance services;

5 a variety of strategies related to the testing of students, including state-developed and -administered competency tests;

6 an array of activities focused on improving the capabilities of the education work force, including new types of teacher proficiency examinations and teacher and administrator professional development training programs; and

7 a host of initiatives aimed specifically at improving mathematics, science, and technology instruction and programs in the schools, including efforts to recruit and retain mathematics and science teachers (Cook, 1984: 8–9, as cited in Borman and O'Reilly, 1990: 115).

For the most part, the above are concerned with credentialing and certification issues with respect to teachers and students. Although there are some curricular issues mentioned, the day-to-day workings of the institution of schooling are left largely intact; the focus for change revolves around better control of the teaching force.

That the various commissions, task forces and reports totally ignored issues of gender inequality is without question (Borman and O'Reilly, 1990). The reports saw as problematic only the relative decline of American test scores, the state of the economy (which they attributed to schools and mainly to teachers), and what they saw as the erosion of America's position in the world economy. The reports did not acknowledge a set of problems relating to the relative position of women and girls and what this implies for schools. It must be made clear here that I am not suggesting that the authors should have focused on issues of gender at the expense of the economy and tests (although I certainly agree with those critics who have rendered much of this analysis problematic to begin with). Rather, I am suggesting that the reports did not even consider the agenda of gender inequality and that this is an important omission.

Here I will argue that schools contribute actively to inequalities by gender, and that the reform movement must take both these inequalities and the ways in which schools contribute to them seriously. Anything less than this is a disservice to the ostensibly egalitarian aims of both American education and the society as a whole.

The Need for Addressing Women's Issues in Educational Reform

There are critical issues with respect to gender that need desperately to be addressed in schools. Women are constructed both discursively and materially as 'less than' men and suffer serious long-term consequences because of this set of social constructions. Why are we so quick to focus on declining test scores and so willing to argue that schools ought to do something about it, and so ready to ignore the fact that at least two million women are beaten by their husbands each year and that as many as 600,000 are severely assaulted by them four or more times a year? (Breines and Gordon, 1983; as cited in Martin, 1991; Langone, 1984). Recent studies suggest that 38 million adults were abused sexually as children and that approximately 22 per cent of Americans fall victim to this dread abuse (Crewdson, 1988, as cited in Martin, 1991). While it is true that both men and women have been abused as children, the vast majority of victims of child sexual abuse have been women. Why are we so unwilling to call this a *problem* – a problem that ought to be addressed, like math scores, in our schools?

The data with respect to job-related outcomes and womens' relative position in the economy must also be discussed here. One of the most striking changes to take place within the last 20 years, in addition to the demise of the capital-labor accord, is the movement of women, on a nontemporary basis, into the paid labor force. Now, over 50 per cent of American women work outside the home in full-time jobs, and a high proportion of these women have young children in the home. It is important to go beyond mere numbers here, however, taking into account the shape of women's participation in the paid labor force. First, as Michael Apple (1986) has noted, women's work reflects a vertical division of labor whereby women as a group receive less pay than men and work under less advantageous conditions. While this is beginning to flatten somewhat given the move into a postindustrial economy under which well paying male laboring jobs are increasingly unavailable, forcing both men and women into the lower paying in-person service sector, the fact remains that men still earn substantially more than women do at every level of schooling obtained. In other words, among high school graduates, men earn relatively more than women and this is equally the case (if not more so) among those men and women who have graduated from college. Second, women's work is differentiated from men's on a horizontal basis in the sense that women are concentrated in particular kinds of work. Seventy-eight per cent of clerical workers, 67 per cent of service workers, and 67 per cent of teachers (and a higher proportion at the elementary level), are women in the United States. Conversely, less than 20 per cent of executive, managerial and administrative workers are women (Apple, 1986: 55). In fact, although women entered the paid labor force at a phenomenal rate recently, they are concentrated in particular kinds of jobs – those with relatively low pay, few benefits and lacking autonomy. For a variety of reasons related to both the needs of the economy for relatively cheap, in-person service labor and the shape of the American family which both needs and demands increased income, the phenomenon of women working outside the home is here to stay. At issue here is the shape of the gendered labor force itself.

Recent studies suggest that job segregation by sex is the principal source of gender differences in labor market outcomes (Bielby and Baron, 1986). Research has shown that gender-based division of labor, although not inevitable, is definitely persistent. The level of occupational sex segregation has changed very little since

1900, despite changes in the sex composition of specific occupations. In point of fact, recent work at the organization level (Bielby and Baron, 1984) suggests that sex segregation is much more pervasive than studies had previously indicated, showing that men and women rarely share job titles within establishments. Such sex segregation leads to massive inequalities in income, a point that Heidi Hartman (1976) attested to some time ago now.

This set of economic realities must be coupled with a rising divorce rate in the United States, which renders low female incomes especially important. It is no secret that divorce rates have risen considerably since the 1950s, leaving many women in virtual poverty as they struggle to bring up their children. This is, of course, even more the case for African-American women, where the divorce rate is much higher than that for whites, and the remarriage rate lower. Nearly three out of 10 black women are divorced. There is also a higher proportion of never-married women among blacks and high separation and desertion rates, often woven through the lives of small children. The incidence of female-headed black households is well documented (Burnham, 1986).

The vulnerability of this segment of the population should be obvious. The median income of female-headed families is less than 40 per cent of husband–wife families to begin with. The connectedness of this with the racism of American society means that more than half (52.9 per cent) of black female householders lived in poverty in 1981 compared to 27.4 per cent of white females in the same situation (Burnham, 1986: 82). The numbers of poor, African-American female-headed households tripled from 889,000 of such families in 1960 to 2.7 million in 1982. Thus, by 1982, two-thirds of all poor black families were headed by women. The data become even more chilling when we look at the community as a whole. As Linda Burnham suggests:

> The impact of impoverishment of female headed households on the economic status of children under the age of eighteen has, of course, been devastating. Of the black children in female-headed households, 67.7 per cent were poor in 1981. The comparable rate for white children in female headed households was 42.8 per cent. But, since the proportion of female headed households is so much lower among whites than among blacks, these figures translated into an even more dramatic differential between black and white children. Nearly one half of all black children, 44.0 per cent, live in poverty while only 14.7 per cent of white children do (1986: 82).

The actual position of women in the family must also be considered at this point. Women have lived under what has been called the Domestic Code, whereby home or family becomes defined as women's place and a public sphere of power and work as men's place. The reality, of course, is that generations of women, both poor and working-class, labored in the public sphere, and that labor also takes place in the home, albeit unpaid. Yet, as Karen Brodkin Sacks points out,

> The Domestic Code has been a ruling set of concepts in that it did not have to do consistent battle with counterconcepts. It has also been a ruling

concept in the sense that it explained an unbroken agreement among capitalists, public policymakers, and later much of organized labor, that adequate pay for women was roughly 60 per cent of what was adequate for men and need be nowhere near adequate to allow a woman to support a family or herself (Sacks, 1984: 17–18).

It was strongly related, then, to the notion of the 'family wage' and the ways in which this notion played out historically in the United States (Kessler-Harris, 1977; Sacks, 1984).

The existence of this powerful domestic code sets parameters within which later lives tend to be lived. Women who do not envision the primacy of wage labor, for example, may not prepare themselves, or argue for the right to be prepared for well-paying jobs with career ladders. If women see the domestic sphere as their responsibility, they may not struggle for the high quality day care centers that would allow them to maintain involvement in the paid labor force to the extent necessary for a career. In fact, the lines between the public and private spheres have blurred considerably in recent years and issues ostensibly private are now, at times, debated in the public arena (for example, the struggle over women's reproductive rights). Action in the public sphere also impacts on the private sphere increasingly, as more and more women work outside the home.

Internalized elements of the domestic code, combined with the reality of women working outside the home, has led to what analysts have called the *double bind*. Women may have defined themselves primarily in terms of home and family, but, in fact, worked outside the home. Rather than alter the nature of the gender inter-actions and division of labor within the home substantially, a double day was instituted in which labor in the home was simply added to hours spent in wage labor. As Ferree notes, 'Women are more and more likely to be in the paid labor force but experience little change in the division of labor at home. Employed women continue to do 4.8 hours a day of housework compared to the 1.6 hours their husbands do' (Ferree, 1984). Recent research on a national sample of couples suggests the rather intractable nature of these arrangements. As Catherine Ross (1987) argues, when the wife is employed, her husband's relative contribution to the housework increases somewhat; well-educated husbands and husbands with less traditional sex role beliefs are more likely to participate in the household tasks. The smaller the gap between the husband's earnings and his wife's, the greater his relative contribution. The wife's education and attitudes, in contrast, do not significantly affect the division of labor at home. Thus, the household division of labor is shaped by the husband's values and the relative power of husband and wife in economic terms. In point of fact, however, this recent research reveals that a full 76 per cent of wives who are employed full time still do the majority of the housework. Given the self-report nature of the data at hand, whereby husband and wives were *asked* about their relative contribution, it might be hypothesized that the actual nature of the household task distribution is skewed even less in favor of a trend toward equalization than Ross suggests (1987: 816).

Although it can be argued that these are societal issues and that schools, therefore, cannot be expected to solve them, the fact is that schools encourage the production of these outcomes in a variety of ways. Although the school allegedly promotes equality along a series of dimensions (gender being only one), there are ways in which schools can be held directly accountable for encouraging vast inequalities – in this case, outcomes highly detrimental to women and, I would suggest, to the society as a whole. I will, in the remainder of this chapter, focus on the ways in which schools encourage these practices. My argument from this point onward is meant to highlight these practices, not to cover the ground with respect to them or to note all the literature related to this topic.[1] Rather than focus on all ways in which schools encourage gender inequality, I will focus on the following: the content of the curriculum, the structure and interactions within schools, and the semi-autonomous level of student identity formation. In each category I will locate what it is about the school that contributes to the outcomes and relations of interest. Some of the literature cited here stems from research done in England. Although the British class structure certainly differs in important ways from the American class structure, in that a more overt set of class antagonisms has always been present in England, issues related to gender identity are quite similar in the two countries. Thus, points raised in England are relevant in many ways to the US context.

How Schools Encourage Gender Inequality

Curriculum

The question here is, How does the formal curriculum represent women and girls, and how, therefore, does it encourage young women to envision themselves as they enter the world beyond school? The evidence here is no longer in dispute. People may argue that it is right that the curriculum be a largely white man's curriculum (witness the argument for great books, and so forth) but it is well documented that the curriculum is androcentric, and white. History is not the history or histories of women's lives, but rather the history or histories of great men. Literature is not the literature of women; it is the literature of men (with some exceptions, of course). The case has been made that science is male centered, and feminists have unpacked the curriculum in terms of gender bias in virtually every subject area. Whole volumes such as *Feminist Scholarship: Kindling in the Groves of Academe* (DuBois *et al.*, 1985); and *Reclaiming a Conversation* (Martin, 1985) are devoted to unraveling the androcentrism of subjects as currently conceived. Thus, the production of knowledge itself, or what we call knowledge at the level of the university, is centered largely on the culture and accomplishments of white men.

This is only intensified as we move downward through the grades. What Raymond Williams (1973) terms 'the selective tradition' ensures that only certain knowledge is packaged into textbook format and distributed to elementary and secondary students. Although feminists have challenged the androcentrism of knowledge as produced and legitimated in the university, little of this challenge finds its way into the elementary and high school text market. While a couple of inserts may be devoted to women, or the temperance movement, or 'women being given the vote', the knowledge distributed to students is extraordinarily male centered. In point of fact, even when texts do attempt some change in this direction, findings from my recent ethnography of white, working-class students indicate that such ostensible change in curricular content is often subverted by teachers themselves at the level of everyday practice. Teachers inform students to 'skip the section on women – it's not on the test', or, as one teacher put it, 'Women's Rights – They have too many rights already'. Students, in turn, dub such class sessions 'American Broads' (Weis, 1990).

In the very early grades, students are exposed to a curriculum that emphasizes the activity and action of boys, and the passivity of girls (Kelly and Nihlen, 1982; Weitzman, 1972; Women on Words and Images Society, 1975). This has, unfortunately, changed less than one might hope, in spite of book publishers' insistence on nonsexist language.

But the gendered nature of the formal curriculum goes well beyond this. Michelle Fine (1988) has explored the ways in which the curriculum about sexuality encourages passivity on the part of young women. The work is informed by a study of current sex education curricula, work on negotiating to include lesbian and gay sexuality in a city-wide sex education program, and interviews and observations gathered in sex education courses in New York City. Basically, Fine argues that the curriculum as conceived and practiced encourages a view of women as victims, while at the same time silences the idea that women have sexual desires as do men. Women, therefore, must be protected and must protect themselves from the approaches of lust-filled males. The corollary here, of course, is that once such 'training' is given, women who fall prey to the unwanted advances of males must take full responsibility for this since they should have known how to protect themselves to begin with. As Fine argues,

> Within today's standard sex education curricula and many public school classrooms, we find 1) the authorized suppression of a discourse of female sexual desire; 2) the promotion of a discourse of female sexual victimization; and 3) the explicit privileging of married heterosexuality over other practices of sexuality. One finds an unacknowledged social ambivalence about female sexuality which ideologically separates the female sexual agent, or subject, from her counterpart, the female sexual victim. The adolescent woman of the 1980s is constructed as the latter. Educated primarily as the potential victim of male sexuality, she represents no subject in her own right. Young women continue to fear and defend in isolation from exploring desire, and in this context there is little possibility of their developing a critique of gender or sexual arrangements (1988: 31).

The Fine paper is important in that it begins to build a notion of dependence for women at the very core of identity – that being sexuality. Women are taught to fear, to protect themselves, to be on the watch for others, and soon, to find that one right man who will protect them within the confines of societally sanctioned marriage. Women are not taught to be actively engaged with self or the external world. This accords with notions of lack of action as distributed through the elementary schools in picture books and texts.

Nancy Lesko (1988) extends the work in this area. Arguing that any analysis of the construction of gender identity must explicitly take into account the body as the site of such identity construction, she focuses on what she calls the curriculum of the body in a Catholic high school. As she argues,

> the curriculum of the body, the total set of intended and unintended school experiences involving knowledge of the body and sensuality, be taken by curricularists, sociologists of education, and feminists as central to the schooling experiences of young women and to the perpetuation of gender identities and inequities in contemporary American society. I am not suggesting that schools are the only sites of messages concerning proper use of the female body, but that schools are important sites in that they are pre-eminent places where adolescents come together during their initial period of sexual identity development. The fact that schools are paternalistic organizations makes their overt or covert attempts to shape the construction of female bodies and, thereby, female identities, an area of concern (1988: 124).

Lesko, in a fascinating study, explores the ways in which the school literally controls womens' bodies through the curriculum; encouraging the female body to be both a social symbol for 'wholeness' or the lack thereof and, as the site of, or material for, identity construction. While this is certainly the case for males as well (witness the tattoos on bulging arms, for example), male bodies are not nearly as regulated as are womens' and, given the constricted nature of womens' identities to begin with, it is virtually impossible to ignore one's body in the construction of identity as a female. Schools, argues Lesko, intensify the direct and explicit attention being paid to the female body by focusing on modesty and so forth. In fact, while there was a dress code for both boys and girls, in practice, it was a girls' dress code, since it demanded little of boys that boys would not do anyway.

For girls, however, there was a tremendous focus on propriety. In particular, young ladies were not allowed to wear sleeveless shirts, sandals or miniskirts. In all respects, they were to cover up their bodies, so as to have proper modesty with respect to bodily appearance. Lesko suggests that such policies indicate that restraint, moderation, niceness and busyness are a code for young women of certain backgrounds. Interestingly enough, student response to this code varied, suggesting the emergence of youth cultural female groupings around the issue of bodily expression, rather than something else (academics, sports, and so forth, as might be the case for boys). Thus, for young women, bodily expression became the central focus for identity construction, even if they rejected somewhat the code of modesty prescribed by the school. The issue of female identity construction is the issue of the body – how it looks, acts, what is covered, what moves how and so forth (see also, Roman, 1988). Thus the curriculum of the body became, in essence, *the* curriculum for young women.

One other point must be considered at this time. While we know to some extent what is in the curriculum with respect to gender, we also must consider those silences that suggest what is not. Jane Roland Martin (1991) has persuasively argued that home and family are effectively eliminated from the legitimate curriculum. Nowhere, except for those few who elect to take domestic science subjects, are students exposed to issues relating to the home. Certainly in social studies, an area that might focus on the private sphere, this is not done since, as noted above, social studies is defined androcentrically, and the private sphere has no place in an andro-centric definition – it is simply a place for men to go back to. The study and consideration of the home and family (not necessarily in its traditional sense) is simply not considered worthy of the formal curriculum. This, once again, devalues the traditionally based work of women, whose job it has been historically to take care of the home and family or private sphere. By not focusing on this sphere in school – by rendering it marginal to the important work of math, reading, and so forth – we are once again devaluing women's contributions to society. Martin calls for an enriched curriculum whereby the private sphere becomes an object of study in order to elevate this sector to rightful legitimacy.

Structure and Interactions within the School

Evidence over the past 20 years suggests that males and females are treated differently in schools. While it is commonly assumed that boys receive more disciplinary action relative to girls in the early elementary grades, research suggests that teachers interact more with boys on each of the four major categories of teaching behavior: approval, instruction, listening to the child and disapproval (Sears and Feldman, 1974).

Similar data were gathered in the early 1980s in England. Focusing on the A-level classes in the humanities department of a college of further education with a large sixth-form intake, Michelle Stanworth (1981, 1983) argues that teachers hold entirely different expectations of their male and female students. Male teachers, in fact, view these two groups of students as totally different, sharing little, and spend much of their own time keeping the two groups discrete. In addition, interviews with teachers indicate an implicit assumption that girls' capacities for efficiency and initiative will be channeled into nurturing or subordinate occupations rather than into less traditional spheres. In addition, teachers, both men and women, view their female students largely in terms of the private sphere, focusing on marriage and parenthood for the girls. As a consequence of this, teachers marginalized female students in the classroom, encouraging the boys to take center stage in virtually every classroom activity. Females were pushed to the edges of such activity, and their existence in these A-level classes, which ostensibly prepared students for entrance into university, was trivialized.

We can obtain further insight into gender relations within schools when we focus on the sports arena. Charles Bruckerhoff (1991) has found that male sports literally overtakes all other functions of schooling in a small midwestern town, rendering male, godlike warriors at the center of peer and adult interactions in the entire community.[2] Certainly this was the case in the recently released popular *Friday Night Lights*, (Bissinger, 1991), a rendition of sports in a small Texas town. While this may not describe sports in all high schools (particularly in larger districts), it is true that sports form the core of the high school experience for many. It must be remembered that this adoration of sports is an adoration of the male body, of the male athlete, and young women enter the scene only as cheerleaders – scantily clad girls jumping up and down as godlike male warriors score points. The function of the cheerleader is to encourage the worship of the men – the prettiest, nicest and most lively are selected to show and encourage adoration. In one school district in western New York, the cheerleaders are assigned a football player each week for whom they have to bring lunch (cooked) and perform other duties (presumably sexual activity is excluded here). Even in the Catholic school that Lesko (1988) studied, all decorum was dropped as scantily clad cheerleaders urged their boys to victory. The social relations implied in this set of gender displays should not be underplayed here. Young women work to encourage young men as center-stage players and they obtain their status from doing so. Although there has certainly been a rise in female sports in the last 20 years, there is no similar gender display when a female team plays. Cheerleading squads may have one male cheerleader, or maybe even more, but an entirely male squad would not be found cheering a female team as they play to crowds of thousands. This would overturn traditional gender definitions and would simply not take place. In point of fact, it is unimaginable.

Along these same lines, authority patterns and staff arrangements must also be scrutinized within schools. The administrative structure of schools is still heavily male, with women comprising the vast majority of teachers at the elementary level (Deem, 1978; Kelly and Nihlen, 1982; Shakeshaft, 1987). A small fraction of superintendents are women, and a relatively small proportion of secondary school principals are women, as well.

There is also segregation of teaching staffs by subject matter. Women tend to be concentrated in language arts, foreign languages, elementary school teaching, and, to a lesser extent, social studies. They are rare in mathematics and the sciences (except biology).

These structural arrangements add up to a separatism in schools, with men largely controlling and monitoring the actions of women. Where women do have an active voice (as teachers, for example), they are workers under the direction of men (Apple, 1986), or, they are traditional helpmates (secretaries in schools, cheerleaders, and so forth). There is little valorization of an active female voice, little sense that women are subjects in their own right outside the structures of male dominance (Weis, 1990). This, of course, parallels the messages communicated through the formal curriculum.

Student Identity

I do not mean to imply here that gender identities and relations are produced totally by the school. Certainly that is not true. Numerous institutions work together to encourage the gender forms we know. However, the school is an active participant in the construction of these forms. Through the curriculum, interaction patterns, and structural arrangements, schools actively encourage certain relations and identities. However, there is also a sense that identity forms and relations, even if embedded within schools, must pass through the semiautonomous level of student identity production before becoming real for the subjects. There is disquieting news on this front, I am afraid. For the most part, this semiautonomous level encourages the production of even more virulent forms of genderized expression than those embedded in schooling itself. The school must begin to interrupt these productions. Anything less than such an interruption is part of the problem.

To begin with, we must explore the issue of language and what must be seen as outright misogyny on the part of young men. Young men are taught to be *men*, and part of this definition is a rejection of everything female. In so rejecting, there is a construction of the female that is often vulgar and certainly increasingly sexualized as boys grow older. In 1989 Derrick Jackson told Boston Globe readers about sixth graders in a public school who had been asked to relay the first word that crossed their mind about the opposite sex (Reynolds, 1987). The girls responses were: Fine, Jerks, Rude, Cute, Ugly, Conceited, Crazy, Boring, Sexy, Dirty Minds, Punks, Sexually Abusive Punks. The boys, on the other hand, had the following to say (remember, please, that these are sixth graders): Pumping ('big tits'), Nasty, Vagina, Dope bodies (big breasts and big behinds), Door Knob (breasts), Hooker, Skeezer ('a girl who will "do it" with 50 guys') (Jackson, 1989, as cited in Martin, 1991).

Data from England and Australia reveal similar misogynistic streaks in males (Clark, 1989; Mahoney, 1989, as cited in Martin, 1991; Wood, 1984). Boys routinely labeled girls 'sluts', 'period bags', 'big tits', 'dogs', 'aids' and so forth. This routine degredation did not stop at the level of language, however. Boys conceptualized the female other in certain terms – terms that led to the plotting of rapes for sheer entertainment; throwing young women into the boys' toilets ('like a dog'); and actual rapes (witness 'date rapes', or 'gang bangs', for instance). The point within male culture was to 'get what they could from a girl and then throw her away'. This form of brutalized sex that involved attacking young women characterized sex talk among boys and is a logical outgrowth of the ways in which young women are conceptualized to begin with. There is no reasonable alternative discourse regarding women in male culture. The discourse of the 'good girl' or 'good woman' demands almost passivity and certainly catering to male needs and desires. The female subject is not a subject in her own right, but only as she caters to men (which, of course, makes her an object). Much of the discourse around women is filthy and brutal and this is an image that young men grow up with. Although it may be coded somewhat differently by social class, I believe that the broad strokes of the imagery are largely similar. While these strokes may soften somewhat as men age, the vestiges of this exploitative and superior attitude toward women do not disappear easily (witness the trials of William Kennedy Smith and Mike Tyson, for example).

Young women, too, produce aspects of gender identity within their own groupings. These gender identities do not necessarily challenge the arrangements within society. In fact, Angela McRobbie (1978) has argued powerfully that although working-class girls in England endorse for the most part traditional femininity, they do so as a creative response to their own lived conditions rather than as a passive acceptance of meanings imposed by either school or family. In spite of the fact that they know, for example, that marriage and housework are far from glamorous, they construct a fantasy future in which both realms are glamorous by elaborating what might be called an 'ideology of romance'. They create an anti-school culture but one that is specifically female in that it consists of interjecting sexuality into the classroom, talking loudly about boyfriends, and wearing makeup. McRobbie raises the following point about the power of the semiautonomous level of cultural production:

> Marriage, family life, fashion and beauty all contribute massively to this feminine anti-school culture and, in so doing, nicely illustrate the contradictions in so-called oppositional activities. Are the girls in the end not doing exactly what is required of them – and, if this is the case, then could it not be convincingly argued that it is their own culture which itself is the most effective agent of social control for the girls, pushing them into compliance with that role which a whole range of institutions in capitalist society also, but less effectively, directs them toward? At the same time, they are experiencing a class relation, albeit in traditionally female terms (1978: 104).

Linda Valli's (1986) study of working class girls in an American high school extends our understanding of the way in which gender cultures take the form that they do. Valli studied a group of girls in a cooperative education program, a vocational program in which senior high students go to school part time and work part time in an office. She explored the ways in which students construct work and family identities and, more specifically, the ways in which ideologies relating to the family and the social and sexual division of labor impact upon the production of cultural reforms.

Valli clearly documents the ways in which gender culture shapes school-related behavior and choices. Deciding to take the office preparation curriculum is

> not the result of either office career aspirations or an oppositional school culture. Instead, it represented a sensible accommodation to their future possibilities and probabilities as the students and their parents saw it. This view of future probabilities resulted not only from a realistic perception of the job market, but also from a notion of what was a good job 'for a woman' (1986: 102).

Thus, students entered this program not because of anything the school necessarily did, but because of what the school did not do, that being the interruption of this set of gender expectations.

Taking the office curriculum was perceived as the best of available options. Job openings exist in the clerical area and most importantly, the work was not seen as derogatory to the students' sense of femininity (see also Griffin, 1985). Once in the program, the training the students received further marginalized their identities as wage laborers. The identity as workers outside the home was presented as secondary to a home/family identity, thus bringing us back to the points about curriculum raised earlier. 'While in some minimal ways the women may have rejected the ideology of male supremacy', Valli argues, 'at a more fundamental level, they affirmed it, granting superiority and legitimacy to the dominance of men in a way that appeared spontaneous and natural' (1986: 252).

The young women's culture must be situated within ongoing social structural arrangements. In many ways, choosing the office preparation program represents a sensible accommodation to sexist structures, in giving women some control over their own labor (there are issues of sexual harassment here as well, see Gaskell, 1983). Unfortunately, of course, such choices feed into the very structures of gender that give rise to them to begin with. As Valli states,

> Given the scarcity of professional level or interesting career type jobs and the difficulty of handling such a job along with home family responsibilities, the emphasis the co-op students place on a traditional feminine code exhibited a certain amount of good sense. Reproducing a traditional culture of femininity can be interpreted as a way of escaping the tedious demands of wage labor and of denying it power over the self. It can even be seen as an unconscious resistance to capitalist domination. The irony, of course, is that this culture both reproduces patriarchal domination and fails to alter capitalist exploitation which is quite amenable to a segment of the skilled labor force having a tangential relation to it (1986: 263).

The point again is that the production of gender identity cannot be read simply from curriculum, interactions, and structures within schools.[3] Not only is it tied to other institutions and cultural forms (see Smith, 1988) in society (such as magazines, newspapers, MTV, films, advertising, toys, and on and on), but it must always pass through the subject to become enacted. Recent evidence from my ethnography (Weis, 1990) and from Mary Fuller's (1980) work in England suggests that there are glimmerings of feminist and liberatory gender consciousness among women weaving through this semiautonomous level as well. There is definitely a sense of pride in being black and female in Fuller's West Indian women, for example, and the young working-class women in my study exhibit a sense that they want something more from life than the gender arrangements exhibited within their own families. Unfortunately, however, evidence from young men suggests no such progressive gender challenges, leaving us with a rather frightening picture as we move into the twenty-first century.[4]

Conclusion

I began this chapter with a look at the reports stemming from the numerous agencies that have recently focused attention on schooling. The reports are uniformly critical (although in different ways) of the current state of American education. The problem to be remedied relates largely to what is seen as America's loss of its preeminent position in the global economy. There is virtually nothing in the reports or in the papers of the many critics of the reports, about the kinds of human beings that are being turned out of schools and identifying that as a problem.[5] I have, in this chapter, suggested that none of the reports focuses on the ways in which schools contribute to certain forms of gender constructions and gender relations, which is a serious omission. It is telling, indeed, that the critics did not see it as such. Women and children are beaten in today's society, not by an enemy from abroad, but by an enemy within – the domestic relations in our own country. In an era where rapes have become material for the national media circus, surely we should begin to ask questions about the ways in which our schools contribute to this deplorable situation, and what we, as educators, can begin to do about it. We cannot afford to take the position that schools simply mirror society and that they, therefore, have no responsibility to address the conditions under which certain forms of gender constructions and relations are shaped. I have suggested here that schools are part of the problem and that it is time for us to take seriously ways in which we can address it. Through the formal curriculum, hidden curriculum (staffing relations and authority patterns, the type of attention paid to the female body and so forth), and ineptitude or plain unwillingness at disrupting certain forms of gender brutality, schools are contributing directly to the gender relations at hand. This is not a question of whether men or women are born with a certain type of wrist movement, or even whether men are naturally more prone to mathematics. This is a question of the ways in which gender comes to be defined and enacted and whether these definitions and enactments are worthy of a supposedly civilized country such as ours. By not defining problems relating to these gender constructions as worthy enough to be commented upon in discussions about what should be done with schools, we are, quite simply, encouraging them to continue. It is time that we take a more active role in considering ways in which schools may be used to construct a positive future for all of us, not just those white males of privilege amongst us.[6]

Notes

1   Some topics such as institutional and programmatic access are not covered here. See Jane Gaskell (1984), Jeannie Oakes (1985), and Lois Weis (1987, 1985) for discussions of these important points.
2   Alan Peshkin (1978) offers similar data on the role of sports in a community.
3   The same point can be made for male culture, of course. See Walker (1988) and Willis (1977).
4   In fact, the opposite is the case. The gender challenge among men is toward more rightest social forms. See Weis (1990).

5 One notable exception here is Borman and O'Reilly (1990). Jane Martin (1991) has recently raised this challenge as well.
6 I am not suggesting that all white men are privileged. Obviously poor men are not so privileged and I agree with Liz Ellsworth's (1989) points here. However, certain deeply structured gender forms and relations tend to cut across the society and we must pay attention to these as well.

References

APPLE, M. (1986) *Teachers and Texts*, New York, Routledge.

BIELBY, W. and BARON, J. (1984) 'A woman's place is with other women: Sex segregation within organizations', in RESKIN, B.F. (Ed) *Sex Segregation in the Workplace*, Washington, DC, National Academy, pp. 27–55.

BIELBY, W. and BARON, J. (1986, January) 'Men and women at work: Sex segregation and statistical discrimination', *American Journal of Sociology*, **91**(4), pp. 759–99.

BISSINGER, H.G. (1991) *Friday Night Lights*, New York, HarperCollins.

BLUESTONE, B. and HARRISON, B. (1982) *The De-industrialization of America*, New York, Basic Books.

BORMAN, C. and O'REILLY, P. (1990) 'The eighties image of girls and women in the educational reform literature: A review of the issues', in SHEA, C.M., KAHANE, E. and SOLA, P. (Eds) *The New Servants of Power: A Critique of the 1980s Reform Movement*, New York, Praeger.

BOYER, E. (1983) *High School: A Report on Secondary Education in America*, The Carnegie Foundation for the Advancement of Teaching, New York, Harper and Row.

BREINES, W. and GORDON, L. (1983) 'The new scholarship on family violence', *Signs*, **8**, pp. 490–531.

BRUCKERHOFF, C. (1991) *Between Classes*, New York, Teachers College Press.

BURNHAM, L. (1986) 'Has poverty been feminized in black America?', in LEFKOWITZ, R. and WITHORN, A. (Eds) *Crying Out Loud*, New York, Pilgrim Press, pp. 69–83.

CLARK, M. (1989) *The Great Divide*, Canberra, Australia, Curriculum Development Centre.

COLLEGE BOARD (1983) *Academic Preparation for College: What Students Need to Know and be Able to Do*, New York, Author.

COOK, E. (1984) 'Sex equity and national reports in education', unpublished paper.

CREWDSON, J. (1988) *By Silence Betrayed: Sexual Abuse of Children in America*, Boston, MA, Little Brown.

DEEM, R. (1978) *Women and Schooling*, Boston, MA, Routledge & Kegan Paul.

DUBOIS, E., KELLY, G., KENNEDY, E., KORSMEYER, C. and ROBINSON, L. (1985) *Feminist Scholarship: Kindling in the Groves of Academe*, Urbana, IL, University of Illinois Press.

EDUCATION COMMISSION OF THE STATES (1983) *Action for Excellence: Task Force in Education for Economic Growth*, Washington, DC, Author.

ELLSWORTH, E. (1989) 'Why doesn't this feel empowering? Working through the repressive myths of critical pedagogy', *Harvard Educational Review*, **59**, pp. 297–324.

FERREE, M.M. (1984) 'Sacrifice, satisfaction and social change: Employment and the family', in SACKS, K.B. (Ed) *My Troubles are Going to have Trouble with Me*, New Brunswick, NJ, Rutgers University Press, pp. 61–79.

FINE, M. (1988) 'Sexuality, schooling and adolescent females: The missing discourse of desire', *Harvard Educational Review*, **58**(1), pp. 29–53.

FULLER, M. (1980) 'Black girls in a London comprehensive school', in DEEM, R. (Ed) *Schooling for Women's Work*, London, Routledge and Kegan Paul, pp. 52–65.

GASKELL, J. (1983) *Course Differentiation in the High School: The Perspective of Working Class Females*, Paper presented at the American Educational Research Association Meeting, Montreal.

GASKELL, J. (1984) 'Gender and course choice: The orientations of male and female students', *Journal of Education*, **166**(1), pp. 89–102.

GOODLAD, J. (1984) *A Place Called School: Prospects for the Future*, New York, McGraw-Hill.

GRIFFIN, C. (1985) *Typical Girls?*, Boston, MA, Routledge and Kegan Paul.

HARTMAN, H. (1976) 'Capitalism, patriarchy and job segregation by sex', *Signs*, **1**(3), pp. 137–70.

HOLMES GROUP (1986) *Tomorrow's Teachers*, East Lansing, MI, Author.

HOLMES GROUP (1990) *Tomorrow's Schools: Principles for the Design of Professional Development Schools*, East Lansing, MI, Author.

JACKSON, D. (1989, June 2) 'The seeds of violence', *Boston Globe*, A1.

KELLY, G. and NIHLEN, A. (1982) 'Schooling and the reproduction of patriarchy: Unequal workloads, unequal rewards', in APPLE, M. (Ed) *Cultural and Economic Reproduction in Education*, Boston, MA, Routledge and Kegan Paul, pp. 162–80.

KESSLER-HARRIS, A. (1977) 'Where are the organized women workers?', *Feminist Studies*, **3**(1–2), pp. 92–110.

LANGONE, J. (1984) *Violence*, Boston, MA, Little Brown.

LESKO, N. (1988) 'The curriculum of the body: Lessons from a Catholic high school', in ROMAN, L., CHRISTIAN-SMITH, L.K. and ELLSWORTH, E. (Eds) *Becoming Feminine: The Politics of Popular Culture*, Basingstoke, Falmer Press, pp. 123–42.

McROBBIE, A. (1978) 'Working class girls and the culture of femininity', in THE WOMEN'S STUDIES GROUP (Ed) *Women Take Issue*, London, Hutchinson, pp. 96–108.

MAHONEY, P. (1989) 'Sexual violence and mixed schools', in JONES, C. and MAHONEY, P. (Eds) *Learning our Lines*, London, The Women's Press.

Making the Grade: Report of the Twentieth Century Fund Task Force on Federal Elementary and Secondary Education Policy, (1983) New York, Twentieth Century Fund.

MARTIN, J.R. (1985) *Reclaiming a Conversation*, New Haven, CT, Yale University Press.

MARTIN, J.R. (1991) 'The radical future of gender enrichment', Mimeo.

NATIONAL COMMISSION ON EXCELLENCE IN EDUCATION (1983) *A Nation at Risk: The Imperative for Educational Reform*, Washington, DC, US Government Printing Office.

NATIONAL SCIENCE BOARD, COMMISSION ON PRECOLLEGE EDUCATION IN MATHEMATICS, SCIENCE AND TECHNOLOGY (1983) *Educating Americans for the 21st Century: A Plan of Action for Improving Mathematics, Science and Technology Education for all American Elementary and Secondary Students*, Washington, DC, National Science Foundation.

NEWMAN, C. (1988) *Falling from Grace*, New York, The Free Press.

OAKES, J. (1985) *Keeping Track*, New Haven, CT, Yale University Press.

PESHKIN, A. (1978) *Growing up American*, Chicago, IL, University of Chicago Press.

POLICY COMMITTEE OF THE COMMITTEE FOR ECONOMIC DEVELOPMENT (1987) *Children in Need: Investment Strategies for the Educationally Disadvantaged*, New York, Committee for Economic Development.

REICH, R. (1991) *The Work of Nations: Preparing Ourselves for 21st Century Capitalism*, New York, Alfred P. Knopf.

REYNOLDS, P. (1987, March 27) 'Violence at home', *Boston Globe*, A15, 17.

ROMAN, L. (1988) 'Intimacy, labor and class: Ideologies of feminine sexuality in the punk

Lois Weis

slam dance', in ROMAN, L., CHRISTIAN-SMITH, L.K. and ELLSWORTH, E. (Eds) *Becoming Feminine: The Politics of Popular Culture*, Basingstoke, Falmer Press, pp. 143–84.

ROSS, C. (1987) 'The division of labor at home', *Social Forces*, **65**(3), pp. 816–33.

SACKS, K.B. (Ed) (1984) *My Troubles Are Going to Have Trouble with Me*, New Brunswick, NJ, Rutgers University Press.

SEARS, P. and FELDMAN, D. (1974) 'Teacher interactions with boys and girls', in STACEY, J., BERAUD, S. and DANIELS, J. (Eds) *And Jill came Tumbling After*, New York, Dell, pp. 147–58.

SHAKESHAFT, C. (1987) *Women in Educational Administration*, New York, Sage.

SIZER, T. (1984) *Horace's Compromise: The Dilemma of the American High School*, Boston, MA, Houghton Mifflin.

SMITH, D. (1988) 'Femininity as discourse', in ROMAN, L., CHRISTIAN-SMITH, L.K. and ELLSWORTH, E. (Eds) *Becoming Feminine: The Politics of Popular Culture*, Basingstoke, Falmer Press, pp. 37–59.

STANWORTH, M. (1981) *Gender and Schooling: A Study of Sexual Divisions in the Classroom*, Pamphlet 7, London, WRRC.

STANWORTH, M. (1983) *Gender and Schooling*, London, Hutchinson.

VALLI, L. (1986) *Becoming Clerical Workers*, New York, Routledge.

WALKER, J.C. (1988) *Louts and Legends*, Boston, MA, Allen and Unwin.

WEIS, L. (1985) 'Progress but no parity: Women in higher education', *Academe*, **71**, pp. 29–33.

WEIS, L. (1987) 'Academic women in science, 1977–1984', *Academe*, **73**(1), pp. 43–7.

WEIS, L. (1990) *Working Class without Work: High School Students in a De-industrializing Economy*, New York, Routledge.

WEITZMAN, L. (1972) 'Sex-role socialization in picture books for preschool children', *American Journal of Sociology*, **77**, pp. 1124–50.

WILLIAMS, R. (1973) 'Base and superstructure in Marxist cultural theory', *New Left Review*, **82**, pp. 3–17.

WILLIS, P. (1977) *Learning to Labour*, Westmead, Saxon House Press.

WOMEN ON WORDS AND IMAGES SOCIETY (1975) *Dick and Jane as Victims: Sex Stereotyping in Children's Readers*, Princeton, NJ, Author.

WOOD, J. (1984) 'Boys' sex talk: Groping towards sexism', in *Gender and Generation*, London, Hutchinson, pp. 187–97.

Chapter 5

Strategic Feminist Research on Gender Equality and Schooling in Britain in the 1990s

Miriam David, Gaby Weiner and Madeleine Arnot

Introduction

In this chapter we, as feminists, address the question of how to research gender equality and schooling. The focus is especially on changes in schooling with reference to equal opportunities, either pupil performances/achievements or equal treatment in school of pupils and teachers. The particular issue is how to develop and design research to map and explain changes in education and particularly those with respect to gender equality from a feminist perspective. Our twin interests are in conceptual matters around equality and research. Both these are complex matters and are not easily defined. In respect of equality, we are concerned to look at the relationships between men and women, boys and girls in terms of educational performances/achievements/outcomes and the processes of equal treatment within school – both the formal and informal curriculum. Our discussion draws on a modest, year-long, research project funded by the Equal Opportunities Commission for England and Wales (EOC) that we have recently completed, which looked at educational reforms and gender equality in schooling over a 10-year period from 1984–1994. We contextualize this research project in the wider arena of commissioned and grant-funded research in Britain today and feminist research perspectives. We argue that policy-oriented research such as this one is too limited to explore the reasons for the cultural shifts in gender equality and we speculate on those reasons.

Feminist Research for Educational Change

Mapping change in relation to gender equality and schooling can be seen as either broad sociological, educational and/or conceptual matters, or as more policy-oriented questions about the state of schooling in relation to a range of policy and/or reform initiatives. In the latter the issue of developing strategies for policy development or change is likely to be more paramount than in the case of more conceptual and/or sociological or educational research. Both sets of questions are susceptible to a range of research methodologies, including feminist approaches. However, feminist perspectives and approaches do not easily map onto these broad distinctions about types of research which contrast pure or fundamental research with strategic research or research for policy strategies.

Feminist approaches are not only analytical but also strategic – concerned with social justice, social change and reflexivity. Indeed, it could be argued that feminist research is crucially about providing the necessary evidence to bring about improvements in women's educational, social and economic roles. Thus feminist research or feminist perspectives can be defined in a variety of ways, linked to wider changes in the social context. The classic definition of a feminist research perspective was provided more than 20 years ago by Ann Oakley, 'A feminist perspective consists of keeping in the forefront of one's mind the lifestyles, activities and interests of more than half of humanity – women' (1974: 10).

Sandy Acker, in an intriguing chapter in her book *Gendered Education* (1994) asks the question 'Is research by a feminist always feminist research?' She argues that

> feminist research, like other research, is shaped by its surroundings, and
> ... in certain circumstances the best that can be expected is work that is
> *covertly* feminist. The implication is that rather than following a list of
> criteria at the design stage in order to determine what is authentic feminist
> research, we might think of feminist work as that which is informed at any
> point by a feminist framework (italics in original) (1994: 550).

She also goes on to argue that 'feminist writers have been fruitful in the production of scholarship and research; moreover, they have engaged in unusually extensive reflection about what it is they do ... the influence of post-modern or post-structuralist thinking has added even greater urgency ...' (1994: 56–7). In the last decade, indeed, such feminist approaches have also begun to come together with post-structuralism or post-modernism, focusing particularly on discourse analysis to understand the shifting nature of public policy debates around public versus private matters.

In a previous study, David, together with other colleagues, defined feminist approaches to policy as follows:

> We, as feminists ... wanted to explore the subtle meanings of policy especially for women as mothers and mothers' experiences of school and
> education for themselves and for their children ... We aimed to show how
> an analysis which looks across the boundaries with regard to the relationships between family and education generally ... reveals an issue – or
> agenda – that has been obfuscated by present policy and academic analysis and research ... Being a mother can mean different ways of knowing
> about and experiencing the world as compared to more official understandings. Policy understandings and educational institutions are constructed on
> 'public' world ways of knowing and a professional agenda, and cannot or

rather do not relate to the realities of women's family-related lives (David, Edwards, Hughes and Ribbens, 1993: 206–7).

A very different gloss is now placed on the relatively traditional concepts that have been the stock-in-trade, so-to-speak, of feminist social analysis, as an increasing focus on discourse analysis as ways of knowing or understanding become more popular. As Skeggs puts it, however,

> Fortunately few educationalists fell for the marketing of postmodernism's seductively easy analysis. However, there has been a move away from the principles of social democracy that informed feminist educational theory and practice (Kelly, 1992). It is now realised that social democratic principles only reinforce individualism and the sexual divisions within and between the public and private domains (Skeggs, 1994: 87–8).

In the changed contexts of higher education and academic research in the 1990s, together with four colleagues, David has begun to extend definitions of academic feminism as follows:

> As feminists we are concerned to explore women's experiences, but taking into account not only their material realities but their diversities and differences . . . For feminists, promoting issues which centre equity and social justice become inextricably bound up with self promotion and struggles for power within academic fields. As Ladwig and Gore (1994) point out reflexivity demands that any discussion of social privilege and power needs to pay attention to 'questions of *academic* power and privilege, competition and contestation' (1994: 236) (in David, Davies, Edwards, Reay and Standing, 1996: 1–2).

Given these changing contexts and definitions, how are we to understand the changing nature of policy and gender relations and of feminist research? There are several interrelated issues. Can feminist research merely consist in self-styled feminists asking questions about gender relations or does such research entail particular methodological approaches? If feminist research is only about setting the initial questions does prior active involvement or immersion in the issues constitute at least a prerequisite? Is feminist research about taking a particular perspective such as Dorothy Smith's 'from the standpoint of women' (1987) or Donna Harraway's (1988) 'situated knowledge'? Harraway suggests that feminist research adopts a partiality of vision in order to account for multiple truths while retaining a sense of structural inequalities. 'We seek those ruled by partial sight and limited voice – not partiality for its own sake, but, rather, for the sake of connections and unexpected openings situated knowledge make possible. Situated knowledge are about communities, not about isolated individuals' (Haraway, 1988: 590).

Can such feminist research be conducted for public bodies such as, in Britain, the Equal Opportunities Commission? Would such research be so constrained by the terms and conditions set by the funding body as to render the evidence and/or analysis problematic? On the other hand, would a feminist perspective preclude immersion in externally funded 'strategic research' or research for policy-strategies, such as those defined by the EOC? Or to take Acker's catholic definition of feminist research, would it be *'covert' research?* Thus it now becomes a more complex question about how to design and develop a feminist research project on gender equality and schooling and for what purpose. It is made all the more complicated by changes in the wider contexts for conducting research whether primarily scholarly or externally funded and commissioned by contractors.

Shifts in the Research Context enabling a Critical Stance

The question of the relationship between research and policy has been a vexed one, particularly so, in the area of social and educational policies where for the past 30 years or so, there has been a growing involvement of individual academics in the policy process. But that growth has not been even, and has been transformed by political changes affecting both the academic and research communities and those defining the terms in government. Moreover, many, including feminist researchers, (cf. David, 1993; Skeggs, 1994) have taken the politically committed stance of being overtly critical of government and policies (cf. Ball, 1990; Bowe, Ball and Gewirtz, 1994) rather than coming to the aid of policymakers, given the right wing stance of the British government over the last 16 years.

This stance has been partly responsible for a shift over the last decade or so, from the definition of what constitutes 'pure' academic research to research that is, in the terms of the British Research Councils, particularly the Economic and Social Research Council (ESRC), 'policy-oriented and/or relevant'. *All* British academic research whether funded directly through the Higher Education Funding Councils (HEFC) or the Research Councils now has to be designed in such a way as to be of use to both academic and the non-academic communities. Moreover, the shifts in the funding of all kinds of research (whether pure or strategic/policy) to customer/contractor types of research and as a consequence of tendering approaches have altered the landscape of research, but especially from this point of view, social scientific research. Whereas the contractors' main aim now is to get value for money, the nature of research and the knowledge generated are also now clearly different, given the discursive shifts in the characteristics of research. Research has now become an industry, especially social and educational research. And thus policy-oriented or strategic research have become more enmeshed, in that it is now difficult to separate out policy-oriented research from the more 'pure' variety with respect at least to what we have now come to call public-policy research.

This shift in research funding and focus has resulted in questions about what constitutes adequate research around policy issues. This is particularly the case, from our point of view at least, on the grounds of promoting gender equality in education. This question, of course, cannot easily be answered in the abstract. Given the changes in the political landscape, those concerned with social justice issues, such as feminists, may have shifted the main focus of their research involvement to a more critical stance on policy and practice involvement as Skeggs (quoted above) has noted. The 'new' approaches to research in the academy may involve externally grant funded projects as much as the now traditional 'scholarly' academic research.

The Design of a Feminist Research Project on Gender Equality in Education

Thus, the question of a more strategic and less analytical and conceptual approach becomes more pressing in a changed research arena where evidence about the nature of policy shifts and changes and their impacts upon gender equality may be raised. Indeed, at the time of writing, these kinds of question had been placed high on the public agenda by, *inter alia*, Chris Woodhead, Her Majesty's Chief Inspector and Head of the Government's Office for Standards in Education (Ofsted). He wrote a column in *The Times* (6.3.96) entitled 'Boys who learn to be losers: on the white male culture of failure' arguing that the question of white working-class boys' poor performance in both primary and secondary schools was a cause for deep concern and required urgent explanation. He drew on evidence from Ofsted inspections but went on to speculate on a wide range of reasons to explain *'the most disturbing problem we face in the whole education system'*. He also argued that '[s]olutions to the problem do not, however, depend upon any all-encompassing psycho-social theory' and went on to present a range of educational policy changes such as raising standards of literacy and numeracy, curriculum developments and education for parenting, especially for 'the problem of boys living in single-parent families who have no role models'. His essential argument was for strategies and/or policies to restore boys' sense of self worth as the foundation of their desire to learn. In other words, he was alluding to what may now be considered 'a crisis in masculinity'.[1]

In other words, Woodhead did not have much regard for the careful explication of the research evidence but rather assumed a crisis, if not a moral crisis, phrased as 'the most disturbing problem'. This crisis is, of course not new, but had surfaced in Britain quite strongly the previous summer. In the press and media in the mid-1990s, during the examination results period, typical headlines included 'The trouble with boys' (*The Sunday Times*, 19 June 94); 'Girls trounce the boys in the examination league table' (*The Times*, 3 September 1994); 'Can girls do better without boys?' (*Daily Express*, 11 November 1994); 'Brainy girls are top of the class' (*Today*, 22 November 1994).

However, the current media debates do not always foreground the question of gender. Woodhead's approach may be contrasted with the British journalist, Will Hutton's full page analysis of 'the looming crisis in education' and his 'recipe for change' in the previous Saturday's *Guardian* Outlook (2.3.96: 21). In his left-leaning account not one word was devoted to issues of gender equality nor equal opportunities more generally. Yet the problem was also seen in terms of a relatively crude social class analysis, and a reversion, in terms of policy solutions, to the recognition of 'differing abilities' and different educational solutions for different classes of children. In this respect, not focusing on strategies to curtail, let alone promote, gender equality may be seen to be equally problematic. However, both pundits identify a crisis in education; one asserts that it has to do with masculinity whereas the other presents a gender-neutral approach but provides a recipe for change that would, implicitly if not explicitly, also promote new forms of masculinity. What this crisis consists of is the problematic issue; what is the nature of the material evidence prompting the accusations of a crisis in education?

A similar moral crisis about boys has surfaced in other countries: for example, in Australia, Foster (1995: 54) identifies a recent 'backlash period' against gains made by girls as a result of a decade of equal opportunities policymaking deliberately aimed at girls and young women. Faludi, in the USA, also notes this perennial process in the media in her interesting study, *Backlash* (1991).

There is at least confusion about whether boys' performance has indeed deteriorated as girls' performance has improved or, on the other hand, whether educational standards are falling or improving and the contribution of shifting gender relations to these patterns. How to map and explain these patterns, as a basis for developing new strategies, is therefore complex and fraught with problems of definitions, politics and analysis. Moreover, there are other questions to consider, which may have to do with processes rather than outcomes of equal opportunities policies and/or educational reforms. A feminist perspective might suggest interest in the policies, processes of policymaking and implementation around equal opportunities rather than the reasons for girls' or boys' performances in examinations and schooling.

Given the confused nature of the public debates, a number of questions can be posed about research on gender equality and schooling. Is the main question one of the following:

- the impact of the changing gender balance in standards and/or performance in examination in schools through tests and public examinations including vocational qualifications;
- assessing the impact of policy changes such as conservative educational reforms on the relations between the sexes in public examinations and/or their processes of schooling;
- evaluating the impact of explicit policies for equal opportunities on both the practices and performances of girls and boys in school and their eventual outcomes;
- assessing and evaluating the impact of wider social changes on what happens in school; or
- assessing the nature of changing gender relations and their sources and influences in families and schools?

The EOC Study: Educational Reforms and Gender Equality in Schools

Two years ago we responded to an invitation to tender for a research project by the Equal Opportunities Commission. The invitation to tender asked for the researchers to collect and collate evidence on educational reforms and equal opportunities in education, specifically schools in England and Wales, since the EOC's research division had not collected such material since the mid-1980s.

In our successful bid we planned to map the policy and educational changes over a 10-year period, from 1984 to 1994, using three different methods:

- an analysis of examination performance data of school leavers especially at 16 + (GCSEs), 18 + (GCE A levels) and 16–18 (vocational qualifications);
- surveys of the perspectives of all LEAs and primary and secondary state maintained schools;
- case studies in a small number of LEAs and schools.

Our proposal was based upon our prior knowledge of, and involvement in, educational matters as feminists, although we each brought to bear differing but complementary perspectives: Arnot as a feminist and sociologist of education, mainly renowned as a theoretician, Weiner as an educational researcher on curriculum and a well-known feminist in equal opportunities and David as one known for her critical, sociological and feminist, policy analysis. This led us to choose, within the constraints of the terms of reference, a set of questions and methodology which would produce both a statistical picture and illustrative examples; macro- and micro-information. However, we found ourselves unable to adopt an explicitly feminist methodology (if there is one) but allowed our prior immersion in the issues to suffuse the ways in which we addressed the questions. Moreover, we were required, as part of our terms of reference, to map trends in gender equality and schooling over a 10-year period and the contexts in which they occurred rather than to provide wider explanations for the patterns that we might uncover. This kind of mapping exercise was required by the funders, since they wanted a basis for recommending new policies, rather than developing a more detailed theoretical explanation: 'strategic' rather than 'pure' research. Thus the limitations of the terms of reference, time and funding has restricted a fuller analysis and explanation.

An Evaluation and Reflection on our Approach

Our research designs, nevertheless, did not lead us straightforwardly to our studies and analysis. Implementation was not without problems because we had reckoned without the enormity of the changes in the political and policy contexts. These in particular affected how we could go about mapping change in a *national context*, given that Wales was experiencing changes that were different from those in England. (Scotland had its own study, published separately – Turner, Riddell and Brown, 1995.) Thus the questions of both examination performance data and the selection of LEAs and schools for the surveys and case studies proved more complicated than anticipated, including the need to translate our Welsh questionnaires into Welsh before administering them. Similarly, given the complex definitions of different databases, our examination performance data analysis may well include some students from Scotland and Northern Ireland. It is not necessarily restricted to England and Wales. Furthermore, changes in the definitions of characteristics of schools, part of the changing policy context towards marketization and choice, rendered the sampling frame for schools problematic in the sense of its constant changes, particularly around the creation of schools opting out of local authority control to Grant Maintained (GMS) status. At the time of implementation there was no one national database of all types of school from which to draw our sample. Thus we had to exclude all private/independent schools (not directly funded by government), Special Educational Needs (SEN) schools, and many schools defined as sixth form colleges for 16–18 year olds. In addition, reform strategies to transform LEA-school relations affected our access to LEAs and schools, and their evidence on changing performance indicators. Nevertheless, these changing databases give some indication of the characteristics of the shifts in public policy over the time period and informed our policy analysis.

It is important to consider, too, whether our research approach would have been different if we had had different funders such as the ESRC rather than the EOC, and if we had not needed to work within the constraints of the terms of reference. In fact, the EOC, as an official government organization, has given us the legitimacy to study these issues and has aided our abilities to obtain access to a range of organizations, schools, LEAs, examination boards, etc. Similarly it afforded us the opportunity, at a critical juncture, to do important and funded research on a topic of intense interest to us, at a crucial time in the changing context of gender relations. However, there have been some limitations to the scope of the investigation, in terms of the time frame of the funding and the overarching political sensitivities to these issues that should not be under-estimated. In some senses the headline of the news article in *The Times* (6.3.96) accompanying Woodhead's column illustrates the real sensitivities to these issues of gender equality: *'Anti-school bias "blights boys for life"'*. Therefore our results need to be set in context and interpreted carefully.

Our Findings

We report below on our three sets of findings, which cover issues which may not necessarily be related to each other but which document clear changes over the 10-year period under investigation, namely improvements in examination performances by gender, developments in equal opportunities policymaking and shifts towards what we have called a 'gender-fair' culture.

Improvements in Examination Performance

Our evidence and that from other studies with which we are familiar runs directly counter to that of Woodhead, and others, in relation to examination performance data. In particular, we have found remarkable evidence of schools' achievements with respect to a range of their pupils. First, the introduction of a National Curriculum in 1988 formalized and strengthened the set of core subjects (to which science was added) taken by all students, and regular and public forms of testing were introduced. There appeared to be fewer possibilities for subject choice at 13-plus though. As a consequence of the Dearing Report (1993), the number of compulsory subjects in the initial National Curriculum has been reduced. At the time of writing, the outcome of the Dearing changes has yet to be evaluated, though it is anticipated that sex-stereotyping will re-emerge alongside increased choice.

At *primary school level* in the mid-1990s, assessment focused on the core subjects (English, mathematics and science) and in the main girls have been achieving at higher levels overall, especially in English, with boys more likely to perform at the extremes.

In terms of *secondary school examination performance*, the introduction of GCSE (in 1985, first examinations in 1988) has led to higher examination entry and performance patterns of both boys and girls, but particularly with girls. This change more than any other, in our view, has caused the shifts picked up in the press. Since 1985, moreover, there has been an *increase in the proportion of year 11 pupils entering public examinations* (from 91 per cent to 96 per cent) but the changes in the cohort sizes of the entries for English reveal a drop in the numbers of male students from nearly half a million to just over 304,000 in 1994. The numbers of female students has dropped proportionately even more (from outnumbering males by over 30,000 in 1985 to 2000 fewer female students than males in 1994). Thus there has been

- *an increased entry and a closing gender performance gap in most subjects* in GCSE apart from chemistry and economics which are still largely taken by boys, and social studies which is largely taken by girls.
- Male students continue to achieve relatively less well in English and the arts, humanities, modern foreign languages and, perhaps more unexpectedly, technology.
- Girls have reversed the gender gap in entry in mathematics and history and there was near equality in male and female performance in maths; girls are consistently outperforming boys in history.
- Single sex girls' schools continue to be particularly successful in examination performance.

Both girls and boys are doing well in terms of entering and passing examinations, and both sets of standards are improving not declining as Woodhead, inter alia, would have us believe.

At *GCE A level*, over the ten year period (1984–1994) the proportion of the age cohort (16–18-year-olds) has changed significantly, *a rise of approximately 12 per cent*. The male cohort has risen from just over 73,000 in 1985 to just under 78,500 in 1994 and females from just under 67,500 in 1985 to just over 87,500 in 1994. The rise in young women choosing A levels has been far steeper than that for young men, so that by 1994 females outnumber males by over 9000. *However, there remain relatively sex-stereotyped patterns of examination entry and performance.*

- There is a higher male entry into sciences (physics, technology, computer studies, geography, chemistry, mathematics) and the level of male entry into English and modern foreign languages is also higher than previously.
- Significantly, there is a higher female entry for arts and humanities.
- *Males gain higher A-level grades in nearly all subjects*, especially mathematics, chemistry, technology, history, English and modern foreign languages. (They also gain the lowest grades, performing at the extremes in examinations – throughout their schooling.)
- This grade superiority is gradually being eroded with a marked improvement in female performance at A level, particularly in biology, social studies, art and design. In the last two there has been a reversal of performance trends in favour of young women.

For those students seeking *vocational rather than academic qualifications*, subject and course choice has remained heavily sex-stereotyped with boys and girls choosing different subjects, and girls less likely to gain higher awards. Young men were more likely to achieve traditional vocational qualifications and young women were more likely to take the new vocational qualifications. Such patterns reflected what was termed a strong gender bias (Felstead, Goodwin and Green, 1995: 55). (This is the subject of Dearing's recent report which predates his invitation into higher education.)

Thus the 10-year period covered by our study is associated with a *considerable rise in achievement of all compulsory and post-compulsory qualifications, especially amongst young women*. School leavers' data suggest that although young women leave school more qualified than young men, there are important national, regional, ethnic and social differences in gender patterns. Gender differences remain in relation to subject entry in post-compulsory qualifications, although there has been a marked improvement in performance of female students in almost all subjects at A level, especially those where male students have tended to be over-represented in entries.

Equal Opportunities Policymaking

We also examined the context in which these changes in gender performance in examinations took place. We surveyed primary and secondary schools and LEAs to obtain a picture of their perspectives on educational reforms and equal opportunities. What appears to be the case in the 1990s is the relatively high level of equal opportunities policymaking nationally. Hitherto, equal opportunities policymaking had achieved a high profile only in certain metropolitan and urban areas. Given the apparent hostility, or at least lack of commitment, of government to equality issues from 1979 onwards, an unanticipated finding of the project was that, in the mid-1990s, most schools surveyed had equal opportunities policies on gender (two-thirds), the majority of which (83 per cent) had been developed after 1988. These policies tend to focus on curriculum practice and employment concerns rather than on pupil or student performance or on parents. A quarter of LEA policies do not apply to pupils and only two out of five policies include parents. The main impetus for the development of equal opportunities policies and practices has come from LEAs and head teachers in the case of primary schools, and from LEAs, head teachers, committed teachers and TVEI in the case of secondary schools. English and Welsh LEAs generally reported an increased role in the development of gender equality in the primary sector since the reforms. Neither parents nor parent governors are reported to have played an active part in the development of equal opportunities policymaking. Equality issues are not viewed as a high priority by most schools and LEAs and less than 10 per cent gave gender issues a high priority. There was also evidence of wide variation in awareness and application of equal opportunities or understanding of changed performance trends relating to girls and boys.

Significantly, where equal opportunities initiatives developed locally, they tended to address the reform context of the Government's regularly required inspections by the Office for Standards in Education (Ofsted), indicators of 'value addedness', raising performance, governor training, and male underachievement. The reduction in the role and influence of LEAs has led to relative isolation in policymaking with little attempt to disseminate beyond the immediate school cluster group or even the individual school staffroom. Thus the equal opportunities culture in the mid-1990s has been one that has tended to have a narrow focus, and to fuse social justice issues with performance standards and improvement, with a greater emphasis on the latter.

Gender-fair Culture

The culture of schooling has, in our view, been transformed in the last ten years. The aim of much early feminist educational work was to encourage a school culture in which girls could prosper and raise their aspirations and achievements (see Byrne, 1978). A sign of its success perhaps is that students in the 1990s seem more aware and sensitive to changing cultural expectations, with many girls and young women exhibiting confidence about their abilities and future, especially in terms of employment, and boys and young men more sensitive to gender and equality debates. Labour market and cultural transformation has led to changed vocational aspirations for both boys and girls with girls tending to see the necessity for paid employment and their improved employment possibilities, particularly in the expanding service sector. The availability of part-time work, though lower paid, tends also to fit in with their traditional family commitments. On the other hand, the employment opportunities of young men have contracted as conventional male manufacturing jobs have disappeared, leading to a higher degree of uncertainty about what the future has to offer, particularly for working-class youth.

However, while schools have seemed to benefit from changing pupil and student cultures, the management of education exhibits no equivalent changes. In fact, schools and LEAs (and also government education agencies, political parties, education quango, higher education institutions, etc.) continue to be shaped largely by the culture of (white) male management (in staffing, governing bodies, institutional hierarchies, etc.) which has demonstrated little interest in equality issues. Unexpectedly, given the high ratio of female staff, this has been a particularly noticeable feature of primary schools.

Reflections on our Conclusions

Summarizing the EOC project

The EOC project reported upon above has been a mapping exercise about patterns and trends in gender equality over a 10-year-period in which we have found three different sets of evidence – about examination performances by gender, about the extent of equal opportunities policymaking and about cultural shifts in approaches to gender issues in schooling. In all three arenas there have been shifts and improvements overall, but we cannot claim that there is any necessary relationship between the three sets of shifts. Nor are we, as feminists, able to claim that the changes may be attributed (solely or at all) to feminist action and activity, but we may speculate that the wider changes in context, in which women and feminists especially have played their part, particularly socio-economic trends and changes may contribute to some of the shifts identified.

First, we have found evidence of great improvements in examination performance of both boys and girls, but particularly with girls 'closing the gender gap'. However, as we have noted, the picture is not as stark as the current political and media pundits would have us believe. Girls are not outperforming boys overall. They are now performing equally well as boys at GCSE, and in a small number of subjects, better than boys; they have closed the gender gap in many subjects at A level, but there remains evidence of considerable sex-stereotyping in subject entry and in performance. In vocational qualifications, sex stereotyping is an enduring feature; and boys on the whole still do better. Nevertheless, we would want to celebrate the achievements of schools in realizing more students' potential and producing these kinds of successes.

This celebration is particularly important since the schools in England and Wales, which we have studied, have been located in the framework of a massively changing social and political context. Moreover, this change has been part of a discourse of derision. The schools have had to operate with constant change in policies with respect to their organization and their curricula. However, curricular changes, especially those associated with the national curriculum, have, it seems from our studies, enabled more students to participate across the curriculum in compulsory schooling; sex-stereotyping tends to re-emerge in post-compulsory courses when choice of subjects is more available. Moreover changes in the policies and practices towards performance indicators and the monitoring of gender equality in schooling have also enabled us to reveal and present these patterns. But the development of systematic data collection and the monitoring of educational processes as well as performance now is an urgent priority. For instance, establishing the part that different types of school play in these processes has been singularly difficult in such a changing environment, with constant moves towards market forces in policy and practice. We have identified pockets of good practice in schools and a changing climate towards what we have called a gender-fair culture. In other words, we have noted changing definitions of the notions of equal opportunities.

However, given the changing political and policy climate which has also suffused the contexts in which research is now conducted, this particular study has not been able to account for the reasons for changes in gender performances or practices in schools. We remain puzzled by some of the evidence that we have uncovered; in particular, the fact that there is a changing climate in schools – a gender-fair culture – with respect to the equal treatment of pupils, if not staff. In addition, we are unable to account for the improvements in examination performance in terms of educational reforms or equal opportunities policies. Many of the changes that we have revealed had already begun before the main period of educational reform, from 1988 to 1994, which itself is only likely to be fully effective in the next century.

However, it seems to us clear that with a feminist approach which foregrounds gender, we have been able to be explicit about changing gender relations and what happens in schools, seeing schools as a success story, especially in the context of heavily constrained resources. Despite this context, we are able to see that girls are doing well and boys only falling behind relatively speaking, not absolutely. The future however remains a concern; how will schools continue to be supported in these kinds of equal opportunities activities, given the changes in LEA-school relations? It is especially the case that LEAs' role has been reduced and they will not be able to provide the kinds of support that they report having provided as they did in the past.

A Reflection on our Feminist Approach

It seems clear to us, with the benefit of hindsight, that despite the constraints of externally commissioned research, we have been able to apply feminist perspectives and approaches to the consideration of our material. We have been able, and indeed been provided with a tremendous opportunity, to map changes in equal opportunities and gender equality in schooling. However, the constraints of time have not yet allowed us to develop any wider explanation for the three sets of changes that we have identified. We have not yet been able to identify linkages between improvements in girls' examination performances, developments in equal opportunities policymaking and shifts towards a gender-fair culture.

What would constitute an adequate explanation for the changes, both positive and negative, that we have witnessed? Inevitably we are drawn back to our intellectual and academic feminist perspectives and now seek an explanation for these changes – changing gender culture in schools and in examination performances – in terms of the wider social and economic contexts, such as the labour market, in changing families and the role of feminist action/activities, rather than in the detail of public policy development, whether equal opportunities or educational reform. In particular, it may be the case that the broader changes in labour markets and

Miriam David, Gaby Weiner and Madeleine Arnot

-especially women's work or new employment patterns can explain why girls now opt to take more public examinations across the board. Girls may also be influenced by their mothers' and other women's lives, seeing the necessity of labour market participation rather than the necessity of marriage, dependence on a male bread-winner and motherhood. There is clear evidence, from other studies, of these other broader shifts.

We are not, however, enamoured with those sociological theories which seek to link changes in intimate and personal life with wider political changes towards choice, seeing these as a new form of democratization, and the creation of new life-style politics, enabling women's greater participation in public life (Beck, Giddens and Lasch, 1994). Although these new developments clearly draw on feminist the-ories they are not adequate, in our view, to explain the uneven developments and changes in gender relations in education, whether amongst pupils or their teachers.

However, a feminist perspective on social and cultural changes might pro-vide us with the ways towards explaining changes in schooling, cultural shifts and examination performance by girls, showing that cultural shifts, rather than specific policy moves and educational reforms, are the motor of social and sexual changes in society.

Note

1   It is interesting to note that this issue was further discussed in *The Guardian* (11.3.96) on the Women's pages (pp. 6–7) rather than in the general section. However, it con-tained only interviews with boys from Tong School in Bradford, and the entire article, by Linda Grant, was devoted to the question of 'white, working class boys . . . at the bottom of the pile'.

References

ACKER, S. (1994) *Gendered Education: Sociological Reflections on Women, Teaching and Feminism*, Buckingham, Open University Press.
ARNOT, M., DAVID, M. and WEINER, G. (1996) *Educational Reforms and Gender Equality in Schools*, Manchester, Equal Opportunities Commission, Research Discussion Series No. 17.
BALL, S. (1990) *Politics and Policy-Making in Education*, London, Routledge.
BECK, U., GIDDENS, A. and LASCH, S. (1994) *Reflexive Modernization*, Cambridge, The Policy Press.
BOWE, R., BALL, S. and GEWIRTZ, S. (1994) 'Captured by the discourse? Issues and con-cerns in researching "Parental Choice" ', *British Journal of the Sociology of Education*, **15**(1), pp. 63–78.
BYRNE, E. (1978) *Women and Education*, London, Tavistock.
DAVID, M.E. (1993) *Parents, Gender and Educational Reform*, Cambridge, The Polity Press.
Daily Express 'Can girls do better without boys?', 11 November 1994.
DAVID, M., DAVIES, J., EDWARDS, R., REAY, D. and STANDING, K. (1996) 'Mothering and

education: Reflexivity and feminist methodology', in WALSH, V. and MORLEY, L. (Eds) *Breaking Boundaries: Women in Higher Education*, London, Taylor and Francis.

DAVID, M., EDWARDS, R., HUGHES, M. and RIBBENS, J. (1993) *Mothers and Education Inside Out? Exploring Family-Education Policy and Experience*, London, Macmillan.

FALUDI, S. (1991) *Backlash: The Undeclared War against Women*, London, Hodder & Stoughton.

FELSTEAD, A., GOODWIN, J. and GREEN, F. (1995) *Measuring Up to the National Training Targets: Women's Attainment of Vocational Qualifications*, Research Report, Centre for Labour Market Studies, Leicester, University of Leicester.

FOSTER, V. (1995) 'Barriers to equality in Australian girls' schooling for citizenship in the 1990s', *Lararutbildning Och Forskning I Umea*, **2**(3/4), pp. 47–60.

HARAWAY, D. (1988) 'Situated knowledges: The science question in feminism and the privilege of partial perspective', *Feminist Studies*, **14**(3) Fall, pp. 575–600.

HUTTON, W. (1996) 'The looming crisis in education', *The Guardian* Outlook, March 2nd, p. 21.

LADWIG, J.G. and GORE, J. (1994) 'Extending power and specifying method within the discourse of activist research', in GITLIN, A. (Ed) *Power and Method: Political Activism and Educational Research*, London, Routledge.

OAKLEY, A. (1974) *The Sociology of Housework*, London, Martin Robertson.

SKEGGS, B. (1994) 'The constraints of neutrality; the 1988 ERA and feminist research', in HALPIN, D. and TROYNA, B. (Eds) *Researching Education Policy: Ethical and Methodological Issues*, London, Falmer Press.

SMITH, D. (1987) *The Everyday World as Problematic*, Milton Keynes, The Open University Press.

The Guardian 'Linda Grant', 11 March 1996, G2, p. 3.

The Sunday Times 'The trouble with boys', 19 June 1994.

The Times 'Girls trounce the boys in the examination league table', 3 September 1994.

Today 'Brainy girls are top of the class', 22 November 1994.

TURNER, E., RIDDELL, S. and BROWN, S. (1995) *Gender Equality in Scottish Schools: The Impact of Recent Reforms*, Manchester, Equal Opportunities Commission, Research Discussion Series.

WEINER, G. (1994) *Feminisms in Education*, Buckingham, The Open University Press.

WOODHEAD, C. (1996) 'Boys who learn to be losers: On the white male culture of failure', *The Times*, 6 March.

Part II

The Politics of Silence and Ambiguity

'It is indeed crucial to locate the "silences" – the absent presences – in all school messages' (Apple, 1994: 353).

Sexist grammar burns into the brains of little girls and young women a message that the male is the norm, the standard, the central figure beside which we are the deviants, the marginal, the dependent variables . . . it . . . leaves men safe in their solipsistic tunnel-vision (Adrienne Rich, 1979: 241).

The unnoticed, quiet students who drop out, the issues that (everyone understands) do not belong in public discourse or on an agenda but nevertheless affect a woman teacher or administrator, and the areas of discretion and ambiguity left when policies and programs are formulated and implemented in a cavalier manner – these are the politics of silence and ambiguity. So, too, are the politics of identity – the negotiations, compromises, cooptation, lobbying, rewards and punishments and covert diversions and game-playing (note the political terminology) going on as children create their identities, influenced by messages from schooling and popular culture. The politics of identity continue for women educators, who must mediate between the pressure to be the good woman teacher and the need to construct a passing identity in order to be seen as having leadership potential. The politics of silence and ambiguity include the microinteractions through which people learn who should and should not speak up, who should and should not have more access to the computer terminal and the teacher's praise. The ensuing chapters in Part II unfold analyses of behind-the-scenes politics.

Singh's analysis of interactions among young schoolchildren exemplifies the value of asking, what are the ramifications of the slippage between the formulation of a gender equity policy and that policy's encounter with the realities constructed through societal power arrangements and understood by even our youngest schoolchildren? In Chapter 6, 'From Software Design to Classroom Practice' we see the pedagogic device embedded in curriculum materials as a vehicle for the cultural production of masculinity, social Darwinism and gendered power relations.

When schools of education, school districts and social agencies declare intentions and policies aimed at sex equity, do they mean it? Do they closely monitor their effectiveness? In Chapter 7 by Wanda Pillow, the researcher *loses* Kathy, her research 'subject'. The irony of Kathy's case demonstrates how, in spite of high political attention to teenage pregnancy, our policy analyses and our social agencies lose their subject/clients, and how adolescent mothers' realities may not connect with those helping agencies.

In 'Toward a Curriculum of Resiliency', Chapter 8, we meet Sharon, whose case illustrates girls' resistance, in the face of identity negotiation, to the constraints of good-girl-ism expected by social agents like educators. Is she to be pitied as a victim and likely drop-out who cannot fit in? Or is she to be admired for intuitively seeing the fallacies of the female version of meritocracy, which sends the message: good girls are chaste, modest, quiet but hardworking and competent and neat, trying to act white middle-class even if they're not, and their reward will be graduation, marriage, a respectable-for-a-woman job, and patriarchal protections by father, husband, courts, legislatures?

Hollingsworth, too, in Chapter 9, 'Feminist Praxis as the Basis for Teacher Education', identifies the issues that take precedence in teacher education, and shows that teacher education makes only token (if any) efforts to prepare educators to take leadership against the silent practices that water down gender equity initiatives. Nor does teacher education give such educators the widened view and sensitivity to support Kathy or Sharon as they sort through the questions about their identities and their futures. By quietly *not attending to* these issues, schools of education fail Sharon, leaving her floundering through risky behavior; they also fail educators, leaving them unable to critique schools' unwritten white patriarchically structured curricula.

Documenting silence and ambiguity is a challenge, often requiring intensive analyses and case studies with few numbers that resist generalizations. Thus, these chapters illustrate the need for different approaches and standards for policy analysis.

> Social constructions are so tightly legitimated that certain questions are unaskable and certain phenomena remain unobservable, making persistent dilemmas of schools' part in racism, classism, sexism, poverty perpetuation into non-issues and non-events (Anderson, 1990: 42).

References

APPLE, M. (1994) 'Texts and contexts: The state and gender in educational policy', *Curriculum Inquiry*, **24**, 3, pp. 349–59.

ANDERSON, G.L. (1990) 'Toward a critical constructivist approach to school administration: Invisibility, legitimation, and the study of non-events', *Educational Administration Quarterly*, **26**, 1, pp. 38–59.

RICH, A. (1979) *On Lies, Secrets, and Silence*, New York, NY, W.W. Norton.

Chapter 6

From Software Design to Classroom Practice: An Australian Case Study of the Gendered Production, Distribution and Acquisition of Computing Knowledge

Parlo Singh

Introduction

During the period of federal Labor government in Australia (1983–1996), numerous education policies referring explicitly to the use of computers in the classroom were developed and implemented in an attempt to reform the schooling system. Generally, these policies were aimed at restructuring educational institutions to meet the social, cultural and technological challenges posed by industrial restructuring.[1] Educators were urged to ensure that students developed the attitudes, skills, and ingenuity to compete in a technologically oriented market dominated by Southeast Asia and the Pacific Rim (Quality of Education Review Committee, 1985). In addition, policywriters encouraged teachers to explore ways in which computers could be used to facilitate teaching and learning by linking geographically distant schools within Australia (Australian Education Council Task Force, 1985; National Advisory Committee on Computers in Schools, 1982; Quality of Education Review Committee, 1985). A key component of official policies produced under federal as well as state Labor governments in Queensland, 1989–1996 was attention to the underparticipation and underachievement of girls in mathematics, science and technology subjects.[2] For example, senior policywriters in the Gender Equity Unit of the Department of Education, Queensland (1991: 14) suggested that the difficulties girls experienced participating in many post-school training, education and employment fields could be attributed to their low enrollments in science, mathematics and technology subjects.

During the years in which these education policies were produced, computer technology was introduced into all government secondary schools. Computer hardware and software purchases were government-funded, and in most cases computers were networked and located in one room designated as the computer laboratory. Specialist curriculum subjects in computing were developed and computer teachers were trained in higher education institutions. At the primary school level, however, government funding for computer equipment was limited. Although subsidies were provided by state departments of education, funds for the purchases of computer equipment were largely raised by teachers, in collaboration with parent and community organizations. When purchased, computer equipment was either networked and situated in a computer laboratory or used as stand-alone equipment – one computer per classroom (see Kenway, 1995).

From the early 1980s then, knowledge about school computing was produced and circulated in multiple education sites, including official education policies, curriculum documents, initial teacher-training institutions, parent and community organizations, teacher and student talk, student interactions with computers and student evaluation records. The emergence of a language about school computing in these sites was significant for three reasons. First, computing was not part of the language of Australian education policies or school talk prior to the 1980s. Second, the language of computing acquired specific educational meanings as it was appropriated and recontextualized from sites outside of schooling institutions. Third, under federal and state Labor governments, the language of school computing was linked not only to the market place, that is, to the production of technologically literate workers for the changing needs of industry, but also to the social justice platform of gender equity.

In this chapter I suggest that a pedagogic discourse about computing was produced, transmitted and acquired within and across various Australian education sites from the early 1980s onwards. I use the term 'pedagogic discourse' in Bernstein's (1990, 1996) sense of an ensemble of rules or procedures for the production and circulation of knowledge within pedagogic interactions. According to Bernstein (1990), discourse consists of the power and control relations that structure the categories of meaning regulating specific pedagogic sites. It is important to note that in Bernstein's theory, power is constituted in the strength of the insulations or symbolic boundaries between categories, rather than in the content of the categories. For example, power relations were constituted in the strength of the insulations between knowledge selected and classified as educational computing and knowledge that was categorized as non-educational.

In the production of Australian school computing discourses, bureaucratic agencies including school computer support centres and software production services were created as sites of knowledge production and distribution. In addition, the production, transmission and acquisition of school computing knowledge created new classifications of educational personnel, namely information technology curriculum writers, software designers, computer consultants, school computer experts, classroom computer teachers and student computer learners. According to Bernstein's theory, this process of reclassification does not prevent personal agency – people negotiate. The negotiations over rules and procedures of a discourse such as educational computing are affected by people's positions in pedagogic and social practices. Moreover, given that the rules or procedures of computing knowledge production and reproduction are constituted in and through social relations, the ways that people position themselves will either reproduce or transform these rules and procedures (see Bryson and de Castell, 1994).

Bernstein (1990) has labeled the principles or rules that structure educational knowledge as 'the pedagogic device'. As a social structure for the distribution, recontextualization and evaluation of knowledge, this device is a relay or vehicle for power relations. Control over the social construction of the pedagogic device is essential to cultural production and reproduction within any given setting. Consequently, control over the pedagogic device becomes the site of struggle and conflict between groups of students, teachers, parents and administrators who attempt to privilege their ways of knowing and interacting within a setting. Consensus among these conflicting interests may be realized through the construction of a hierarchy of discourses regulating classroom practice. For example, conflict over models of best educational computing practice was resolved in policy which stipulated that the stand-alone model was consistent with child-centered theories of progressive primary school education. Similarly, while teachers and students were encouraged to use many different software packages, these were organized hierarchically so that adventure games, problem-solving packages, data base programs, word processing packages, and Logo were discursively constructed as educationally sound, while drill and practice software was constructed as unsound. By categorizing educational computing software as progressive and child-centered, the pedagogic device worked to mask conflict.

Case Study of Computing Practice in an Australian City

The data reported in this chapter were collected during a study of computing practice in four state schools located in a major Australian city.[3] The computing programs of the four schools were nominated by education department officials as exemplary. The majority of students attending the four schools were from families in which both parents were tertiary-educated professionals. Many of the students believed that education was to their benefit and intended to enter a private secondary school and then to complete a professional degree at university. Three-quarters of the student clientele had access to a computer at home. In most cases, the home computer was technologically more sophisticated than the school computer. Only one teacher involved in the study had access to a home computer.

Over a six-month period, data about pedagogic practice involving computers were collected from six classrooms. The interactions of students at the computer were audio-taped and transcribed for analysis. In addition, students were interviewed in groups of three about their perceptions of communication in interactions around computers. Classroom teachers, software designers and computer consultants were also interviewed. Interview questions addressed the ways in which computers were used in classrooms, the educational skills attained by students, differences in student interaction with computers and the structure or design of software packages.

The following section of this chapter presents analyses of the interview data collected for the study. Analysis focuses on the rules or principles regulating school computing knowledge. The analysis examines three discursive sites: software producers' understandings of curriculum design, teachers' theories of computer education and students' perceptions of classroom interactions around computers. I argue that each discursive site was regulated by a gendered division of labor that positioned people to take up specific institutional identities during the production and reproduction of school computing knowledge. Moreover, I propose that gendered identities were not simply reproduced from one discursive site to another. Rather, power relations involving computing knowledge were negotiated at each educational site. As discourses shifted between sites, a space was created for ideological struggles over what constituted valid school computing knowledge, what counted as valid transmission of this knowledge, and what counted as valid realization of this knowledge on the part of the student (Bernstein, 1975: 85).

Bernstein's (1996) principles of recontextualization explains this dynamic. According to Bernstein, recontextualization occurs when a given specialized discourse is delocated, relocated, and refocused; brought into new relations with other specialized discourses and reordered internally. Power and control relations are relayed through these pedagogic relations of reordering school knowledge. One effect of this internal ordering of curricula is marginalization or silencing of certain groups of teachers and/or students. Consequently, an adequate analysis of exclusion within the discourse on school computing demands more than identification of which groups are excluded. It also demands attention to the principles by which curricula are produced, transmitted and evaluated.

Constructing a Universal Discourse of Computing: Software Theory

All of the schools participating in the study used a software program called *Treasure Mystery*, which was designed by John Patel, a classroom teacher seconded to the position of software designer within the Department of Education, Software Production Services Unit. *Treasure Mystery* is an electronic novel designed to develop students' problem-solving skills. In an electronic novel, students move around locations in a micro-setting, solve problems and puzzles and become part of the story. The problems are designed so that one leads to another. In other words, the program involves cumulative problem solving. *Treasure Mystery* asks students to play the role of a marooned pirate. The player is left on an island by a group of pirates and commanded to find the Spanish treasure within a set time. To locate the treasure the player has to solve a number of problems, such as passing through a maze of caves, removing leeches and escaping from falling stones. Players are allowed to carry six items (flint, rope, salt, compass, bag, water) to assist them on their journey. They have to be selective in their choice of items as they must overcome many difficulties on this journey. The game can be played at four skill levels, beginners (60 moves per time period – 420 moves total); medium (40 moves per time period – 280 moves total); expert (23 moves per time period – 161 moves total) and hardest possible (22 moves per time period – 154 moves total).

In the following extract, Patel explained how he constructed the package.

Patel: . . . with adventure games by and large, that environment is set.
PS[4]: Do you think that the environment that you have chosen could have alienated some students?

Patel: I shouldn't think so because I tried to design – obviously, we consciously design things without sex bias, it's important to us . . . but you find that any sort of theme that you are going to choose can be construed in some sort of way by someone as being biased and there have been some disasters in the past, where people have tried to produce software particularly for a certain population. I've never seen a piece of software – to be honest, a piece of adventure software designed for boys – that comes out and says this is designed for boys. But I have seen some that comes out and says this is designed for girls. The Reannon range of software *Jenny on the Prairie, Claire of the . . .*

PS: And is it effective?

Patel: Ghastly. And girls are probably more turned off it than boys. It was a range of software with graphics, adventure software . . . But very patronizing stuff. Where the whole adventure focused around some little girl playing in the forest with her pet fox and gathering berries and things like that. Nothing happens, you know it's dull, deadly dull. And it was like, let's make a piece of adventure software without the adventure. And to me it was ghastly. Anyway with *Treasure Mystery* I didn't set in my mind too, didn't set to make the central character a boy, or girl necessarily. I mean there were plenty of female pirates around. The problems or situations that the child finds himself in the game don't refer to either sex. They're problems that kids, it's supposed to, it never stated that the pirate is an adult or a child in there, that's something left up to the imagination . . .

His stated intentions notwithstanding, Patel constructed a micro-environment based on a pirate theme that was friendly to boys and distinctly unfriendly to girls (Clarricoates, 1987). In all four schools, a majority of boys were intrigued by the pirate mystery, imagined themselves as pirates seeking treasure, and monopolized the game during class and recess times. By contrast, the girls rarely ventured near the game and did not imagine themselves as pirates searching desperately for treasure. These observations of gendered pedagogic interactions in classroom computing are consistent with the findings of research studies on masculine bias within scientific and technical knowledge. Numerous research studies have concluded that curricula texts such as school science and mathematics were designed to appeal to boys rather than girls (Clarricoates, 1987; Walkerdine, 1989; Whyte, 1985). In particular, Clarricoates' (1987) study revealed that popular themes such as dinosaurs and pirates used in progressive primary school pedagogy catered to male, rather than female, interests. However, teachers assumed that these themes were universally popular amongst all children.

Similarly, the software designer John Patel produced a progressive software text oriented to capture boys' interest because it was based on a pirate theme. However, Mr Patel attempted to legitimize the masculinist micro-environment through the fictional construction of a universal class- and gender-neutral child, the pedagogic object of progressive, liberal or child-centered educational discourses. The power of progressive pedagogy to construct a truth about cognitive development is based on its claims of objective, measurable, scientific legitimacy. The universal learner of progressive pedagogy is the white middle-class male (Walkerdine, 1990). This learner is discursively constructed as the norm in terms of healthy cognitive development. Students who are Other to this norm, for example, girls, are measured as deficit. Drawing on the premises of healthy cognitive development within progressive pedagogy, John Patel argued, 'I didn't set in my mind to . . . make the central character a boy, or girl necessarily . . . the problem or situations that the child finds himself in the game don't refer to either sex . . . they're problems that kids . . .'. However, even in his earnest attempt to legitimize masculinist knowledge as neutral, universal and essential to the development of problem solving skills, John Patel constructed the child as male. Further, Mr Patel argued that the software program *Treasure Mystery* was not explicitly labelled as masculinist knowledge. By contrast, software designed for girls clearly attempted to be 'girl-friendly' (Whyte, 1985), and was categorized by Patel as exclusionist to boys, because it was 'designed for girls' and therefore 'produced for a certain [group]'. In an attempt to legitimize masculinist knowledge as essential to the development of logical and rational thinking skills, John Patel belittled adventure software designed specifically for girls as 'dull, deadly dull', a curricula which did not meet the needs of girls – 'girls are probably more turned off it than boys'. The criticism of feminine stories was continued by John Patel, with the discursive construction of a dichotomy which associated masculinist narratives with 'real adventure', and female chronicles as the antithesis of the 'real adventure'; 'a piece of adventure without the adventure'.

This does not imply that the fiction constructed by Mr Patel about boys' and girls' adventure games was contrary to empirical truth. Indeed, adventure games designed explicitly for girls may have been construed by both boys and girls as deadly dull. That is to say, girls may have rejected the feminine knowledge forms of the girls' software (Davies, 1989a; 1989b). This is not the point that is being made here. Rather, the point is that girls as well as boys may reject feminine knowledge because feminine knowledge is constructed as inferior to male knowledge. This opposition between valorized masculine knowledge and denigrated feminine knowledge is central to the production and reproduction of a gendered regime of power relations. These relations are masked by constructing masculinist knowledge as neutral, technical and universal. For example, John Patel constructed *Treasure Mystery*, an explicitly 'boy friendly' piece of software, as neutral knowledge; 'it never stated that the pirate is an adult or a child in there, that's something left up to the imagination'. Within the progressive discourse of individual creativity and personal development, failure or poor performance was attributed to the individual child's lack of interest or imagination. The individual child who 'lacked imagination' in this context represented the lacking 'Other' posited by the adventure-loving male; namely the female.

In addition to the software disk, the *Treasure Mystery* curriculum package included a teacher's manual which provided information about the software, teaching ideas, and a full solution to the game. Display posters, student work sheets and award certificates were also included in the curriculum package. The aim of providing additional educational resources, all based on the theme of pirates, was to give teachers and/or student instructors the opportunity to be selective and innovative in their use of the resource. John Patel stated:

> my advice for people using software in schools is always be adventurous in the use of the software, don't be afraid to take any kit no matter how wonderful it looks or how structured it appears to be, tear it to bits, and re-do it to suit your own needs. Re-do it to suit the needs of your kids and the needs of your school . . . All of this has to be pulled apart and you use as much of it or as little of it as you want and build your own stuff to go with it.

John Patel placed the responsibility for effective use of the software curriculum package on the individual teacher and student. The set environment of the text produced by Mr Patel and his team of designers was constructed as completely malleable in the hands of the professional educator. And yet, Mr Patel clearly stated that the micro-environment for adventure games 'is set' and that 'any sort of theme that you are going to choose can by construed in some sort of way by someone as being biased'. The significance of this contradiction between a 'structured' learning environment and one that teachers can 'tear . . . to bits, and re-do . . . to suit the needs of your kids' is its foundation in child-centered progressive pedagogy. Within this pedagogic model, the teacher as facilitator is responsible for creating a flexible child-centered learning environment that supports the healthy cognitive development of each individual student. However, the individual child who is the center of this progressive pedagogy, and for whom the learning environment is constructed, is the 'white middle-class male' (Walkerdine, 1990).

Clearly, Mr Patel attempted to resolve this contradiction of catering to the needs of all students and creating a structured learning environment conducive to the development of the normal learner's problem-solving skills. He appropriated divergent learning theories such as behaviorist program design[5] and progressive, child-centered education to produce a recontextualized discourse about software curricula.

The principle of drill and practice catering to individualized tuition had dominated software design on the commercial market. Adventure games were produced to meet the demands of progressivist educators who urged for curricula designed specifically to facilitate individual creativity and critical problem-solving skills in the context of small group discussions. These educators often evaluated drill and practice programs as 'unsound' educational materials. In addition, many of the students who participated in this study assessed drill and practice language and mathematics programs as 'terrible' and 'not educational'. Thus a dichotomy was established within the discourses of school computing. Adventure games based on progressive educational theories were educationally sound, and drill and practice software programs were educationally unhealthy. This fiction about the educational value of progressive pedagogy realized in the form of adventure software was based on a desire to liberate children from the power of teachers and routine computer programs.

However, within progressivist discourse the education of girls presents something of a dilemma. Progressive pedagogy, in its most liberal form, denies difference and treats girls 'as if' they were boys, that is, as 'honorary boys'. Within this discourse, feminine difference is distinguished as the negative or deficit Other of the universal masculine child. Masculinity is associated with creativity, rule-breaking and rationality. Femininity signifies the 'Other' of masculinity and consequently is connected with rote-learning, rule-following, irrationality, passiveness, silence and neatness. Aspects associated with the 'Other' of masculinity are taken to be harmful to psychological and moral development. Thus, John Patel constructed real adventure software as characterized by masculinist attributes, and 'Other' software (i.e., software designed specifically for girls) as detrimental to the healthy cognitive development of all students.

Classroom Teachers: Recontextualizing Agents of the State

In the first instance, the pedagogic practice of computing is regulated by the internal order of specific software programs. This does not imply that the structure of software programs mechanically positions students and teachers to behave and act in specific ways. Rather, teachers are active agents who have the pedagogic space to appropriate and challenge the masculinist bias within specific software programs. In other words, as they enter positions within the regulative practices of schooling institutions and recontextualize discourses of computing from these positions, teachers are active agents. As agents they negotiate social relations within pedagogic practice. For example, in the process of recontextualization, they select, organize and pace knowledge. During this pedagogic process, an ideological space is created for teachers to challenge gendered power relations. To reiterate, while the preceding analysis indicated that child-centered adventure game software programs were structured by masculinist power relations, these gendered relations are not simply or deterministically reproduced in classroom practice.

The next section of this chapter analyzes the instructional computing theories of three teachers who were categorized as exemplary practitioners by school administrators. Two of the teachers, Mrs Rossi and Mr Hansell, taught upper grades at Samerton Primary. The third, Mr Sullivan, taught middle grades at Murwin Primary. All three teachers used the software package *Treasure Mystery* in their classroom. The teachers were asked about computing practice in their classrooms and the computing skills they expected students to acquire at school. All three teachers nominated '*risk-taking*' as the most important skills that students needed to become proficient computer users, and also suggested that working with computers would enable students to develop the skills and attributes of risk-takers. The concept of risk-taking was defined as an instructional skill that required the development of critical and lateral thinking. However, the regulative discourses structuring the development of risk-taking skills were gendered. Gloria Rossi talked about student learning in the context of school computer work.

> *Mrs Rossi*: what we are basically trying to do in all the subject areas is trying to teach the children to think. To teach them to think you have to have them motivated to some extent. And to have them motivated you have to have some sort of sustained motivation, not just a one off, just a half-hearted type of thing . . . you could use a focus from something from a computer program . . .
>
> *PS*: What do you mean by thinking? What types of thinking skills would you expect the students to be developing from the computer?
>
> *Mrs Rossi*: Well problem-solving skills for a start. Analysis right. Synthesis, evaluation, making judgments . . .
>
> *PS*: And you see computers as helping to develop those higher level skills?
>
> *Mrs Rossi*: I think so, because first of all it is a risk-taking type of thing.
>
> *PS*: How is it risk-taking?
>
> *Mrs Rossi*: Risk-taking because until you, I mean some people feel that they know computers very well but the majority of kids don't know much about it. I guess it is because they don't have enough use and they don't have enough use because they don't have enough programs. But they are a little bit sort of frightened, not really frightened, but they are not wholeheartedly familiar with either the computer or the program. Now if everything goes smoothly that is fine. If it says 'press return', they press return and the next thing comes up. But I think that is a risk-taking type of thing. You could wipe the whole thing, wreck the computer, wreck the program . . .

Mrs Rossi positioned herself within the discourses of progressive education, computer education, and compliance with bureaucratic dicta – 'we have to be guided by the top echelon of the Education Department'. Of crucial importance is the way in which Mrs Rossi selected and organized disparate discourses to construct a pedagogic discourse regulating professional practice. In the process of recontextualization, the ideological and political form of incompatible discourses changed as they were ordered hierarchically around a central signifier: 'risk-taking'. Risk-taking behavior was linked with the progressive educational concept of higher-order thinking skills and with the technological concept of familiarity with the computer. For Mrs Rossi, 'higher-order thinking skills' signified problem solving, analysis and synthesis. Citing Bloom's Taxonomy of cognitive skills, Rossi stressed the importance of teaching students concepts and processes rather than facts. Facts, she argued, dated rapidly. Students therefore needed to learn the process of gathering, analyzing and synthesizing information. In the context of computer use, however, higher-order thinking skills were associated with not being afraid to use the computer. Through the process of appropriating and recontextualizing educational discourses, Mrs Rossi produced an instructional discourse of computing that emphasized the importance of risk-taking and overcoming fear of computers through familiarity.

Warren Hansell also taught at Samerton Primary, and during the course of this study was seconded to the position of computer consultant for the school region or district. Although he was a capable computer user, Hansell planned to acquire further computing skills by specializing in computing in the education degree he was completing part-time. In the role of computer adviser at Samerton Primary, Hansell had contributed significantly to the formulation of school computing policies. After taking on the role of regional computer consultant, he continued to advise Samerton staff about the computing curriculum. When interviewed for the present study, Mr Hansell was asked to define the skills he expected students to learn with computers.

> *PS:* What types of computer skills would you be hoping to teach?
> *Hansell:* The computer skills again would be keyboarding skills, accessing information, that's basically what I am aiming for with that particular program (database game).
> *PS:* What types of computer skills do you think these students should have by the time they leave primary school?
> *Hansell:* I think that they should be familiar with the computer.
> *PS:* What does that involve?
> *Hansell:* Well again not being frightened of the computer. Secondly, I think they should be able to come to a computer, be able to boot it, run a program. Not necessarily be an expert on it, but just generally have those basic skills of getting a program started.

Like Rossi, then, Hansell constructed students as apprehensive computer users. This representation was produced through the structuring of strong symbolic boundaries between the everyday or mundane knowledge of classroom participants and esoteric computer knowledge. This classification implied that computing knowledge could only be acquired gradually and through systematic instruction. Thus, Hansell argued that it was of utmost importance that students gain familiarity with computers. 'Familiarity' was associated with 'not being frightened of the computer'.

Herein lies a profound contradiction: interviews with the students involved in the study indicated that they generally experienced little or no apprehension in using computers. Two-thirds of the students who attended Samerton Primary had access to a computer at home. In many cases, students acquired difficult computer skills from reading manuals, or from parents who used computers on a daily basis in their professional occupations. Many of the students claimed that they learnt more about computers at home than at school.

In a classroom setting regulated by discourses that positioned students as 'fearful' of computers, three boys, Anthony, David and Bruce, managed to enter positions of power in relation to computing discourse. The three boys were able to appropriate the discourse of 'computer expert' because the classroom teacher, Mrs

Rossi, and the school policy coordinator, Mr Hansell, did not position themselves within this discourse. Mrs Rossi admitted that she knew little about computers, and often deferred to the male student experts in the class. Computing for Mrs Rossi was a 'risk-taking type of thing. You could wipe the whole thing, wreck the computer, wreck the program.'

Like the classroom teachers at Samerton Primary who constructed a discourse of the universal child as a 'risk-taker', Sullivan, the classroom teacher at Murwin Primary constructed a discourse of the universal child as 'confident' and able to front up to any challenge. In both cases, male and female teachers positioned the female student in the institutional discourses of schooling as 'Other' to the student who was a risk-taker, confident and challenging.

> *Sullivan*: children today need that confidence. Whether they are over-confident or not is irrelevant. The very fact that they are able to front up to any challenge with the preconceived idea that 'I am going to beat this', that is going to support them all the way through their development days . . . Ah, I think probably girls today too, I'm not quite sure whether the computer has had any specific effect on girls, ah, in their developmental role of how they see themselves in society. I find that given the chance the girls will be less reluctant or more reluctant I should say, more reluctant to come towards the computer to use it, where the boys will always say at eight o'clock: 'Can I use the computer?'; after school: 'Can I use the computer?' Last year I had an experiment where I noted a week about computer usage, boy, girl, boy, girl. But the girls' week fell apart very quickly, to the extent where during girls' week the computer was never used. But it was forbidden for the boys to use it. All this went on for about six weeks, then I had to rearrange the whole thing. The girls just weren't interested.

Sullivan discussed the theory of learning he used to structure computing practice in his classroom. All children were constructed within this discourse as confident and willing to confront challenges and take risks. However, girls were positioned outside the socially constructed 'universal child'. Girls represented the Other to the modern subject who was willing to confront and take on any challenge. In this discourse boys naturally accepted challenges and asked to use the computer, while girls were 'more reluctant' to use the computer. Girls 'just [weren't] interested' in computers despite the interventionist strategies adopted by Mr Sullivan.

Mr Sullivan's interventions to reform classroom practice did not challenge the existing gender regime and division of labor that constructed computing as boys' work. To allocate space for girls to use the computer, without challenging the rules and procedures that produced this discourse, was ineffective. Girls avoided using the computer during their allocated period because outside of the teacher's gaze they were chided by the boys who had made claim to technological expertise who resented giving up the classroom computer for a entire week to the girls. Because Sullivan did not challenge these masculinist techniques of domination and control, his intervention strategy reproduced, rather than challenged or transformed, gendered power-knowledge relations.

The next section of this chapter considers student perceptions of computer pedagogy. While software designers and teachers have been described as active agents of recontextualization, this does not imply that students were merely passive objects of instructional discourses. Indeed, students often assumed the identity of computer expert, instructor or teacher within the classroom. This was most apparent in those situations where teachers had little or no knowledge of computing.

Constructing Male Technological Expertise: Competence and Hierarchy

At Murwin Primary, a team of seven male players attempted to control the game *Treasure Mystery*. Three student-players, David, James and Justin, were often nominated as the best computer users by the classroom teacher and other students. David and James had initially organized a team of boys to solve the problem of *Treasure Mystery*. Collective efforts of the team were saved onto a disk under a file composed of their initials. As newcomers into the group gained acceptance, their initials were added to the file name. With seven players, the file name became lengthy, and mirrored the hierarchical division of labor within the team. That is, the file name JJUDCATL.DOC, represented in order of importance, James (J), Justin (JU), David (D), Charlie (C), Andrew (A), Troy (T) and Luke (L). The key players, James, Justin and David, always attempted to maintain their position as producers of new knowledge about the game.

Justin: We looked it up in the book and told Mr Sullivan . . .
James: No one taught us. We looked it up in the book. Mr Sullivan just said, 'you can save it'. He looked it up in the book as well.
PS: What are you going to do once you have got to the end?
James: We'll do it again.
Justin: We'll get a paper and write down all the ways to get through things, just in case we forget.
James: I don't forget.
Justin: I know, but sometimes you can forget.
James: I remember everything . . . about the disk that is in there. How to get past all of the things . . .

Justin and James negotiated a position in the pedagogic practice of classroom computing from which they could exercise control over power/knowledge relations. The boys generally, and James in particular, were hesitant to relinquish their hold over specialized software knowledge. By not exchanging information about the software package *Treasure Mystery*, James attempted to maintain his position as computer expert within the hierarchical division of labor for problem solving strategies.

Although the classroom teacher had access to privileged knowledge about computers, the boys in this team challenged the teacher's power and authority to know. However, there was no simple rule about who was positioned where within the hierarchical, gendered regime of computer use. Rather, control over the production and transmission of 'new knowledge' about computing was always a site of struggle between the classroom teacher and the boys, between the boys and girls, and within the groups of boys and girls.

Bernstein (1990) proposed that the pedagogic device (the structure underlying the production, transmission and evaluation of school knowledge) is the crucial site for social and cultural reproduction. Interest groups are likely to engage in struggles to control the pedagogic device that structures the production and reproduction of 'legitimate or thinkable' school knowledge. In this case, although Mr Sullivan distributed software resources to the students, he had little knowledge of the internal structure of the texts. Consequently, he placed himself as a learner in relation to the boys, who took the position of instructors. In this way, the seven players, with James and David in the lead, gained first and thereby privileged access to software packages. Often the boys would sneak up to the classroom during recess times so that they could gain exclusive use of the computer. The boys would also cheat by finding answers to game problems in the teacher's resource manual. Boys who had learned how to program also used hacking strategies to bypass difficult sections in game activities and thereby finish the game in the fewest possible moves. All of these actions can be seen as attempts to maintain social relations of computer dominance.

But within the masculinist technocratic discourses of computer use, each boy was positioned, and positioned himself, in different relations to the discourses. While James and David struggled to maintain their position as experts of the game *Treasure Mystery*, Luke, Charlie, Troy and Andrew vied to gain acceptance within the group. Charlie and Andrew would often spend considerable time during recess sessions working at the computer. The same commitment to group membership was not expressed by Luke and Troy. Indeed, Troy experienced intense emotional and physical distress in attempting to negotiate a position for himself within the group of male computer experts. One afternoon, he was physically assaulted for not measuring up to the standards of masculine computer and sporting ability constructed by the team. His initials were erased from the password used to denote group membership. However, Troy persisted in negotiating for reacceptance into the team of computer experts.

> *Sullivan*: Last year these two boys took that boy behind the shed and bashed him up after a game.
>
> *PS*: True. What, that was David and Andrew bashed up James.
>
> *Sullivan*: Yes. No bashed up Troy. His mother was up here. And she was very angry. So there is a lack of tolerance in physical attributes . . .

Similarly, Luke often talked about how bored he was with the software and how he really wanted to go outside and play games with the other boys. After he gained acceptance as part of the male computer club, he desired approval from the male sporting elite. James and David had already gained membership within the discourses of technocratic, sporting and academic masculinity. However, Justin was marginalized from both the academic and sporting spheres. Much of his time during recess sessions was devoted to solving software problems and trailing new programs. Justin aspired to a career which would allow him to draw graphs and simulations on computers.

PS:	Who would you say was the best at computers in your class?
Daniella:	David Jones and Justin.
David F:	Justin's really good at the computer. He spends hours on his computer.
PS:	What type of computer has he got at home?
David F:	I don't know. It is a really good one. His dad uses it a lot . . .
PS:	Why do you think David Jones and Justin are so good at computers?
David F:	Because they have got one at home and they are always using it . . .
Danny:	Justin and David Jones are only good at games. They don't know where the keys are . . .
David F:	Justin's smarter than him (Danny) at computers, but not at work.
Daniella:	Yes. Not at work.

Justin's knowledge of computers, particularly with respect to solving game problems was acknowledged by his peers. This is important because Justin did not receive recognition within the academic discourses of the classroom. For Justin, positioning within the discourses of school computing enabled him to gain some recognition for his cleverness from fellow students and the classroom teacher. Through the discourses of computing, Justin's identification as 'not clever in schooling' was partially modified so that he was positioned as an 'expert' computer user. Justin successfully managed to negotiate a position within the classroom where he could recontextualize and embed instructional discourses of computing acquired in the home setting into the regulative structures of the classroom. These regulative structures had been partially constructed by the team of seven male computer experts through the language of technocratic masculinity. Instructional skills associated with computer use were likely to gain recognition only when they were embedded in these discourses (Walkerdine, 1990). It is probable then that computer instructional skills embedded in voices Other to technocratic masculinity may not be recognized as legitimate school knowledge.

Discourses of masculinity associated with the use of the computer were socially constructed in and through the daily practices of the classroom, positioning each boy who entered the group of computer experts. The classroom teacher, Sullivan, also colluded in the production of a dominant or hegemonic masculinity (Connell, 1990a, 1990b).

Sullivan: Whether boys see that it is all very well to be confident, to get in there with the best of them, to do your best. Maybe they see that to do that well you have got to be also agile. As in sports. To be able to pass as a successful male, you have to be physically strong. Now if this is the case there is *nothing* that I can do about it. Because it *is happening*. It is an under-thing that is happening with the development of kids. Maybe that is what life is all about. Maybe throughout the ages people have had to strengthen themselves physically as well as mentally.

In this comment Sullivan naturalized strongly insulated gender categories through recourse to biologically-based theories of instruction. Mr Sullivan appropriated and reorganized theories of learning to structure a regulative discourse of masculinity. Within the social fiction of this regulative discourse, male violence and aggression was legitimated as the product of innate and natural development. Aggressive and competitive masculinity was, in Mr Sullivan's words, 'what life is all about'. By constructing regulative discourses of social Darwinism in the instructional rules, Sullivan colluded with the boys in reproducing patriarchal structures. Within this classroom setting, acquisition of computing skills was dependent on the ability of students to pass as 'successful males'. Students who were positioned within pedagogic practice as Other to successful males, were expected to 'strengthen themselves physically as well as mentally'. Competition and explicit aggression associated with controlling the computer were naturalized as 'an under-thing that is happening with the development of kids'. The onus for deconstructing the regulative patriarchal structures of the classroom, and for constructing a regulative discourse that would enhance the opportunities of all students for learning, was removed from the classroom teacher; 'there is nothing that I can do about it.'

The social construction of a patriarchal discourse regulating classroom practice at Murwin Primary enabled seven male students to organize a team of adventure game players that monopolized the computer. Each team player negotiated a different form of masculinity within the constraints of the regulative discourse. Despite the difference in forms of masculinity, the structure of the software program *Treasure Mystery*, allowed all seven students to position themselves as computer experts. In the following interview extract, five of the boys from the team spoke about their relations to the internal structure and categories of the game.

PS: You know when the story starts and it says you're left on the island and you have to get the treasure before the pirates come back, do you think that the pirates are all men? Do you think that there would be any women pirates?

Andrew: Oh there might be. But I don't think so.

Troy: No.

PS: Do you think the person who is playing the game is a man or a woman?

Boys: A man.

James:	Because you can see yourself on it, sometimes.
Andrew:	Yes.
Justin:	Yes like when you . . . it has a picture of you drowning.
PS:	And it is a man drowning is it?
Boys:	Yes.
PS:	Do you think girls would like that if the whole game was about men and there weren't any girls in it?
James:	I don't think that they see it or anything.
Charlie:	They don't even want to go near it. {Laughter}
Andrew:	They don't take much notice.
James:	If it is a man or a lady.
Justin:	They spend so long um trying to fiddle around with the book trying to go where is this? How do we go this way?
James:	Only a really experienced man if they didn't have a book could get through the computer game really.

The boys' perceptions of gender differences in social relations around the computer can be analyzed in terms of the structure of the pedagogic relay. The temporal, internal ordering of knowledge within software texts marginalizes or silences certain groups of teachers and/or students. Within adventure game software, a symbolic pedagogic relay or carrier of messages was constructed by software designers. The pedagogic voice internal to the game *Treasure Mystery* carried numerous ideological messages. In this setting, the voice of the pedagogic carrier was recognized as masculine and positioned boys in relations of power and control, excluding girls. Boys identified with the message of the pedagogic relay – the male image. They saw themselves in the image of the character stranded on the island and were therefore included in the game. Moreover, the boys suggested that girls were excluded from interacting with the software because they could not identify with the characters or storyline: 'They don't even want to go near it.'; 'They don't take much notice.' Thus, the boys were clearly aware of the girls' absence from the computer environment. They explained this absence in terms of girls' lack of interest in adventure software computer games. This explanation constructs girls as deficient or lacking and consequently draws attention away from the exclusionary rules or principles structuring the content of adventure game software. It will be recalled that this software was designed specifically to facilitate students' problem-solving skills in a progressive computer-based learning environment.

Another interpretation of girls' absence from this learning environment is that they experienced difficulty identifying the problem to be solved: 'I don't think that they see it or anything.' Because the content of the adventure game was based on the theme of pirates, many girls may have felt excluded from this male semiotic system. They simply did not have the prior content knowledge of pirates or the skills of arcade-type software to interact effectively with adventure game computer programs. Students need some knowledge of the content of software texts in order to recognize and work through problems.

Another explanation for girls' absence in the classroom computing environment is that they experienced marginalization because the content and rules of the pirate game were designed to appeal to boys (Fox Keller, 1986; Luke, 1996; Spender, 1995). When girls interacted with the computer software program they entered a ready-made structure based on 'male virtues' and 'manly games' such as competitiveness and self-assertiveness. The rules for proceeding through the problem-solving components of the game, as well as for improving proficiency, were defined by men and were based on masculine norms such as those developed in arcade game cultures. For girls to succeed in solving problems in this computer micro-environment they had to become 'like boys' (Walkerdine, 1990). Taking up masculine identities is difficult for girls because they may desire to be like female teachers and mothers, who are discursively positioned as the passive 'Other' of the active masculine child. In other words, girls come to desire in themselves qualities that appear to be the opposite of those of the universal child that the progressive pedagogy of school computing is set up to produce.

The team of Justin, James, Andrew, Troy and Charlie was hailed by the pedagogic messages in the software text. A fundamental aspect of adventure games and other software packages used in primary schools is that they set up a competitive or 'beating' relationship between the student, the computer and the collection of people, usually males, who have played and recorded their score either in the game or elsewhere. In this way, the framing relation between boys and specific software games, that is, the controls on communication in pedagogic relations, is structured by male power relations of selection, sequencing, pacing and criteria. The competition between the boys needs to be understood in terms of a socially and historically constructed text of masculinity. The boys were not only competing with each other, but also with the records of previous game players, which had been recorded into the software text (Apple and Jungck, 1991; Connell, 1987). The power relations of masculinity were structured into the software text (Bernstein, 1990; 1996). Computing technology as curriculum has unique memory capacity that reifies and institutionalizes the power relations created by recording the progress of males through the game program.

This is not to imply that if the central character in the computer game program *Treasure Mystery* was a female, pirate girls' interactions with the text would alter. The important point here is not whether the central character is male or female; the point is that socially and historically constructed gender relations are relayed through the structure of the pedagogic device. To reiterate, girls were marginalized not only by the content of the game, but also by the construction of computing as a masculine activity in various pedagogic sites. In addition, the active participation of boys in the adventure game cannot be attributed simply to interest generated by masculine images and story lines. The team of male players did not enter the software micro-world simply because they were hailed by a male figure, which carried their procedures and commands. The social relations established between this team of boys and the computer cannot be attributed solely to the fact that boys relate better to pirate themes, camping activities, action adventures, or being stranded alone on an island. Rather, the boys were included and the girls marginalized by the general structure of the pedagogic carrier that set the limits and created the possibilities for pedagogic competence in the computing classroom. In other words, the very structure of the pedagogic text contributed to the silencing of girls and the construction of 'inherent male superiority' in computing. The rules or procedures of selection, organization, transmission and evaluation were controlled at various sites by software designers, classroom teachers and male computing experts. At each site an ideological space was created for the challenge and contestation of masculinist dominance in school computing, but this opportunity went unrealized.

The next section of this chapter focuses on girls' perceptions of computing pedagogy. In the discourses of software designers, classroom teachers and male student computer experts, girls were constructed as hesitant computer users. However, this does not suggest that girls passively accepted these pedagogic identities in their classroom computer use. Rather, as the following data indicate, girls struggled continuously to negotiate positions of power and gain recognition for the computing competences that they acquired. This difficult struggle took place within an educational computing discourse structured by masculinist, technocratic power–knowledge relations, as previous sections of this chapter have shown.

Feminine 'Deficit' and Challenge

The three girls mentioned in the following series of extracts, Trisha, Julie and Wendy, also attended Murwin Primary and considered themselves to be adept computer users. They knew how to turn on a computer and how to access and use word processing, data base, drill and practice and game programs. All three girls acquired most of their knowledge about computers from outside the classroom setting. Julie used her cousin's computer, while Trisha and Wendy had access to a home computer. In addition, the girls enjoyed working with computers and spoke of the importance of gaining computer skills so that they could increase their chances of securing a well-paid and interesting job in the future. The girls were from two-parent working families. Julie's mother was a secretary, Wendy's mother was a computer programmer, and Trisha's mother was a pre-school teacher aide. The girls spoke about the gendered form of interactions in the classroom, specifically in terms of computing.

Trisha:	When Mr Sullivan, ah, when something goes wrong with the computers he always chooses one of the boys. Like he'll say, 'Come on James, come and fix up the computer. What's wrong with it James?'
PS:	Does Mr Sullivan ever choose anybody else?
Julie and Trisha:	Oh, David and Justin. Justin's like a smart aleck type of person, because he's got a computer at home, and he sort of, well when we're doing work on the computer he always says, 'Well if you need any help call me.' He sort of likes . . .
Julie:	Mr Sullivan always picks David to do things. And he's

	nervous about him in his school work and other things, because David understands everything he says. And he's smart.
Trisha:	He thinks he's great and he knows everything about computers and that.
PS:	Who thinks that, Mr Sullivan or David?
Trisha:	Mr Sullivan.
Wendy:	David.
Julie:	Mr Sullivan and David.
PS:	Does Mr Sullivan think that any girls are experts at computers?
Julie:	No, not at computers.
Trisha:	No, he never asks girls to come up to the computer and help. He uses us as messengers.
Julie:	Yeah, he does. He uses us as messengers, but he uses the boys for all the hard things.
PS:	Is that an important thing to use girls as messengers?
Julie:	No, not really.
Trisha:	No.
Julie:	Because I don't think Mr Sullivan should choose girls to do different things. Because, ah, say for instance I was up here and Mr Sullivan had something wrong with the computer and I was up here because my cousin's got a computer and I have used the computer a lot. And I was up here but he didn't want me, he wanted James and he was down on the oval.
PS:	Did you understand what Mr Sullivan wanted you to do? Did you understand the question he asked James?
Julie:	Um, not really because the things Mr Sullivan asks James, some of the girls don't understand because he doesn't let the girls try to understand.

Powerful knowledge associated with the use of the classroom computer was appropriated by a group of boys with the support of the classroom teacher. After gaining teacher recognition for this knowledge, the boys constructed a gendered division of labour for the production and transmission of computing skills. The classroom teacher, Mr Sullivan, assisted the boys in developing a computer gender regime in the classroom. By positioning these three boys as producers of knowledge, Mr Sullivan temporarily gave up his own power position to know. His pedagogic relation with the boys was characterized by nervousness because the boys challenged his knowledge of computing.

Mr Sullivan continually reinforced the boys' position of power in relation to computing knowledge. In the classroom, the boys were positioned within the invisible pedagogy of progressive or child-centered discourse. Bernstein (1975) proposed that invisible pedagogy encouraged the verbal exploration of individual motives and identities (i.e., personal relations). Through the use of nicknames, Mr Sullivan personalized his relations with the computer experts and thereby promoted and rewarded individual talent. Bernstein (1975) theorized that the discourse of individuality strongly regulates the social, linguistic and cognitive development of each child positioned within the code of invisible pedagogy. However, the boys did not individually produce or construct technical knowledge, technological identities and spatial/temporal relations around the classroom computer. Technocratic masculinity was collectively produced, but naturalized through the discourse of individuality.

Mr Sullivan's using personal language with the male students was one realization of the invisible pedagogic code. In addition, the fantasy simulation adventure game was designed on the pedagogic principles of invisible or progressive pedagogy, designed to facilitate the development of students' individual and group problem-solving strategies. Thus, adventure software curricula represented a text which realized multiple pedagogic codes – a visible pedagogy embedded within a modified invisible pedagogy.

This problem-solving computer micro-environment created classifications – symbolic boundaries between categories of knowledge – between girls' knowledge and boys' knowledge, for example. This micro-environment also framed sharply distinguished forms of communication within and between symbolic categories – the personalized interactions between the boys and the teacher and the more formal interactions between the girls and the computer. One example is Mr Sullivan removing himself from the position of authority – the position of knower and the boys' freedom to by-pass entire sections of the software.

According to the girls, Mr Sullivan only recognized the computer knowledge and expertise of male students in the class. That is, only males were positioned within the progressive or invisible pedagogic discourse of adventure software computing. Girls' knowledge of computing was recognized within pedagogic practice, but in a remarkable play of power/knowledge relations. Sullivan, a teacher who knew less about computing than his students, disavowed the girls' computer competence and positioned them within discourses of domesticity. In other words, the girls were expected to carry messages from the classroom teacher to the male student computer experts. They became reproducers rather than active producers of knowledge. Girls were positioned as Other to the masculine producer of knowledge.[6] For the girls, discourses of domesticity – messengers between the teacher and male computer experts – constructed subordinate pedagogic relations. They were recognized only as 'carriers of meaning'; transmitters or reproducers of technological knowledge.

This positioning within discourses of domesticity further prevented the girls from gaining access to elaborate forms of computer-based problem solving. In not asking them to solve computer problems, Mr Sullivan denied the girls opportunities to explore and discover; that is, he failed to create a learning environment conducive to the development of the girls' problem-solving strategies. The girls were denied access to esoteric forms of computer knowledge. Bernstein (1986) suggested that instructional discourse is realized in two distinctly different orientations of knowledge, namely esoteric (unthinkable) and mundane (thinkable). Esoteric knowledge provides students with access to the procedures or rules for the production of new knowledge. Julie argued that Mr Sullivan denied the girls opportunities for solving computer-based problems. Yet all three girls were competent computer users, enjoyed playing with computers, and visualized a future to which computing skills were central. However, in the classroom, the computing competence of these three girls was not fostered or recognized. In realizing discourses of technocratic masculinity, the particular ensemble of rules or procedures for the production and circulation of knowledge – the pedagogic device – effectively managed to silence and change the feminine voice from computer-competent to computer-incompetent and to change the girls' identities from technologists to domestics.

To reiterate, technocratic discourses of masculinity allowed boys to enter social relations of knowledge production, specifically, solve adventure game problems. By contrast, discourses of feminine domesticity constructed subordinate identities during knowledge transmission. Girls rarely engaged in social relations where they assumed positions as producers of knowledge. Furthermore, positioning with the discourse of domesticity further removed the girls from gaining access to elaborated forms of computer-based problem solving. This analysis does not imply that girls' identity was unified, fixed or remained static in the pedagogic contexts of school computing. For the girls, pedagogic identity shifted from a passive, victimized femininity to an active, aggressive, rational femininity. Their silence was a negotiated silence; a suppressed anger. At home, when they got frustrated with the computer, they walked away and tried to solve the problem at a later stage. When their brothers usurped the computer, they felt like 'strangling them'. When they were not positioned within the progressivist pedagogy of personal relations and discovery learning, they negotiated alternative positions. Girls worked at and succeeded with word processing and keyboard tutor software packages and spent their spare time playing, rather than engaging with computer work disguised as play (I wish we could hear more about the girls' preferences, successes, and activities!).

The silence and inactivity of girls in the school computer setting was not based on a simple acceptance of male superiority with computers. Rather, power and control over the structure of the pedagogic device, realized as technocratic masculine discourse in the classroom studied, was the site of contestation between the students. Power was ultimately realized in the sites of evaluation. The boys constructed social relations in which Others would accept the fiction of their technological mastery. Deconstructing the fiction of male technical superiority in the computer context enabled the girls to contest male control over the pedagogic device. Initially Julie positioned herself within the discourse of technocratic patriarchy and claimed '. . . David understands everything he says. And he's smart.' However, later in the same conversation, Julie contested this positioning. She argued that David's technological expertise was not simply the result of a natural superiority with computers. Rather, his expertise was discursively constructed through his classroom displays of competence, self-promotion as a technological expert and the recognition he received from the classroom teacher, Mr Sullivan. Julie's ideological switch in these two sentences was remarkable. In the space of one conversation, she managed to shift from a position within the fiction of David's natural technological competence to a position which enabled her to question the social relations by which David appropriated and displayed technological knowledge. The girls thus contested the illusion or fiction of male supremacy in computing. They started to recontextualize male technological competence from a discourse of innate ability to one cognizant of the fictionalized construction of this competence, and thereby momentarily shifted the power and control relations of the pedagogic device.

Conclusion

This limited case study explored the social construction of computing discourses and the negotiation of positions within these discourses by software designers, classroom teachers and students. It was suggested that the selection, organization, transmission and evaluation of educational computing knowledge at each discursive site relayed relations of power and control. Moreover, each site occasioned an ideological struggle over the construction of gendered power relations within computing knowledge. Through the process of recontextualization, discourses of educational computing were delocated and relocated so that a new internal ordering of knowledge was produced at each pedagogic site.

Within the classroom practices of two Australian primary schools, a group of boys negotiated positions of power to construct gendered forms of computing knowledge. By recontextualizing discourses of computing, gender equity and theories of instruction, the boys and the classroom teachers constructed a masculine norm of computing practice. Males were positioned within the discourses regulating classroom practice as risk-takers and as willing to accept challenges. Girls were positioned as Other to the socially constructed male norm.

Although constructed as the Other of the male computer expert, girls managed to contest and negotiate power relations within the classroom. Julie and Trisha constructed a femininity oppositional to the hegemonic technocratic masculinity dominating computing practice. They refused to be positioned within the fiction of male competence and female ineptitude in computing. By deconstructing the fiction of male superiority with computers, a fiction socially constructed and maintained in the classroom, they gained some ground in interrupting gendered power-knowledge relations.

However, the subjection of girls to the position of domestic labor and as facilitators for the intellectual labor of boys operated not only at the level of physical and conscious control. Boys may well have blocked girls from computers through physical and verbal abuse, but subjugation was most effective when it penetrated unconscious desires and emotional attachments. Although girls may have resisted their positioning as domestics, they also struggled to please the classroom teacher and the boys. This meant bowing to the boys' supposed superiority.

Although this case study was necessarily limited by the small number of schools, school classes, software designers, computer consultants, teachers and students and by the local contexts, I suggest that the social constructions revealed by the detailed analyses in this chapter hold currency in an environment far greater than that of Australian primary education.

Acknowledgments

Basil Bernstein's assistance with the study and ongoing encouragement, particularly during his May 1996 Australian visit, are most gratefully acknowledged.

Notes

1   See Australian Education Council Task Force on Education and Technology, 1985; Department of Education, Queensland, Curriculum Services Branch, 1984; Department of Education, Queensland, 1985, 1987; National Advisory Committee on Computers in Schools, 1983; Quality of Education Review Committee, 1985.
2   See Commonwealth Schools Commission, 1984; Department of Education, Queensland, Ministerial Advisory Committee on Gender Equity, 1992; Department of Education, Queensland, Gender Equity Unit, 1991; Department of Education, Queensland, Gender Equity Unit, Studies Directorate, 1992; Department of Employment Education and Training, 1988, 1989, 1990.
3   The names of all software designers, software packages, classroom teachers, students and schools have been changed to ensure the ethical requirements of research anonymity are maintained. This is in strict accordance with the requirements of the Ethics Committee, Griffith University.
4   PS is Parlo Singh, the researcher.
5   Richard Creswick, a software designer working with John Patel, was asked to describe the theory of instruction used to select, organize and pace curriculum content. Creswick stated:

> I have a long association with the Army Reserves and I was specifically involved in the Army training system, which is based on criterion-based training and evaluation, where you have to go and look at the job . . . You look at every aspect of . . . training . . . And it is all done in terms of behavioural objectives, and very specific behavioural objectives, not waffly objectives like in the education system, very wishy-washy.

6   Historically the women's roles have been confined to the reproduction or transmission of knowledge. As wives, teachers and mothers they pass on cultural and social traditions rather than produce new knowledge or cultural forms.

References

APPLE, M. and JUNGCK, M.W. (1991) 'Is participation enough? Gender, teaching and technology in the classroom', *Curriculum Perspectives*, **11**(2), pp. 1–13.
AUSTRALIAN EDUCATION COUNCIL TASK FORCE ON EDUCATION AND TECHNOLOGY (1985) *Education and Technology*, Melbourne, Australian Education Council.
BERNSTEIN, B. (1975) *The Structuring of Pedagogic Discourse: Class, Codes and Control*, **3**, London, Routledge & Kegan Paul.
BERNSTEIN, B. (1986) 'On pedagogic discourse', in RICHARDSON, G. (Ed) *Handbook of Theory and Research for the Sociology of Education*, New York, Greenwood Press.
BERNSTEIN, B. (1990) *The Structuring of Pedagogic Discourse: Class, Codes and Control*, **4**, London, Routledge.

BERNSTEIN, B. (1996) *Pedagogy Symbolic Control and Identity: Theory, Research, Critique,* London, Taylor & Francis.

BRYSON, M. and DE CASTELL, S. (1994) 'Telling tales of school: Modernist, critical, and postmodern "true stories" about educational computing', *Journal of Educational Computing Research,* **10**(3), pp. 199–221.

COMMONWEALTH SCHOOLS COMMISSION (1984) *Girls and Tomorrow. The Challenge for Schools, Report of the Working Party on the Education of Girls,* Canberra, AGPS.

CLARRICOATES, K. (1987) 'Dinosaurs in the classroom. The "hidden" curriculum in primary schools', in ARNOT, M. and WEINER, G. (Eds) *Gender and the Politics of Schooling,* London, Unwin Hyman.

CONNELL, R.W. (1987) *Gender and Power,* Sydney, Allen & Unwin.

CONNELL, R.W. (1990a) 'An iron man. The body and some contradictions of hegemonic masculinity', in MESSNER, M. and SCHO, D. (Eds) *Sport, Men and the Gender Order,* Campaign, IL, Human Kenetics Books.

CONNELL, R.W. (1990b) '"A whole new world": Remaking masculinity in the context of the environmental movement', *Gender and Society,* **4**(4), pp. 452–78.

DAVIES, B. (1989a) *Frogs and Snails and Feminist Tales,* Sydney, Allen & Unwin.

DAVIES, B. (1989b) 'The discursive production of the male/female dualism in school settings', *Oxford Review of Education,* **15**(3), pp. 229–41.

DEPARTMENT OF EDUCATION, QUEENSLAND, CURRICULUM SERVICES BRANCH (1984) *Towards a Rationale for the Instructional use of Computers in the Classroom,* Brisbane, Queensland, Department of Education.

DEPARTMENT OF EDUCATION, QUEENSLAND (1985) 'Education 2000', A discussion paper, Brisbane, Queensland, Department of Education.

DEPARTMENT OF EDUCATION, QUEENSLAND (1987) *P–10 Curriculum Framework,* Brisbane, Queensland, Department of Education.

DEPARTMENT OF EDUCATION, QUEENSLAND, GENDER EQUITY UNIT (1991) *Gender Equity Information,* Brisbane, Queensland, Department of Education.

DEPARTMENT OF EDUCATION, QUEENSLAND, GENDER EQUITY UNIT, STUDIES DIRECTORATE (1992) *Gender Equity in Education Policy Statement,* Brisbane, Queensland, Department of Education.

DEPARTMENT OF EDUCATION, QUEENSLAND, MINISTERIAL ADVISORY COMMITTEE ON GENDER EQUITY (1992) *Social Justice (Gender) Suggested Strategies and Indicators for the Achievement of Gender Equity in Queensland Schools,* Brisbane, Queensland, Department of Education.

DEPARTMENT OF EMPLOYMENT, EDUCATION AND TRAINING (1988) *The National Policy for the Education of Girls in Australian Schools,* Canberra, AGPS.

DEPARTMENT OF EMPLOYMENT, EDUCATION AND TRAINING (1989) *Girls in Schools 2. Report on the 'National Policy for the Education of Girls in Australian Schools',* Canberra, AGPS.

DEPARTMENT OF EMPLOYMENT, EDUCATION AND TRAINING (1990) *Teaching girls (2),* Canberra AGPS.

FOX KELLER, E. (1986) 'How gender matters, or, why it's so hard for us to count past two', in HARDING, J. (Ed) *Perspectives on Gender and Science,* Lewes, The Falmer Press.

KENWAY, J. (1995) 'Reality bytes: Education, markets and the information superhighway', *Australian Educational Researcher,* **22**(1), pp. 35–65.

LUKE, C. (1996) 'ekstasis@cyberia', Unpublished paper, Graduate School of Education, The University of Queensland, Brisbane, Australia.

NATIONAL ADVISORY COMMITTEE ON COMPUTERS IN SCHOOLS (1983) 'Teaching–learning and the application of computers in primary schools', A discussion paper prepared for the Commonwealth Schools Commission, Canberra.

QUALITY OF EDUCATION REVIEW COMMITTEE (1985) *Quality of Education in Australia*, Commonwealth of Australia, Canberra, AGPS.

SPENDER, D. (1995) Nattering on the net, Sydney, Spinifex Press.

WALKERDINE, V. (1989) *Counting Girls Out*, London, Virago.

WALKERDINE, V. (1990) *Schoolgirl Fictions*, London, Verso.

WHYTE, J. (1985) 'Girl friendly science and the girl friendly school', in WHYTE, J., DEEM, R., KANT, L. and CRUIKSHANK, M. (Eds) *Girl friendly schooling*, London, Methuen & Co. Ltd.

Chapter 7

Decentering Silences/Troubling Irony: Teen Pregnancy's Challenge to Policy Analysis

Wanda S. Pillow

Pregnancy, Schooling and Policy Analysis

As someone who is involved in working with young women and invested in creating effective and equitable educational policies, I often find myself mired in the dilemmas and tensions of how to interpret data, take account of public sentiment and develop effective policy. Nowhere have I found this more difficult than in my research on teen pregnancy. Teen pregnancy has captured national attention as a personal and political issue and created a call for reform that Constance Nathanson characterizes as a 'minor industry in the US' (1991: 145). Billed as an indication of 'a failure of American society' (NCHS, 1992), teen pregnancy is increasingly described as a problem of epidemic proportions and is portrayed as a defining example of what is morally and socially wrong in American society today.

Teenage pregnancy is increasingly targeted as a policy problem and specifically an educational policy problem. Teen girls[1] who become pregnant are of course usually school-age, and nearly half of all teens who have children before the age of 18 do not finish high school (Foster, 1986). Schools have thus been expected to design programs and policies to deal with the teen pregnancy problem. This task however has not proven easy. While a wealth of research exists on identifying characteristics of teenagers at risk for pregnancy[2] there is little agreement on what to do with this information.

Programs set up to provide help and guidance to teen mothers soon run up against entrenched ideological and moral issues. Specifically, the accepted pervasiveness of teenage pregnancy as a public problem has contributed to pre-existing moral concerns surrounding issues of contraception, abortion, single parenting and female sexuality (Lesko, 1995; MacIntyre and Cunningham-Burlay, 1993; Nathanson, 1991). Tied to these concerns are questions and conflicting beliefs about schools and the purpose of schooling. Should schools be involved in discussions of and education in such areas as sexuality and birth control? If so how? To what extent? By whom? These questions and concerns have resulted in debates at national and community levels on the provision and content of sex education ('Just Say No' versus informational programs), on whether pregnant teens should be able to attend regular schools or be placed in a separate program, and on whether daycare should be provided for the pregnant teen. (Will daycare increase school attendance or will it encourage teen pregnancy?) This configuration of issues has resulted in a response to teen pregnancy in the USA that Nancy Lesko describes as 'erratic, marked by tenuous funding and little political support' (1995: 179).

Compounding this situation are findings that many existing programs demonstrate little or no effect on the rates or consequences of teen pregnancy. Additionally, little research has focused upon teen parents themselves, allowing news magazines and popular myths to construct the popular image of teen parents.[3] In these ways, teen pregnancy is a complicated and political policy issue which offers a challenge to our current methods of research and analysis. On the one hand, we have a proliferation of data, information, research and moral outrage surrounding the issue of teen pregnancy; yet ironically, on the other, we have a lack of programs, contextual information, support and effective interventions.

This chapter focuses on the ironic tensions surrounding teen pregnancy by considering how traditional forms of policy development and analysis participate in a process of proliferation and silencing. What assumptions does traditional policy analysis make? What/who is silenced in the naming of teen pregnancy as a policy problem and how does this silencing affect intervention programs? What methodologies can aid in tracing, naming and decentering these silences?[4]

In order to pursue these questions, I present the story of a teen girl who is pregnant as a basis for analyzing the problematics of policy analysis.[5] Upon first analysis, Kathy's[6] story may seem to affirm what we think we know about teen pregnancy. However, through a closer examination, Kathy's story leads to the consideration of silenced outliers and of policy assumptions embedded in programs for teen mothers. I conclude with a discussion of how critical, feminist and poststructural methodologies are useful in the task of decentering the silences perpetuated by traditional policy theory.

Kathy

Kathy struck me particularly because she *was* the teen mother in *Time* magazine. She was quite thin and pale and spoke in a soft voice; she seemed unassuming, at times shy, holding her head down and hiding behind her hair. She completely fit the demographic profile of a teen mother – troubled home environment, mother and siblings who were teen parents, low self-esteem, poor student, seemingly unambitious, unsteady relationship with her boyfriend, previous involvement with drugs, and sexually active as a victim at an early age (Flick, 1984).

Here is an excerpt of a journal entry I made after meeting Kathy the first time:

Kathy sat, moved and spoke in a very unassuming manner. Her hair is strawberry blond; thin and wispy, framing her face and falling to her shoulders. Her skin is so pale it at times looked luminous (she has been having trouble with morning sickness). She wore little or no make up – umm, black eyeliner I think. She had dark circles under her eyes and her skin is taut – she is very thin – almost gaunt. She has several nervous gestures and looks in need of a cigarette (she says she is trying to stop smoking but that it is driving her crazy). She made short bursts of eye contact, sometimes nodding so that the small frame of her whole upper body swayed. She wore tight faded jeans, gripped below her waist on impossibly narrow hips that belied her pregnancy. A little scoop necked tee covered with a short black motorcycle-type leather jacket; her shoes were old and worn tennis shoes, worn without socks . . . she spoke several times today of wanting confirmation and acceptance from her boyfriend, mother, teachers. Kathy said she was confused and alone – she was eager to talk (February 20, 1992).

Kathy and I met at least twice every week for a little over two months. We talked. She shared stories with me about her life, her dreams, her fears. I shared my life, my dreams, my fears and information when I could provide it. We talked as women, who despite a 15-year age difference, found similarities across our lives related to class, relationships and pregnancies. Kathy was new to the city we were both in at that time. Her mother and her mother's boyfriend and also Kathy's boyfriend had moved to that city for employment reasons. Kathy said she was unhappy in her new home and missed where she used to live.

> *K:* It's really bad here. The drugs here are really bad – right out on the streets they're selling crack all around us.
>
> *WP:* It wasn't like that where you used to live?
> *K:* No – not where we lived. I mean my boyfriend and his family have always been involved in drug dealing but it's worse here and my family doesn't do that.

Kathy and I often discussed her relationship with her boyfriend (she had just turned 15, he was 21). She was disturbed that she and he were still living with his mother and that he did not have a job. She thought he should go get a job and be more responsible especially since they had a baby on the way. She seemed very confused and close to tears at several points.

> *K:* I just don't know what I'm going to do – it's just not right the way he's acting and I told him so. He's not taking any responsibility and then we fight and he and his mom call the police on me and tell them to take me out of the house – it's just not right them treating me like that while I am pregnant.
>
> *K:* I just don't know what to do. I can't stay with him if this is the way he's going to be. I told him that too. I don't know it's really hard.

Kathy told me that she and her mother had had trouble getting along in the past but that since Kathy had been pregnant her mother had been 'real nice and more understanding'. Kathy shared with me that her other brothers and sisters all had children at young ages. Her brother, at age 20, had four children each 12 months apart. This led into the following discussion on having children and birth control:

> *K*: I just don't know how some people can wait so long to have kids. I mean why do it when you are in your 30s and so old. Well, I guess what I mean is how do people go that long without getting pregnant. I mean how do you stop accidents?

Kathy had minimal information about birth control methods and maintained a 'they don't work anyways' attitude toward most of them. She discussed how she and her boyfriend had not used birth control because:

> *K*: You see my boyfriend was worried that he would not be able to have a baby because he had been with a girl for 9 months but she never got pregnant, so he wanted to see if he could have a baby.
> *WP*: Did you want to have a baby too?
> *K*: Well, I did until I got pregnant and now I'm not sure – I'm really scared.
> *WP*: Why did you want to have a baby?
> I guess just to have something to love; something that would be my own. I really wanted that, but now it seems really scary.

As I got to know Kathy better I began to understand how important this typical cliche 'I want something to love' was to her. Kathy did not just say this; she lived it. In her mind, pregnancy was a time that should embody the best about being a woman, a time when she should be treated well and feel fulfilled. In Kathy's family, pregnancy was part of an initiation to adult status and respect; her mother was a teenage parent to five children who in turn have been or are now teen parents.

Kathy was involved with a counselor at a youth services program. One day she told me that she had to take a drug test later that day. This disturbed her, because she had told the counselor she had not done drugs since she had become pregnant, but the counselor did not believe her.

> *K*: I told her I was not doing drugs since I've been pregnant and it's hard cause it's dealing all around me, but I'm not going to do it. But she doesn't believe me and I've already done one test and now I have to do another.

Kathy would seek me out if she heard I was at her school. I worked at a parent center/playroom also housed in the school and often was at the school with my own children. One day, Kathy came into the playroom after she had been released from testing. We talked about her health – she looked a little pale and was still having trouble with morning sickness. Kathy stayed in the playroom and watched for a while – there were a couple of other mothers there with their kids playing. I introduced her to the other mothers and the children. We talked about her due date and she said she wasn't sure if she would be able to come back to school after she had the baby because of childcare. She told me that the school wants them back three weeks after birth and at 7:45 a.m.[7]

In our continuing conversations, it became apparent that Kathy was struggling; struggling to balance her need to assert herself and her voice against her need and desire to be taken care of, to be loved. She was resorting to threats with her boyfriend and her voice revealed the tremulousness of those threats. Although she was getting along better with her mother, she said, 'Your mother isn't who you want to be with when you are pregnant.'

Kathy never did 'fit in' with the school. She was always alone whenever I saw her – she never formed a support group of peers. She never overly affirmed herself with any of the teachers. I watched her flat stomach swell into a slight mound. I felt such an inadequacy to (re)present her life, even in my journal notes. One day Kathy just did not show up at school. Kathy's homeroom teacher could not contact anyone at Kathy's listed address or telephone number; who knew where she might have gone. I attempted calling and asking around about her myself. I 'knew' Kathy for only about two months – but she marked a space in my life which I hope I never forget. I read over some of my old journal notes and remember:

> Kathy and I are in the playroom together with my two children and 3 other moms and their kids. We sit on the floor – Kimmy runs to give me 'huggies' and Kathy gives Kimmy a toy. 'She is so cute,' Kathy says. She is wistfully watching the kids play – 'I hope it will work out for me.'

Kathy and I were reading Sandra Cisnero's *House on Mango Street* before she left. The following section was one Kathy particularly identified with – we read it together four times. I often heard her speak similar words herself. One time I read this section out loud to Kathy as she closed her eyes and relaxed her body:

> Sally, do you sometimes wish you didn't have to go home? Do you wish your feet would one day keep walking and take you far away from Mango Street, far away and maybe your feet would stop in front of a house, a nice one with flowers and big windows and steps for you to climb up two by two upstairs to where a room is waiting for you. And if you opened the little window latch and gave it a shove, the windows would swing open, all the sky would come in. There'd be no nosy neighbors watching, no motorcycles and cars, no sheets and towels and laundry. Only trees and more trees and plenty of blue sky. And you could laugh, Sally. You could go to sleep and wake up and never have to think who likes and doesn't like you. You could close your eyes and you wouldn't have to worry what people could make you sad and nobody would think you're strange because you like to dream and dream. And no one could yell at you if they saw you out in the dark leaning against a car, leaning against somebody without someone thinking you are bad, without somebody saying it is

wrong, without the whole world waiting for you to make a mistake when all you wanted, all you wanted, Sally, was to love and to love and to love and to love, and no one could call that crazy (Cisneros, 1989: 82–3).

I continued to attempt to 'find' Kathy for several months but to no avail. To this date I do not know where Kathy went, if she had her baby and if they are both healthy and safe. Kathy was never recorded as a drop-out of the school program she was in because she did not officially sign herself out of the program. Her name was kept on the attendance roll for one month, after which her name was removed and her folder filed under 'inactive'.

Policy and Silences

Normative Silences

I repeatedly struggle with the writing and (re)presenting of Kathy's story because I was able to meet and talk with Kathy for only 10 weeks, compared to a minimum of six to 20 *months* I spent with other young women. I wondered, should I not talk about Kathy because I do not have enough data? All researchers and program evaluators at some point have to confront the issue of data 'outliers' – those statistics or stories that just do not quite fit. Quantitative researchers can often rely on statistical manipulation to 'out' the 'outlier'. However, what do we do with participants who for whatever reason did not complete the research, who become lost? Qualitative and field-based inquiry experience lost data on a personal level. What do we do when the data we compose are lives – individuals we have talked to, talked with, sought out, observed, laughed, cried and shared a meal with? What do we do with a story that disappears before its conclusion or before we understood the plot? Is this story now irrelevant? Does its incompleteness mean that it should not be told?

When I began moving through data from my research with young women who were pregnant and/or parenting, I found I had several lost data stories. These stories were necessarily incomplete and could have been easily dismissed as such. However, upon discovering a pattern among these lost stories, I felt troubled at the ironic effects of normative assumptions on these teen girls' lives. For example, like Kathy, many of the young women on whom I had incomplete information, women who became lost when they left the school program, were the young women who best fit the profile of a teen mother (Pillow, 1994). Why would the girls whose voices, mannerisms and even physical being most embodied the public and research personae of teen pregnancy become 'lost' – why would they drop out of the teen pregnancy program designed with exactly them in mind?

What kind of ironic silencing is occurring in these *not* tellings?[8] Would I participate in this silencing by not telling their stories because the stories were incomplete? Who is being silenced? Michelle Fine (1991) identifies the power of silences as follows: 'Silencing shapes language, representations, and even the forms of resistance permitted and not' (Fine, 1991: 9). Fine challenges us to uncover these silences and thereby name 'policies and practices of exclusion' (p. 8). What different tales would our pieces of missing data tell us? As Lather asks, 'What are their silences telling us?' (1987: 12).

In Kathy's case, we should investigate the power of a normative silence – of a silence which perpetuates itself because it so affirms what we think we know that we feel no need to hear (or assume we already have heard) the voice it obscures. For a long time I wrote *around* Kathy's story. There already seemed to be a wealth of stories about teen girls like Kathy represented in media, public and research arenas. Indeed, through those discourses[9] girls like Kathy had become the norm of a teen girl who is pregnant.[10] But how should we react when a norm is nevertheless lost – perpetuated, yet silenced? I could shatter the silence of Kathy's story by analyzing it through a feminist lens, but for what purpose? For whose representation?

It is easy to demonstrate how patriarchy perpetuates her abuse and role as victim. Kathy's story can readily be analyzed through a feminist lens, demonstrating how patriarchy perpetuates her abuse and role as victim. Such critiques are necessary and needed to name the silences present in discourse surrounding teen pregnancy. However, 'victim narratives' are easily converted into policies and programs which only seem to perpetuate the silences and become immersed in moralistic sermonizing.

In an effort to implode the normative practices of silencing evident in my experiences with Kathy, I began to explore what would it mean to re-situate Kathy's story, to emphasize the irony[11] of her status as outlier, outsider, and ultimately exile from a program designed expressly for women supposedly just like her. The teen pregnancy program in which Kathy participated thematized her 'difference' and set it into programmatic regulation and resolution. The program should have provided exactly the space, support and help she needed, yet she remained outside. How did this happen? And importantly for the interest of this chapter, what kind of critique does the irony of Kathy's story offer to how we make, implement and analyze policy?

First, as discussed above, the telling of Kathy's story and how Kathy reinforces what we think we already know raises the question: What are we silencing through normative assumptions and practices? Second, a feminist analysis which considers the impact of gender, class and patriarchy on Kathy's life would yield further insight into how teen programs are not meeting the needs of the young women in them. Third, a postmodern genealogy can aid in this process by further tracing the silences surrounding the discourse of teen pregnancy, explicating Kathy's story as an ironically normative outlier. The remainder of this chapter will explicate these last two points, concluding with a discussion of how the combination of these forms of analysis – feminist and postmodern – requires a shift in our thinking about how we do policy theory and analysis.

Feminist Analysis and Decentering Feminist Narratives

Feminists who engage in policy analysis encounter a challenging dilemma: As Kathy Ferguson asks, 'How can we simultaneously put women at the center and decenter everything, including women?' (1993: 3). Some may of course question this need to decenter women. Why decenter ourselves just when we are claiming a place and space in theory and in knowledge-making; isn't this another instance of women losing their voice?[12]

Most feminist efforts have centered on women – dislocating men as the center, challenging claims of self-evidence and knowledge – claiming an 'us too' space. Women have asserted the existence of 'women's ways of knowing' (Belenky *et al.*, 1986) and women's leadership styles (Shakeshaft, 1986). However, as much as these findings and assertions have filled in gaps and absences in women's *herstory*, they have also fallen into a mire of essentialist[13] claims which have served to exclude some women (i.e., along class, racial and ethnic lines). Additionally, these empowering essentialist identities have also served to draw boundaries which continue to limit women's participation; for example, if women are *naturally* more caring then men, then women are better suited for parenting, child care, teacher and other service-oriented, low-paying positions.

Thus, while women-centered analysis may be beneficial in that it dislocates or inverts hierarchical identities, it also depends upon some foundational, common space of women's experiences and thus does little to interrupt dominant power structures (Ferguson, 1993). Often such feminist tellings end up becoming what I term 'tragic invokings' or 'victim narratives' (those stories which seek to show how truly oppressed and tragic women are) and/or 'victory narratives' (those stories which celebrate an unproblematized heroine who finds previously unknown strength against the patriarchy). Such tellings remain as polemical as the hegemonic[14] structures many feminists seek to subvert and thus fall prey to the same modernist dilemmas as any other polemic.[15] If we acknowledge that the tools, discourses, and practices of theory, methodology, and analysis 'already belong to the organization of knowledge in the service of the master' (in this case modernity, hegemony, or patriarchy) we must accept the challenge not to engage in inquiry which simply develops an inverted hierarchy of knowing (Godzich, 1994: 21). Many postmodern and feminist writers point to the dilemmas of doing such resistant dismantling (Trinh, 1989, 1991). Trinh Minh-Ha reminds us that '"breaking rules" still refers to rules' (1991: 59).

Julia Kristeva in 1977 exhorted feminists to 'stop making feminism into a new religion, undertaking or sect and begin the work of specific and detailed analysis which will take us beyond romantic melodrama and beyond complacency' (see 1986: 298). McNay suggests that feminist research needs to look beyond artificial polarities and 'explore ways in which theory can be made compatible with the local' (1992: 8). What would it mean to decenter 'woman' in a feminist analysis of teen pregnancy? What additional questions might be asked, stories uncovered, strategies provoked by such a form of subversive analysis?

Teen pregnancy is critically in need of a feminist voice, critique and analysis that can move beyond polemic in its findings and stories. The focus of teen pregnancy discourse and research is already predominantly upon the female. So here, the problem is not how to put the teen woman into the picture but rather how to decenter the role of gender in teen pregnancy, so that the silences related to issues of gender, female parenting and female sexuality can be analyzed and discussed. Butler terms this process the task of 'a *feminist genealogy* of the category of women' (1990: 5).

Feminist Genealogical Inquiry as Policy Analysis

The notion of a *feminist genealogy* stems from Foucault's reformulation of Nietzsche (1977/1984). The form of critical inquiry Foucault calls *genealogy* provides a forum for decentering what we think we know and for tracing how we came to know it. Judith Butler states that:

> A genealogical critique refuses to search for the origins of gender, the inner truth of female desire, a genuine or authentic sexual identity that repression has kept from view; rather, genealogy investigates the political stakes in designating as an *origin* and *cause* those identity categories that are in fact the *effects* of institutions, practices, discourses with multiple and diffuse points of origin (1990: ix).

Genealogy pays implicit attention to details, thus unmasking and questioning what traditionally may seem innate or natural; it exposes the 'power of the norm'.

Genealogy as a form of analysis interrupts simple reversal strategies of displacement. As Ferguson states 'Genealogical reversals do not restabilize cause/effect relations in the opposite direction so much as they unsettle any effort to conceptualize singular or linear relations between events and practices' (1993: 4). Shapiro characterizes genealogy as disclosing 'the operation of power in places in which familiar, social, administrative and political discourses tend to disguise or naturalize it' (1992: 1). Gutting describes genealogy as the analysis of 'the development of bodies of knowledge out of systems of power' (1989: 6). Foucault calls this attempt to identify, locate and analyze discourses and practices of knowledge and power 'the genealogy of the modern subject' (1977/1984: 7).

Foucault thus brings notions of subjects, agency and bodies into genealogy as inquiry, stating that his goal 'has not been to analyze the phenomena of power' but, instead, to 'create a history' of how 'human beings are made subjects' (Foucault, 1977/1984: 7). Genealogy provides a means to situate and understand the discourses of power and practice that influence the naming, defining and living of teenage pregnancy. This process interrupts traditional notions of subjectivity, takes into account the 'politics of the gaze' (who studies whom) and focuses attention on not only the politics of *what* gets said about girls who are pregnant but *how* what is said about girls who are pregnant defines what we say.

A feminist genealogy of teen pregnancy as a policy issue would, for example, not only name and question the impact of the polemical dualism of male and female, but also attempt to trace how we define what we think we know about teen pregnancy through that dualism. This emphasis on and consideration of what Foucault terms 'power-knowledge' creates the possibility for questioning what we would not normally question and additionally calls into question how we perform our analysis. A feminist analysis in this sense would seek to interrupt and disrupt the circularity of assumptions about the authentic experiences of teenage pregnancy by examining assumptions about gender roles and sexuality.

In a society that assumes heterosexuality, assumes childbearing as part of a woman's life and assumes male power, dominance and sideline participation in responsibility for these actions, teen pregnancy programs are developed with little or no attention given to both the normative and proliferative affects of gender on teen pregnancy. Many current policies and practices surrounding sex education and teen pregnancy programs fail to critically examine or acknowledge the current and historical power relations prevalent in the construction of male and female identities and sexuality (McRobbie, 1991; Weiler, 1988). How is it that the sexualized, fetishized issue of teen pregnancy has remained a women's issue with immense backlash against women, single parents, etc., without the effects and power of gender expectations and roles coming into question?

By ignoring and thus silencing issues of gender and female sexuality related to teen pregnancy, policy programs for teen girls who are pregnant have remained entrenched in normative assumptions and moralistic ideology. For example, stories about low self-esteem among pregnant teen girls appear frequently in teen pregnancy research, but are never connected to the paradoxical and embedded gender and cultural roles facing young women in our society. Thus, teen pregnancy programs continue to emphasize changing the girls themselves – helping them learn to take 'morally defensible positions'[16], to redeem themselves for their mistakes, and to be 'good mothers' (Lesko, 1990, 1995; Pillow, 1994).

Even in programs for teen girls who are pregnant and thus have obviously been sexually active, information about sexuality focuses upon sex education only – the biology, the mechanics, the dangers – ignoring topics related specifically to female sexuality, like the double bind in which women often find themselves (good girl/bad girl), expectations and delimitations, gender roles, or pleasure (Pillow, 1994). Michelle Fine (1988), upon a review of sex education curriculum in the US, has documented what she calls a 'missing discourse of desire' for teen girls. This silencing of gender roles and sexuality and how these issues impact teen pregnancy is a silencing of women's concerns. Understanding how these silences are perpetuated while at the same time women's sexuality is being constantly marketed and proliferated is crucial to intervention programs that serve teen women.

In this analysis, the irony of Kathy's story calls into question the process through which we define a policy problem and traces the power relations between macro- (the policy/program) and micro-subject (in this case, Kathy), demonstrating how they regulate and produce each other. The simultaneous silencing and proliferation of discourse surrounding teen pregnancy creates and reinforces both the subject and the policy developed for the subject.

As discussed earlier, Kathy embodied the prototypical client of teen pregnancy policy and programs (poor, 'white trash', drug abuser, in an abusive relationship with a man six years her senior, family history of teen pregnancy compounded by low self-esteem). Beyond that, Kathy even said the 'right things' once in the program

– she spoke in the liberal humanist voice the program espoused and desired set gender roles. For example, she wanted to dress her child neatly and live in that two-story white house; she admitted she made mistakes and wanted to be 'better'; she realized that she needed help and asked for it; in short, she presented a lived authenticity that mirrored the program's expectations. Yet, in this lived authenticity she remained an exile.

Kathy's differences – ironically both silenced and proliferated – were engulfed by and fed into the program in simplistic, rationalistic ways without any real analysis of the impact of gender roles on teen sexuality, pregnancy and self esteem. However, the more troubling irony is that Kathy did take on the regulative discourses and practices of the program and of larger social constructions of teen pregnancy. She changed herself – in fact, she struggled to do so.

However, in changing herself, Kathy was silenced, exiled. She was at once a guarantee of the program's need to exist, a polemic around which to build such programs, and a threat to its success. A feminist genealogy of teen pregnancy points to the proliferation of normative assumptions in the presence of normative silences. Such an analysis also points out the dependency of these proliferations and silences on each other – they perpetuate each other as a form of 'power-knowledge' (Foucault, 1977/1984).

The telling and analyzing of Kathy's story as 'troubling irony' decenters the normative silencing of the (re)presentation of her life and creates a place from which to trace the power and impact gender has on teen pregnancy. This analysis points out many absences in teen pregnancy research and policy interventions, absences which cause us to ask, how is it that programs set up to help girls exactly like Kathy fail to do so? Why is it that images of girls like Kathy were evoked in program material, yet overwhelmingly these are not the girls the program actually served? These questions raise broader insights and issues in the arena of policy theory and offer both a critique and a call for a reframing of policy analysis.

Reframing Policy Analysis

While policies are usually produced with well-meaning intent, institutional policies often have many shortcomings and may even serve to debilitate the exact condition they wish to advocate (Elmore, 1983; McLaughlin, 1990). How is it that policies can, at times, fail to serve exactly those who they are set up to help, as I have shown in this chapter? Contributions from researchers employing critical, feminist and/or postmodern theories have highlighted the inadequacies of our current social policy practices and have focused attention on the negative impact of racism, classism and sexism on many of our current policies.

In particular, as a part of the larger critique of modernity, recent attention has been paid to the consequences of the attachment of policy theory to scientific models for developing and implementing policy. Increasingly, researchers have scrutinized the dependency of policy upon rational, scientific models for the explanation for policy problems and the creation of interventions (Ball, 1990; Carlson, 1993; Griffith, 1992; Scheurich, 1995). Some researchers have blamed faulty assumptions within such scientific models for the establishment of normative and regulative social policies that yield minimal results (Carlson, 1993; Hewitt, 1991; Kelly and Maynard-Mooney, 1993).

Hewitt (1991) emphasizes the significance of this process by demonstrating how modernist discourse creates forms of knowledge that achieve a normative and legitimate status and which are then used to structure problems and interventions in limiting ways (Hewitt, 1991). A legitimized knowledge allows us to polemically structure some issues as policy problems (this is acceptable, this is not), define the problem (what and who the problem is), and prescribe an intervention (fix what is wrong), all within an aura of facts and truth. This process can and does occur without consideration of the normative practices and assumptions embedded in the policy process and without knowing or acknowledging for whom the policies are supposedly developed.

Donna Deyhle and Frank Margonis (1995), in research on Native American education, emphatically point out the differences between the aims of educational policy and the young Navajo women it serves: 'Educational discussions produce analyses that stand in sharp contrast to the familial orientation of Navajo women' (1995: 136). Deyhle's and Margonis' work dramatically points out the dilemmas of traditional theories of analysis which tend to look, consider and, most importantly, judge educational results and practices only through the lens of ideal middle-class student and worker. Michelle Fine, in her study on high school drop-outs found herself changing the origin of the policy problem from why a student would drop out to 'why so many would stay in a school committed to majority failure' (1991: 7). Deyhle and Margonis critique traditional theories of analysis and, echoing Fine, conclude that, 'Many Navajo women's less-than-enthusiastic response to schools is better viewed as a stable, ethically based disagreement than as a reaction to the dominant group' (1991: 158).

Such analyses point to the dilemmas of continuing to think about educational policy through a normative, modernist lens. Their findings point to a need for a *re*thinking and an *un*thinking of our current practices. How do researchers engage in such a difficult endeavor? How does one position power, subjectivity and legitimacy both as modernist discourses and as sites of disruptive analysis? Specifically, knowing that difference is used as a point of departure calling for a need for intervention and reform (Fine, 1991; Singer, 1993), how can we tell stories of difference that resist polemical tellings and thus polemical responses?

I have presented feminist genealogy as one means through which normative assumptions/polemical tellings can be traced, questioned and decentered. Feminist genealogy questions the process of naming and defining teen pregnancy and shows how attempts to find monocausal links are overly simplistic. Sally MacIntyre and Sarah Cunningham-Burley cite one of their favorite conclusions of teen pregnancy research: '*Probably* one of the most immediate causes of adolescent births is intercourse itself' (1993: 63). Such research ignores the complexity of teen pregnancy within a larger societal framework (including issues of gender, race and class), allowing contributing factors to be distorted or denied (Sidel, 1990). Thus we have a popular and scientifically constructed view of teen mothers as sexually immoral and irresponsible, bad mothers, and emotionally unstable, wrought with a feeling of hopelessness in their lives (Lesko, 1990). Social and educational policies set up to help teen girls who are pregnant take up and reflect these beliefs.

Traditional policy theory's modernist reliance upon use of statistical and research data participates in the naming of teen pregnancy as an 'epidemic', out of control, in need of regulation. While the figures for teen pregnancy rates in the USA and the predictions for poor outcomes for both the teen mother and her child are indeed alarming, these figures can be misleading when taken out of context. For example, when comparing teen birth rates in the USA with those of other western nations, little consideration is given to the impact of the presence of integrated systems of social, health and child care in nations which have lower teen pregnancy rates. Nor are differing attitudes toward gender, sexuality and sexual practices, the availability of sex information, or the availability and acceptability of contraceptives taken into account.

Additionally, the surge of public concern about the teen pregnancy problem ironically occurred at a time when teen pregnancy rates were declining (NCHS, 1992). Nathanson (1991), upon closer analysis of birth rates for women of all ages, found that teen pregnancy rates follow the pregnancy rates for women of other ages. The above critique is not meant to discount the dilemmas young mothers face in our society but to suggest that what we think we know about teen pregnancy is incomplete. The entrenchment of discourse surrounding the issues of teen pregnancy in moral arguments and modernist theory has limited the scope and shape of both research and possible policy options (Lesko, 1995).

By refocusing/reframing the origin of a policy problem through a feminist genealogy we can begin to make visible and question assumptions which go into the making of the policy problem. For example, if we take into account that public and political attention on teen pregnancy surged during a time of *lower* birth rates for teen girls and that, indeed, teen pregnancy rates follow birth rates in the USA for women of all ages, how does this shift our perception of the problem of teen pregnancy? How do issues of race and class impact what we think about who should be pregnant or who should *not* be? Is teen pregnancy the problem or *unwed* teen pregnancy the issue?

If the unwed pregnancy of a wealthy, white, mature fictional character like Murphy Brown[17] can ignite a debate about family values, what happens when the unwed mother is also poor, young and minority? Through this analysis it becomes apparent that teen pregnancy confronts our fears and beliefs about who should be having sex and having babies. Rhode explain the 'sense of crisis' surrounding teen pregnancy in the USA as 'less the rate of births to teenage women than the socio-economic context in which those births occur and the cultural ideology they challenge' (1993: 3).

A reliance upon binaries (good/bad, responsible/irresponsible) used to define the realms of female gender roles and female sexuality aids in the characterization of teen pregnancy as 'deviant'. The naming of teenage pregnancy as deviant, as a problem of 'epidemic' proportions, 'provides access to bodies and a series of codes for inscribing them, as well as providing a discourse of justification' (Singer, 1993: 117). Thus, who should be pregnant or not, who should be a parent or not, who should be sexual in what way or not, become social/political issues which when they are 'out of control', like teen pregnancy, require regulation. The discourses we use to define the problem of teen pregnancy both identify and justify teen pregnancy as a social problem and do so through what these discourses simultaneously proliferate and silence.

Hence, teen pregnancy research and policy interventions can be understood as entrenched in the dilemmas of modernism, resulting often in normative assumptions that reflect our paradoxical attitudes and practices concerning female sexuality. This chapter specifically addresses challenges to this process and asks how policy analysis results might figure differently when issues of power, subjectivity and the 'politics of the gaze' are utilized as points of analysis. In this chapter, I have suggested that a combination of feminist and postmodern theories – a feminist genealogy – can challenge the policy researcher to shift the focus of attention, to question what is assumed to be normative or given.

Such an analysis creates the possibility for both revealing and decentering silences and engaging in a multi-layered and subversive analysis. In conclusion, I would like to revisit the use of 'irony' as a means of analysis and the 'troubling irony' of Kathy's story. A genealogical, theoretical form of analysis was important to this type of telling. Through this form of analysis, Kathy's story takes on a power that is troubling and ironic, a power which would have been silenced in another type of telling. Kathy's story could certainly have been told and heard only as a victim narrative that recapitulates her as the poor, tragic other. What would we silence in such a telling? Genealogy scrutinizes the political process of policy development and analyses that perpetuate polemical images of girls like Kathy only to be unable to 'reach' them. Genealogy also forces the telling of a story so seemingly simplistic that the depths of regulatory power relations can only be observed with a twist of irony.

Telling a story like Kathy's also acts to 'break and decenter silences' – to get at the complexity of the telling of stories of teen pregnancy. Kathy's story asks: Who is being served by this teen pregnancy program? Who is the policy set up to really benefit and what hegemonic power relations operate in this process? On a larger scale, this analysis also calls into question traditional means of policy analysis and names reliance upon modernism as part of the problem. Kathy's story does not fit, because she was both the norm and the exception; thus the telling of her story serves to fragment, to complicate, to divide.

When I think of Kathy I imagine other stories not told and what it would mean to trace the tellings of the silences, to imagine the unthinkable and the unarticulated and to pursue their possibilities. From the telling of a troubling irony, I find hope in the rendering of the unthinkable in all of its complicitous multiplicities. As Ferguson asserts: 'the effort to incite multiplicity against the somnolent hand of totalization and to mobilize the arts of irony to do so, need not weaken feminisms' strategies of political struggle; rather, it may multiply the levels of knowing and doing upon which resistance can act' (1993: 157).

Notes

1   It is important, interesting and telling to note that the data and findings about teen parents have been focused and based upon teen *mothers*. Because pregnancy and parenting are engendered as female issues, research and policy reform have focused on who the teen mother is, why she became pregnant and what kind of parent she will be. When fathers of teen pregnancies are targeted by research and policy programs it is predominantly without the blame and stigma prevalent in literature surrounding teen mothers (Lawson and Rhode, 1993; Nathanson, 1991; for information on programs for teen fathers see: Lawson and Rhode, 1993; Lindsay and Rodine, 1989; and Whatley, 1991).

2   Louise Flick (1984) is credited with developing five categories of 'at-risk' factors which are commonly used to identify teens at risk for teen pregnancy and to develop preventative intervention programs. The categories include: demographics, family, individual, peer group and couple characteristics.

3   One myth which has recently received national attention is the age of the father involved in teen pregnancy. Contrary to popular belief the age of the male tends to be 7–8 years older than the female, usually men in their 20s. However, response to this acknowledgment has remained caught in simplistic family values rhetoric, ignoring larger issues of gender expectations and sexuality, with the most recent call being to identify who 'these men' are and put them in jail unless they marry the teen mother (National Public Radio evening edition report, January 8 1995).

4   I have chosen the phrase 'decentering the silences' not to suggest that we replace some current *center* with a new one but, as I explain later in this chapter, to point to the irony of how teen pregnancy research and policy interventions silence gender issues while simultaneously proliferating gender – in terms of sex role stereotyping – in a normative way. I wish to attempt here, then, to engage in an analysis which *decenters* an unspoken, assumed center in a way which is additive, disruptive and subversive.

5   This data story is from research I conducted on teen pregnancy policy from 1991–1994.

6   *Kathy* is a pseudonym chosen by the young woman for use in publications or presentations.

7   These policies and the lack of childcare provision is reflective of the 'tough-love' disciplinary approach of this program's policies and curriculum (Pillow, 1994).

8   The statewide policy program for teen girls I studied had identified girls who left the program as 'inactive or absent'. These girls were not considered drop-outs unless they themselves notified the program that they were dropping out. In this way, the girls who left the program were rendered even more invisible in their impact because they were not counted nor compiled in local or state program reports.

9   'Discourse', as used in this article, may be understood as the content, practices and talk which constitute the social and the subject (in this, case teen pregnancy and the teen mother), creating 'discursive fields' of influence impacting what we think we know and how we know it – that is, the production of knowledge. An analysis of discourse considers how knowledge is produced, for whom, by whom. See Henriques *et al.* (1984) for a thorough reading of 'discourse', 'subjectivity' and 'power-knowledge'.

10 Kathy as described here represents a small minority of the young women I came to know over my three-year study with young pregnant women. A majority of the young women who I met countered popular constructions of young single mothers with their self-esteem, education attainment/achievement, goals and sense of their future (see Pillow, 1994). Thus, Kathy and other young women like her stood out as outliers not in their difference from what we expect of teen mothers but in their sameness.

11 In situating Kathy's story as irony I am attempting to move beyond a voice of cynicism and despair to an embracing of irony that in its 'doubleness [that] can take many forms' (Ferguson, 1993: 30).

12 Many would characterize this debate and controversy as being about the relationship between feminism and postmodernism. For explication of this controversy and further discussion of this relationship refer to Linda Nicholson (1990) and Chris Weedon (1987).

13 The relationship between essentialism and feminism is complicated and controversial. I use essentialism to refer to the identification of a common characteristic of what it is to be a woman – as in 'women are more caring' or 'women need love more than they desire sex'. Such characterizations of what is 'essential' about women, although they may feel true, exclude other possibilities and other groups and ignore the role larger power relations play in creating essential categories. For example, perhaps males equally need love in addition to sex; if so, what is it about our categories of 'male' and 'female' that reinforce the essential belief to the contrary? What do we gain by claiming essential differences between the categories of female and male? What power is working through these categories and how, to whose benefit and to what effect?

14 Hegemony refers to the predominant relations of domination (through language, knowledge and power), relations which make a particular representation of the world seem natural and universal. The power of hegemony is that it acts invisibly and involves not our coercion but complicitous consent – it remains unquestioned.

15 Modernism refers to an ideological belief in and reliance upon science – the idea that we can know and name what is real and find truth. Modernism allows us to name what is unnatural, perverse or 'other', as established through hegemony, with the confidence of scientific reasoning. Modernism functions through the use of polemics, dualisms, and opposites – one good, the other bad; one true, the other false.

16 This phrase comes directly from the mission/purpose statement of the teen pregnancy intervention policy I studied.

17 The attention the fictional character Murphy Brown attracted as a female who chose to be a single mother is a telling example of how strongly discourse about women's sexuality and gender roles is entrenched in a polemical morality capable of capturing a nation's attention. The fact that the Murphy Brown character is a working, upper-middle-class, heterosexual, Caucasian professional did nothing to alleviate claims of her character as a bad role model and a threat to American family values.

References

BALL, S.J. (1990) *Politics and Policymaking in Education: Explorations in policy sociology*, London, Routledge.

BELENKY, M.F., CLINCHY, B.M., GOLDBERGER, N.R. and TARULE, J.M. (1986) *Women's Ways of Knowing: The Development of Self, Voice and Mind*, New York, Basic Books.

BUTLER, J. (1990) *Gender Trouble: Feminism and the Subversion of Identity*, New York, Routledge.

CARLSON, D. (1993) 'The politics of educational policy: Urban school reform in unsettling times', *Educational Policy*, **7**(2), pp. 149–65.

CISNEROS, S. (1989) *The House on Mango Street*, New York, Vintage Books.

CONWAY, D.W. (1994) 'Genealogy and critical method', in SCHACHT, R. (Ed) *Nietzsche, Genealogy, Morality: Essays on Nietzsche's Genealogy of Morals*, Berkeley, CA, University of California Press, pp. 318–33.

CUSSICK, T. (1989) 'Sexism and early parenting: Cause and effect?', *Peabody Journal of Education*, pp. 113–31.

DAVIDSON, A.I. (1986) 'Archaeology, genealogy, ethics', in HOY, D.C. (Ed) *Foucault: A Critical Reader*, New York, Basil Blackwell, pp. 22–33.

DEYHLE, D. and MARGONIS, F. (1995) 'Navajo mothers and daughters: Schools, jobs and the family', *Anthropology and Education Quarterly*, **26**, 2, pp. 135–67.

ELMORE, R.F. (1983) 'Complexity and control: What legislators and administrators can do about implementing public policy', in SHULMAN, L.S. and SYKES, G. (Eds) *Handbook of Teaching Policy*, New York, Longman, pp. 342–69.

FERGUSON, KATHY E. (1993) *The Man Question: Visions of Subjectivity in Feminist Theory*, Berkeley, CA, University of California Press.

FINE, M. (1988) 'Sexuality, schooling and adolescent females: The missing discourse of desire', *Harvard Educational Review*, **58**, 1, pp. 29–53.

FINE, M. (1991) *Framing Dropouts: Notes on the Politics of an Urban Public High School*, Albany, NY, State University of New York Press.

FLICK, L. (1984) *Adolescent Childbearing Decisions: Implications for Prevention*, St. Louis, MO, The Danforth Foundation.

FOSTER, S.E. (1986) *Preventing Teenage Pregnancy*, Washington, DC, The Council of State Policy and Planning Agencies.

FOUCAULT, M. (1977/1984) in RABINOW, P. (Ed) *The Foucault Reader*, New York, Pantheon Books.

FOUCAULT, M. (1974/1990) *The History of Sexuality: An Introduction*, **I**, New York, Vintage Books.

FRASER, N. (1989) *Unruly Practices: Power, Discourse and Gender in Contemporary Social Theory*, Minneapolis, MN, University of Minnesota Press.

FURSTENBERG, F.F., BROOKS-GUNN, J. and MORGAN, S.P. (1987) 'Adolescent mothers and their children in later life', *Family Planning Perspectives*, **19**(4), pp. 142–51.

GIROUX, H.A. (Ed) (1991) *Postmodernism, Feminism and Cultural Politics*, Albany, NY, SUNY.

GODZICH, W. (1994) *The Culture of Literacy*, Cambridge, MA, Harvard University Press.

GRIFFITH, A.I. (1992) 'Educational policy as text and action', *Educational Policy*, **6**(4), pp. 415–28.

GUTTING, G. (1989) *Michel Foucault's Archeology of Scientific Reason*, Cambridge, England, Cambridge Press.

HENRIQUES, J., HOLLWAY, W., URWIN, C., VENN, C. and WALKERDINE, V. (1984) *Changing the Subject/Psychology, Social Regulation and Subjectivity*, London, Methuen.

HEWITT, M. (1991) 'Bio-politics and social policy', in FEATHERSTONE, M., HEPWORTH, M. and TURNER, B.S. (Eds) *The Body: Social Process and Cultural Theory*, London, Sage, pp. 225–55.

HOLLWAY, W. (1984) 'Fitting work: Psychological assessment in organizations', in HENRIQUES, J., HOLLWAY, W., URWIN, C., VENN, C. and WALKERDINE, V., *Changing the Subject/Psychology, Social Regulation and Subjectivity*, London, Methuen.

KELLY, M. and MAYNARD-MOODY, S. (1993) 'Policy analysis in the post-positivist era: Engaging stakeholders in evaluating the economic development districts program', *Public Administration Review*, **53**, 2, pp. 135–42.

KRISTEVA, J. (1986) in MOI, T. (Ed) *The Kristeva Reader*, New York, Columbia University Press.

LATHER, P. (1991) *Getting Smart Feminist Research and Pedagogy with/in the Postmodern*, New York, Routledge.

LAWSON, A. and RHODE, D.L. (Eds) (1993) *The Politics of Pregnancy: Adolescent Sexuality and Public Policy*, New Haven, Yale University Press.

LESKO, N. (1990) 'Curriculum differentiation as social redemption: The case of school-aged mothers', in PAGE, R. and VALLI, L. (Eds) *Curriculum Differentiation/Interpretive Studies in US Secondary Schools*, Albany, NY, State University of New York Press, pp. 113–36.

LESKO, N. (1995) 'The "leaky needs" of school-aged mothers: An examination of US programs and policies', *Curriculum Inquiry*, **25**(2), pp. 177–205.

LINDSAY, J.W. and RODINE, S. (1989) *Teen Pregnancy Challenge: Book Two: Programs for Kids*, Buena Park, California, Morning Glory Press.

MACINTYRE, S. and CUNNINGHAM-BURLEY, S. (1993) 'Teenage pregnancy as a social problem: A perspective from the United Kingdom', in LAWSON, A. and RHODE, D.L. (Eds) *The Politics of Pregnancy/Adolescent Sexuality and Public Policy*, New Haven, CT, Yale University Press, pp. 59–73.

MCLAUGHLIN, M.W. (1990) 'The Rand Change Agent Study revisited: Macro-perspectives and micro-realities', *Educational Researcher*, **19**(9), 11–16.

MCNAY, L. (1992) *Foucault and Feminism: Power, Gender and the Self*, Boston, MA, Northeastern University Press.

MCROBBIE, A. (1991) *Feminism and Youth Culture*, Boston, MA, Unwin Hyman.

NATHANSON, C.A. (1991) *Dangerous Passage/The Social Control of Sexuality in Women's Adolescence*, Philadelphia, PA, Temple University Press.

NATIONAL CENTER FOR HEALTH STATISTICS (1992) *Vital Statistics of the United States*, **1**, Table 1–67, p. 64.

NICHOLSON, L.J. (Ed) (1990) *Feminism/Postmodernism*, New York, Routledge.

PILLOW, W. (1994) 'Policy discourse and teenage pregnancy: The making of mothers', unpublished dissertation, Ohio State University.

RHODE, D.L. (1993) 'Adolescent pregnancy and public policy', in LAWSON, A. and RHODE, D.L. (Eds) *The Politics of Pregnancy/Adolescent Sexuality and Public Policy*, New Haven, Yale University Press, pp. 301–335.

SCHEURICH, J.J. (1995) 'Policy archaeology: A new policy studies methodology', *Journal of Policy Studies*, p. 253.

SHAKESHAFT, C. (1986) 'A gender at risk', *Phi Delta Kappan*, (March), pp. 499–503.

SHAPIRO, M. (1992) *Reading the Postmodern Polity: Political Theory as Textual Practices*, Minneapolis, MN, University of Minnesota Press.

SIDEL, R. (1990) *On Her Own: Growing up in the Shadow of the American Dream*, New York, Penguin Books.

SINGER, L. (1993) *Erotic Welfare: Sexual Theory and Politics in the Age of Epidemic*, New York, Routledge.

SPIVAK, G.C. (1990) in HARASYM, S. (Ed) *The Post-colonial Critic: Interviews, Strategies, Dialogues*, New York, Routledge.

TRINH, M.T. (1989) *Woman Native Other*, Bloomington, IN, Indiana University Press.

TRINH, M.T. (1991) *When the Moon Waxes Red: Representation, Gender and Cultural Politics*, New York, Routledge.

WALKERDINE, V. (1990) *Schoolgirl Fictions*, London, Verso.

WEEDON, C. (1987) *Feminist Practice and Poststructuralist Theory*, Cambridge, Basil Blackwell.

WEILER, K. (1988) *Women Teaching for Change: Gender, Class and Power*, Boston, Mass, Bergin & Garvey.

Wanda S. Pillow

WHATLEY, M.H. (1991) 'Raging hormones and powerful cars: The construction of man's sexuality in school sex education and popular adolescent films', in GIROUX, H.A. (Ed) *Postmodernism, Feminism and Cultural Politics: Redrawing Education Boundaries*, New York, SUNY Press, pp. 119–43.

WOLPE, A. (1988) *Within School Walls: The Role of Discipline, Sexuality and the Curriculum*, London, Routledge.

Chapter 8

Toward a Curriculum of Resiliency: Gender, Race, Adolescence and Schooling

Natalie Adams

Embedded in the pervasive rhetoric of schooling is the assumption that schools are apolitical sites where identity-less students gather, absorb the same information, and share the same opportunities to succeed. However, extensive research (see Sadker and Sadker, 1994) has demonstrated that female students continue to be 'shortchanged' in school (AAUW, 1992). As Fine and MacPherson, 1992, Fordham, 1993, and others (Lesko, 1988; Roman, 1988; Tolmon, 1994) have argued, we must be careful in making any claims that females simply by virtue of their sex experience the same forms of oppression. In reality, young women are subjected to different forms of oppression based not only on their gender but also on their race, class, ethnicity and sexual orientation. Furthermore, the manner in which adolescent girls make sense of their own lives, how they view oppression, and how they elect to counter that oppression is impacted by what Alcoff defines as 'positionality' (1986: 324). Yet schools tend to define in very monolithic terms what constitutes an appropriately raced and gendered individual, thereby situating some girls as being clearly more deviant (i.e., more at-risk) than other girls (Adams, 1994).

The purpose of this chapter is to analyze how the multiple discourses of femininity, adolescence and whiteness manifest themselves in the policies and practices of schools. My approach to this analysis is based on two theoretical assumptions: First, there is no inherent truth in any discourse. Rather, all discourses are contrived and can thus be made and understood in a multitude of ways. I argue that schools, whether consciously or not, choose to enact a specific discourse of femininity and adolescence that often dismisses the lived experiences of many of their female students. Second, any discussion of discourse must be specific and contextualized in the lives of ordinary people. Thus, I focus specifically on one adolescent female[1] at one particular school to illustrate that adolescent girls do not unproblematically absorb the definitions of femininity, adolescence and whiteness that the school presents to them – rather negotiation, struggle, compromise and resistance play key roles in their construction of self. Using three different metaphors that emerged in the stories told by this one adolescent female – 'The gangster', 'The black girl trapped in the white girl's body', and 'The good women' – I intend to illuminate how, as Davies explains, 'individuals, through learning the discursive practices of society, are able to position themselves within those practices in multiple ways and to develop subjectivities both in concert with and in opposition to the ways in which others choose to position them' (1989: xi).

The Gangster

In a world in which the ideal woman is slim, blonde, beautiful, blue-eyed, and has gorgeous teeth, hair and complexion, Sharon Freeman[2] fails miserably. Sharon towers over most of her peers – both male and female – and she is overweight. Her hair is brown, short and often unruly; she has acne, and her teeth are chipped and a dullish brown. Furthermore, Sharon is neither quiet nor passive. In class, she shouts out answers without raising her hand. She verbally challenges teachers when reprimanded and frequently engages in physical fights. During our first interview, Sharon told me, 'I just can't act like a young lady cause I'm loud and like to be active and stuff.' I responded, 'Do you think those are male or boy traits?' Sharon quickly replied, 'No, they're more gangster-like acts.'

Her appropriation of the term *gangster* stems from her keen interest in rap artists (most of whom are male and black) who seem to defy authoritative figures (parents and teachers) and established institutions (white policemen). In this context, the gangster represents a sense of power typically not accrued to adolescents in our culture. For Sharon being a gangster reflects an emotional and physical survival strategy that demonstrates that she alone is in control of her fate, thus responsible for what she does and who she becomes.

Whether her stories are about fighting . . .

> Yeah, I've been in trouble with the police for fighting with an armed weapon. When they found me, I had a knife in my shoe, a knife on my side, a gun on my side, a gun in my hand.

relationships with adults:

> I was about to fight in this classroom with Katie Cassman cos she went back and told somebody I was a whore for dating black boys. And Mr Donell [the principal] told me that I had no business confronting her, and I said, 'What else I'm supposed to do? Let people talk about me? I don't think so. Nobody's going to talk about me and get away with it.'

relationships with men:

> I asked him [a boyfriend] for some money on the phone cos he wanted me to skip school yesterday and come to his house and spend the night with him. He said he didn't have no money. 'You don't have no money but still you want me to come spend time with you; that's time I could be spending with somebody else that gives me money.' I didn't go.

or having a baby at age 13:

> I don't care what people be saying. I should know what comes in me and what comes out me. There's nothing wrong with having a child. I wanted it; I had it; I'm going to keep her, and I'm not getting rid of her.

Sharon positions herself as one always on the outside of the dominant culture yet always in power and in control.

Although Sharon's school has no *stated* policy about its responsibility for social-izing girls into appropriate gender roles, behaviors, and attitudes, the 'micropractices of regulation' (Foucault, 1980) operating at her school (teacher talk, classroom interactions, enforcement of disciplinary procedures) serve as powerful reminders about what constitutes correct feminine behavior. Consequently, at school being a gangster is not acceptable behavior – especially for a white girl – and although Sharon does not view her behavior as being either masculine or feminine, the teachers and administrators interpret Sharon's gangsterlike behavior as 'trying to be a boy'. In explaining why Sharon is such a discipline problem at school, her social studies teacher said, 'Sharon tries to be tough; you know be a boy. She's always getting in fights. She even wants to try out for the football team.' similarly, her PE teacher described Sharon as 'having big problems. She wants to be a boy.' Clearly, Sharon's articulation of what is typically viewed as masculine behavior marks her at school as being an abnormally gendered adolescent. In short, as her social studies teacher reminded her in the hall one day after she entered the class very boister-ously, Sharon does not act like a 'proper little lady'.

The gangster metaphor is one in which the marginalized seize power without the endorsement of the dominant culture. As Sharon changed from a quiet seventh-grade girl whom nobody noticed to an eighth-grade girl who demanded that her presence be acknowledged, she gained a sense of power that her teachers found deplorable. It is her nonconformity to the dominant normative understandings of femininity that gives her this sense of power. However, such empowerment comes with a price. Like the working class youth in the early twentieth century who did not conform to the 'model of adolescence that schools and youth organizations presented to them' (Gillis, 1981: 177), poor, white girls in the late twentieth century who use their body, voice and intellect in ways that challenge the school's preoc-cupation with the passive, docile adolescent body are marked as deviant female adolescents and often labeled 'at-risk'.

The Black Girl Trapped in a White Girl's Body

Although Sharon is considered a discipline problem because she acts like a boy, she is described by her teachers as a bright student who scores above average on standardized tests, who makes good grades and completes all her work. According to her social studies teacher, 'Sharon's really smart; she does her work, makes A's on my tests, but she is so annoying.'

Clearly, it is not Sharon's academic well being that concerns her teachers; it is her social and emotional well being that her teachers question, for in addition to defying normative understandings of an appropriately gendered being, Sharon also challenges traditional notions of what constitutes an appropriately raced being: Sharon is a white female who wants to be black. As she proudly tells teachers and peers, 'I'm a black girl trapped in a white girl's body.' Sharon's friends are black, her boyfriends are black, and the father of her baby is black. For most of the study, she lived with a black friend in an all-black neighborhood.

However, for white girls, acting black is not an option in a contemporary society based upon the supremacy of whiteness. Bell hooks (1995) describes white supremacy as a taken-for-granted assumption that having white skin is a privilege giving one not only the right but the obligation to be superior and act in superior ways. As Toni Morrison (1992) reminds us, part of the power of white supremacy lies in the construction of whiteness and blackness as dualisms. This is exemplified by the language used by two of Sharon's teachers in talking about Sharon:

'Sharon's vocabulary and the way she talks is so black. I've never seen anyone so much *act the other way.*'

'Sharon doesn't know who she is. She's trying to associate with blacks. She runs around with *them*; she talks like *them*; she even lives with *them*.'

Because of Sharon's actions and associations, she is viewed as a failure to her race. In other words, she has shunned what her teachers view as the privileges and obligations accrued to whiteness.

By assuming what the school considered to be both a male identity and a black identity, Sharon is judged much more harshly than either her white male or black female counterparts. The teachers state that they have tried everything – punishment work, talking to her mother, time out room, and even suspension – to get Sharon to behave appropriately (i.e., like a white girl should). Indeed, the teachers at her school repeatedly attribute Sharon's problems in school to what her French teacher termed, 'a lack of home training'. Traditionally, it has been the responsibility of parents to teach their children what constitutes appropriately raced and gendered behavior. Yet, when parents are perceived to have failed, as has Sharon's mother, to teach these lessons, the school clearly assumes the right to intervene. For example, when Sharon was sent to the office for writing love letters to a black male who did not want her attention, the principal called Sharon's mother and asked her if she were aware that her daughter was dating black boys. In this instance, the principal chose to address the implications of Sharon's actions rather than the action itself.

Sharon herself is well aware that her identification with blacks is at the root of her problems with both her teachers (all of whom are white) and with white students. She relates the following story about how the lessons of white supremacy are taught to erring white students:

One teacher at this school called me out of class and told me what I'm doing is embarrassing us. And I said, 'Who do you mean by us?' and she said, 'the whites', and I said, 'Whatcha mean by that? Look you can teach me at school but you can't tell me if I want to date a black man or a white man. You don't tell me nothing about my love life.'

Sharon realizes that her refusal to 'be a lady' coupled with the fact that she 'acts black' marks her as deviant. Sharon copes with this inability to meet the standards of white femininity by rejecting these ideals as irrelevant to her life, since she is, after all, a 'black girl trapped in a white girl's body'.

The Good Woman

Although Sharon's teachers have chosen to interpret her actions as evidence of an abnormally gendered and raced individual, an alternative reading of Sharon's story would suggest that in many ways Sharon acts just like a good, heterosexual white girl. Sharon often completes both classwork and punishment work for her male peers. She is also very loyal to those whom she cares about and places a primacy on relationships and connections to others. When a white boy called her a 'nigger lover' because she was talking to a black boy in class, Sharon stood up, hit the boy hard enough to knock him down, and told him, 'don't call him a nigger'. On numerous occasions, Sharon has fought to prove her loyalty to her best friend India. Sharon explains this special bond and her willingness to fight for India as follows:

> If somebody wants to fight India, I'm going to be India's back. I'll beat anyone up that messes with India cos India's my baby's godmother. I don't want nobody hurting her cos if something happen to me, my baby going straight to her.

India lauds Sharon's willingness to fight for her:

> Me and Sharon got the relationship of a lifetime. I really don't think nothing could break me and Sharon's relationship. Because if I'm ready to fight somebody, Sharon's got to say, 'Don't fight them. I'll handle it.' She'll fight for me. Sharon will get suspended for me.

In fact, Sharon was finally suspended from school for fighting for India. Interestingly, upon suspending her, the principal told Sharon, 'Sometimes you can care too much.'

On the day she was suspended, I found Sharon sitting on the couch crying. Next to her were several small pieces of facial tissues which she was using to dab at her eyes. During her explanation of why she was getting suspended, Sharon poignantly articulated what she saw as the crux of her problems in school:

> You know when I was in sixth grade, I never said a word, and I never got in trouble; I kept all my feelings inside til I was about to bust. You know

I can't do that no more, I've got to express myself, and seems like when
I do, I get in trouble. I can't even be myself here.

Ironically, as long as she conformed to the acceptable codes of behavior for a white
girl (i.e., being quiet, keeping feelings inside, avoiding conflict), she was not considered abnormal or a problem; however, when she stepped outside those restric-
tions and embraced a view of herself as an empowered being (or a 'gangster'), she
was considered to have severe identity problems. By age 14 Sharon has learned a
lesson about her identity that is implicitly taught to girls all over – being silent and
disconnected has its rewards from the dominant culture. However, the cost of being
'nobody' is too high and one Sharon no longer cares to pay.

Sharon's stories illustrate the struggle many girls experience in trying to meet
conflicting expectations of what it means to be an adolescent, what it means to be
white, and what it means to be a female in today's society. Ironically, when Sharon
does conform to normative understandings of females as caring and in connection
with others, she often comes into conflict with the school's emphasis on individuation,
isolation and control (typically viewed as masculine characteristics), thus breaking
school rules, such as copying the punish work of others or fighting, or the school
code of acceptable white female behavior – passing love notes to a black boy.

Unlearning the Truth

Barone asserts that stories have the power to move people in ways that research articles and technical monographs do not, because stories disrupt 'implicit, habitual,
taken-for-granted beliefs . . . [and] normative ways of seeing' (1992: 17). If we
believe (as do I) that storytelling is a powerful tool for bringing about educational
reform, what then can we glean from Sharon's stories that might illuminate our work
with adolescent girls who are viewed by their school as being 'at-risk' or 'problem
students'? I would contend that the discontinuities between Sharon's struggle to construct an identity that defies erasure and the policies and practices at her school that
seek to define what constitutes an appropriately raced and gendered individual forces
us to question the following: 1) How do schools attempt to teach young women the
discursive practices of society that often become constructed as the truths about
femininity, adolescence and whiteness? 2) Realizing that discourses can be made
and understood in a multitude of ways, how can we unlearn the truths embedded
in the dominant discourse of gender, race and adolescence so that schools can be
transformed into places that value a non-unitary understanding of what constitutes
an appropriate adolescent identity?

Unlearning the Truth about Gender

First of all, stories like Sharon's challenge the very notion that there are indeed
monolithic characteristics that distinguish one as feminine or masculine. Indeed, the

notion of femininity and masculinity as essentialized and opposite traits – the notion typically constructed in the dominant discourse of gender, the discourse that gets played out in this school – has little meaning in many girls' everyday lives. In Sharon's lived experiences, these binaries become blurred, reversed or obliterated, as Sharon's reference to gangster traits as being neither male nor female illustrates. Consequently, Sharon does not necessarily negotiate her identity against traditional binary understandings of male–female, masculine–feminine. Rather, gender for her is a continuum, always in flux, and has little to do with passively accepting either a feminine or masculine role.

This rejection of a binary notion about gender is most evident in Sharon's stories about fighting and aggression. In the dominant discourse of gender, fighting is identified as a masculine behavior; thus fighting is viewed as the most symbolic form of deviancy for girls. Clearly, this belief was upheld at the school Sharon attended. Neither administrators nor teachers knew how to deal with the growing number of girls who were engaging in physical fights. Comments such as 'where I come from' or 'when I was growing up, nice girls didn't fight' were made repeatedly by both male and female faculty. However, Sharon rejected the belief that fighting and assertiveness was a masculine trait. She dismissed such ideas as sexist and argued that in no way should her fighting be construed as imitating boys. Sharon stated, 'When I fight, I ain't trying to act like no boy; I'm just acting like myself.' She then quickly added, 'I mean I'm just being myself.' Her quick change of the word *acting* to *being* highlights the struggles young women encounter in trying to construct a gendered identity in a culture that situates normalized femininity and masculinity as dualisms. Often they are expected to *act* in ways that are antithetical to their sense of *being*.

While the dominant discourse, which equates femininity with passivity and submission, situates Sharon as resisting or rejecting femininity, Sharon does not view her behavior as such. Quite the opposite; she perceives herself to be quite feminine. In fact, Sharon and her friends often refer to girls who do not take up for themselves or who allow others to push them around as not 'being womanish enough'. Unlike the adults at her school who view girls fighting as abnormal behavior, Sharon and her friends and family perceive girls who allow others to control them, either physically or emotionally, to be the ones who are *abnormal*.

Unlearning the Truth about Identity

Second, unlearning the truth about identity (as illuminated by Sharon's stories) forces us to acknowledge the multiple positionings that all of us take up based on the multiple intersections of race, class and gender. Yet, schools tend to promote an understanding of identity as being fixed, monolithic and unitary. Rarely is there space in classroom discourse to examine the contradictions, tensions and ambiguities embedded in the multiple intersections of identity. For example, what does it mean to simultaneously be white, heterosexual, working-class, female, southern and adolescent? The value of focusing on these sometimes contradictory positions is that 'we are able to see individuals not as the unitary beings that humanist theory would have them be, but as the complex, changing, contradictory creatures that we each experience ourselves to be, despite our best efforts at producing a unified, coherent and relatively static self' (Davies, 1989: xi).

By acknowledging that our identities are multiple, shifting and always discursively positioned in relation to race, gender, class and other salient features of personal life, schools would be forced to interrogate a pervasive myth in American public education – one built on the ideals of self-determination, free will and hard work. In her stories of being a gangster and a black girl trapped in a white girl's body, Sharon fights to make her voice heard, her presence felt, and to validate her sense of self. In many ways, however, Sharon reinforces the myth about identity construction that suggests we can be anything we want to be. Indeed, throughout my interviews with Sharon, she continuously repeated comments such as 'I can do anything I want to do' and 'nobody tells me who to be.'

In reality, who Sharon can be is severely limited by the material realities of her life: she is poor, her mother has a drug problem, her step-father is an alcoholic, she has a 1-year-old baby and receives no financial help from the father. Therefore, she fights hard to create a sense of identity that defies vulnerability. Unquestionably, her insistence upon taking control of situations before they control her often contributes to the reproduction of her own oppression. By having sex for money with multiple partners, she is subjecting herself to the dangerous and often life-threatening consequences of promiscuity; by challenging the school rules that assert that fighting is inappropriate behavior, she places herself in jeopardy of being expelled. By resisting the schools' attempts to educate her, she runs the risk of dropping out of school, in which case her dream to become a zoologist would remain just a dream.

Furthermore, by positioning herself as a woman fully in charge of her own life, one invulnerable to pain and the criticisms of others, she is forced to hide another part of her life from both her teachers and her peers. Like most stories, as we peel away the layers, we inevitably uncover other texts – the ones that speak poignantly of the mysteries, paradoxes, tensions and conflicts that make us human. It is in Sharon's private personal writing that another facet of her identity surfaces – not as a gangster unconcerned with the opinions of others but as a vulnerable adolescent female struggling with her sense of self:

Feelings

Happy,
Sad,
Mad,
Hurt,
Upset,
Alone.
Why do they change on me?
One day I might be one

> The next day I'm another
> Why do they change on me?

These moments of self-doubt, these times of loneliness, and the feelings of vulnerability remain unspoken truths about Sharon's identity – truths she dare not reveal to her teachers or her peers.

School folks rarely engage in serious discussion about schooling for identity, even though schools operate in very explicit ways to regulate appropriate identities (i.e., a female identity, a white identity). Unlearning the truth about gender, race, and identity in school forces us to recognize that schools are powerful transmitters of the dominant discourse of femininity and whiteness, and that this transmission often occurs in subtle ways, as illustrated by the ways in which Sharon's school seeks to regulate what constitutes appropriate behavior for a white girl. Yet, schools typically operate under the guise that gender and race make no difference (beyond equal access), despite the reality that adolescent girls experience schooling very differently than do boys, just as white students experience school very differently than do non-white students. As a result of the rhetoric of 'everybody's equal here', adolescent females like Sharon are denied access in school to a language for critiquing the dominant discourse of femininity, white supremacy and the patriarchal structure of schooling.

Unlearning the Truth about Adolescence

Third, unlearning the truth about gender, race and adolescence requires us to interrogate the construct of adolescence itself. Historical accounts of adolescence (Gillis, 1981; Ketts, 1977) show that since its institutionalization in the nineteenth century, this stage of development has been situated as a time of inevitable 'storm and stress'. All adolescents (regardless of race, class or gender), in their search to form an identity separate from their families and parents, supposedly undergo emotional trauma and distress. Regardless of studies (Adelson, 1986; Bandura, 1964) that document that adolescence is no more and no less stressful than early childhood or late adulthood, the belief that adolescents (by virtue of their age) need to be protected not only from themselves but from the evils of society pervades most discussions of adolescence.

Missing in this dominant discourse of adolescence is a consideration of how race, class and gender impact the normatively situated concept of 'storm and stress'. Unlearning the truth about adolescence, as Sharon's story demonstrates, requires us to question the discourse of storm and stress itself: Why has adolescence continued to be characterized as a time of storm and stress? What constitutes normative storm and stress? How do schools through their control of time, knowledge and power reinforce our traditional understandings of adolescence as a time of storm and stress? What does the construction of adolescence reveal about power structures in our society as a whole? Most importantly, how are adolescent females like Sharon situated as abnormal or at-risk students when they fail to meet the conflicting expectations of being adolescent, female and white?

Dealing with the storm and stress of adolescence is an expected role of most middle and secondary schools. However, at Sharon's school a distinction clearly exists between what is considered *normal* storm and stress and what is considered *abnormal* storm and stress. Talking back to the teacher (within reason) is considered normal adolescent storm and stress. However, girls fighting is not considered normal adolescent behavior as reflected by teachers' comments that 'girls should be able to talk out their problems' and 'it's immature for girls to fight'. Teenage girls passing notes in class is considered normal behavior. White girls giving love notes to black boys is abnormal adolescent behavior, as evidenced by Sharon being sent to the office for writing a love note to a black male and by the school's subsequent call to her mother, asking her, 'Do you allow your daughter to date black boys?' In school, storm and stress is allowed as long as those behaviors are viewed as age-related deficiencies. However, those girls whose adolescent identity challenges the dominant discourse of femininity and whiteness and breaks cultural rules, those individuals who fail to meet the expectations of the dominant culture, are labeled deviant, abnormal at-risk.

Toward a Curriculum of Resiliency: Unlearning the Truth about Gender, Race, Adolescence and Schooling

Describing resilient youth as good problem solvers who possess social competence and have a sense of identity, independence, and control over their own environment, the Western Center for Drug-Free Schools and Communities (1994) argues that the focus on disadvantaged youth must change from a focus of at-risk students to one of resilient students. Ultimately, unlearning the truth about gender, race and adolescence challenges us to envision a curriculum for resiliency rather than a curriculum for deficiency, which is the implicit focus when students are labeled 'at-risk', 'deviant', or 'abnormal'.

Envisioning a curriculum of resiliency based on the positive characteristics students like Sharon bring to school requires us to unlearn the traditional model of schooling. A curriculum of resiliency invites an understanding that legitimizes the lived experiences of all students, rather than those of a privileged few. Such a curriculum would acknowledge that students come to school with identities who have acquired a way of seeing the world that may differ from that of the dominant culture. A curriculum of resiliency would allow students to bring their out-of-school subjective realities into the classroom (including their own raced, gendered and classed self-definitions) and would focus on the lives of students and their cultures. Furthermore, a curriculum of resiliency would acknowledge the many ways in which individuals construct meaning.

However, a curriculum of resiliency would demand much more than simply acknowledging multiple ways of being and knowing. This understanding of curriculum would challenge both teachers and students to critically analyze power and domination in our society, and by so doing, become critical agents in the reconstruction of that society. Most importantly, a discourse of resiliency rather than deficiency would offer a way of reading Sharon's life in a way that would validate that she is indeed *somebody*.

Undeniably, unlearning the truth about gender, race, adolescence and school- ing forces a fundamental rethinking of the discourses that govern policies and prac- tices. Yet, such an undertaking is imperative – especially in schools which continue, despite their numerous attempts at reforming and restructuring, to be alien places for girls like Sharon.

Notes

1   This chapter is based on data gathered from an ethnographic study I conducted from 1993–1994 in a middle school located in the Deep South. The majority (60 per cent) of the 792 students at this school were black; socioeconomically they came from predomin- antly working-class and lower-middle-class families. The majority of the students were males (55 per cent) and of the 358 females, the majority were black. The teachers, how- ever, were predominantly white (60 per cent) and female (80 per cent). The three admin- istrators were male. Although white females comprised the lowest percentage of the student population, the teachers at this school were predominantly white females (53 per cent).
2   This is a pseudonym, although Sharon wanted me to use her real name. The research agreement with her school, however, prohibited my using any real names.

References

ADAMS, N. (1994) '"A proper little lady" and other twisted tales of adolescent femininity', unpublished doctoral dissertation, Baton Rouge, LA, Louisiana State University.
ADELSON, J. (1986) *Inventing adolescence*, New Brunswick, NJ, Transaction Books.
ALCOFF, L. (1986) 'Cultural feminism versus poststructuralism: The identity crisis in femin- ist theory', in MALSON, M., O'BARR, J., WESTPHAL-WIHL, S. and WYER, M. (Eds) *Fem- inist Theory in Practice and Process*, Chicago, IL, The University of Chicago Press, pp. 295–326.
AMERICAN ASSOCIATION OF UNIVERSITY WOMEN (AAUW) (1992) *How Schools Shortchange Girls*, Washington DC, Author.
BANDURA, A. (1964) 'The stormy decade: Fact or fiction', *Psychology in the Schools*, **1**(3), pp. 224–31.
BARONE, T. (1992) 'The limits of theory: Critical storytelling and the deep persuasion of the polity', Paper presented at the annual meeting of the American Educational Research Association, San Francisco, California.
DAVIES, B. (1989) 'The discursive production of the male/female dualism in school settings', *Oxford Review of Education*, **15**(3), pp. 229–41.
FINE, M. and MACPHERSON, P. (1992) 'Over dinner: Femininity and adolescent female bod- ies', in FINE, M. (Ed) *Disruptive Voices*, Ann Arbor, MI, The University of Michigan Press.
FORDHAM, S. (1993) '"Those loud black girls": (Black) women, silence, and gender "pass- ing" in the academy', *Anthropology and Education Quarterly*, **24**(1), pp. 3–32.
FOUCAULT, M. (1980) *Power Knowledge: Selected Interviews and Other Writings, 1972– 1977*, Sussex, Harvester Press.

GILLIS, J. (1981) *Youth and History*, New York, Academic Press.

HOOKS, B. (1995) Interview with CNN *Booknotes*, 17 November.

KETTS, J. (1977) *Rites of Passage: Adolescence in America 1790 to the Present*, New York, Basic Books.

LESKO, N. (1988) *Symbolizing Society*, Basingstoke, The Falmer Press.

MORRISON, T. (1992) *Playing in the Dark: Whiteness and the Literary Imagination*, Cambridge, MA: Harvard University Press.

ROMAN, L. (1988) 'Intimacy, labor, and class: Ideologies of feminine sexuality in the punk slam dance', in ROMAN, L. and CHRISTIAN-SMITH, L. (Eds) *Becoming Feminine; The Politics of Popular Culture*, Basingstoke, Falmer Press, pp. 143–84.

SADKER, M. and SADKER, D. (1994) *Failing at Fairness: How our Schools Cheat Girls*, New York, Simon and Schuster.

TOLMAN, D. (1994) 'Doing desire: Adolescent girls' struggles for/with sexuality', *Gender and Society*, **8**(3), pp. 324–42.

WESTERN CENTER FOR DRUG-FREE SCHOOLS AND COMMUNITIES (1994) 'Kids who cope and schools that help them', *High Strides*, **6**(2), p. 2.

Chapter 9

Feminist Praxis as the Basis for Teacher Education: A Critical Challenge*

Sandra Hollingsworth

In this chapter, I want to address three interrelated ideas: First, I want to argue for the intersection of feminist analyses of lived educational experience and the action research movement – or feminist praxis – as the basis for teacher education. Second, I want to argue that this intersection suggests not only a critical theoretical framework for educating teachers – but underscores a practical argument for turning our attention, resources and energy in teacher education away from preservice education toward teachers in practice. Third, I want to look critically at what we're doing as feminist educators that may be contributing to the conservative nature of schooling and think about how we might do it differently.

The Case for Feminist Analyses of Lived Educational Experience

Let me begin with the argument for educational practice coming from both John Dewey[1] and feminists of the second and third waves of the 1960s to 1990s. We, as students and teachers, come to know and understand through the filters of our experiences, our social positions in life and work and our senses of personal (and political) agency. I think most of us here would agree. I am a feminist educator because I have lived feminist experiences throughout my life. From the time I had to fight 'more knowledgeable' authorities (older and more powerful) to get the right to write about racial inequities in the 1960s as editor of my high school paper, to the time I realized, as a graduate student, the rage that I felt from being taught world history from the perspective of only white, Euro–American men, or from being refused entry to advanced math classes because 'girls didn't need that level of mathematics', I have understood what feminist issues in education are. Living my adult life as a lesbian academic hones feminist questions about knowledge and experience even more sharply. I suspect many of you have related stories.

I also imagine that most of us would theoretically agree with the current social constructivist position on knowledge acquisition, and see transmitting information

* Hollingsworth, S. 'Feminist praxis as the basis for teacher education: A critical challenge', Portions were previously published as 'The problem of gender in teacher education', *Mid-Western Educational Researcher*, **8**(2), pp. 3–12 (1995). Reprinted with permission.

as pedagogues as ineffective. Yet so often we find ourselves unwittingly in trans-
mittive modes. As feminists, we want to educate our undergraduate students to be
aware of educational injustices with respect to race, class, gender and other differences. Yet most of our students come to us without experience in the classroom,
or having given serious and personal thought to the politics of injustice. So, we
hope to inculcate and indoctrinate them. And we're frustrated when we can't.

Many of us have tried to educate our students with the help of critical or
poststructural theories. Liz Ellsworth (1989), Jennifer Gore (1992), Patti Lather
(1991), Mimi Orner (1992), Valerie Walkerdine (1986) and others have embraced
the construction of critical feminist pedagogies to liberate the voices of the Other.
However, they found the application of critical theory to classrooms problematic;
it seemed they were still trapped within modernist enlightenment epistemologies.
Thus, efforts to create 'emancipatory classrooms' within a unitary or transcendental
(if critical) view of emancipation failed.

For me, the problem of critical pedagogy hinges on two issues: insufficient
theorizing by critical scholars about the nature of knowledge with respect to gender, and my personal investment in having students see things as I want them to.
I will talk about the problem with knowledge first.

Dorothy Smith (1987) reminds us that knowledge, *the* economic commodity
produced by academics, is constitutive of relations of *ruling* as well as of relations
of *knowing*. Though many other critical sociologists and political scientists have
spoken to us about the problematic nature of knowledge as a political act (see especially Bourdieu, 1977; Foucault, 1980; Freire, 1970), those challenges did not resonate
with my own experience until I heard them articulated from feminist stances. The
omission of the gendered experience left me reading (and feeling) as though I (as
woman) still did not have a right to know, to speak, to question, to challenge, to
change. The generic *man* in *man*kind, and hu*man*ist, and hu*man*ity, had not historically included me (as child-abuse survivor, female student who wanted to study
mathematics, wife and mother, single female parent, woman professor, lesbian community member). Like many black American women's critiques of feminism (see
hooks, 1990), I was not certain, without specifically naming my own experience,
that I would be included in the 'new and post' conceptions of knowledge. As long
as my particular woman's viewpoint was seen as too threatening to bring into the
conversations *on knowledge*, much less illuminate the potential for *reconstructing
knowledges*, I was not sure at all that my knowledge would count. That my teaching
and my research would count. Further, I was not certain that children and students,
unnamed in most poststructuralist critiques of knowledge, would be any better off
than they were before. Finally, I have noticed throughout my career as a teacher educator that *unless teachers examine and name their own knowledges and questions,
they have difficulty becoming critical consumers of other-formulated knowledge.*

Most poststructuralists in the United States critique the metanarratives written by others which have controlled our collective education – such as those of
Bloom (1964), Schon (1982), Schwab (1972), Shulman (1987), and Tyler (1949) (see
Cherryholmes, 1988, for a partial overview.) Poststructuralists are sometimes self-
critical in critiquing poststructural models of knowledge against more structured

approaches (again, see Cherryholmes, 1988). And yet, they rarely name their own personal positionings inside of their theories: their struggles with pedagogy and ideology, how their students and peers have turned their theories upside down, their own doubts about the validity of their positions. Nor do they ask me about similar occasions and positions in my lived theories. Thus, those seamless depictions of poststructural theory leaves me skeptical and fearful. Critical theories could also leave me feeling as if I hadn't found the right theory yet, except for the continual messages I've received across my life that there is no right theory. Here's an example.

In a very telling moment as a religious young woman of 22, I went to my Anglican priest for help to restore my faith in a unitary creator. 'I'm beginning to doubt my faith in God', I confessed. The priest responded not as I'd hoped, but with a response which validated my uncertainty and shaped the questions of my life: 'You know, I think I am too.' That early example of what I'd now call a feminist postmodern contribution to eroding the 'theorizing subject' left me with a sense of agency. It still does. You may have had similar experiences.

The distinctions between poststructural and feminist theories are of special importance, since it took so long for feminist theorizing to be recognized. Who speaks, after all? Where is the point of departure when it comes to knowing? Who speaks for whom? For Judith Butler, the subject is constituted at certain points where power overlaps action and knowing. Never predetermined, these subjectivities identify various theoretical positions, 'working the possibilities of their convergences and trying to take account of the possibilities they systematically exclude' (Butler, 1990: 9). And, as subjects whose power shifts as we are repositioned daily in our collaborative work with others, we can continually remember *how it feels to know and not know.*

I have to admit that my personal investment in having students 'come to know' has often hindered their knowing, perhaps in excess of any concerns with knowledge. I suspect that investment has gone beyond my own classroom. Perhaps, as part of a community of feminist educators, our right-minded stances on knowing how our students should know and act has contributed to the backlash against feminist theory. We have to acknowledge that there is a definite correlation between *the rise of the radical right and critical feminist traditions in education* (Arnot, 1993: 186). Though the reasons are complex, I wonder what we can do to avoid contributing to the increasingly conservative nature of schooling. I guess what I'm arguing for here is a use of feminist theory with our students in the way that it came to us – through conversation, two-way (at least) critique, and slowly rethinking our own experiences. I'm not sure a semester course is enough. And, moving too fast may not only be alienating for students, but devastating for us. Let me give an example.

I've often convinced my students that it is appropriate to critique authority, and then feel confused or even angry when they challenge *me!* One full class of preservice teachers at Berkeley was ready to mutiny over my suggesting that they construct their own knowledges too fast. Shulamitz Reinharz reminds us that to hear another's voice, we have to be willing to hear what someone is saying, even when it violates our expectations or threatens our interests. 'In other words, if you want someone to tell it like it is, you have to hear it like it is' (Reinharz, 1992: 16). Many times feminist projects of praxis to illuminate the voices of the oppressed women hope to empower them as well as represent their lived conditions, while the oppressed Other simply wants to join in the emancipators' critiques of schooling. Michelle Fine reports on such an experience: 'With all of their suspicions of public education (and they expressed many), they still saw public schooling as the only possible vehicle for their children's futures. For many, the risks of voicing critique were simply seen as too great' (Fine, 1992: 217).

Sometimes, my students are too privileged to identify with feminist descriptors. One teacher, married to a multi-national corporate vice-president told me after one class that she just didn't 'get' the feminist message. 'I went home and told my husband, "I've tried and I've tried, but I just don't feel oppressed!"' At other times, what I hear in my classes and my collaborations is unacceptable to me, rendering conversation and collaboration impossible. Sometimes empowered students and teachers advocate interventions and strategies that we organizers can't support (Fine, 1992: 217). A group of teachers I worked with in an urban school wanted to eliminate lower-track failure by barring entry to students from single-parent homes! I eventually left that collaboration.

One of my greatest lessons in this work is to learn that others may not share the same emotional, intellectual or occupational experiences that make them ready to take on the risks that I do. I need to constantly keep in mind that I am positioned as a tenured faculty member, a single mother with grown children, a partner in an increasingly stable relationship, and a friend to many strong women and men. My risks are not as costly as others' might be. Further, it is often difficult to remember that an ultimate goal of emancipatory research and pedagogy is to establish conditions wherein the Others can represent themselves, and not be represented by advocates. Yet that's not the norm in educational research and practice. I know, however, that my best indicator of success comes each time a student joins a conversation on feminist issues voluntarily, then goes out to reconstruct what she's learned in personal, rewarding and different ways for herself.

The Case for Feminist Teacher or Action Research as a Pedagogical Medium

I became interested in the action research literature as a guide to educational praxis when I took my first faculty position as a teacher educator at UC Berkeley in 1986. My first course was called 'Teaching as Research'. I still teach it now, both at Michigan State University (MSU) and internationally. However, the course has changed substantially – along with my own understanding of how to better integrate it with feminist theory. To get ready to teach the class each year, I read various conceptions of action research, such as Lawrence Stenhouse's (1975) conception of teachers as researchers; John Elliott's (1991) notion of action research as a pedagogical paradigm or form of teaching; descriptions of the task as a 'systematic self-reflective scientific inquiry by practitioners to improve practice' (James McKernan, 1991); or a philosophical stance toward 'the inter-dependency of knowledge and action, of educational theory and educational practice' (Bridget Somekh, 1993). John Elliott, for example, a colleague of Stenhouse in the Humanities Project, emphasized the interpretive-hermeneutic nature of inquiry in this work. Elliott argued that teachers in England in the 1960s invented action research as a reaction to streaming or tracking systems in which large numbers of students would fail.

> Faced with both passive resistance and active rebellion, teachers in the secondary modern had two choices. The first was to develop and maintain a system of coercive control: to turn secondary moderns [or schools where the majority of students went at age 11 who were not selected for academic or technical educations] into 'concentration camps'. The second was to make the curriculum more intrinsically interesting for the students and transform the examination system to reflect such a change (1991: 4).

I was impressed with both the personal and political praxis of action research. Thus, it seemed to me that cooperating with groups of teachers engaged in action research was the way to facilitate their learning to teach. Perhaps promoting action research could solve both the problems of knowledge and my personal investment in teachers' beliefs and practices.

Modeling after Elliot and others' non-feminist, but critical approaches, I learned that even *action research, situated apolitically at the intersection of knowledge and practice, was not enough.* Positioned as teachers in the hierarchy of educational responsibility, where abstracted knowledge of teaching is more valued than useful knowledge (see Labaree, 1993), preservice teachers, in particular, did not perceive themselves to be powerful enough to 'create and critique knowledge' that action research required. Even while they realized that external and generic research findings – abstracted from their specific persons and practices – were insufficient to successfully teach urban students, they did not experience the *agency* to construct alternative knowledges. So I taught them that they did have the agency, if they could only realize how it has been constrained by their positions as teachers-to-be in a women's profession (Laird, 1988). I had them read Glorianne Leck:

> Of central importance in the feminist critique is the examination of the primary assumption of patriarchy – that activities of male persons are of a higher value than activities of female persons. This precept is woven into the entire intellectual paradigm that is foundational to current schooling practice. For this reason the feminist critique orders a challenge to the epistemological roots of educational theory as we know it (1987: 343).

Reading this literature with the students, I began to see clearly that teachers, as a class, work under less-than-professional conditions with increasingly complex demands for academic, social and psychological expertise in demographically diverse settings. I found that teachers are asked to comply with a narrowly constructed set of ideological standards which shape their rights to know and evaluate their practices. These standards – stated as credentialing requirements, teacher and student evaluation measurements, curricular mandates, and even appropriate research paradigms for advanced degree work – are historically established by people outside of the classroom in positions of power (mainly men) without benefit of teachers' (mainly women) voices and opinions (see Apple, 1985). *I* was convinced, but the preservice teachers, positioned in a short-term effort within a larger program which ignored feminist theory and action research, were not.

Many other courageous efforts are underway to programmatically address action research, with varying degrees of feminist analyses (see Cochran-Smith, 1994, and Liston and Zeichner, 1991), yet they are similarly frustrated. Even if preservice students do come to realize the need to teach for social change, they seem to lack the experiences which transform that realization into their behaviors and beliefs. When they finally get into classrooms, they are overwhelmed by the conservative education system. Of the 58 teachers (with solid political consciousnesses) I followed from UC Berkeley into their classrooms after a graduate-level credential program, only 7 either did not conform to school practices or drop out. It's with those 7 that my work really began. It was only after they were experienced in the political system of school, that they could begin to ask the questions and take action to transform education for children of all races, classes and genders (see Hollingsworth, 1994a).

I concluded that teachers have to live such experiences to understand them. They cannot absorb others' experiences *a priori* before entering the classroom. Once there, when they realize the feminist positioning of teacher, they need us – as teacher educators – to educate them as classroom or action researchers, so that they can transform their own practices, if not their schools and communities.

Rethinking Teacher Education to Redirect the Conservative Nature of Schooling

What I'm leading to, as you can see, is that although using feminist pedagogy and action research in teacher education is a good idea, we may be directing our energies inefficiently when we focus our attention only on preservice education. Yet how can we influence change? For most of our universities, credential students are the economic foundation of schools of education. Masters programs across the states are under attack because of budget cuts. Further, most of our colleagues are unfamiliar with the literature on both feminist theory and action research. So how can we, as feminist educators, engage in action research to transform teacher education so that we have a mass of professionals teaching for change. I have three risky but potentially reformational ideas towards those ends. First, we might re-educate our non-feminist colleagues as well as our students to gain a larger base of support. Second, we can begin to conceptualize how we might apply various approaches to feminist praxis across the continuum from preservice to inservice education. Finally, we might write about our own challenges in teaching for change.

*Educate our Colleagues about the Need to Attend to Gender, Race,
Class, in Every Aspect of Program Design and Experience*

Recently I prepared a paper on The '"Problem" of Gender in Teacher Education'
(Hollingsworth, 1994b). I questioned why we, as a field, basically ignore the feminist arguments which could teach us how to better educate our primarily female student body.[2] I e-mailed my colleagues at MSU to help sort out the problem. Most had
not thought about it at all !!! Those who did aligned with one or more of six hypotheses on why we don't take gender into account in preservice teacher education:

Hypothesis A) 'It's women's work': The normative position of the teacher. As
noted above, Susan Laird (1988) suggests that one predominant view of teaching
is that it is a woman's profession and therefore the positioning of women close to
children is both normal (needing no analysis) and acceptable (needing no critique).
One of my female colleagues offered this provocative explanation:

> Teacher education entered the academy [wanting] to be seen as a body
> of professional knowledge ... it was a scientific knowledge – not what
> any mother or care-giver would know just from being alive and functional
> in the world ... If we explore either adult development or what gender
> adds to the knowledge base, we fear our status as a special knowledge
> will vanish. Looking at how gender has guided research, problem framing,
> questions that are rewarded if asked – this could be BAD news. We might
> find out that women's ways of thinking parallel the knowledge base and
> then we might have to discount any pieces of that knowledge base that
> have crept in because women were involved! If we find that there has been
> no parallel, that women have been excluded from the development of the
> knowledge base, that's worse. Then we'd have to ask whether teaching
> involves something valuable and as yet unexplored. If so, we're right back
> to the awful space where teaching and the minds of women are linked in
> some way. Where does that leave us as a profession? A science? If teach-
> ing is a decidedly female component, then any mother could teach – the
> slippery slope to avoid at all costs.

*Hypothesis B) 'We're busy with other things': The focus on subject matter and
generic 'reflection'.* The establishment of schooling around the structure of the
disciplines and research on teacher education being primarily subject-matter oriented doesn't leave much room for cross-disciplinary issues such as gender.

Hypothesis C) 'There's no need': The objective nature of educational research. The
dominant methodological paradigm which has been used to study teacher education has stressed objectivity and neutrality. Therefore, a good research design is
expected to account for personal differences, rendering gender non-significant. Since
the research doesn't address it, there's not need to bring it up in preservice teacher
education.

Hypothesis D) 'It's not in our best interests': A research focus away from girls and women. Although the balance is changing following the civil rights and women's movements of the 1970s and 1980s, most researchers in education are still white and male (AERA, 1989; Campbell, 1981). Further, funding opportunities for studies on women and girls in education have been historically limited. Not only has the US Department of Education failed to widely support specific programs, but gendered relationships are not a significant part of any study within major government funded research centers, such as the National Center for Research on Teacher Learning at Michigan State University.

Hypothesis E) 'I'm doing it, already!' The inclusiveness of multicultural education. Many researchers and teacher educators are including diversity and multicultural issues in their current work, and believe they are also attending to gender in that category.

Hypothesis F) 'It's taboo': Emotion and controversy. Attention to gender is also minimalized in teacher education because of its emotional, controversial and sensitive nature (Britzman, 1991; Miller, 1990). Some of my colleagues and many of my students suggest that research on girls as women is purposely ignored by both women and men, because men might find it threatening and offensive. Taking a different angle, one of my colleagues courageously told me about the unspoken practice of males teaching young adult females while struggling with (often uninvited) thoughts about sexual relations. He also lamented that there is no forum for addressing his confusion and concern over gendered roles and relations, because that part of his practice 'goes without the discipline that might be afforded by conversation'.

Additionally, because of the backlash against feminist critiques of society led by the popular press (Faludi, 1991) and the perceived radical nature of a unified feminist movement, scholars of teacher education are less likely to have read or engaged in conversation about feminist analyses of education. Yet ideally, feminism and education have much in common – both aim to empower all people and to provide opportunities for the full expression of human potential (Gaskell and McLaren, 1991). Further, the feminist literature has impacted so many areas of life in recent generations[3] that teacher educators can no longer afford to ignore it – no matter how uncomfortable we may be with gendered issues. Deborah Britzman tells us that the journey is not easy, but is do-able:

> the category of gender becomes even more controversial when we consider how gendered selves are tied to specific histories of social justice, civil rights, colonialism, economic struggles, social positions and to the emotional commitments that are built because of these histories. Exploring the contradictory meanings of gender requires a second and more complex look at how received discourse, stereotypes and social practices make gender a significant site of identity struggle . . . To become open to topics routinely considered 'taboo', 'political' or 'too controversial' for classrooms, educators must come to terms with the messiness of emotional commitments

as they work through their own fear that inviting controversies means not being in control (1993: 28).

It seems essential that our colleagues read and consider critical analyses of feminist literature.[4]

Draw upon the Various Feminist Stances to Educate Preservice and Inservice Teachers Differently

Here's where we might brainstorm and become proactive in rethinking teacher education in terms of feminist praxis. I'll take the first cut at it, although it is simply one of many possible suggestions. Borrowing from the stances Michelle Fine uses to situate feminist psychologists in the texts they produce – ventriloquist, voice and activism (1992), I would organize preservice and inservice teacher education along those lines, with teacher educators studying the effects of such pedagogy. I would spend a short time at the preservice level (let's say one year) teaching from the stances of ventriloquy and voices, and the bulk of our time (maybe two years) addressing the stance of activism at the inservice level. The program length (and course credit income) would remain about the same, but the focus and timing would shift.

Making Preservice Teachers Aware of the Ventriloquist Nature of Research on Teaching and Learning

The first step in encouraging teachers to consider feminist praxis is to help them become aware of the problematic nature of knowledge – and become critical of external experts (who often treat knowledge unproblematically) that they've come to see as authority across their lives. Beginning with a critique of mainstream psychology which flattens, neutralizes and objectifies personal and political influences upon its 'discoveries of natural laws of human behavior', Michelle Fine, for example, uncloaks researchers who 'pronounce truths while whiting out their own authority, so as to be unlocatable and irresponsible' (1992: 214). She reminds us of Donna Haraway's caricature of this epistemological fetish with detachment as a 'God trick ... that mode of seeing that pretends to offer a vision that is from everywhere and nowhere, equally and fully' (Haraway, 1988: 584). She quotes Lilian Robinson:

> Once upon a time, the introduction of writings of women and people of color were called politicizing the curriculum. Only *we* had politics (and its nasty little mate, ideology), whereas *they* had standards (Robinson, 1989: 76) ... Ventriloquy relies upon Haraway's God trick. The author tells Truth, has no gender, race, class, or stance. A condition of truth telling is anonymity, and so ventriloquy (Fine, 1992: 212).

Again, simply telling preservice teachers or having them read Haraway and Robinson won't convince those who have not experienced the God trick. Longitudinal action research across programs (not just in isolated classes), looking critically at all knowledges in practice (even those we revere) is required.

Educating Preservice Teachers to the Research on Voices

Becoming aware of the blanket silencing which comes with ventriloquy, many feminist researchers began to reject its neutral stance in research, and to articulate and amplify feminine voices. Beginning with Carol Gilligan's moral critique of human development, *In a Different Voice* (1982) and Sandra Harding's epistemological critique of knowledge (1986), both of which, in turn, drew upon such feminist object relations theorists as Nancy Chodorow (1978), these feminists have engaged in theorizing gendered subjectivity from a *difference* perspective. They argue that the socialized experiences of girls and women teach them to view identity, morality and even education differently from boys and men. In fact, it has been my experience (and the experience of many other feminist teachers and teacher educators) that preservice and inservice teachers initially began to internalize feminist critiques of knowledge and education through an awareness of difference. One of Magda Lewis' students reports:

> In history we never talked about what women did; in geography it was always what was important to men. The same in our English class, we hardly ever studied women authors. I won't even talk about math and science . . . I always felt that I didn't belong . . . Sometimes the boys would make jokes about girls doing science experiments. They always thought they were going to do it better and made me really nervous. Sometimes I didn't even try to do an experiment because I knew they would laugh if I got it wrong. Now I just deaden myself against it, so I don't hear it anymore. But I feel really alienated. My experience now is one of total silence. Sometimes I even wish I didn't know what I know (Lewis, 1992: 173).

Of course, we must be cautious when are teaching from a voices perspective. Through researching my teaching, I've learned that attending to difference feminism is not convincing to those who don't feel different – at the preservice or inservice level. Here's an example.

In a graduate course for teacher educators at UC Berkeley, I asked the teachers to read Lewis, Laird and others, then to analyze graduate curriculum, teacher exams, teacher evaluation protocols and teaching reward structures to get a sense of the values they represented and to recommend changes. Routinely, the values generically attributed to women – such as care, inclusion, compassion and multiple perspectives were underrepresented when compared to values generically attributed to men such as detachment, independence, consistency, principled knowledge and leadership. Even though the bias inherent in teacher education, evaluation and reward structures became clear in these studies, teacher educators were reluctant to conclude that gendered relations were problematic. One student wrote

> After reading Laird's article, I found I did not relate to it at all, in terms of the theses that underlie the whole thing – like that [teaching] is demeaning because it's woman's work. I just didn't resonate with that at all. I guess as a teacher, I never thought of myself as a woman. I thought of myself as a human being who had a real interest in kids and learning. I always felt respected and treated very professionally by men and women. The only [feminist issue] I can connect to is the pay difference. I don't think differential pay for 'men's jobs' and 'women's jobs' is right at all.

Without resonating experiences, exposure to information about cultural feminism does not appear to lead to action.

The best way I've found for dealing with such cases is to begin classes auto-biographically, so that our various positions on feminist theory can be situated in our life stories; then explain how and why I see critical feminist pedagogy as a means to uncover and critique our own and others' theories; make the course evaluation problematic; and let go of class outcomes. I have to keep reminding myself that whether students adopt my current stance on feminist theory or not is *not* the goal of feminist pedagogy – it is to open us all up (even me) to new ways of seeing the familiar and challenging injustices.

Some of the methods I use in my classes to make space for everyone's voice – such as extended conversation where I am a participant as well as a facilitator – are reminiscent of Belenky, Clinchy, Goldberger and Tarule's (1986) description of 'connected' classrooms. Janice Raymond and others are critical of the 'equitable voice' approach. Raymond's book on female friendships suggests that such non-hierarchical practices can prevent women from discovering and using their own strength, and also encourage them to endeavor to achieve their goals through the exercise of indirect power or even manipulation within a group. 'No real power emerges from a group that silences its best and brightest voices for a false sense of group equality. And certainly no strong friendships can be formed among women who have no power of being' (1986: 197).

Further, the critiques raised in assessing the 'voices' category of feminist research argue against 'swimming in the murky waters of essentialism' (Stanley, 1990: 14). Liz Stanley continues (with my emphasis):

> I am referring to a specifically feminist ontology, not an ontology attached to the category '(all) women'. *I make no claims that 'women' will share this state of being; patently, most do not* . . . That it is the experience of and acting against perceived oppression that gives rise to a distinctive feminist ontology; and it is the analytic exploration of the parameters of this in the research process that gives expression to a distinctive feminist ontology . . . My concern is with the conditions under which some classes of people, but not others, are treated as, or come to feel they are treated

as, 'other'; and consequently construct . . . a distinctively sociological epistemology. There is also nothing about the acknowledgment of 'difference'
that precludes discussion, debate and a mutual learning process (Stanley,
1990: 14–15. See also Britzman, 1992 for another excellent critique of
gendered essence.)

And, as Fine reminds us about feminist scholarship:

> this critique of voices is by no means advanced to deny the legitimacy of
> rich interview material or other forms of qualitative data. To the contrary,
> it is meant for us to worry collectively that when voices – as isolated and
> innocent moments of experience – organize our research texts there is a
> subtle slide toward romantic, uncritical, and uneven handling and a stable
> refusal by researchers to explicate our own stances and relations to these
> voices (Fine, 1992: 219).

These cautions might guide our pedagogy in preservice teacher education.

Working with Inservice Teachers from a Perspective of Activist Feminist Research or Praxis

A third stance toward theories and projects of feminist research takes into consideration the critiques of both the ventriloquy and voices research, and thus raises new
questions. One is the nature of our own research and pedagogical methodologies.
How can we position ourselves as researchers committed to critical, self-conscious
and participatory work dedicated to change, engaged with but still respectfully separate from those with whom we collaborate and teach? *How can we not only know
differently from how we were educated, but continue to know differently? How can
we teach so that our students can teach us?* This is tough stuff – for us as well as
for our students. Therefore, I am suggesting that we employ this level of inquiry
into activist feminist praxis with inservice teachers.

For Michelle Fine (1992) and Patti Lather (1991) images of activist feminist
scholarship share three distinctions:

> First, the author is explicit about the space in which she stands politically
> and theoretically – even as her stances are multiple, shifting, and mobile.
> Second, the text displays critical analyses of current social arrangements
> and their ideological frames. And, third, the narrative reveals and invents
> disruptive images of what could be (Fine, 1992: 221).

Feminist activist research consciously seeks to break up social silences to make
spaces for fracturing the very ideologies that justify power inequities – *even feminist ideologies*. It takes on a form of praxis from critical theory – and more. In accounting for the conditions of its own production, it becomes 'unalienated knowledge'

(Stanley, 1990: 13). 'In such work, researchers *pry open social mythologies that others are committed to sealing*' (Fine, 1992: 221, emphasis mine). Contradictory loyalties are exposed. Gender is no longer a unifying concept, nor is collaborative action research; nor is the abstract knowledge; nor is it the reward of breaking the silences for all participants.

Critical legal scholar Regina Austin (1989) problematizes the cost of breaking the legal silence surrounding African-American women's bodies within white men's law. Though it is hard for many of us to accept the risks which come from adopting such a position, for example, the professional vulnerability it occasions, particularly since such positions are easily dismissed by less marginalized academics, some of us might resonate to her words:

> When was the last time someone told you that your way of approaching problems . . . was all wrong? You are too angry, too emotional, too sub-jective, too pessimistic, too political, too anecdotal and too instinctive? How can I legitimate my way of thinking? I know that I am not just flying off the handle, seeing imaginary insults and problems where there are none. I am not a witch solely by nature, but by circumstance, choice, [and gendered label] as well. I suspect that what my critics really want to say is that I am being too self consciously black (brown, yellow, red) and/or female to suit their tastes and should 'lighten up' because I am making them feel very uncomfortable, and that is not nice. And I want them to think that I am nice, don't I? (Fine, 1992: 221–2).

Magda Lewis reminds us of one other caution for this work, a caution which is hard to find in non-feminist critical theory.

> We cannot expect that students will readily appropriate a political stance that is truly counter-hegemonic, unless we also acknowledge the ways in which our feminist practice/politics creates, rather than ameliorates, a feel-ing of threat: the threat of having to struggle within unequal power rela-tions; the threat of psychological/social/sexual, as well as economic and political marginality; the threat of retributive violence – threats lived in concrete embodied ways (Lewis, 1992: 187).

I've recently helped design a master's program in curriculum and teaching at MSU based not only on these guidelines, but a belief in an inquiry approach to continuing teacher education, a commitment to tackling gendered relations from the perspective of postmodern feminists and others who think similarly, and some research on my own preparation of teacher educators at UC Berkeley. We begin the first course by deconstructing the notions of woman, man, teacher, knowledge, and research. We learn to see those concepts differently. We explore our own biogra-phies to determine the narrative construction and reconstructions of our own values, preferred paradigms, teaching and learning styles, identities relative but not uniformly connected to gendered notions of values, or learning and teaching paradigms. We engage in action research through questions that are personally meaningful *both to our lives and our practices*. In the course we come to see that, even though we have participated in similar education programs and were taught a similar truth or know-ledge base, that our own experiences and ways of making sense of the world led us to construct or give meaning to that truth in different ways – that we continue to reconstruct our knowledge given our shifting positions across personal histories. This approach does appear to lead to action. We begin to see ourselves as teachers and our students as learners in different ways, then to act on those understandings. One teacher educator at UC Berkeley had this to say about the course two years after it had ended:

> To have the opportunity to come together with others whose life work is to enhance the development of teachers and engage in the construction of knowledge was transforming and emancipatory. Letting go of my concep-tions of the 'official' occupational role of teacher educator, I was able to move from a notion of myself as intermediary between the knowledge base and the novice teacher to an appreciation for the power of biography and the function of the self in teaching and learning to teach . . . (see Gallagher, 1992).

Programs which look critically at gendered and positional relations of teaching and learning seem to hold much promise for developing knowing, critical, action-oriented, reflective teachers of all students.

Write about What We're Learning as Feminist Teacher Educators

We need more literature, more voices, more energy and more challenges to turn the tide of the increasingly conservative nature of education. Interest in feminist schol-arship is growing in many other disciplines outside of education. I predict that there will soon be a growing interest in feminist analyses of education. Yet, of course (I can speak from personal experience), such authorship is risky.

Michelle Fine concludes her analysis of using activist research to reframe fem-inist psychology by asking us to take more risks in our research. To state up front and throughout our research projects that we are speaking with 'partial knowledges'. To take acknowledged, contradictory, argumentative, and shifting positions in re-search 'positioned explicitly with questions and not answers; as mobile and multiple, not static and singular; within spaces of rich surprise, not predetermined "forced choices"; surrounded by critical conversation, never alone' (Fine, 1992: 230). To do so, we have even to expose our own vulnerabilities – and challenge our supporters.

Endnote

How has my discovery of feminist readings of action research affected my current sense of self – as teacher educator, academic, action researcher and critical friend?

I no longer need to seek authoritative permission to construct and critique the possible in educational reform.[5] I still need to learn more about respectful collaborative relations – recognizing when others are not ready or willing to take the risks I do. I am often regarded as too impatient and too impassioned. Worse, I am more often ignored. Yet, I believe in the project. I am inspired by a quotation from Susan B. Anthony which hangs above my desk:

~~Cautious, careful people, always casting about to preserve their reputation and social standing, never can bring about a reform.

~~Those who are really in earnest must be willing to be anything or nothing in the world's estimation, and publicly and privately in season and out, avow their sympathies with despised and persecuted ideas and their advocates and bear the consequences.

I have witnessed radical changes take place in teachers' self-descriptions, their urban school classrooms, schools, and districts. I've seen teachers devise new pedagogies for bringing their children's lives into the classroom and curriculum. I have seen school boards and state policies change because of feminist action research.

And I am (today) in the company of good and critical friends. I find new friends who hear me, and then invite me into their spaces to continue the conversation. The price for this work, though, also involves estrangement and strange reconnections. The teachers with whom I work regularly outgrow me in their praxis and move on. Karen Teel won a Spencer Fellowship for teacher research. Mary Dybdahl took a teacher–leadership position in the long-lasting strike for collective voice in her school district. Anthony Cody has written critiques of popular (and expensive) inservice programs which don't apply his understanding of feminist praxis in his urban middle school. Jo Anna Mulhauser has created a space as an adjunct in a community college to teach and write and speak about the gendered nature of early childhood education. I'm heading for Asia to continue longitudinal work on activist feminist research with teachers in social studies. Our professional lives have expanded in different directions – as they should. Sometimes I miss the conversations, though, when we were all on the same page.

Someone recently asked me, 'If these feminist action research projects succeed, what will teacher educators do?' I take comfort in the closing of Michelle Fine and Pat Macpherson's story of their communal and contradictory explication of feminist experience with a group of teenagers. The authors had anticipated that their adolescent guests would represent an after picture which depicts all the gains of the women's movement. The teenagers failed to live up to their fantasies. Their embodied (and heard) stories shattered the hoped for ideological framing of the research dinners.

After our last dinner, stuffed and giggly, tired but still wanting just one more round of conversation, we – Pat and Michelle – realized that the four young women were getting ready to drive away. Together and without us

...We turned to each other, realizing that even our abandonment was metaphoric and political. These four young women were weaving the next generation of feminist politics, which meant, in part, leaving us. We comforted ourselves by recognizing that our conversations had perhaps enabled this work (Fine and Macpherson, 1992: 202).

I invite you to share in the potential of your own contributions and engage with me in conversation about the possibilities for the intersection of feminist theory and action research, and the resultant opportunities for societal, as well as educational change.

Notes

1 I suspect that Dewey must have been influenced by the first wave of feminism at the turn of the century, although I don't know anyone who has written about that.
2 I chose gender, not in isolation of other life positions such as race and class, but because that is the characteristic most likely to be ignored in preservice education.
3 See the National Women's Studies Association 16th Annual Conference program, 1994, for a list of those contributions; see also Britzman, 1992, and Liston and Zeichner, 1991, for a discussion of those contributions to teacher education.
4 This part of the manuscript was previously published, as 'The problem of gender in teacher education', in 1995 in the *Mid-western Educational Research*, **8**(2), pp. 3–12.
5 A colleague of mine, Diane Holt-Reynolds, told me at a recent American Educational Research Association meeting that I acted as though I were 'entitled' to knowledge.

References

AMERICAN EDUCATIONAL RESEARCH ASSOCIATION (AERA) (1989) 'Annual Report, 1988–89', *Educational Researcher*, **18**(6), p. 20.
APPLE, M.W. (1985) 'Teaching and "women's work": A comparative historical and ideological analysis', *Teachers College Record*, **86**(3), pp. 461–81.
ARNOT, M. (1993) 'A crisis in patriarchy? British feminist educational politics and state regulation of gender', in ARNOT, M. and WEILER, K. (Eds) *Feminism and Social Justice in Education*, London: Falmer Press, pp. 186–209.
AUSTIN, R. (1989) 'Sapphire bound!', *Wisconsin Law Review*, **3**, pp. 539–78. (Cited in REINHARZ, S. (1992) *Feminist Methods in Social Research*, pp. 221–2).
BRITZMAN, D. (1992) 'Decentering discourses in teacher education: Or the unleashing of unpopular things', in WEILER, K. and MITCHELL, C. (Eds) *What Schools Can Do: Critical Pedagogy and Practice*, Albany, NY, State University of New York Press, pp. 151–76.
BELENKY, M.F., CLINCHY, B.M., GOLDBERGER, N.R. and TARULE, J.M. (1986) *Women's Ways of Knowing: The Development of Self, Voice and Mind*, New York, Basic Books, Inc.
BLOOM, B.S. (1964) *Stability and Change in Human Characteristics*, New York, Wiley.
BOURDIEU, P. (1977) 'Cultural reproduction and social reproduction', in HALSEY, H. and KARABEL, J. (Eds) *Power and Ideology in Education*, New York, Oxford University Press, pp. 487–551.

BRITZMAN, D.P. (1993) 'Beyond rolling models: Gender and multicultural education', in BIKLIN, S.K. and POLLARD, D. (Eds) *Gender and Education* (Ninety-second Yearbook of the National Society for the Study of Education), Chicago, IL, University of Chicago Press.

BRITZMAN, D. (1991) *Practice Makes Practice: A Critical Study of Learning to Teach*, Albany, NY, State University of New York Press.

BUTLER, J. (1990) *Gender Trouble: Feminism and the Subversion of Identity*, New York, Routledge.

CAMPBELL, P.B. (1981) *The Impact of Societal Biases on Research*, Washington, DC, National Institute of Education.

CHERRYHOLMES, C.H. (1988) *Power and Criticism*, New York, Teachers College Press.

CHODOROW, N. (1978) *The Reproduction of Mothering*, Berkeley, CA, The University of California Press.

COCHRAN-SMITH, M. (1994) 'Teacher research and teacher education', in HOLLINGSWORTH, S. and SOCKETT, H. (Eds) *Teacher Research and Teacher Education Reform*, (Yearbook of the National Society for the Study of Education), Chicago, IL, University of Chicago Press.

ELLIOTT, J. (1991) *Action Research for Educational Change*, Buckingham, Open University Press.

ELLSWORTH, E. (1989) 'Why doesn't this feel empowering? Working through the repressive myths of critical pedagogy', *Harvard Educational Review*, **59**(3), pp. 297–324.

FALUDI, S. (1991) *Backlash: The Undeclared War Against American Women*, New York, Doubleday.

FINE, M. (1992) *Disruptive Voices: The Possibilities of Feminist Research*, Ann Arbor, MI, The University of Michigan Press.

FINE, M. and MACPHERSON, P. (1992) 'Over dinner: Feminism and adolescent female bodies', in FINE, M. (Ed) *Disruptive Voices: The Possibilities of Feminist Research*, Ann Arbor, MI, The University of Michigan Press.

FOUCAULT, M. (1980) *Power/knowledge*, New York, Pantheon.

FREIRE, P. (1988) *Pedagogy of the Oppressed*, New York, Continuum.

GALLAGHER, P. (1992, April) 'Toward a habit of inquiry: Teacher questions and the "difficulty of seeing"', Paper presented at the Annual Meeting of the American Educational Research Association.

GASKSELL, J. and McLAREN, A. (1991) *Women and Education*, 2nd Ed, Calgary, Alberta, Canada, Detselig Enterprises, Ltd.

GILLIGAN, C. (1982) *In a Different Voice: Psychological Theory and Women's Development*, Cambridge, MA, Harvard University Press.

GORE, J. (1992) *The Struggle for Pedagogies*, New York, Routledge.

HARDING, S. (1986) *The Science Question in Feminism*, Ithaca, NY, Cornell University Press.

HARAWAY, D. (1988) 'Situated knowledges: The science question in feminism and the privilege of partial perspective', *Feminist Studies*, (**14**), pp. 575–99.

HOLLINGSWORTH, S. (1989) 'Prior beliefs and cognitive change in learning to teach', *American Educational Research Journal*, **26**(2), pp. 160–89.

HOLLINGSWORTH, S. (October, 1994b) 'The problem of gender in teacher education', Invited address at the Midwestern American Educational Research Association, Chicago.

HOLLINGSWORTH, S. (1994a) *Teacher Research and Urban Literacy Education: Lessons and Conversations in a Feminist Key*, New York, Teachers College Press.

HOOKS, B. (1990) *Yearning: Race, Gender and Cultural Politics*, Boston, MA, South End Press.

LABAREE, D.F. (November, 1993) 'The lowly status of teacher education in the United States: The impact of markets and the implications for reform', Paper prepared for the Rutgers Invitational Symposium on Education (RISE) conference on 'Promise and Challenge in Teacher Education: An International Perspective'.

LAIRD, S. (1988) 'Reforming "women's true profession": A case for "feminist pedagogy" in teacher education', *Harvard Educational Review*, **58**(4), pp. 449–63.

LATHER, P. (1991) *Getting Smart: Feminist Research and Pedagogy With/in the Postmodern*, New York, Routledge.

LECK, G.M. (1987) 'Review article – Feminist pedagogy, liberation theory, and the traditional schooling paradigm', *Educational Theory*, **37**(3), pp. 343–55.

LEWIS, M. (1992) 'Interrupting patriarchy: Politics, resistance and transformation in the feminist classroom', in LUKE, C. and GORE, J. (Eds) *Feminisms and Critical Pedagogy*, New York, Routledge, pp. 167–91.

LISTON, D.P. and ZEICHNER, K.M. (1991) *Teacher Education and the Social Conditions of Schooling*, New York, Routledge.

MCKERNAN, J. (1991) *Curriculum Action Research: A Handbook of Methods and Resources for the Reflective Practitioner*, New York, St. Martin's Press.

MILLER, J. (1990) *Creating Spaces and Finding Voices: Teachers Collaborating for Empowerment*, Albany, NY, State University of New York Press.

ORNER, M. (1992) 'Interrupting the calls for student voice in "liberatory" education: A feminist poststructuralist perspective', in LUKE, C. and GORE, J. (Eds) *Feminisms and Critical Pedagogy*, New York, Routledge, pp. 74–89.

RAYMOND, J. (1986) *A Passion for Friends: Toward a Philosophy of Female Affection*, Boston, MA, Beacon Press. (Cited in LUKE and GORE (1992) p. 162).

REINHARZ, S. (1992) *Feminist Methods in Social Research*, New York, Oxford University Press.

ROBINSON, L. (1989) 'What culture should mean', *The Nation*, September, pp. 319–21.

SCHON, D.A. (1982) *The Reflective Practitioner*, New York, Basic Books.

SHULMAN, L.S. (1987) 'Knowledge and teaching; Foundations of the new reform', *Harvard Educational Review*, **57**(1), pp. 1–22.

SCHWAB, J.J. (1972) 'The practical: A language for curriculum', in PURPEL, D.E. and BELANDER, M. (Eds) *Curriculum and the Cultural Revolution*, Berkeley, CA, McCutchan, pp. 72–9.

SOMEKH, B. (Spring, 1993) 'Thinking about CARN in March, 1993', *CARN Newsletter*, **1**, Bournemouth, Bourne Press.

SMITH, D. (1987) *The Everyday World as Problematic: A Feminist Sociology*, Boston, MA, Northeastern University Press.

STANLEY, L. (1990) *Feminist Praxis: Research, Theory and Epistemology in Feminist Sociology*, New York, Routledge.

STENHOUSE, L. (1975) *An Introduction to Curriculum Research and Development*, London, Heinemann.

TYLER, R.W. (1949) *Basic Principles of Curriculum and Instruction*, Chicago, IL, University of Chicago Press.

WALKERDINE, V. (1986) 'Progressive pedagogy and political struggle', *Screen*, **27**(5), pp. 54–60.

Part III

New Politics, New Policy

My hope is that our lives will declare
this meeting
open.
(June Jordan, *Metarhetoric*, 1976)
What happens in policy arenas, programs and political maneuvering when women have power, when women's concerns begin to be addressed, when women redefine how knowledge is constructed and what knowledge is valuable? Counternarratives, subaltern politics, are noticed, named, given credence and legitimacy and democracy becomes a word that includes something hopeful for women.

Part III's chapters offer possibilities of expanded agendas, paradigms, feminist politics, although each is a story of struggle, with anticipated and powerful resistance. The early simplistic maneuvers to create inclusive curricula included drawing dresses and shading the skin on illustrations of scientists in textbooks. Chapter 10, A Model for Gender-inclusive Science . . . takes a more theoretical stance and unmasks the western masculinist bias in science, revealing the deep social, historical and political context, including how the ideology of modern science gave men 'a new basis for masculine self-esteem and male prowess' (Keller, 1985: 64) while also sanitizing and neutralizing. In this chapter, Parker shows how a feminist science would provide new tools of inquiry and connection.

Two chapters move from the politics of knowledge back to the formal arenas of politics and policy, providing a glimpse at new politics, new policy. Studies of policy formulation sometimes track how an issue gets on the agenda and how it is defined. So, when sexual harassment is named, put on the formal policy agenda for a school board, how well can a traditional school policy system formulate policy that will address what women know and live? Will women's groups' participation and women's testimony suffice to bend policies and practices? Laible's Critique of the Ideal of Community (Chapter 11) sets a feminist and critical standard, demonstrating what can and cannot be attained through traditional political power structures. In Chapter 12, Mawhinney's Canadian teachers constructed a devilishly unladylike sense of their own worth, power and rights, taking charge of their own destinies by creating a women's teachers' union and defending that control in spite of challenges from the men's union and from the court system. The chapter demonstrates that attaining the power, money, votes, memberships and persevering in the political system may not be enough. For, as MacKinnon demonstrates, the current system is arranged to maintain patriarchy. Speaking of the need for a new jurisprudence, MacKinnon cautioned:

> Law that does not dominate life is as difficult to envision as a society in which men do not dominate women . . . To the extent feminist law embodies women's point of view, it will be said that its law is not neutral. But existing law is not neutral. It will be said that it undermines the legitimacy of the legal system. But the legitimacy of existing law is based on force at women's expense. Women have never consented to its rule – suggesting that the system's legitimacy needs repair that women are in a position to provide. It will be said that feminist law is special pleading for a particular group and one *cannot* start that – or where will it end? But existing law is already special pleading for a particular group, where it has ended. The question is not where will it stop, but whether it will start for any group but the dominant one (MacKinnon, 1989: 249).

The Canadian case illustrates MacKinnon's point. The master's tools retain regulative and judicial power, tearing down new constructions. Even policies and political strategies with clout, money, theory, methodologies, astute political maneuvers and energetic support groups will be challenged by those whose advantage is threatened. As Kuhn observed: 'Political revolutions aim to change political institutions in ways that those institutions themselves prohibit' (1970: 93).

Finally, Chapter 13, by Wynand Wilson, provides the method for analyzing the efficacy of girl-friendly policies. Such policies should have cultural and material outcomes ranging from personal dignity to workplace equality.

References

JORDAN, J. (1976) 'Metarhetoric', reprinted in RICH, A. (1979) *On Lies, Secrets, and Silence*, New York, NY, W.W. Norton.

KELLER, E.F. (1985) *Reflections on Gender and Science*, New Haven, Yale University Press.

KUHN, T.S. (1970) *The Structure of Scientific Revolutions*, (2nd edn), Chicago, University of Chicago Press.

MACKINNON, C.A. (1989) *Toward a Feminist Theory of the State*, Cambridge, MA, Harvard University Press.

Chapter 10

A Model for Gender-inclusive School Science: Lessons from Feminist Scholarship

Lesley H. Parker

Introduction

In many parts of the world, programs have been introduced to encourage girls and women into science, but the numbers participating, particularly in the physical sciences and in science-related careers, are still small. This raises the question of whether there is a better way for educationists to rethink the interaction of gender and science. In this chapter I suggest that the work of feminist scholars, particularly in relation to the image of science, provides an appropriate starting point for such rethinking.

In 1985, Alison Kelly argued that there are four ways in which schools contribute to the construction of a masculine image of science: first, disproportionately large numbers of males study, teach, and are identified as practitioners of science; second, the presentation and packaging of curriculum materials display a masculine bias; third, classroom interactions follow male-oriented patterns; and, fourth, the type of thinking commonly labeled scientific embodies a Western masculinist world view (1985: 133). In this chapter I focus on the fourth dimension of Kelly's (1985) schema. My purpose is to develop, from the work of scholars who are part of the postmodernist feminist critique of science, a theoretical view of what a more gender-inclusive school science might look like. Following an initial overview of the major strands within this critique, I focus specifically on the strand concerned with the definition of science. I heed the warning of Young that such definitions should not be taken as given, for 'what "does" and "does not" count as science depends on the social meaning given to science, which will vary not only historically and cross-culturally but within societies and situationally' (1971: 21).

My critique of the definition of science is based on the work of Keller (1978, 1982, 1983, 1985, 1989) and the contributions of other postmodernist feminists in relation to specific aspects of Keller's work. It leads into a discussion of the place of the dualisms that are ubiquitous in western philosophical traditions. Arguing that these dualisms need to be interpreted as complementary rather than oppositional, I present a summary image of gender-inclusive science distilled from my analysis. In the concluding section of the chapter I then translate this image into a picture of a gender-inclusive school science curriculum.

The Feminist Critique of Science

Mapping the Territory

Scholars focusing on science and gender have come from many different disciplines and have taken many different approaches to their studies. Within this highly diverse context, at least three feminist scholars (S. Harding, 1986; Rosser, 1989; Schiebinger, 1987) have attempted to map the various strands within the literature. Their analyses have shown that, generally, studies fall into one of four major categories. One of these categories, concerned with the institutionalized, structural barriers to women's participation in science, has been explored, from the perspective of school education, by Parker, Rennie and Harding (1995). In this chapter, I explore the other three categories – categories which have produced research that has considerable potential to inform a theoretical definition of gender-inclusive science.

The 'her-story' of science. The first category embraces what is sometimes called the 'her-story' of science, as distinct from what O'Brien (1981) has termed 'male-stream' history. Typified by the work of Margaret Rossiter (1982), it documents the previously obscured, undervalued and devalued contribution of women to science. It highlights the gendered nature of knowledge, in that women's activities and discoveries in areas such as horticulture and chemistry were not defined as science, although men engaging in similar kinds of activities (from a less practical or domestic point of view), were accepted as scientists. It points to the need, not only for a broader definition of 'science', but also for a recognition of the value system centered on the concept of gender. It draws attention also to the work of the women scientists who have been successful in traditional science, and of the many whom Rosser (1989: 4) called the 'lost women of science', and it makes the names and contributions of all of these women accessible.

'Scientific' definitions of women. In the second category are critiques of the studies of *scientific* definitions of women's nature, studies that emphasize differences between men and women, and studies that trace these differences to immutable biological differences. Such studies date back at least to Aristotle (who argued that women's weaker nature justified their inferior social status), but they also encompass the more recent work of the craniologists, who, as shown by Gould (1981), linked an alleged male intellectual superiority to males' heavier brains, and the arguments of the social Darwinists, who alleged that woman was man whose evolution had been arrested in a primitive stage (Morgan, 1972). There have also been, as indicated by Sayers (1982) in her critical review of the area, many who either argued

or assumed that women's intellectual gains could only be made at great cost to their reproductive capacities, and many others who sought to provide scientific proof of women's inferior nature through research on hormones or on brain lateralization.

Several critiques of these 'uses and abuses of biology', as Sandra Harding (1986: 21) has called them, demonstrate the value-laden nature of the research. Feminists from many different backgrounds, for example the neurophysiologist Bleier (1984); the biologists Birke (1986a, 1986b); Hubbard and Lowe (1979); and Lewontin, Rose and Kamin (1984); the mathematical biologist Keller (1985); and the historians of science Fee (1976) and Haraway (1981) have been joined in 'lifting the argument about sex differences out of the realm of "pure" science and placing it within its social context' (Schiebinger, 1987: 327). Together these researchers have been able to demonstrate the lack of validity of assumptions about the value neutrality of science, as well as the lack of validity of arguments that used anatomical differences between the male and the female body to justify social and educational agendas, agendas which ensured that males retained privileged access to scientific knowledge and the practice of science.

The definition of science. A third strand of research addresses the definition of science and the ways in which the definitions of 'science' and 'not science', in terms of both content and methodology, operate to exclude women from science. It incorporates Schiebinger's (1987: 328) discussion of 'gender distortions in science', and Rosser's (1989: 8–10) two categories of 'feminine science' and 'feminist theory of science'. It also incorporates Sandra Harding's (1986: 23–4) discussion of whether the design and interpretation of research can be value-neutral, whether gender politics shapes the cognitive form and content of scientific theories, and whether beliefs about 'what we honor as (scientific) knowledge' can be understood satisfactorily through feminist epistemologies. Although a number of different approaches have been taken in this category of work, that of Keller (1985) is a particularly fruitful source for the development of a theoretical definition of gender-inclusive science.

Keller: The Reclamation of Science

In some of her many 'reflections on gender and science', Keller (1978, 1982, 1983, 1985, 1989) sought to explore the conjunction between science and masculinity and the disjunction between science and femininity. In an elaborate historical, philosophical and psychoanalytical analysis, she traced systematically the origins of androcentrism in science back to the very beginnings of western knowledge. She identified, in her historical analysis, three critical periods in the evolution of contemporary scientific thought and practice, namely, Platonic thought, Baconian science and the 'new' scientific thought prevailing around the time of the founding of the Royal Society. She demonstrated that the model of gender relations and the culturally bound definitions of valuable knowledge prevailing during each of these periods ensured the exclusion of females from the evolving definition of science.

Keller argued that the ideology of modern science gives men 'a new basis for masculine self-esteem and male prowess' (1985: 64). In addition, she saw science as both responding to and providing crucial support for the polarization of gender required by industrial capitalism. She commented that:

> [i]n sympathy with, and even in response to, the growing divisions between male and female, public and private, work and home, modern science opted for an even greater polarization of mind and nature, reason and feeling, objective and subjective; in parallel with the gradual desexualization of women, it offered a deanimated, desanctified, and increasingly mechanized conception of nature (Keller, 1985: 63).

In the third, psychoanalytical section of her analysis, Keller, like Chodorow (1978), employed object relations theory to argue that an association between objectivity and masculinity was produced through a process which resulted in girls having a sense of self as connected to the world, and boys having a sense of self as separate from the world. She forged the links between science and masculinity by highlighting this connection between masculinity and objectivity, and the consequent self-selection of scientists as people who gain emotional satisfaction from their belief that they are objective, neutral and able to stand back, as it were, from their subjects.

Keller also explored the relationships amongst objectivity, power and domination. She challenged the familiar, relatively static, unilateral definitions of autonomy and objectivity, and put forward a model of both of these concepts which was dynamic and interactive, taking account of rather than neglecting a human being's connection to other human beings. The implications of her model for science are far-reaching. What emerges is a picture of science premised not on the desire to dominate, to master and to exercise power over nature, but on interaction with and internalization of the object of enquiry. Keller noted, too, that such a picture, while not entirely legitimated by the rhetoric of science, is not totally foreign to the practice of science. Her reference to Goodfield's account of Anna Brito's research on tumors provides an excellent example of such an approach: 'If you really want to understand a tumor, you've got to *be* a tumor' (Goodfield, 1981: 213, quoted in Keller, 1985: 125). Her detailed and sensitive documentation of Barbara McClintock's approach to research, based on 'a feeling for the organism' (Keller, 1983), provides an even better example.

In her work on McClintock, Keller presented an account of the practice of 'different' science, and of the contribution to scientific knowledge made by this kind of practice. She touched eloquently on the dilemma, even identity crisis, that confronts women endeavoring to practice science within the currently dominant paradigm. Further, she raised the question of the cost to a woman, in personal identity terms, of trying to 'share masculine pleasure in mastering a nature cast in the image of woman as passive, inert and blind' (1985: 174). She demonstrated how McClintock's solution (because she wanted to be a scientist, not because she was a woman) lay essentially in her interactive, non-hierarchical definition of the relationship between subject and object. Keller also expanded on the scientific/ philosophical aspects of her argument, using other cameos drawn from the annals of scientific research, in particular from her own experience as a practicing scientist and philosopher of science. Through these examples, she explored the possibilities for paradigmatic change within science, with special emphasis on the impetus for any such changes which do appear to have taken place.

Four points of major importance to this chapter emerge from Keller's analysis. The first throws new light, from a feminist perspective, on some of Young's (1971) statements about the social definition of science. In Keller's terms, gender ideology is manifested in the selection, by scientists, of what counts as science, and the recognition, by both scientists and non-scientists, of who counts as a scientist. The second and third points concern the limits and possibilities of change to the dominant paradigm of science. As Keller saw it, despite science's overall imperviousness to change, change does take place, even if always in the face of what she called, in terms reminiscent of Kuhn (1970), 'a web of internal resistance' (1985: 136). Further, she emphasized that if a changed or different science is to be accepted, it must emerge from within science by growth and not by discontinuity. The fourth point concerns the nature of this changed or different science. Keller saw it as predicated on the transcendence of the bias that she had identified in science, and the reclamation of science as a human instead of a masculine activity. Pluralism and eclecticism were fundamental to her vision of a scientific paradigm that 'allows for the productive survival of diverse conceptions of mind and nature, and of correspondingly diverse strategies' (1985: 178).

Other Feminist Researchers: Keller Reinterpreted

For the purpose of generating a theoretical perspective on gender-inclusive science, it is helpful to consider Keller's work in the context of that of other feminists in this area. The work of many of these scholars has been informed by the research of Gilligan (1982), who suggested that women speak 'in a different voice' from men (and thus from the discourse of science) and by the research of Belenky, Clinchy, Goldberger and Tarule (1986), who posited that there are 'women's ways of knowing' that are quite distinct from those of men. However, while there appears to be agreement amongst all of these scholars that there are gendered ways of relating to knowledge and that the current definition of science is masculinist and exclusive, there are markedly different interpretations regarding whether this is a phenomenon or a problem. As shown in the following discussion, those who see it as a problem tend to place it in the context of rival paradigms and of irresolvable conflict and competition, a position that would not appear to augur well for effective social or educational change. Those like Keller, however, who see it as a phenomenon, are more likely to recommend the acknowledgment and constructive accommodation of this diversity, and the ultimate enrichment of science through diversity, a position that seems likely to hold much more promise for effective social and educational change.

Gynocentric Science – A Competing Paradigm?

As indicated above, Keller's solution to the androcentrism of science was to reconceptualize science so that it accommodates alternative ways of viewing and studying the natural world. Of the feminists who are not in agreement with this solution, some, such as Ginzberg (1989), have developed the Kuhnian principle of competing paradigms, making contrasts between traditional androcentric science and what they call 'gynocentric' science. Ginzberg (1989) picked up the Kuhnian proposition that 'the proponents of competing paradigms practice their trades in different worlds' (Kuhn, 1970: 150). Like Keller, Ginzberg argued that gynocentric science, such as midwifery, has always existed alongside androcentric science, such as obstetrics. She argued also that, again like Kuhn's competing paradigms, these two ways of practicing the science and craft of childbirth 'disagree not only about the list of problems to be resolved, but also about the theories, methodologies, and criteria for success that will be used to assess the results achieved' (Ginzberg, 1989: 79).

In a further analogy to Kuhn's description of the resistance with which the dominant paradigm meets a competing paradigm, Ginzberg argued also that gynocentric science, has been at best overlooked because it was defined as everyday women's work and at worst suppressed and discredited, sometimes violently, because of alleged associations with superstition or even evil. Overall, Ginzberg remained ambivalent, however. On the one hand she saw a more gynocentric definition of science as one way to make the world 'better for everybody' (Kuhn, 1970: 82) but on the other she was resistant to any association at all with the 'baggage' of traditional science.

Challenging the Dominant Paradigm: Can Others 'Do' Science?

Much of the feminist critique of science has dwelt on the exclusive, self-perpetuating, self-reflexive nature of those who are acknowledged as scientists, and their predominantly white, male, upper-middle class status. Hubbard (1989: 120) is amongst those who have pointed out that wider public accountability is not built into the current system of science knowledge-making. She argued that other kinds of people have a role in the making of science. She suggested that the inclusion of women in science needs to take place not by making women's domestic work more scientific in the traditional sense, but by 'acknowledging the scientific value of . . . the facts and knowledge that women have accumulated and passed on in our homes and volunteer organizations' (1989: 128). She argued also that a major contribution of women to science is at the political level, where they help to expose the political content of science and its political role. Her vision was of a socially responsible science, involving a much wider range of people than at present in the setting of agendas and the identification and answering of relevant questions – a science *by* the people, rather than a science *for* the people.

Another question explored by others besides Keller concerned whether or not there can be a 'feminist science'. In attempting to answer this question, Longino (1989), like Keller, saw the categories of 'feminine' and 'science' as socially constructed. She emphasized, also like many others, that to define *a single* feminist anything is not valid, because gender is experienced differently by different groups and individuals, according to the way it interacts with other variables such as class, race and ethnicity. On both of these grounds, Longino argued, like Sandra Harding (1986), against the idea of a feminist science. She suggested, however, that the focus should be shifted from the construction of a feminist science to the process of doing science as a feminist. In this sense, Longino saw feminist scientific practice as 'highly interactionist, highly complex' (1989: 55). She noted with concern that such a model of scientific practice is not the preferred one, and that, without changes to the current social, political and economic climates and to the current views of legitimate scientific research, there is only a limited future for this model.

Irigaray (1989) has also contrasted a possible feminist science with science as conceptualized currently, focusing on a set of presuppositions which she saw as separating the scientific from the non-scientific. These presuppositions include:

- the presumption of a reality distinct from the knower;
- the imposition of models and grids, not as tools, but as reality itself;
- a privileging of the visible, to the virtual exclusion of inputs from other senses;
- an assumption of the neutrality of technological equipment;
- an assumption that repeatability (irrespective of the sameness of two experimenters) is the fundamental criterion for objectivity;
- the equation of the ability to manipulate and control with progress and knowledge.

While Irigaray's presuppositions are arguably characteristic of what many would call 'bad' scientific practice, her analysis nevertheless is useful in identifying the features assumed to be prerequisite for scientific rigor. She argued that three of these features – the substitution of symbols for proper nouns, the focus on the quantitative rather than the qualitative and the use of formalized language – act to seal science from the everyday world and to make it an activity exclusive to those who prefer to deal in symbols, numbers and formalized language.

The Language of Science

In the context of language, there has been considerable debate as to whether or not the language of science allows for the emergence of alternative ways of doing science. In this context, Irigaray (1989) argued convincingly that 'the language of science, like language in general, is neither asexual nor neutral' (1989: 58). She pointed out that the subjective *I, you* and *we* do not appear in the traditional language of science, and that, overall, the discourse of science is much more comfortable with relationships of negation, conjunction and disjunction than it is with reciprocity, exchange, permeability or fluidity. Keller's example of the 'master cell' has demonstrated the prevalence of concepts of power and control in the metaphors of science. Irigaray went further, showing how the very discourse of traditional science imposes limits on what is accepted as science.

Are Scientists Made?

The object relations perspective on human development that underpins much of Keller's theorizing is supported strongly by several other feminists. From a theoretical perspective, Weinreich-Haste (1986) used it as a fundamental plank of her argument that a 'new form of rationality' is evolving which allows for 'differences in how scientific activity is conceived and how the products of science and technology are evaluated' (1986: 121). From a science education point of view, Jan Harding (J. Harding, 1986; Harding and Sutoris, 1984) and John Head (1980, 1985) also based their arguments with respect to girls' and boys' choice of science as a career on object relations theory. They drew on empirical research, (such as Roe, 1952), which claimed that practicing scientists tend to be emotionally reticent and minimally oriented to people, apparently because of isolation due to trauma or loss in early childhood. They highlighted the implications of these characteristics (in other words these kinds of people and this kind of image of science) for science curricula and the choice of these curricula by boys and girls. They argued that the presentation of science 'as a system of generalizations and immutable laws, divorced from the problems of the world' (J. Harding, 1986: 163) reflects the documented personality characteristics of practicing scientists. Further, in support of their argument, they demonstrated empirically that science appeals to boys who tend to be emotionally immature and who see it as a subject separate from human relationships, but that the girls who choose science tend to be of above average maturity and tend to have made their choice in the hope that they will be able to apply their scientific learning to improve the quality of life.

Is Neutrality Enough?

To some, Keller's argument for more diversity in science can appear to be an argument for science to be *gender neutral*. As argued emphatically by Martin (1982, 1985), however, gender neutrality is a flawed concept. Martin discussed a number of traditions in women's education. She pointed out that the sex neutral tradition is derived from Plato and was espoused by most curriculum theorists until the beginning of the 1970s. This tradition maintains that curriculum offerings should not be differentiated according to sex, an argument which on its own could be acceptable. However, as Martin (1982) pointed out, this presumption that sex was irrelevant to learning was operationalized within a concept of learning as detached from everyday life. It ignored what Martin called the 'reproductive' aspects of life (domestic and interpersonal life) and it focused on the 'productive' aspects of public life, aspects which culturally were denied to women. Thus, as Martin argued, this concept of learning was not sensitive to the reality that 'men and women in the past and the present do not have identical experiences and are not seen as identical by the culture . . . Treating them as if they were the same is not to treat them equally' (1982: 107).

The Place of Dualisms

A Cautionary Note

I return now to one of the consequences of the kind of analysis carried out by Keller, a consequence associated with the issue of competing or compatible paradigms that I discussed earlier. This consequence, which has been identified with some concern by several feminists (see Bleier, 1984; Glennon, 1979; MacCormack and Strathern, 1980; Weinreich-Haste, 1986) is that such an analysis can lead to a set of dichotomies or dualisms. Feminized science, contrasted to a picture of traditional masculinist science in terms of such dualisms, can be seen as science premised on:

- an holistic rather than an atomistic approach;
- order rather than law;
- mutual respect and interaction rather than domination;
- a non-hierarchical continuum of difference rather than a dichotomy and polarization;
- involvement rather than detachment;
- understanding rather than predicting;
- empowerment through understanding rather than power to manipulate;
- broadly defined rather than highly specialized scientific knowledge;
- scientific knowledge contextualized in history and in contemporary society, rather than ahistorical and decontextualized scientific knowledge.

Sets of dualisms such as these are ubiquitous in western philosophical traditions. As Schiebinger has pointed out:

> The basic categories of modern thought have taken shape as a series of dualities: reason has been opposed to feeling, fact to values, culture to nature, science to belief, the public to the private. One set of qualities – reason, fact, object – came to represent constituents of rational discourse and scientific knowledge. The other set of qualities – feeling, value, subject – have been defined as unpredictable and irrational. When the dualism of masculinity and femininity was mapped onto these categories, masculinity

became synonymous with reason and objectivity – qualities associated with participation in public spheres of government, commerce, science and scholarship. Femininity became synonymous with feeling and subjectivity – qualities associated with the private sphere of hearth and home (Schiebinger, 1987: 331).

Many feminists see such dualisms as dangerous. First, they take the view that the mapping of identifiable categories of human beings on to any set of dichotomies such as these denies the variation within those categories, denies the holistic nature of humanity and carries with it all the risks known to be associated with stereotyping. Second, as noted by Collins (1993a), they see this as an example not only of the way that language works through oppositional concepts such as those identified above by Schiebinger, but also of the way the value relation built into each binary pair of constructs tends to valorize the masculine and to define the feminine simply in terms of what is not masculine. Third, they point out that, although such dualisms represent one kind of tool for describing the world, they are not used as such. The dualisms are posed not as hypotheses to be investigated, or as ends of a continuum, but as self-evident truths with predictive and definitional significance. As Bleier has noted (1984: 197), 'we tend to mistake our cognitive techniques to comprehend the universe for the universe itself' and, as emphasized by Lemke (1994), the *disjunction* read into dualisms ensures that the two poles of the duality are mutually exclusive.

In educational terms, clearly it is highly problematic if these dualisms are enforced as reality itself, rather than only as representative of reality. If 'science' and 'not science' are defined strictly in terms of this set of dualisms, and if the set includes 'masculinity' and 'femininity', then inevitably young people are forced to risk an identity crisis at the point in their schooling when they make their choice of future study or occupation. In Keller's words, 'any scientist who is not a man walks a path bounded on one side by inauthenticity and on the other by subversion' (1985: 174). Arguably, if these dualisms are embedded unquestioningly in school science, the point at which females and males choose whether or not to continue with science, and if so, which science, will continue to be a 'critical event' in the science education of all students (Parker, 1987).

Dualisms as Complementary rather than Oppositional: A Theoretical Model of Gender-inclusive Science

I argue here that these dualisms have served a valuable intellectual purpose in the past, and may continue to do so in the future. They have helped feminist scholars to expose some of the problems inherent in a narrowly defined science. Further, most feminists are aware of the trap posed by dualistic modes of viewing the world. Longino (1989: 47) noted the fallacy inherent in rejecting one approach to science as incorrect and embracing another as the way to a truer understanding of the natural world, or, in her terms, trading 'one absolutism for another'. Like Sandra Harding

(1986) and Lorraine Code (1993), she pointed out that women's backgrounds and experiences are too diverse to justify the generation of a single cognitive framework for either feminine science or feminist science. Similarly, Alcoff (1989) argued that simply removing the masculine will not purify science. Keller herself, despite the many contrasts she set up, recognized nevertheless the trap in substituting feminine science for masculine science or, as she put it, substituting 'one form of parochiality for another' (1985: 178).

As indicated earlier, Keller's vision was pluralistic and eclectic, based on a transcendence of the bias she identified in science, and on the reclamation of science as a human, instead of a masculine activity. Weinreich-Haste (1986) asked the question, 'Does rationality overcome a dualistic world view?' Keller's answer would appear to be a resounding 'Yes!', as would that of Weinreich-Haste herself, who, in alignment with Keller's view of reformed science, proposed that her new form of rationality is '*in complement to* the traditional form' (1986: 121, emphasis added) not in competition with it, or replacing it.

In accepting this pluralism, the picture of science presented in oppositional terms earlier in this chapter becomes a picture of a discipline premised not on an holistic *rather than* an atomistic approach, but on

- an holistic *as well as* an atomistic approach;
- order *as well as* law;
- mutual respect and interaction *as well as* domination;
- a non-hierarchical continuum of difference *as well as* a dichotomy and polarization;
- involvement *as well as* detachment;
- understanding *as well as* predicting;
- empowerment through understanding *as well as* power to manipulate;
- broadly defined *as well as* highly specialized scientific knowledge;
- scientific knowledge contextualized in history and in contemporary society, *as well as* ahistorical and decontextualized scientific knowledge.

In accepting this version, however, the caveat of Weinreich-Haste must be heeded: because of the deeply rooted dualisms in western culture, the emerging, more holistic, less control-oriented conception of rationality 'has been mapped onto the gender dichotomy' (1986: 129) or, in the terms of the theoretical model advanced elsewhere, it has become 'gender-coded' (Parker, 1995).

Implications for a Gender-inclusive Science Curriculum

The Problem for School Science

Although the work of Keller and most other feminists does not deal directly with school science, it has considerable application to this area. In this sense, some postmodernist analyses (see Collins, 1993) provide important background to the place of science in the school curriculum. These analyses identify science, as traditionally taught, as one of the more recently emergent lynch-pins of the kinds of school curricula that have dominated the English-speaking world during most of the twentieth century. They argue that these curricula have been, and for the most part still are, based on modernist assumptions about the world, assumptions which became hegemonic during the nineteenth century. As Collins pointed out, 'modernism was about empirical evidence and the rule of reason' (1993b: 5), and, in this context, one of the strands which is historically traceable concerns 'the rise in the prestige of physical science, the kind of totally predictable science which can be used to control, to the pinnacle of preeminence' (1993b: 5). Collins emphasized that, even in the 1990s, the school curriculum remains dominated by 'technocratic, modernist priorities: mathematics, physics, chemistry and more recently economics (*taught as positivist truth*)' (1993b: 10, emphasis added).

The positivist truth Collins alludes to is essentially part of what Keller (1985: 125) called the 'dominant rhetoric' of science. As demonstrated by Malcolm's (1989) description of school science, the problem for school science appears to be that it has tended in the past to replicate this dominant rhetoric; indeed, it has tended to replicate it much more faithfully than have scientists in the practice of science. Scrutiny of high school science syllabus policy documents typical of the 1980s demonstrates that school science knowledge, in the late twentieth century, represents a distillation of what is seen as the essence of the discipline of science, a representation which is, in many cases, an outdated oversimplification.

In attempting to characterize science as an area of study, school curricula appear to have emphasized what is alleged to make science different from other areas of human activity rather than what science might have in common with other human activity. Control, objectivity, reasoned argument and value-free 'truths' of science have been presented in opposition to chaos, subjectivity, irrationality and value-embedded 'not science'. The hierarchical orderings and fixed approaches to scientific enquiry that are part of many traditional science curricula reinforce a simple, competitive, individualistic, linear view of science, rather than a complex, egalitarian and interactive view. Science is presented as 'the tale of better control of the natural environment . . . the story of triumph of the rational, of the rule of the head' (Collins, 1993a: 4). As Birke commented, 'impersonal, reductionist kind of science . . . is still the backbone of school and college biology' (1986a: 195). She pointed out that, 'if girls (and some boys) are opting out of science at school because they want to see nature in terms of relationships and connectedness, then we have to change the image of science that is conveyed in schools' (1986a: 196). First, however, we need to clarify the ways in which that image needs to be changed.

Change to What? The Reconstructed Image of School Science

Keller's arguments for science to be reclaimed as a fully human rather than a masculine activity have just as much validity in relation to school science as they do in relation to the practice of science by scientists. Thus, her vision of an eclectic, pluralistic science, which accommodates diverse ways of thinking about and doing science, needs to be fundamental to any reconstructed image of school science. In terms of curriculum theory, such a transformation is consistent with the culmination of the developmental, sequential model of curriculum transformation proposed by Schuster and Van Dyne (1984) for the liberal arts. The sixth and final stage of Schuster and Van Dyne's model portrayed, like the curriculum advocated here for science, a transformed, balanced curriculum and an inclusive vision, based on diversity of human experience, not sameness and generalization. In operational terms, it is insufficient for diversity simply to be facilitated or provided for in this reconstructed school science curriculum, however. Diversity needs to be *embedded* in the curriculum, the pedagogy and the assessment.

First, with respect to content, the reconstructed curriculum would need to include the 'her-story' of science and the work of the lost women of science alluded to earlier in this chapter. It would need to expand the boundaries of science and the definition of legitimate scientific knowledge to include science which takes place in contexts of domesticity or nurturance. It would need to project an holistic, non-hierarchical view of science – a view quite at odds with the division of science into a hierarchy of separate subjects such as occurs currently in most high school science curriculum structures. It would need to include, as an essential part of scientific knowledge, a discussion of how that knowledge has evolved, and how it has been used and abused. Overall, in doing all of this, it would need to ensure that androcentric and gynocentric science are not presented as competing paradigms, with the former valued more highly than the latter, but as a single global entity, where diversity is part of the integrity of the discipline.

Second, with respect to pedagogy, this reconstructed curriculum would need to allow for discussion of the extent to which science is value neutral and objective, and to provide opportunities for personal involvement of students with science, in the manner of Keller's description of Barbara McClintock. In addition, the pedagogy would need to allow for different entry characteristics of students, different ways of viewing the world, ways of knowing other than western male ways, different voices from western male voices and the doing of science by people other than western males. Further, and at the very least in the interests of validity, the assessment procedures would need to match the pedagogy faithfully and would need to reflect the diversity embedded in the teaching strategies.

Concluding Comments

The picture of gender-inclusive science that has emerged from my analysis in this chapter is very similar to that which emerged from empirical evidence of the kind of curriculum that appears to be associated with increased participation and achievement by females (Parker, Rennie and Harding, 1995). Clearly, this kind of science curriculum does not conform to Irigaray's set of preconditions for scientific rigor, conditions associated with the detached, symbolic, numerical and formalized representation of reality. This raises questions regarding whether such a changed science

Lesley H. Parker

can be accepted as real and rigorous science and whether, indeed, rigor itself is an ideology. Such questions warrant further exploration in the context not just of dismantling the master's house, but also of rebuilding it.

References

ALCOFF, L. (1989) 'Justifying feminist social science', in TUANA, N. (Ed) *Feminism and Science*, Bloomington, IN, Indiana University Press, pp. 85–103.

BELENKY, M.F., CLINCHY, B., GOLDBERGER, N.R. and TARULE, J.M. (1986) *Women's Ways of Knowing*, New York, Basic Books.

BIRKE, L. (1986a) 'Changing minds: Towards gender equality in science?', in HARDING, J. (Ed) *Perspectives on Gender and Science*, Lewes, Falmer Press, pp. 184–202.

BIRKE, L. (1986b) *Women, Feminism and Biology: The Feminist Challenge*, New York, Methuen Inc.

BLEIER, R. (1984) *Science and Gender: A Critique of Biology and Its Theories on Women*, New York, Pergamon Press.

CHODOROW, N. (1978) *The Reproduction of Mothering: Psychoanalysis and the Sociology of Gender*, Berkeley, CA, University of California Press.

CODE, L. (1993) 'Taking subjectivity into account', in ALCOFF, L. and POTTER, E. (Eds) *Feminist Epistemologies*, New York, Routledge, pp. 15–48.

COLLINS, C.W. (1993a) 'A conference silence: Where are the debates on knowledge and personhood?', Paper presented at invitational conference, *Creating our Future: A Curriculum for the Twenty-first Century* (Convenor: P.W. HUGHES), Hobart, January.

COLLINS, C.W. (1993b) 'Approaching the history of education with a postmodern consciousness', Paper presented at the annual meeting of the American Educational Research Association, Atlanta, GA, April.

FEE, E. (1976) 'Science and the woman problem: Historical perspectives', in TEITELBAUM, M. (Ed) *Sex Differences: Social and Biological Perspectives*, Garden City, NY, Anchor Press, pp. 175–223.

GILLIGAN, C. (1982) *In a Different Voice: Psychological Theory and Women's Development*, Cambridge, MA, Harvard University Press.

GINZBURG, R. (1989) 'Uncovering gynocentric science', in TUANA, N. (Ed) *Feminism and Science*, Bloomington, IN, Indiana University Press, pp. 69–84.

GLENNON, L.M. (1979) *Women and Dualism*, London, Longman.

GOODFIELD, J. (1981) *An Imagined World*, New York, Harper and Rowe.

GOULD, S.J. (1981) *The Mismeasure of Man*, New York, W.W. Norton and Co.

GROSZ, E.A. and DE LEPERVANCHE, M. 'Feminism and science', in CAINE, B., GROSZ, E.A. and DE LEPERVANCHE, M. (Eds) *Crossing Boundaries*, Sydney: Allen and Unwin, pp. 5–27.

HARAWAY, D. (1981) 'In the beginning was the word: The genesis of biological theory', *Signs*, **6**(3), pp. 469–82.

HARDING, J. (1986) 'The making of a scientist', in HARDING, J. (Ed) *Perspectives on Gender and Science*, Lewes, Falmer Press, pp. 160–7.

HARDING, J. and SUTORIS, M. (1984) 'An object relations account of the differential involvement of boys and girls in science and technology', Paper presented at IPN Symposium, Kiel, April.

HARDING, S. (1986) *The Science Question in Feminism*, Ithaca, NY, Cornell University Press.

HARDING, S. (1989) 'Is there a feminist method?', in TUANA, N. (Ed) *Feminism and Science*, Bloomington, Indiana University Press, pp. 17–32. Reprinted from *Hypatia*, **2**(3).

HEAD, J. (1980) 'A model to link personality characteristics to a preference for science', *European Journal of Science Education*, **2**, pp. 295–300.

HEAD, J. (1985) *The Personal Response to Science*, Cambridge, Cambridge University Press.

HUBBARD, R. (1989) 'Science, facts and feminism', in TUANA, N. (Ed) *Feminism and Science*, Bloomington, IN, Indiana University Press, pp. 119–31.

HUBBARD, R. and LOWE, M. (Eds) (1979) *Genes and Gender II: Pitfalls in Research on Sex and Gender*, New York, Gordian Press.

IRIGARAY, L. (1989) 'Is the subject of science sexed?', in TUANA, N. (Ed) *Feminism and Science*, Bloomington, IN, Indiana University Press. (Translated by CAROL MASTROANGELO BOVE), pp. 17–32.

KELLER, E.F. (1978) 'Gender and science', *Psychoanalysis and Contemporary Tought*, **1**, pp. 409–433. Reprinted in KELLER, E.F. (1985) *Reflections on Gender and Science*, New Haven, CT, Yale University Press.

KELLER, E.F. (1982) 'Feminism and science', *Signs*, **7**(3), pp. 589–602.

KELLER, E.F. (1983) *A Feeling for the Organism: The Life and Work of Barbara McClintock*, New York, Freeman.

KELLER, E.F. (1985) *Reflections on Gender and Science*, New Haven, CT, Yale University Press.

KELLER, E.F. (1989) 'The gender/science system: Or, is sex to gender as nature is to science?', in TUANA, N. (Ed) *Feminism and Science*, Bloomington, IN, Indiana University Press, pp. 33–44.

KELLY, A. (1985) 'The construction of masculine science', *British Journal of Sociology of Education*, **6**(2), pp. 133–45.

KUHN, T. (1970) *The Structure of Scientific Revolutions* (2nd ed), Chicago, IL, University of Chicago Press.

LEMKE, J. (1994) 'Postmodernism as a resource for science education?', Panel Discussion (with BRICKHOUSE, N.W., HARDING, S. and GOOD, R.), Annual Meeting, National Association for Research in Science Teaching, Los Angeles, March.

LEWONTIN, R., ROSE, S. and KAMIN, L. (1984) *Not in Our Genes: Biology, Ideology and Human Nature*, New York, Pantheon Books.

LONGINO, H.E. (1989) 'Can there be a feminist science?', in TUANA, N. (Ed) *Feminism and Science*, Bloomington, IL, Indiana University Press, pp. 45–57.

MacCORMACK, C. and STRATHERN, M. (1980) *Nature, Culture and Gender*, Cambridge, Cambridge University Press.

MALCOLM, C. (1989) 'Trends in school science curriculum and their implications for teacher education', in SPEEDY, G., ANNICE, C., FENSHAM, P.J. and WEST, L. (Eds) *Discipline Review of Teacher Education in Mathematics and Science*, **3**, Canberra, Department of Employment, Education, pp. 210–29.

MARTIN, J.R. (1982) 'Excluding women from the educational realm', *Harvard Educational Review*, **34**(4), pp. 341–53.

MARTIN, J.R. (1985) *Reclaiming a Conversation: The Ideal of the Educated Woman*, New Haven, CT, Yale University Press.

MORGAN, E. (1972) *The Descent of Woman*, New York, Stein and Day.

O'BRIEN, M. (1981) *The Politics of Reproduction*, London, Routledge and Kegan Paul.

PARKER, L.H. 'The gender code of school science', Doctoral dissertation, Perth, Curtin University of Technology.

PARKER, L.H. (1987) 'The choice point: A critical event in the science education of girls and

Lesley H. Parker

boys', in FRASER, B.J. and GIDDINGS, G.J. (Eds) *Gender Issues in Science Education*, Perth, Australia, Curtin University of Technology, pp. 13–18.

PARKER, L.H., RENNIE, L.J. and HARDING, J. (1995) 'Gender equity', in FRASER, B.J. and WALBERG, H.J. (Eds) *Improving Science Education: International Perspectives*, (pp. 186–210), Chicago, IL, National Society for the Study of Education and University of Chicago Press.

ROE, A. (1952) *The Making of a Scientist*, London, Dodds Mead.

ROSSER, S.V. (1989) 'Feminist scholarship in the sciences: Where are we now and when can we ever expect a theoretical breakthrough?', in TUANA, N. (Ed) *Feminism and Science*, Bloomington, IL, Indiana University Press, pp. 3–14.

ROSSITER, M. (1982) *Women Scientists in America*, Baltimore, IL, The Johns Hopkins University Press.

SAYERS, J. (1982) *Biological Politics: Feminist and Anti-feminist Perspectives*, London, Tavistock.

SCHIEBINGER, L. (1987) 'The history and philosophy of women in science', *Signs: Journal of Women in Culture and Society*, **12**(2), pp. 305–332.

SCHUSTER, M. and VAN DYNE, S. (1984) 'Placing women in the liberal arts: Stages of curriculum transformation', *Harvard Educational Review*, **54**(4), pp. 413–28.

WEINREICH-HASTE, H. (1986) 'Brother sun, sister moon: Does rationality overcome a dualistic world view?', in HARDING, J. (Ed) *Perspectives on Gender and Science*, Lewes, Falmer Press, pp. 111–31.

YOUNG, M.F.D. (1971) 'An approach to the study of curricula as socially organized knowledge', in YOUNG, M. (Ed) *Knowledge and Control*, London, Collier Macmillan.

Chapter 11

Feminist Analysis of Sexual Harassment Policy: A Critique of the Ideal of Community

Julie Laible

Introduction

Sexual harassment is a serious concern for educational administrators. Recent media attention on the Anita Hill/Clarence Thomas hearings[1] along with the well-publicized American Association of University Women's (AAUW) report (1993), *Hostile Hallways*, on the wide-spread existence of sexual harassment in public schools has caused many school districts to begin developing a sexual harassment policy. Eighty-five per cent of all female students report being harassed in school – most frequently in the halls and in the classroom. Because of the harassment, nearly 40 per cent of adolescent girls do not want to go to school and do not want to speak out in class (AAUW, 1993: 7, 15).

Often policymakers at the district level are charged to produce a draft sexual harassment policy through a study of the problem and consideration of competing policy solutions (Cornbleth and Waugh, 1993). Policymakers, now more than ever, are attempting to include members of the community; such as teacher and administrator associations, parent groups, students in the development of policy (Ingram and Smith, 1993; Koppich, 1993). Although the rhetoric surrounding this process heralds the 'spirit of community' (Etzioni, 1993), Young (1990) argues that persons involved tend to suppress differences among themselves or implicitly exclude from their political group, for example, the policy advisory committee persons with whom they do not identify (Young, 1990). Many feminists argue that the ideal of community in the policy arena has actually led to the suppression and devaluation of women's voices, especially when the committee developing the policy is dominantly male (Yates, 1993).

Studies of the educational policymaking process seldom examine the question of whose voices are heard in the process. Even fewer examine issues focusing primarily on women and the 'private sphere'. Many policies, such as sexual harassment policies, are developed which do not take into consideration the needs, values and ways of knowing of girls and women, half the school population (Belenky, Clinchy, Goldberger, and Tarule, 1986). This study seeks to qualitatively examine the development of a sexual harassment policy in a school district in a mid-size city in the Southwest and to identify whose epistemologies are valued during the process.

Literature Review

Sexual Harassment

Sexual harassment is not a new phenomenon. Like date rape and spouse abuse, it is thoroughly ensconced in our society but seldom receives scholarly attention or public acknowledgment, concern and action. Only very recently have topics such as sexual harassment punctuated the discourses comprising social, academic, institutional and legal realms of life (Wood, 1992).

Once attention was paid to sexual harassment, its pervasiveness was consistently and unequivocally documented.[2] In one of the first national studies (*Redbook*, 1976 as cited in Wood, 1992), 92 per cent of 9000 clerical and professional women reported experiencing some form of sexual harassment on the job. In 1987 the US Merit Systems Protection Board discovered that 42 per cent of the women working for the federal government reported having been sexually harassed in the workplace (Edmunds, 1988). Studies of academic (post-secondary) environments, too, disclosed a disturbingly high incidence of sexual harassment: up to 50 per cent of students and up to 30 per cent of faculty members reported they had been sexually harassed (Dey, Korn and Sax, 1996; Hoffmann, 1986; Rubin and Borgers, 1990).

More recently a 1993 nationwide survey of 1632 randomly selected public school students in grades 8 through 11 found that sexual harassment in schools is epidemic (AAUW, 1993). Eighty-five per cent of the girls and 76 per cent of the boys reported having been sexually harassed in school. One-fourth of the students said they were harassed 'often'. The most common forms of harassment reported were sexual comments, jokes, and gestures (66 per cent); being touched, grabbed or pinched in a sexual way (53 per cent); and being intentionally brushed up against in a sexual way (46 per cent). The most common academic effects of harassment reported by female students in the AAUW survey were 'not wanting to come to school', 'not wanting to talk as much in class', and 'finding it hard to pay attention in school' (AAUW, 1993: 7–15). Nan Stein (1993) reports similar findings from her *Seventeen* magazine survey in which female teenagers were asked to describe their experiences of sexual harassment in schools. Other studies have documented the harassing nature of adolescent peer relationships and the uncaring culture of schools in which alarming frequencies of harmful words and actions are directed at girls and 'feminine' boys (Shakeshaft, Barber, Hergenrother, Johnson, Mandel and Sawyer, 1994).

The growing awareness of sexual harassment and the research documenting its existence has led to legal response. In addition to the passage of the Civil Rights Act of 1964 and Title IX in 1972[3], a recent ruling (i.e., *Franklin v. Gwinnett County Public Schools*, 1992), surprising in both stance and unanimity, held that an individual may sue a school for both compensatory and punitive damages resulting from sexual harassment. Not only districts but individual school administrators can be held personally liable if they learn of a pattern of abuse by one of their employees and show 'deliberate indifference toward the constitutional rights of a student by failing to take action that was obviously necessary to prevent or stop the abuse' (quoted in Walsh, 1994: 6; see *Doe v. Taylor Independent School District*, 1994). Districts and administrators may also be held liable for *student* behavior if districts and administrators are aware of student sexual harassment of another student and fail to take action (*Doe v. Petaluma City School District*, 1993).

In spite of the increased awareness and legal responses to sexual harassment, however, school personnel and students often have difficulty defining sexual harassment. According to most definitions, sexual harassment is 'any unwanted sexual attention from peers, subordinates, supervisors, customers, clients or anyone the victim may interact with in order to fill job or school duties. The range of behaviors includes: verbal comments, subtle pressure for sexual activity, leering, pinching, patting and other forms of unwanted touching' (Eaton, 1994: 9).[4]

Unfortunately, males and females are often unaware of these definitions. Many boys and men do not understand why their behavior is defined as harassment. Part of this may be due to the fact that the types of behavior known as sexual harassment are taken for granted as part of the natural order (Hoffman, 1986). Donna Eder (1995) found in her study of adolescent culture and language, for example, that boys viewing girls as sexual objects is routine and that informal activities of sexual aggression by boys are often viewed as being natural and typical orientations toward sexuality and are seldom challenged (1995: 100). Similarly, powerful male policymakers and school administrators frequently refuse to acknowledge the problem of sexual harassment in schools, or they redefine the value of the problem, especially when it conflicts with their ideological assumptions, values or needs. Sexual harassment, to them, is often not a legitimate issue which needs to be addressed in schools (Ortiz and Marshall, 1988; Riger, 1991). Girls and women, on the other hand, have always known sexual harassment exists, but have had no legitimated way to label what occurs, much less enlist others' help with this 'problem that has no name' (Wood, 1992: 352). Formerly, each individual victim worked alone to make sense of her experience without culturally sanctioned vocabularies and interpretations.

It was only in the late 1970s that pioneer scholars such as MacKinnon (1979) and others (see Farley, 1978; Working Women United Institute, 1975) began to define and devise remedies for the range of behaviors which constitute sexual harassment. These researchers abandoned the earlier assumption that sexual harassment stemmed from individual attitudes and behavior, connecting sexual harassment closely to the following structural conditions and historical patterns of sex-role interaction: 1) notions of male and female sexuality interwoven with legal doctrines; 2) cultural definitions of gender differences; 3) a sex-segregated occupational structure; and 4) bureaucratic forms of decisionmaking and control that give rise to the possibility (likelihood) of sexual harassment.

This reframing, and the lawsuits, resulted in beginning efforts by universities and schools to develop official policies to stop sexual harassment in their organizations.

Most organizations' sexual harassment policies, for example, include institutional statements condemning sexual harassment and outline grievance procedures for victims. These remedies bring to public scrutiny what has previously been taken for granted and provide a political and ideological climate in which exploitative forms of behavior can be analyzed and addressed institutionally. Few complaints, however, are reported (Riger, 1991). Researchers questioning this phenomenon suggest that policies developed to eliminate sexual harassment actually reinforce the hierarchical, sex-segregated structure and power differentials between men and women (Hoffman, 1986), reducing the phenomenon of sexual harassment to its behavioral manifestations and to bureaucratic grievance procedures but neglecting broader institutional efforts to address the disadvantaged status of women (Hoffman, 1986). Moreover, it is usually the male definition of harassment that predominates since men typically have more power in organizations (Kanter, 1977) – even though men and women define sexual harassment differently (Riger, 1991).[5] As MacKinnon states,

> objectivity – the nonsituated, universal standpoint, whether claimed or aspired to – is a denial of the existence or potency of sex inequality that tacitly participates in constructing reality from the dominant point of view ... The law sees and treats women the way men see and treat women (1987: 136, 140).

Sexual harassment policies which require grievance procedures to be formal and public, which contain no clause concerning retaliation or confidentiality, and which designate supervisors, not third parties, to handle complaints are examples of MacKinnon's point. Young children and women who normally hold less power in organizations – those for whom the policy is supposedly designed – in reality, then, have much more to lose by reporting occurrences of sexual harassment than by remaining silent. This is especially true if organizational attention is not given to making connections between sexual harassment and the broader inequalities that exist between men and women in which sexual harassment is embedded (Hoffman, 1986).

Policy slippage serves to further oppress those for whom the policies are developed to protect. Implementation of sexual harassment policies is problematic since no federal, state or local government agency is required to assess the efficacy of sexual harassment policy implementation (Ortiz and Marshall, 1988). Without sanctions for ineffective implementation, sexual harassment policies are merely symbolic.

Policy Analysis

If most sexual harassment policies are discriminatory to those who traditionally have less power in organizations (i.e., women and children) or are ineffectively implemented, one must question whose voices are being heard in the development of policy or in policy analysis. Traditional policy analysis (i.e., those currently used to develop and evaluate sexual harassment policies) includes the following steps: 1) define the problem; 2) talk to stakeholders; 3) develop criteria for evaluating the policy alternatives; 4) develop policy alternatives, and 5) choose and implement the best policy option (Cornbleth and Waugh, 1993). Traditional policymakers assume there is an objective reality – that the problem is viewed in the same way by all people and that power issues and the values of the policymakers have no impact on the definition of the problem nor on the development of the alternatives (Fischer and Forrester, 1986; Majone, 1989).

In contrast, more recent interpretivist or post-positivist policy analysts are recognizing that values and interpretations are part of the policymaking process. For example, Kelly and Maynard-Moody call for policy analysts as outsiders to facilitate bringing together all 'insider' interpretations of the story so that all concerned can gain a 'better understanding of the larger narrative of which they are all a part' (1993: 136). Although they and others (see Hawkesworth, 1988) acknowledge that there is no objective truth and that reality is socially constructed, they also believe that an intersubjective agreement can be reached in the policy process to facilitate a solution (albeit, an interpretive, symbolic solution).

Feminists and other critical theorists have developed alternative, contextually-oriented epistemic stances which have expanded the discursive context of policy analysis. Critical feminist policy analysis, for example, examines policy from women's lives, generates links with social constructions of reality, recognizes a diversity of standpoints, and emphasizes the importance of context in policy analysis (Rixecker, 1994: 133). In contrast to interpretivist policy analysts, feminists and critical theorists argue that intersubjective agreement *cannot* be met when all stakeholders' interpretations of the problem or reality are not equally heard in the interpretivist or positivist policy analysis (Marshall and Anderson, 1995; Yates, 1993), especially when the majority of policymakers/analysts are male. Others have demonstrated how the structures, rules, language and patterns of dominance in organizations, including policymaking, serve to control women, keeping them there to contribute to their work while repressing their alternate ways of talking, valuing and living their lives (Ferguson, 1984). Young (1991) claims, for example, that the ideal of community – including the ideal of a community of policymakers – presumes that subjects can understand one another as they understand themselves. It thus denies the difference between subjects. 'The desire for community', states Young, 'relies on the same desire for social wholeness and identification that underlies racism on one hand and political sectarianism on the other' (1990: 302).

Most recently, Scheurich (1994) has developed a new policy studies methodology, *policy archeology*, based on the works of the postmodern theorist Michel Foucault. This radical and complex policy analysis goes beyond critical/feminist policy analysis to examine the social construction of specific education and social problems. It also identifies the network of social regularities across education and social problems[6] and examines how those regularities are constitutive of the social construction of social problems and the range of acceptable policy solutions. Finally, it questions the social functions of policy studies itself (1994: 5).

In my examination of the development of a sexual harassment policy in a school district in a mid-size city in the southwest, I used a combination of both feminist and postmodern policy analyses. My use of a feminist epistemology challenged traditional conceptions of knowledge creation by asking how a woman might alter traditional 'ways of knowing' (Alcoff and Potter, 1993). I also chose to utilize feminist epistemology because it clearly espoused and accepted its situated orientation – thus, as a *woman* I analyzed a policy that directly impacted *women* and addressed feminist concerns. Traditional policy analysis, even interpretivist policy analysis, I argued, could not adequately serve the victims of sexual harassment (i.e., women and children). As Hawkesworth argues, 'feminist scholarship reveals that androcentrism routinely undermines the claims of policy analysts to produce objective accounts. Tacit gender bias leads policy scientists to . . . fail to notice that the hypotheses they advance about women are inadequately warranted' (1994: 110). Status quo policy analysis frameworks that did not recognize context and situational reality, I knew, would guarantee continued fragmented policy – fragmented policy that would omit the experiences of half the population (Rixecker, 1994).

Second, in addition to feminist epistemology, I used postmodern policy analysis to bring women's voices from 'margin to center' (hooks, 1984) and to show how the emergence and existence of a social problem (i.e., sexual harassment), for which a policy is developed to alleviate, is a social construction process. Additionally, using policy archeology or postmodern policy analysis, I could determine what function the policy served, for as Scheurich (1994) has argued, many policies may actually reinforce normalcy, productiveness and (patriarchal) order and revictimize those persons whom the policy was designed to protect.

Research Design and Methodology

My research design was a case study with indepth qualitative interviews as the main data source. Both the design and the method of data collection provided the opportunity to develop a detailed contextual picture of the school district and the policymaking community. I interviewed the primary policymaker (male) in the central administration of the school district, legal counsel (male) to the district, the local union president (female) for classified employees who was invited to give input during the policy development, and three local and national members of a university women's organization who were also invited to participate in drafting the policy. The interviewees were asked to describe the following: 1) their perceptions of why sexual harassment is now receiving a great deal of attention; 2) their knowledge of reported cases of sexual harassment in the district or stories of personnel or students being harassed (by faculty or students); 3) their definition of sexual harassment; 4) their role on the policy advisory committee and descriptions of what took place at the working sessions to develop the sexual harassment policy. Interview transcriptions were then analyzed by units using the following research questions:

- Do the policymakers differ in their explanations of the emergence and frequency of sexual harassment as a problem in the district?

- Whose voices were dominant in the policymaking process? Clair (1993) and Mumby (1988) claim that the relationship between organizational communication (in this case, school district communication) and meaning formation (in this case, policy development) can only be adequately studied through a conceptual assimilation of issues of power and domination.
- What function does the policy serve? Is it just a symbolic function; does it reinforce normalcy, productiveness, and (patriarchal) order? Does the policy seriously and plausibly attempt to educate students and staff about harassment with penalties for violations, or does it maintain status quo?

Findings

Data Analysis

Four themes or clusters emerged as I analyzed the interview data. They are the following:

1 the emergence and frequency of the problem;
2 the problem in defining sexual harassment;
3 the voices heard in the policymaking process;
4 the function of the policy – whose interests are served by current policy language?

Differing Interpretations of the Emergence and Frequency of the Problem

Various explanations were given for the reason that sexual harassment was now being seen as a problem and given attention nationally and at the district level. All interviewees mentioned recent court cases at the national level. Mark, the policymaker, discussed the recent (December 1993) Supreme Court case *Harris v. Forklift System Inc.* which reaffirmed a lower court's decision that sexual harassment is gender discrimination and that the burden of proof of psychological damage does not lie with the person who has been harassed. Allen, the attorney, discussed a sexual discrimination lawsuit that took place in the district in the 70s that received national attention and the maternity leave cases of the 80s.

All interviewees mentioned the Anita Hill incident and the role that media played in many of the recent sexual harassment cases. Denise, one of the members of the university women's organization (AAUW), was very familiar with the national cases, commenting on specific names and court cases around the country. Janet, the union president, claimed that it had a lot to do with the women's movement and a growing awareness of what is inappropriate behavior at the workplace. She doubted that there was more sexual harassment occurring now than before.

Interestingly, however, there was a difference between the male and female interviewees regarding the frequency of sexual harassment occurring in the district and the events leading to the local district seeing the need for a policy. On one hand, when asked if the district had many complaints or grievances filed recently which would prompt the school board to advise a policy be drafted, the men interviewed claimed that incidents of sexual harassment were isolated and the development of the policy was just a sign of the times that they needed to complete as administrators in a bureaucracy.

On the other hand, the women interviewed were much more vocal about the frequency of sexual harassment occurring in the schools and could cite recent incidents in the district that led the district to see that a problem needed to be addressed. As union president, Janet told stories of her involvement in the investigation of alleged sexual harassment of many female (and male) classified employees and pointed to the large filing cabinets where such records are kept. In addition, she was upset with the phone calls she received from women being sexually harassed on the job but who were afraid to come forward because of retaliation.

Denise stated,

> I do know that someone has filed a Title IX complaint against the school district for sexual harassment and I have seen the findings and they were found in violation of Title IX. And then all of a sudden I hear that they are going to draft this policy. Dr Green[7] has never said anything like that and I've never heard it anywhere else. But I've seen the findings because I taught the victim how to file against them.

Additionally, Mary, the retired teacher and administrator for the university women's organization, spoke of her personal experience of being sexually harassed, and Denise described her daughter's experience of being harassed on the school bus.

Most interviewees' social constructions of the emergence of the problem of sexual harassment at a national level, then, was similar. In essence, the national court cases, the women's movement, and a general awareness of inappropriate behavior at the workplace was how the interviewees viewed sexual harassment to have become more visible at a national level. Regarding the frequency of sexual harassment at the local level, however, and the emergence of a problem within the district, a difference existed between the men and women interviewed. The women were able to cite recent and frequent incidents of sexual harassment in the district while the men constructed a different reality in which sexual harassment existed at a low frequency and was not of a serious nature.

Differences in Definitions of Sexual Harassment

A second recurring theme in the interviews was that of the difficulty in defining sexual harassment. All were aware that sexual harassment is a form of gender discrimination, yet Mark, the primary policy developer, was having difficulties nailing down the definition:

[it's] difficult to find exactly the right wording to umbrella all the various groups [students, staff, and community volunteers] . . . there is a subjective component. Someone has something up on the wall, someone says something, someone tells a joke, and someone is very offended by it. Someone else isn't. You are not required by law to confront the person. You don't have to tell them that 'it offends me, don't do it again'. You could just sit there and listen to that stuff for weeks and weeks and months, and just all of a sudden – boom. You come to your supervisor and say that guy is sexually harassing me. Well, that is kind of hard for people to mentally get around because where's the trail? And you don't have to have a trail. It could be a one shot deal, or it could be a little bit everyday. So trying to put all of that into a definition is very difficult.

Allen feared going too far in describing sexual harassment. The subjective component of the definition, 'the other person's perception', was difficult to put into law. He claimed that the district needed to write a policy with generalities that recognized people have different perceptions. According to Allen, the policy could not be too specific. Additionally, he thought that 'the cases that have been publicized have such horrible facts that they really make bad law.'

In contrast, the women of the university group and Janet did not have difficulty in defining sexual harassment. Denise stated that it was

a behavior that is unwelcome that is unsolicited [defined by the perception
of the receiver, not by the intention of the perpetrator] that can be verbal
or physical and that is directed at you because of your sex.

Janet stated almost the same definition and was able to give a list of verbal comments and physical actions that were off-limits for classified employees.

Still, both Janet and Denise claimed that defining sexual harassment was a real problem in schools. Denise was able to define and recognize the sexual harassment of her daughter on the school bus because of her familiarity and prior experience at the rape crisis center. She said, 'I was able to define it, which I see as a huge problem in the schools. There is no . . . people cannot define it. They confuse it with other things.' When she asked teachers in her district if sexual harassment occurred in their classrooms or hallways, for example, they said no. But when she asked if they see 'this behavior and this behavior and . . .', they readily agreed that they did.

The members of the university women's organization, like Allen, also spoke of the role law played in defining sexual harassment:

What you see are those cases that set the precedent legally that make other
schools or other people or companies fall into line . . . [they] have to be so
severe and the victim has to be so perfect because no one will take it [the
case] unless you have that. Because if a woman failed to report a criminal

act like flashing or assault, then it's her fault. She accepted this behavior. And they don't take into account the dynamics.

As Mary said, 'The prevalent Clayton Williams mentality is that the women bring it on themselves – that their blouses are cut too low and that they shouldn't wear such pretty high heel shoes and that they are . . . asking for it.'
Interview data within this theme indicated that those persons being sexually harassed are left with a bad case law that sets few legal precedents to protect them from harassment and a general ignorance and apathy from public school administrators and state officials as to the actual definition of sexual harassment. Students and teachers who were victims of sexual harassment, it appeared, had few options for receiving assistance. Those with power to enforce policy, therefore, were unaware of or unwilling to define sexual harassment in a serious and specific manner, leaving student and teacher victims unprotected.

Voices Heard in the Policymaking Process

There was a wide range of people involved in the making of the policy. The primary policymaker, Mark, in his interview, discussed the group of representatives that he 'kept informed and in dialogue with' about the policy development. They included teachers' unions, teachers' organizations, a professional school administrator group, a university women's organization, classified personnel union and the city-wide PTA. The largest group, the students, those with the least power, were being defended and spoken for by the university women's organization in their draft recommendations to Mark. The recommendations included incorporating elements into the policy such as prevention, notification, confidentiality, retaliation, support services and the right to an alternative complaint procedure – all of which would give power to students and teachers who were currently afraid to come forward to file complaints against persons sexually harassing them.
Ironically, Mark, the powerful central office policymaker, failed to incorporate the suggestions in the third draft of the policy. Thus, the three women were forced to seek power in higher places. Networking with two board members was one counter-hegemonic strategy they employed, discussing with the board members the necessity of including their recommendations in the policy for the sake of protecting children and staff who had less power and who were intimidated by the proposed bureaucratic method of filing a sexual harassment complaint.[8] Mary asked the board to consider her 7-year-old granddaughter filling out the complaint form and asked what provisions there were in the policy to help young children do that. Similarly, Janet, the classified employee union president, reported to the board that

usually with the blue collar workers that I represent, they are used to losing any battle that they fight with the higher-ups. And if you're a single parent who has kids and this is your only source of support, you can't afford to lose . . . So even when there is a policy in place and there is protection, there is still a lot of fear when [the harasser] is someone in a supervisory position.

In the end, although the primary policymaker rejected the voices of the women, the school board did not when the third draft of the policy was proposed to them. After hearing Denise and Mary oppose the current policy, the board requested that the central office staff and legal counsel develop two separate policies – one for children and one for adults – with more of the university women organization's suggestions incorporated.

The Function of the Policy – Whose Interests Are Served?

The proposed policy's function, it appeared, was to maintain the status quo of the dominant middle-class patriarchy that defined the ideology of the district. Without the assistance of the members of the women's university organization, female (and male) students and faculty and staff who were not part of the district policymaking process were, perhaps unconsciously, allowing those in power in the district to frame the issue and the policy solutions which reinforced basic structural and social inequalities.

According to the male interviewees, the policy drafted would adequately serve all victims of sexual harassment in the school district. Allen, the legal counsel, stated, 'The policy is going to basically prohibit sexual harassment. It's going to give an enforcement mechanism. It is going to provide a way that a person can report and get a remedy and still feel protected.'

In contrast, Janet, the union president, and the representatives of the university women's organization argued the proposed policy would *not* protect the victims of sexual harassment. They felt that different content and wording of the policy could be used that would protect students and other workers with less power than would the language and forms included in the draft of the proposed policy. Denise believed, for example, that the final goal was to develop a policy that was legally sound and that also addressed items beforehand such as prevention, support services, and punishment for retaliation so that an investigation would not be fumbled through and the children or staff person making the complaint would not be revictimized.

And although Janet did not believe that policy would solve all problems dealing with sexual harassment, she did feel that two very central elements were not contained in the proposed policy. The first was the informal grievance procedure which allows a classified employee to just pick up the phone and call someone at central office to tell about harassment they are receiving. This would remove the arbitration or investigation from the hierarchy of the school in which the employee works. The second element was education or training for awareness about the seriousness of sexual harassment for all students and staff included in the policy. Nowhere in the proposed policy draft was education about sexual harassment mandated for students, faculty, staff and parents.

Discussion

As evidenced by the examination of the development of sexual harassment policy in this study, the use of feminist and postmodern epistemologies demonstrates that a community of policymakers does not necessarily hear all stakeholders' voices equally. *Even with current discourse praising participatory policy development, I found the community of policymakers in the school district studied was characterized by male dominance and a hierarchic, top-down structure that did not value input from all of its members, especially women.* Although a community of policymakers is an understandable dream, the ideal of community, in this study, suppressed the voices of women and children and privileged unity over difference. This phenomenom was demonstrated by the male members of the community of policymakers who did not recognize the limits of their understanding women's experiences and who, thus, drafted a policy that did not adequately protect women and children who were victims of sexual harassment.

These findings, I claim, would not have been possible without my use of a situated policy analysis – that is, feminist policy analysis – in which I was not value-free, but located within my own gender studying a women's issue. Observing the development of one district's formulation of a sexual harassment policy, I was able to document how the voices, needs, and concerns of the women and children were not adequately defined, portrayed or heard in the policy community. Traditional positivist or interpretivist policy analysis which claim that policy development is rational, ahistoric, universal and fully objective would not recognize these findings.

Similarly, combining feminist policy analysis with policy archeology, I discerned that:

- the emergence of the problem of sexual harassment was a social construction process;
- sexual harassment was viewed as occurring substantially more by the females interviewed;
- as originally drafted by the male policymakers, the policy did not protect the victims of sexual harassment but served to reinforce the status quo, normalcy, and (patriarchal) order.

If schools are to teach, nurture, and serve *all* of their students equally in a safe and positive environment, new policy methodologies, such as those utilized in this study, must continue to be developed and employed by researchers and policy analysts. Feminist and postmodern analyses of the policy examined in this study allowed me to place the voices of women and children, not in the margins of the policy discourse, but in the center.

Critiquing the ideal of community in policy development, as well as incorporating a broader spectrum of methods, is necessary if more inclusive educational policies are to be generated. As Rixecker claims, 'Whether these critical components of policy design [and analysis] will be attained is now dependent upon the degree to which tolerance and respect exist in the academic, professional, and political arenas' (1994: 137).

Notes

1   In 1991, well-publicized congressional hearings took place concerning the allegations of Anita Hill that Clarence Thomas, a United States Supreme Court nominee, had sexually harassed her in the workplace. Thomas was appointed despite Hill's testimony of harassment.

2   According to Julia Wood (1992), the first wave of reports appeared almost exclusively in popular magazines, rather than in academic journals. Only after there was general interest in the issue did substantial academic research on sexual harassment emerge.

3   Title IX of the Education Amendments, decided by the US Supreme Court in 1972, bound educational institutions not to discriminate on the basis of gender.

4   The courts also recognize two categories of sexual harassment in the employment context and in schools. The first is *quid pro quo* harassment which occurs when a supervisor (or teacher/coach/administrator) conditions the granting of a benefit upon the receipt of sexual favors from a subordinate or punishes the subordinate for rejecting the offer. The second type of harassment is *hostile environment* harassment which occurs when one or more supervisors or coworkers (or student peers) creates an atmosphere that has the purpose or effect of unreasonably creating an intimidating, hostile, or offensive work (or school) environment (National School Board Association, 1993).

5   Riger (1991) has found that the variable that most consistently predicts variation in people's definition of sexual harassment is the sex of the rater. She states that men label fewer behaviors at work as sexual harassment, and even when men do identify behavior as harassment, they are more likely to think that women will be flattered by it. Men are also more likely to blame women for being sexually harassed.

6   Social regularities, according to Scheurich (1994), are 'powerful "grids" or networks of regularities (a kind of grammar or economy similar to Foucault's "complex group of relations") that are constitutive of the emergence or social construction of a particular problem as a social problem . . . [they] constitute what is labeled as a problem and what is not labeled as a problem' (1994: 7). Schuerich has identified five regularities in his application of policy archeology to the policy of coordinated children's services: race, class, gender, professionalization, and governmentality.

7   Pseudonym.

8   See Ferguson, K.E. (1984) *The Feminist Case against Bureaucracy*, Philadelphia, PA, Temple University Press and MacKinnon, C. (1989) *Toward a Feminist Theory of the State*, Cambridge, MA, Harvard University Press.

References

ALCOFF, L. and POTTER, E. (Eds) (1993) *Feminist Epistemologies*, New York, Routledge.

AMERICAN ASSOCIATION OF UNIVERSITY WOMEN (1993) *Hostile Hallways*, Washington DC, Author.

BELENKY, M., CLINCHY, B., GOLDBERGER, N. and TARULE, J. (1986) *Women's Ways of Knowing: The Development of Self, Voice and Mind*, New York, Basic Books.

CLAIR, P.C. (1993) 'The use of framing devices to sequester organizational narratives: Hegemony and harassment', *Communication Monographs*, **60**, pp. 113–136.

CORNBLETH, C. and WAUGH, D. (1993) 'The great speckled bird: Education policy-in-the-making', *Educational Researcher*, **22**, pp. 31–7.

DEY, E., KORN, J. and SAX, L. (1996) 'Betrayed by the academy: The sexual harassment of women college faculty', *Journal of Higher Education*, **67**(2), pp. 149–73.

Doe v. Petaluma City School District, I–103, 838 F. Supp. 1526, 1534 (W.D. OKLA, 1993).

Doe v. Taylor, 15 F. 3d. 433.

EATON, S. (1994) 'Sexual harassment at an early age: New cases are changing the rules for schools', *The Harvard Education Letter*, (ISSN 8755–3716).

EDER, D. (1995) *School Talk: Gender and Adolescent Culture*, New Brunswick, NJ, Rutgers University Press.

EDMUNDS, E. (1988) 'Unwelcome advances', *Atlanta Magazine, September*, pp. 90–3.

ETZIONI, A. (1993) *The Spirit of Community: Rights, Responsibilities, and the Communitarian Agenda*, New York, Crown Publishers.

FARLEY, L. (1978) *Sexual Shakedown: The Sexual Advances of Women on the Job*, New York, McGraw-Hill.

FERGUSON, K.E. (1984) *The Feminist Case against Bureaucracy*, Philadelphia, PA, Temple Press.

FISCHER, F. and FORRESTER, J. (Eds) (1986) *Confronting Values in Policy Analysis: The Politics of Criteria*, Newbury Park, CA, Sage.

Franklin v. Gwinnett County Public Schools, 112 S. Ct. at 1037.

Harris v. Forklift Systems Inc., 60 Empl. Pr. Dc., Paragraph 42,070 (US Dist. Court, Middle Dist. Nashville).

HAWKESWORTH, M.E. (1988) *Theoretical Issues in Policy Analysis*, Albany, NY, State University of New York Press.

HAWKESWORTH, M.S. (1994) 'Policy studies within a feminist frame', *Policy Sciences*, **27**, pp. 97–118.

HOFFMAN, F.L. (1986) 'Sexual harassment in academia: Feminist theory and institutional practice', *Harvard Educational Review*, **56**(2), pp. 105–21.

hooks, b. (1984) *Feminist Theory: From Margin to Center*, Boston, MA, South End Press.

INGRAM, H. and SMITH, S.R. (1993) *Public Policy for Democracy*, Washington DC, The Brookings Institute.

KANTER, R. (1977) 'Some effects of proportion on group life: Skewed sex ratios and responses to token women', *American Journal of Sociology*, **82**, pp. 965–90.

KELLEY, M. and MAYNARD-MOODY, S. (1993) 'Policy analysis in the post-positivist era: Engaging stakeholders in evaluating the economic development districts program', *Public Administration Review*, **53**(2), pp. 135–42.

KOPPICH, J.E. (1993) 'The politics of policymaking for children', *Journal of Education Policy*, **8**(5 and 6), pp. 51–62.

MACKINNON, C. (1979) *Sexual Harassment of Working Women*, New Haven, CT, Yale University Press.

MACKINNON, C. (1987) 'Feminism, Marxism, method and the state: Toward feminist jurisprudence', in HARDING, S. (Ed) *Feminism and Methodology: Social Science Issues*, Bloomington, IN, Indiana University Press.

MAJONE, G. (1989) *Evidence, Argument, and Persuasion in the Policy Process*, New Haven, CT, Yale University Press.

MALEN, B. (1995) 'The micropolitics of education: Mapping the multiple dimensions of power relations in school polities', in SCRIBNER, J. and LAYTON, D. (Eds) *The Study of Educational Politics: The 1994 Commemorative Yearbook of the Politics of Education Association (1969–1994)*, London, Falmer Press, pp. 147–68.

MARSHALL, C. and ANDERSON, G. (1995) 'Rethinking the public and private spheres: Feminist and cultural studies perspectives on the politics of education', in SCRIBNER, J.

and LAYTON, D. (Eds) *The Study of Educational Politics: The 1994 Commemorative Yearbook of the Politics of Education Association (1969–1994)*, London, Falmer Press, pp. 169–82.

MERRIAM, S.B. (1988) *Case Study Research in Education: A Qualitative Approach*, San Francisco, CA, Jossey-Bass.

MUMBY, D. (1988) *Communication and Power in Organizations: Discourse, Ideology, and Domination*, Norwood, NJ, Ablex.

NATIONAL SCHOOL BOARD ASSOCIATION (NSBA) (1993) *Sexual Harassment in Schools: Preventing and Defending Against Claims* (Revised ed.), Alexandria, VA, NSBA.

ORTIZ, F.I. and MARSHALL, C. (1988) 'Women in educational administration', in BOYAN, N. (Ed) *Handbook of Research in Educational Administration*, New York, Longman, pp. 123–41.

PATTON, M. (1990) *Qualitative Evaluation and Research Methods*, Newbury Park, CA, Sage.

RIGER, S. (1991) 'Gender dilemmas in sexual harassment policies and procedures', *American Psychologist*, **46**(5), pp. 497–505.

RIXECKER, S. (1994) 'Expanding the discursive context of policy design: A matter of feminist standpoint epistemology', *Policy Sciences*, **27**, pp. 119–42.

RUBIN, L.J. and BORGERS, S.B. (1990) 'Sexual harassment in universities during the 1980s', *Sex Roles*, **23**, pp. 397–411.

SCHEURICH, J.J. (1994) 'Policy archeology: A new policy studies methodology', *Journal of Educational Policy*, **9**(4), pp. 297–316.

SHAKESHAFT, C., BARBER, E., HERGENROTHER, M.A., JOHNSON, Y., MANDEL, L. and SAWYER, J. (1994, October) 'Conceptions of community: Peer harassment and the culture of caring in the schools', Paper presented at the annual convention of the University Council of Educational Administration, Philadelphia, PA.

STEIN, N. (1993) 'It happens here, too: Sexual harassment and child sexual abuse in elementary and secondary schools', in BIKLEN, S.K. and POLLARD, D. (Eds) *Gender and Education*, Chicago, IL, National Society for the Study of Education, pp. 191–203.

WALSH, M. (1994) 'Principal can be held liable in sexual abuse of student, court rules', *Education Week, March 16*, p. 6.

WOOD, J.T. (1992) 'Telling our stories: Narratives as a basis for theorizing sexual harassment', *Journal of Applied Communication Research*, **20**(4), pp. 349–62.

WORKING WOMEN UNITED INSTITUTE (1975) 'Sexual harassment on the job: Questions and answers', unpublished manuscript, Ithaca, NY.

YATES, L. (1993) 'What happens when feminism is an agenda of the state? Feminist theory and the case of educational policy in Australia', *Discourse: The Australian Journal of Educational Studies*, **14**(1), pp. 17–29.

YOUNG, I.M. (1990) 'The ideal of community and the politics of difference', in NICHOLSON, L. (Ed) *Feminism/Postmodernism*, New York, Routledge, pp. 300–23.

Chapter 12

Institutionalizing Women's Voices, Not Their Echoes, through Feminist Policy Analysis of Difference

Hanne B. Mawhinney

Compared to the longer history of feminist political activism, policy studies within a feminist frame are a comparatively new focus for political inquiry. With the recognition of gender as an analytical category, feminist scholars have sought to institutionalize women's voices in their respective disciplines. After recently reviewing the state of policy study within a feminist frame, Mary Hawksworth (1994) observes that 'the goal of feminist scholarship is to transform traditional disciplines, purging them of androcentric bias, reshaping dominant paradigms so that women's needs, interests, activities, and concerns can be analyzed and understood systematically' (1994: 98). Of the traditional disciplines political science, the grandparent of policy studies, has been slower than most social sciences in incorporating feminism into its conceptual storehouse. Compounding the effect of this hesitancy has been a tendency for feminist political analysts to argue among themselves. In their recent analysis of gender power, leadership and governance, feminist political scientists Georgia Duerst-Lahti and Rita Mae Kelly observe:

> debates occur around how to treat difference. Should we recognize gender differences, acknowledge their consequences, and in strategies for change seek special treatment that accounts for differences? Or should we concentrate on treating women and men exactly the same and advocate only equal pay for equal work, for example, arguing that to do anything else is to reimpose gender demarcations where none need exist? Or, alternatively, should we advocate comparable pay for comparable worth on the grounds that men and women differ, particularly in their working situations? (1995: 2)

Unfortunately, while these positions weave through the important conceptual debates among feminist political theorists, gender effects continue to disadvantage and even harm women in their private and public lives. The new generation of feminist scholarship in education has shown that despite their dominance in the teaching profession, and the emergence of a new awareness of gender effects, women teachers continue to suffer disadvantages created by gender effects (Acker, 1989;

Arnot and Weiler, 1993; Bell and Chase, 1993; Blackmore and Kenway, 1993; Marshall, 1993; Marshall and Anderson, 1994). Accounting for the issues of difference that Durest-Lahti and Kelly (1995) have identified is of critical importance for a new feminist policy analysis.

The Purpose and Methods of this Chapter

In this chapter I take up a unique opportunity to explore the arguments of a feminist legal and policy analysis that have been brought to the debates around how to treat difference that continue to bedevil the feminist policy studies. In this exploration I share the experiences of the elementary women teachers of the Federation of Women Teachers' Associations of Ontario (FWTAO) as they have fought to maintain their status as one of the world's few all female teachers' unions. In recent years the Federation has fought through the Canadian courts the challenges from their counterpart male organization. In the tradition of emerging feminist scholarship, I have transformed into the analysis of this chapter, the voices and arguments of the women leaders of the FWTAO, the feminist scholars and policy analysts who they have called upon as expert witnesses, and the feminist lawyers who have defended their status in the face of the challenges the Federation has faced in the courts of Ontario and at the province's Human Rights Commission.

Since it was established by a small group of women teachers in 1918, the autonomy of FWTAO has been challenged by the federation representing the male elementary teachers of Ontario, the Ontario Public School Teachers Federation (OPSTF). FWTAO was the first of the five Ontario teachers' federations to be established. It functioned with a voluntary membership from 1918 until the passage of the Teaching Profession Act of Ontario in 1944. The Act made membership in a single federation, the Ontario Teachers' Federation (OTF), mandatory for all teachers in Ontario, and gave the five pre-existing teachers' federations (including the FWTAO) equal power and representation as affiliates on the OTF board of governors. The five affiliates represented teacher groups in place prior to the formation of the OTF, including secondary school teachers, teachers in the publicly funded Catholic school system of the province, teachers in the publicly funded French language schools, male elementary teachers in public schools and the female teachers in elementary public schools represented by the FWTAO. These groupings reflect the governance and organization of public education in the province of Ontario specifically, because education in Canada is a provincial responsibility. They also reflect the constitutionally guaranteed collective rights of Ontario's Catholics Francophones to their own publicly funded schools.[1]

Throughout the history of the Ontario Teachers' Federation, the elementary men teachers' federation (OPSTF) has challenged the need for an affiliate structure and particularly the need for a separate federation representing the interests of women elementary teachers in the province. In recent years it has funded several challenges in courts to the right of FWTAO members to be represented by this autonomous organization of women teachers. This chapter examines the arguments that the

FWTAO has brought to the problem of accounting for difference. These arguments are offered as a model of feminist legal analysis and feminist policy analysis at work in the courts constructed in the 'masters' house'.

The chapter presents one part of my ongoing study of women in leadership at the margins of power in education.[2] The chapter focuses on the experiences of gender power, leadership and control of one of the groups of women leaders in teachers' federations across Canada that I am currently interviewing. My analysis is informed by the hours of tape-recorded and transcribed interviews I conducted during the winter and spring of 1996 with several women who have been leaders in the FWTAO. The policy documents, legal arguments and reports which they have shared with me offered insights into the thinking of women at the frontier of feminist thinking in law in Canada and the United States (Eberts *et al.*, 1991). The records of the affidavits the FWTAO elicited from experts in various disciplines offered me an opportunity to examine feminist thinking. It enabled me to explore research on key aspects of the argument the federation presented showing how its practices and policies contributed to the elimination of women's inequality.

My intention is both narrative and conceptual. I make no pretext at presenting the full depth and complexity of the arguments that these women brought to successive court challenges. Nor will I present an unbiased analysis of their claims. Rather I describe from the arguments they have brought to debates on meaning of equality and equity, the history of a group of feminists struggling with how to treat difference in policy, law and practice. My methods are those of a woman researching women. Susan Victor (1995) describes these methods by quoting Chevigny (1984) who states, 'I suppose that it is nearly inevitable that women writing about women will symbolically reflect their internalized relationships with their others, and in some measure, re-create them' (quoted in Victor, 1995: 175). According to these feminist scholars the identification with subjects is 'both a risk and an opportunity; the understanding of the subjects is enhanced by an awareness of their effects on the self of the researcher' (1995: 175).

In the spirit of this feminist methodology I acknowledge my identification with the arguments offered by feminist legal analysts and policy experts in the texts of these debates and with the women leaders of FWTAO who shared their thoughts with me. They take the position that the collective choice of women to work in their own organization is a more reasonable one in view of the gender dynamics operating in mixed sex organizations of all kinds, including the traditional trade unions. I acknowledge this stance less as a prelude to advocacy, than in the spirit of modeling a feminist policy analysis of difference which rejects the tendency of traditional policy analysis to view with suspicion such apparent subjectivity.

In the following discussion I first situate the problem of social justice for women teachers in the context of the practice of democratic education. I offer a brief historical account of the development of the FWTAO and the role that it has played in fighting for equity for women elementary teachers in the province, for women teachers throughout the country and internationally, and in reaching out to support equity policies and practices for all women in Canada. I then review the history of the legal challenges which the Federation has faced during the past two decades, before examining the arguments which feminist legal analysts and experts in various disciplines presented in these challenges to support the conception of substantive equality which acknowledges the problems of systemic inequality. I describe the contradictions and dilemmas created by the gender effects operating in courts confronted by feminist legal advocates engaged in collective lawyering for substantive equality. I suggest some implications of an advocacy orientation for a new feminist policy analysis of difference which focuses on the practices and discourses of power. I conclude by outlining seven lessons for a new feminist policy analysis and advocacy.

Women Educators' Stance Toward Democratic Education

In recent years feminist scholars of education have begun to examine the meaning of democratic education and social justice for the lives of women teachers. There is a growing body of international research of a significant range and depth on the work and lives of women teachers reported in such editions offered by Sandra Acker (1989), Madeleine Arnot and Katherine Weiler (1993), Jane Gaskell, Arlene McLaren and Myra Novogrodsky (1989), Cecilia Reynolds and Beth Young (1995). This research has provided an alternative to the educational reform discourse currently dominated by an agenda of excellence through accountability by assessment, privatization, choice and charters. Commenting on the alternative feminist discourse, Katherine Weiler (1993) argues that feminist theorists of the 1990s have challenged the discourse of excellence with a renewed focus on the struggle for democratic education. They have attended to the ways in which women teachers have in the past, and continue to construct a democratic education for all students.

Weiler acknowledges the long history of activism for social justice in education by women educators, begun in the United States by women like Margaret Haley, the elementary school teacher and organizer for the Chicago Teachers Federation, a powerful early teachers' union composed of women elementary school teachers. Weiler cites a speech Margaret Haley made in 1904 before the National Education Association which identified the contested nature of schooling in capitalist systems:

> Two ideals are struggling for supremacy in American life today: one the industrial ideal, dominating through the supremacy of commercialism, which subordinates the worker to the product and the machine; the other, the ideal of democracy, the ideal of the educators which places humanity above all machines; and demands that all activity shall be the expression of human life (cited in Weiler, 1993: 211).

Haley argued that educators played a vital role in 'encouraging critical education both for individual growth and for the achievement of a more generous and inclusive democracy' (cited in Weiler, 1993: 211). Reflecting this activism for social justice, in the early 1900s Haley helped organize the Chicago Teachers

Federation around not only issues of teachers' wages and working conditions, but also around the political and philosophical questions of what education should be in a democracy like the United States.

About the same time, across the border in Canada, a group of women teachers in Toronto, also concerned with conditions of work for women, organized the Women Teachers' Association of Toronto constituted 'to encourage social and professional union of women teachers [so that] the standing of women teachers shall be duly recognized, to encourage a professional esprit de corps, and the free discussion of all questions affecting the profession' (cited in Labatt, 1993: 8). The charge to discuss all questions affecting the profession has been carried out by members of the FWTAO who have not wavered from a vision of equity in education expressed by the Federation President on the 75th anniversary of the Federation that 'teaching is an act of love [and] Women teachers are caring, dedicated to the welfare of children and to the enhancement of learning' (cited in Labatt, 1993: 330). Since its formation in 1918, the Federation has actively sought to fulfill this commitment to the purpose of equity by influencing the development of pedagogical practices of democratic education in the province. In the course of a century of collective action the Federation has become a national leader in developing curriculum and in promoting pedagogical practices for inclusive education, mainstreaming, cooperative learning, gender equity in the classroom, computers in the classroom and a host of other aspects of democratic education in action.

The FWTAO has always had a broad vision of democratic education, and has used its resources strategically and politically to fulfill that vision. Federation leaders have informed policymaking locally, provincially, nationally and internationally. Federation leaders were among the first to register shock and dismay that Canada was in contravention of the United Nation's Convention on the Rights of the Child. Criticism by the Federation in 1991, contributed to Canada's subsequent decision to ratify the Convention. The Federation was guided by a feminist agenda for democratic education in its policy advocacy to publicly support the principle of first call on society's resources for all the world's children. It used its award-winning journal, the *FWTAO Newsletter*, to focus the attention of women teachers on the plight of the world's children and how teachers can take part in development education for a global education. As an all women's federation, the FWTAO has been able to direct its resources to supporting a global feminism. Since the early 1960s the Federation has educated young women in third world countries through a program of overseas scholarships. Through this program thousands of women in developing countries have received education not otherwise possible. Mary Labatt (1993) who has documented the history of these efforts, observes that 'one special example is the many black women in South Africa who have been to Teachers' College on FWTAO Overseas Scholarships who are now poised to contribute to an equal society by providing quality education for children who will grow up as full participants in a new democracy' (1993: 330).

At the same time, like other women teachers across North America, Federation members have experienced the contradictions and tensions of working in schools organized in ways not always consistent with the principles of democratic education espoused by Haley. Haley had in mind a conception of democratic education that Weiler describes as resting on 'the ideal of a society that is inclusive and celebrates the rich diversity of human beings, not as "capital", but as creative, intelligent, and feeling beings open to the rich possibilities of human life' (Weiler, 1993: 223). This view of democracy encompasses the inclusion and participation of all groups and individuals. It is a view that, according to Weiler, has been under attack by elites who have repeatedly

> attempted to narrow democracy to a limited sphere of individual interests, while leaving political discussion and power to the few. Thus women's concerns and women's lives have been excluded from neo-conservative discourse about education. But over and over again women and others who have been excluded by this narrow definition of democracy have organized and demanded inclusion in the political process and redefined what it means to be an active member of civil society. They have argued for a conception of democracy that is more than simply individual freedom for private choices, but implies as well the participation of all members of the society in the rights and responsibilities of citizenship (1993: 224).

The FWTAO has led the way in fighting for a conception of democracy grounded in a recognition of the group-based social inequalities they face themselves as women teachers. According to Catherine MacKinnon,[3] unlike American and British women, women teachers of Ontario have been able to take advantage of constitutional guarantees provided by the Canadian Charter of Rights and Freedoms. The Equality guarantees in the Charter center on the 'notion of discrimination on disadvantage imposed on a group basis, or arbitrary detriment delivered through a group-based differentiation' (cited in Eberts *et al.*, 1991: 363). MacKinnon observes that in legal and political discourse on equality, the terms 'disadvantaged' and 'disempowered' are used to refer to groups whose life chances society unfairly restricts. Members of those groups are 'typically paid less well and advanced less regularly and have less social status, resource, security, and respect' (MacKinnon cited in Eberts *et al.*, 1991: 364). According to MacKinnon:

> women, compared to men, are such a subordinate group in most societies. Women teachers in Ontario, both as women in society and as women within the teaching profession in Ontario, are not, in general, exceptions to this description (MacKinnon cited in Eberts, *et al.*, 1991: 364).

MacKinnon's observations were made in her affidavit to the Supreme Court of Ontario on behalf of the FWTAO in a claim supported by the men teachers' federation of the province (OPSTF) that the mandatory membership to the Federation set out in By-Law I of the Ontario Teachers' Federation violated the Charter, specifically provisions of freedom of association and equality. Under challenge was the theory of sex equality which underpins the collective character of the FWTAO and its purpose of promoting not only democratic education, but also social justice for women teachers.

Women Teachers Struggling for Equality

I now turn to examine the arguments for and the challenges to, the sex equality theory which provides the *raison d'etre* of the FWTAO. This is a gender-specific theory of equality which responds to the question of how to account for gender differences by arguing that 'equality is best sought by measures which recognize women's inequalities in order to eliminate them' (Eberts *et al.*, 1991: 21). I focus on the equality arguments brought by feminist legal and political analysts in defending FWTAO's gender-specific model of equality, and the judicial arguments discounting and upholding the feminist analysis in three legal actions brought by the OPSTF against the FWTAO. The key legal arguments presented by the FWTAO are simple: all-women organizations that promote women's equality do not violate the Charter equality guarantees. The arguments, demand, however, a reconceptualization of conventional political theories of power, and social justice. This new conception acknowledges the importance of group membership in the constitution of human identity, and recognizes and attends to the question of social justice raised by group-based patterns of disadvantage such as those that characterize the conditions which have historically disadvantaged women elementary teachers in Ontario.

During the past century women elementary teachers in Ontario, Canada have been active participants in the political movement which continues today to develop and implement policies to eradicate gender-based injustices. Along with other women they have used strategies including mobilization, public demonstrations, lobbying, litigation and constitutional amendments. In doing so they have confronted political institutions and ideologies created by men in an era of strict demarcation between the political and domestic spheres. Political parties, courts, bureaucracies and legislatures all developed in a context in which women were legally excluded as political actors, being largely restricted to domestic roles. Thus, throughout the past century, Canadian women have had to search for ways to participate in institutions created for, and by men, and structured in ways consistent with the life circumstances of a small strata of dominant men (Vickers, Rankin, Appelle, 1993, preface).

In the early years of this century women began to focus their efforts to achieve change in their lives increasingly on groups that they themselves created, as women, and that operated in ways that accommodated and reflected women's life circumstances. They also began to emphasize the development of stable, women-centred institutions (Vickers *et al.*, 1993, preface). Women teachers in Ontario joined other groups of women in creating alternative institutions to raise awareness of gender inequities and to rectify blatant injustices (Hawkesworth, 1994). One outcome of their efforts was the formation in 1918 of the FWTAO, which along with other women's organizations fought for the equity policies that are now part of education in Ontario. Women teachers were mobilized to join together in a voluntary federation for the specific and financial status of women teachers. Similar concerns motivated male elementary teachers in 1919 to form the Ontario Public School Men Teachers' Federation (now the Ontario Public School Teachers' Federation OPSTF) and secondary teachers to form their own federation.

Gender politics of the era prior to the formation of FWTAO disadvantaged women significantly. Not only were women not offered similar opportunities for promotion to those offered men, but women were not permitted to negotiate for their salaries. Salary equity was, however, particularly important for women teachers at the turn of the century, who were paid only 73 per cent of the average male teacher's salary (Eberts *et al.*, 1991: 6). The activism of the early leaders of the federation grew out of the experiences many had in the suffrage movement and their understanding of the clearly divergent interests of men and women teachers. That understanding and experience stood organizers in good stead in their struggles to enroll members, particularly during the depression when desperate teachers underbid each other for jobs. Although the conditions of work and of life for many women teachers during that decade were stark, the federation worked systematically to establish employment exchange services, to introduce a sick benefit plan and to extend legal services to its members.

By the early 1940s the difficulties of sustaining such efforts while at the same time continuing to enroll new teachers led the Federation to join with the elementary men teachers' federation and the secondary teachers' federation in lobbying the government of the day to mandate that all teachers belong to and contribute financially to their professional associations. The Premier of the province would only agree to this policy change if all teachers in the province were represented by a single federation. Agreement was reached as result of the political negotiations between the government and teachers in these three federations, and two other groups; teachers in English Catholic schools and teachers in the schools for the province's minority French language speakers, that the five groups would become affiliates to a single federated body. In 1944 Ontario's Teaching Profession Act was passed with regulations anticipating the creation of the Ontario Teachers' Federation (OTF) to whom statutory fees are paid, and five affiliated bodies with representation in running the affairs of the OTF. The legislation mandates the compulsory membership of all teachers teaching in publicly funded schools in Ontario into the OTF, but membership in the affiliates is determined by an OTF By-Law I determined by the organization's board of governors. The OTF membership By-Law I allocates teachers among the five affiliates teachers on the basis of their historical origins and in recognition of the federated nature structure of the Teaching Profession Act (1944). Any change in affiliate membership is decided by the OTF executive in conjunction with the executives of the affiliates concerned. The OTF represents teachers on matters which affect all teachers in the province, and the affiliates represent teachers who are their members on matters which are of relevance to them specifically. Thus women teachers in elementary public schools are assigned membership to the FWTAO.

Mandatory members furthered the capacity of the Federation to promote the interests of women. During these early years the FWTAO began to exercise a leadership and influence that continues to this day, in the development of elementary curriculum, and in promoting pedagogy emphasizing cooperative rather than competitive learning. During these years the Federation did not lose sight of its mandate to promote salary equity. Its leaders gained expertise in negotiating on the behalf of women in communities across Ontario, and the salary scale which they developed gradually gained acceptance. Gaining some degree of salary equity was a slow process and even after the Legislature of Ontario passed a bill to mandate equal pay for work of equal value in 1951, school boards continued to pay married male teachers an additional allowance. Leaders of the FWTAO recognized that the salary differences between male and female elementary teachers in Ontario that could be found until the 1980s reflected the unequal access women teachers had to the principalship. The Federation developed a program of fellowships and bursaries to assist women seeking to gain the baccalaureate qualifications which became required for positions of responsibility in the province's schools by 1961.[4]

The Federation recognized early that while such supports for individual teachers were essential they were not enough to open opportunities to assume leadership positions for most women teachers in the province's elementary schools. As a larger institution, the Federation was able to marshal its financial and human resources to lobby governments and school boards for policy changes to promote affirmative action. It developed documents for school boards on affirmative action, and as a result of its efforts the provincial government in 1984 adopted a policy that required school boards to promote affirmative action for women in their employment relations and in their curriculum.

Since 1970 the Federation has run concentrated leadership training courses for women who are typically not mentored by male principals, and often excluded from the informal networks which breed such relationships. The FWTAO leadership courses have provided particularly important opportunities for women in small and isolated rural communities who would not otherwise have had such support. During this decade the consolidation of small rural schools into larger administrative units resulted in a dramatic reduction in the number of women holding responsibilities as principals. The effect was dramatic as the larger schools were assigned male principals and the proportion of women in principalships dropped from 26 per cent in 1967 to 8 per cent just three years later in 1970 (Eberts *et al.*, 1991: 9). The effect was also longlasting, since as late as 1988 only 13.6 per cent of elementary teachers were women. Declining enrollments and the amalgamation of small school boards during these years reduced the opportunities for the women prepared for the principalship through the efforts of the Federation.

The Federation has also used its resources and expertise to promote the interests of women generally in local communities, provincially, nationally and internationally. The Federation has historically fought violence against women. In recent years it has funded shelters for abused women throughout the province. Federation researchers presented a brief to the government of Ontario's legislative committee on the status of pensions pressing for the inclusion of homemakers in the Canada Pension Plan. In the 1970s recognizing the importance of a national lobby for all Canadian women, the Federation provided office space, supplies and secretarial assistance for the organization that has become the National Action Committee on the

Status of Women as it struggled to begin its work. The Federation made a crucial and most important contribution to the status of Canadian women by providing similar assistance to the Women's Legal Education and Action Fund (LEAF), a group which sponsors legal cases crucial to the development of women's equality jurisprudence.

The Federation's commitment to sex equality led it to join with other women's groups in demanding that the federal government include strong and effective sex equality guarantees when the Charter of Rights and Freedoms was finally enshrined in the Canadian constitution in 1985. It is ironical that the day after the sex equality provisions came into effect, the very first steps were taken filing a legal action against the FWTAO for discrimination on the basis of sex by an Ontario women elementary school backed by the men's union. The action turned out to be the first of several legal challenges, including one that has not yet been heard.[5] During each of these challenges arguments were offered by Federation lawyers outlining the principles of a substantive theory of equality which demonstrates that a woman's right of self-determination – as exemplified in collectively chosen public all-women and women-only settings-promotes actual sex equality. I turn next to examine the arguments used to support this theory.

Interpreting Equality Rights for Women Teachers

On April 17, 1985, Margaret Tomen, a female elementary school principal supported by OPSTF funding, applied for a judicial review in Ontario Divisional Court seeking an order to quash the OTF By-Law I which mandates membership to affiliate federations, on the basis of historical groupings on the grounds that it was discriminatory and contrary to the Canadian Charter of Rights and Freedoms. Along with another elementary school teacher, Linda Logan-Smith, Margaret Tomen also filed an application to the Ontario Human Rights Commission for a ruling that the membership rules violate the nondiscrimination provisions set out in the Ontario Human Rights Code. Although these actions overlapped, I will examine each separately, beginning with the case for discrimination brought by Tomen only under the *Charter of Rights and Freedoms.*

Margaret Tomen's application asserted that the Ontario Teachers' Federations membership rules requiring that all women elementary school teachers belong to FWTAO and all men elementary teachers belong to OPSTF discriminated against her on the basis of sex. She claimed OTF By-Law I was discriminatory because it prevented her from joining the union of her choice, the OPSTF, because she was a woman. Margaret Tomen was in fact, a voluntary member of OPSTF, a status which gave her virtually all rights of statutory membership. Although OPSTF was not her official bargaining agent, it had always bargained jointly with the FWTAO, and Tomen had herself negotiated on behalf of OPSTF.

The application to the Ontario Divisional Court, which raised arguments that the OTF By-Law I discriminated on the basis of sex and religion and violated freedom of association, was eventually heard before the Supreme Court of Ontario. During the two weeks of hearings, the feminist legal arguments, backed by evidence

Hanne B. Mawhinney

from feminist scholars from a broad range of disciplines presented a gender-specific theory of equality in the context of Canadian Charter law. The model of equality developed focuses attention 'directly on the ways in which women's inequity is constructed through male dominance behaviours, male control of institutional power and resources and male opposition to sex equality' (Eberts *et al.*, 1991).

In keeping with this thrust of feminist policy analysis, Federation lawyers presented affidavits from leaders of the FWTAO documenting the decades of attempts by the men teachers' federation (OPSTF) to persuade FWTAO to amalgamate. Although local OPSTF groups, reflecting the policies of the federation had consistently opposed meaningful local affirmative action policies, and had not been in favor of equity legislation, the Federation had changed its By-Laws to admit women as members, and had changed its name from the Ontario Public Men Teachers' Federation to the Ontario Public School Teachers' Federation. FWTAO lawyers argued that in challenging the OTF By-Law allocating mandatory membership to the five affiliates, the mens' Federation was attempting to secure its political goals of amalgamation of the Federations. They charged that OPSTF's constitutional claims should be examined with skepticism, and appealed to the Court to dismiss the applications and send the dispute 'back in the political arena where it belongs' (Eberts *et al.*, 1991: 30). Lawyers for the FWTAO also called on the Court to examine the real nature of the constitutional rights and freedoms as they apply to claims made by Margaret Tomen and the OPSTF.

The allegation by Ms. Tomen, that in denying her the right to choose her own bargaining agent, By-Law I violates Charter of Rights and Freedoms guarantees of freedom of association was dismissed as incorrect by FWTAO lawyers, Elizabeth Shilton Lennon and Mary Eberts. Freedom of association, Lennon argued, protects the rights of individuals to join together in groups to pursue common goals, whereas Ms. Tomen asked for the right to choose her bargaining agent on an individual basis. Freedom of association protects the freedom of individuals to join together in groups to pursue common goals. Lennon noted that the fundamental purposes of freedom of association would be negated if Ms. Tomen's claim were permitted to undermine collective goals and interests without compelling constitutional justification. She concluded that:

> The freedom of association of FWTAO's members is entitled to greater constitutional protection than the association claims, if any of [Margaret Tomen] inasmuch as FWTAO's members have associated to pursue sex equality, a goal protected by section 15 of the Charter [of Rights and Freedoms] (cited in Eberts *et al.*, 1991: 68).

Mary Eberts responded for the Federation to the charge that Ms. Tomen's equality rights were breached by her assignment to the FWTAO on the basis of her sex with a unique presentation. Eberts' summary of the evidence presented by the experts into a number of general categories supports the model of substantive equality upon which the Federation rested its response to the OPSTF challenge. I have abstracted directly from Eberts' summary the key points of evidence in the affidavits of expert's called to testify by FWTAO, in order to provide readers of this chapter with the gist of the arguments supporting this model of substantive equality for women (Eberts *et al.*, 1991: 75–80).

Eberts' evidence confirms that women elementary school teachers continue to be disadvantaged in terms of salaries, promotions and other opportunities for advancement, relative to men, as are women in Canada generally. Experts called by the Federation explained the disadvantage by demonstrating the social and psychological processes by which male dominance is reproduced. They showed how men, regardless of their numbers in organizations, possess disproportionate authority in, and control of, mixed gender interactions. Experts in psychological processes explained that enhanced authority is constructed through sex-differentiated approaches to verbal interactions, and group tasks, and by stereotyping the leadership role as masculine. This psychological structure is evident in educational systems where male authority, values, interests and achievements are affirmed. More directly coercive evidence was presented suggesting that when single-sex organizations have amalgamated, men tend to take over leadership positions previously held by women, to reallocate resources previously committed to women, and to block initiatives that redress women's inequality. Evidence showed that men use their enhanced authority in professional, educational and labor organizations to prevent women from raising concerns about women's equality, and when those concerns are raised, to invalidate them. One of the specific strategies used by men to resist women's equality claims has been to employ legal and political processes to prevent women from forming women's organizations.

The FWTAO also presented comparative evidence demonstrating that evidence that all-women's organizations, including all-women teachers' unions are more effective than mixed sex organizations in representing the interests of women. Moreover the status of organized women, including women teachers, improves with organizational autonomy. A measure of women's autonomy in unions is the extent to which they can pursue sex equality issues. Several affidavits presented by experts in a number of disciplines agreed that all-women associations promote women's equality in numerous ways. In such organizations women are free to allocate their own resources to women's issues. According to several affidavits, the policies and practices of the FWTAO specifically had the effect of increasing awareness of sexism in education, and the Federation had the power to allocate resources to combat it.

The evidence which I have briefly reviewed was called forth by the FWTAO in order to respond to the legal question posed by Tomen to the Ontario Supreme Court: Does the existence of all-women organizations discriminate on the basis of sex? Eberts observes that the legal argument had to establish two points: first, that all-women organizations actually promote equality; and second, that such organizations are legal under constitutional equality law. Affidavits of experts in legal theory and other disciplines were offered supporting the legality of the FWTAO membership rules. Evidence offered by several lawyers concerned with legal issues affecting women showed that all-women organizations are legal in other countries. Ruth Anker-Hoyer confirmed that Norway, Sweden and Denmark all explicitly recognize that all-women organizations that promote women's equality cannot be considered to violate sex equality guarantees (Eberts *et al.*, 1995: 275). The cornerstone the model of substantive (actual) equality which framed the arguments presented by FWTAO in this case, implies that women-only organizations can be consistent with promotion of sex equality, and eliminating women-only organizations is inconsistent with achieving sex equality.

Decisions on Equality under the *Charter of Rights and Freedoms*

In September, 1987, Mr Justice Ewaschuck of the Ontario Supreme Court rejected the arguments presented on behalf of Margaret Tomen challenging the validity of the portions of By-Law I of the Ontario Teachers' Federation (OTF) in the face of equality and right of free association provisions in the Canadian *Charter of Rights and Freedoms*.

The case was prepared and argued early in the development of Charter equality doctrine. The Supreme Court of Canada had not yet made substantive rulings on key sections of the Charter, but some more expansive approaches to interpreting the implications for human rights legislation were emerging in jurisprudence in lower courts. Lawyers and advisors for the FWTAO concluded that this new and more open context offered an opportunity for facts presented by experts supporting FWTAO's theory of substantive equality to be considered in Charter-related jurisprudence.

The Federation was successful in placing in Charter equality jurisprudence a record of facts of the substantive conditions of women's equality presented by the experts supporting the status of FWTAO as an all-women's organization promoting sex equality. However, although, Mr Justice Ewaschuck did dismiss the application by Ms Tomen to invalidate By-Law I on the basis that it violated Charter equality and freedom of association provisions, he did not choose to base his ruling on equality provisions. Rather he determined that the Canadian *Charter of Rights and Freedoms* did not apply to the by-law of a non-governmental organization. He reasoned that 'The Charter was primarily designed solely to protect individuals from government abuse . . . [and] By-Law I is a private law internal to the Ontario Teachers' Federation and its five affiliates' (cited in Eberts, 1991: 609–10). Federation lawyers argued that the judge could have made legal history by basing his ruling directly on equality grounds. The judge did, however, recognize the basic principle that the Charter does apply to group rights. Mr Justice Ewaschuck ruled:

> The Charter was designed to restrain governments from abusing fundamental individual (and more limited group) rights and freedoms, but only those rights and freedoms particularized in the Charter. The Charter was designed to protect individuals from government tyranny. The Charter was not designed to permit individuals to tyrannize other private individuals or groups in the name of individuals' rights. The Charter was not designed to permit absolute individual freedom so as to result in unbridled anarchy as opposed to ordered liberty (cited in Eberts *et al.*, 1995: 609).

The subsequent appeal by OPSTF of this decision to the Ontario Court of Appeal was dismissed with costs to the FWTAO. A further appeal by OPSTF seeking leave to bring the matter before the highest court in Canada, the Supreme Court of Canada, was also dismissed with costs. The team of feminist legal and policy experts assembled to support the challenges brought against FWTAO had successfully intervened in one of the first cases appealing to the equality rights and freedom of association rights of the new Canadian *Charter of Rights and Freedoms*. Presented as a claim for sex equality, Margaret Tomen's application was based on a gender neutral theory of equality. It is a theory which responds to the problem of accounting for difference which was first raised in this chapter by considering that 'equality is best sought by treating women and men the same, without regard to existing social inequalities' (Eberts *et al.*, 1991: 21). If it had been successful, it would have had the effect of undermining and perhaps eventually eliminating the FWTAO.

Claims to the Human Rights Code

One of the many lessons to be taken from this case is that legal and political challenges to institutions and structures promoting women's equality are rarely resolved definitively. New arenas of challenge are found to replace those exhausted by particular actions. In this case, denial of the appeal to Charter provisions by the Ontario Divisional Court did not affect the efforts of the OPSTF to compel the Federation to amalgamate through the legal venue offered by the Ontario Human Rights Code. The OPSTF supported the complaints of Margaret Tomen and Linda Logan-Smith, another elementary school teacher to a Board of Inquiry of the Human Rights Commission. The two women complained that they were discriminated against because of their sex, because they were required as a condition of membership in the OTF, and specifically as a result of the OTF By-Law I, to become statutory members of the FWTAO. They claimed that they were thus denied the right to become statutory members of the OPSTF, the association of their choice. They specified in their claim that they did not challenge the right of the FWTAO to exist as a female-only association, rather they directed their complaints against compelled statutory membership on the basis of sex.

FWTAO was an active intervenor in the claim brought by Ms Tomen to the Board of Inquiry, presenting a case based on the theory of substantive equality and supported by testimony from experts in various aspects of sex equality and discrimination similar to the case they successfully presented to the Ontario Divisional Court. In the case of the Board of Inquiry, the approach was not successful. In March 1994, Dr Daniel J. Baum found for the Board of Inquiry that By-Law I of the OTF represented unlawful discrimination on the basis of gender because it contravened section 6 of the Ontario Human Rights Code, RSO 1990, c.H.19.Section 6 which reads as follows:

> Every person has a right to equal treatment with respect to membership in any trade union, trade or occupational association or self-governing

profession without discrimination because of race, ancestry, place of origin, colour, ethnic origin, citizenship, creed, sex, sexual orientation, age, marital status, family status or handicap.

In his analysis Dr Baum argued that Tomen and Logan-Smith suffered injury to their dignity interests due to discrimination flowing from compulsion. He reasoned that Tomen and Logan-Smith claimed they were discriminated against because they were denied statutory membership in OPSTF on the basis of their sex. This denial resulted from the requirement that they take statutory membership in FWTAO as a 'matter of compulsion, like all other female public elementary school teachers' (Baum, 1994: 13). In a preliminary finding Dr Baum concluded that:

> Having viewed all the relevant facts, a reasonable person could conclude that there was a rational basis for finding that there was discrimination against the Complainants on the basis of gender which offended their dignity interest: They were denied the right to become statutory members of OPSTF, which wanted to be a mixed-gender association, because they were compelled to be statutory members of a single-sex teaching association (1994: 22).

In the final phase of the proceedings of the Commission of Inquiry, expert testimony was presented by FWTAO, OPSTF and the Counsel for the Commission on the nature of injury to dignity interests. Dr Baum consistently discounted expert testimony provided by witnesses brought forward by FWTAO. For example, the testimony of Dr Jill Ker Conway, accepted as an expert in nineteenth and twentieth century American history concerning the relationship between education and access to professional achievement, was given limited weight on the matter of compulsory membership in FWTAO because, Dr Baum argued:

> Her comments concerning compulsory membership were not central to the primary thrust of her testimony concerning single-sex educational institutions and associations . . . [and] indeed, the bases for her comments appeared to be grounded in her experience in Australia and with the union movement there (Baum, 1994: 42).

Baum cites the following dialogue concerning the compulsory membership mandated by By-Law I between Dr Conway and the Counsel of the Commission as evidence for his reason for giving limited weight to her testimony:

> JC: I have indicated that I think the issue here is whether or not a group whose purpose is to maximize the career potential of women teachers in the elementary system can maintain its base of resources is a very serious one for its future. I take the question of compulsory membership as a very important one on which I believe there are some arguments that can be made.

Question: You see this as relating to the continuation of the institution?

JC: I think it can probably continue with very limited resources, but I don't believe that is a particularly beneficial thing for women teachers.

Question: With respect, Professor Conway, you don't know how many women would choose to belong to a mixed [gender] organization or a single-sex organization given the choice?

JC: I do know how strong the cultural pressure is for women to affiliate with men's organizations and strong pressure that is exerted, which I have experienced for ten years running a single-sex institution, and historically that [the pressure] has been very effective (Baum, 1994: 42).

Dr Baum, judged Professor Conway's comments to be unrelated to the issue of compulsion. He discounted her comments because, in his view, she offered 'no significant analysis relating to the effect of compulsion on individuals subject to such power'. He indicated that she, thus, had nothing to contribute to the primary concern of the proceedings.

Using similar assessments of the value of other expert testimony offered by FWTAO witnesses, Dr Baum effectively discounted the model of substantive equality put forward by the Federation. In the end he ruled that female teachers could not be forced to join an all-female union. Linda Logan Smith, one of the complainants, agreed with the judge's conception of equality, commenting to the press after the decision: 'You do not solve a problem by isolating yourself and trying to work in isolation. You have to get in there with a group as a whole to make the changes' (Daly, 1994: A9).

A Dissenting View: Differentiation Not Discrimination

To Federation leaders the decision represented a narrow interpretation of legal equality, one untouched by the evidence offered by experts. Barbara Sargent, the President of FWTAO at the time, commented to reporters: 'there appears to be no comprehension about the lack of equality for women and about the role this federation has played for 75 years' (Daly, 1994: A9). Evidence gathered from women who in recent years have researched the problems of accounting for difference was simply not judged to be relevant to the judgment of discrimination in the arena of Ontario's Human Rights Commission. Nor was the evidence given weight by the majority of the Ontario Divisional Court to which FWTAO appealed Dr Baum's decision. In its appeal the Federation asked to Court to review whether the Board of Inquiry under Dr Baum erred in concluding that By-Law I violated section 6 of the Code, and whether it erred in its management and consideration of the evidence. The latter question reflected the Federation's concern with the manner in which Dr Baum called evidence from both sides of the case. The Court upheld Dr Baum's methods noting that:

Hanne B. Mawhinney

While it may have been appropriate to call all of the evidence that both sides called in this case in what turned out to be the longest human rights case in Canadian history, in the final analysis the evidence of the history and of the experts was of very little assistance in determining the legal issues involved (Toronto Divisional Court, Court File No. 271/94, 273/94: 36).

The decision was not unanimous. J. Boland, the sole female judge dissented with the majority judgment. She argued that By-Law I did not contravene section 6 of the Ontario Human Rights Code, rather:

What we have here is not discrimination, but rather distinction without disadvantage. I believe that the Board erred in law in determining there was discrimination in the absence of a disadvantage or a real, material, and objective prejudice (Ontario Divisional Court, Court File No. 271/94, 273/94, J. Boland, dissenting: 2).

Madame Justice Boland observed that the evidence established that such disadvantage was not evident because Margaret Tomen and Linda Logan-Smith, like all elementary teachers in the province have extensive opportunities for professional interaction with their male colleagues, and additionally that they are not required to participate in the programs of FWTAO. She noted that while the complainants objected to being associated with affirmative action measures, the evidence established that 'amending By-Law I to provide for choice of affiliate membership for women public elementary teachers would have detrimental impact on FWTAO's ability to represent its members and carry out its agenda' (Ontario Divisional Court, Court File No. 271/94, 273/94, J. Boland, dissenting: 7).

Madame Justice Boland charged that the Board of Inquiry further erred in its interpretation of 'dignity interests' in the Human Rights Code. She argued:

The preamble [of the Code] simply confirms that dignity of the person lies at the heart of all human rights legislation . . . In other words, every act of discrimination is an affront to dignity but not every affront to dignity is a discriminatory act (Ontario Divisional Court, Court File No. 271/94, 273/94, J. Boland, dissenting: 1995: 7).

She further charged that Dr Baum erred in not following the direction of the Supreme Court of Canada which has stated that a finding of discrimination cannot be made in a vacuum. She observed that, 'Context is important. The context should be examined to clarify the rights and freedoms that are truly at stake and to properly assess any completing values . . . Dr Baum heard considerable evidence with respect to all of these factors and failed to take them into account and evaluate them in their historical, social and legal context' (p. 8). Madame Justice Boland concluded by observing that

Dr Baum may have lost sight of the real issues before him resulting in an interpretation of the Code that appears to give exclusive recognition to the rights of individuals and thereby reducing the equality rights of the other affiliates protected by the Code (1995: 11).

Lessons for Feminist Advocacy and Policy Analysis

The dissenting decision of Madame Justice Boland released June 21, 1995, left open the door for the FWTAO to mount an appeal to the judgment of the majority of Ontario Divisional Court. That appeal will be heard in November 1996, over a decade since the OPSTF first supported the model of equality and vision of how to deal with difference held by Margaret Tomen. The legality of compulsory membership in an all-women federation in face of equality provisions in Canadian jurisprudence remains undecided.

Although the story is unfinished, the advocacy approach which sustained the lawyers and leaders of FWTAO in these challenges offers important insights into a new feminist policy analysis supporting equality jurisprudence. The lawyers representing the Federation have described the preparation of the defense against the challenges of the OPSTF as a unique effort to develop a model of equality and a practice of legal argument and women's advocacy to support that model (Eberts *et al.*, 1991: 613–16). The question posed by the Tomen challenge is fundamental to, but also contested in, feminist thinking: how do we account for difference. Federation leaders decided to answer the question with an approach consistent with the principles of equality and social justice for women. They rejected the common practice of disadvantaged groups of hiring members of privileged groups to represent their interests in the courts. Instead of hiring male lawyers, the federation hired as co-counsels, Mary Eberts and Elizabeth Shilton Lennon, lawyers from different firms with complementary expertise respectively in women and equality and labor law. Instead of relying on clerks, the Federation provided these lawyers with access to the resources of a large group of feminist researchers and consultants. Moreover, Federation leaders became actively involved in every step of the case.

In the following concluding discussion I describe seven lessons for feminist policy analysis that can be taken from the efforts of the Federation:

- collective lawyering offers a 'power with' approach to feminist legal policy analysis;
- collective analysis of evidence creates a thoughtful basis for the development of feminist equality theory;
- feminist legal and policy analysis can be supported by archival evidence kept by women's organizations;
- oral advocacy by feminist legal and policy analysts is not genderless;
- advocates for women's equality in law can overcome the gender effects operating in courts by presenting evidence with authenticity and self regard;
- feminist policy analysis and advocacy can contribute to a reconstructed political theory based on a commitment to equality and the absence of oppression;

- an advocacy approach to feminist legal and policy analysis informed by theories of substantive equality can help to institutionalize women's voices in all domains of social life.

The case illustrates a refinement of collective lawyering processes that Canadian women lawyers have been developing particularly since the *Charter of Rights and Freedoms* became law. In a number of projects collectives of lawyers, law students and experts from the feminist research community have scrutinized existing law for barriers to women's equality. The FWTAO used its independence as an all-female organization to allocate its resources to support workshops bringing together these collectives, and to sponsor academic research on issues of relevance. Reflecting again a feminist conception of 'power with', the differences between legal advisors and federation advisees were invisible. A commentary on the process by participants observes: 'as the work progressed, practitioners evaluated academic work, academics made strategic suggestions, policy analysts directed research efforts and administrators participated in discussions of legal and political theory' (Eberts *et al.*, 1991: 614).

The collective lawyering process evolved during the two years of preparation for defense. Early on there was an anticipation that determining a conventional theory of equality would resolve the direction that lawyers could subsequently take. During the course of the preparation the focus of collective meetings shifted from more abstract discussions of constitutional law, to considerations of particular aspects of the FWTAO context and case. Eventually it became clear to those involved that a theory of equality was emerging from the particular functions of FWTAO. The legal and theoretical dimensions of the case developed from collective examinations of concrete evidence. The collective analysis of evidence created a more thoughtful basis for subsequent theoretical development.

The experiences of the collective which defended the OPSTF challenge to the Ontario Divisional Court, offer important directions for feminist policy analysis. The membership case reveals the importance of women's organizations being 'archival, to record their own reality, so that it can be analyzed as well as provide tools with which women can analyze other data and theory' (Eberts *et al.*, 1991: 616). The careful record which FWTAO had kept of its activities and the research on the status of women elementary teachers over the years which it had supported and recorded enabled the legal team to develop a historical argument for the special role it had played in promoting equality and social justice for women. Most important for all women, that historical record, and the analysis of it, joins the research sponsored by the Federation to support its case, in the case law on equality theory and women's rights.

An important lesson for feminist legal analysis is the judgment by Eberts and Lennon, based on their experience with the membership case, that oral advocacy by women lawyers is never genderless. In the case of women lawyers representing an all-women's federation's claim that it promotes equality, gender effects in the courtroom are particularly evident. Eberts and Lennon describe lawyering in this context as an exercise in advocacy for women. Yet in the law, they point out that the authority to speak comes from being credentialed in the male designed and dominated systems of training and jurisprudence. In the collective lawyering undertaken by FWTAO, the authority of the women advocates was 'grounded in research that had been designed by, for, and about women' (Eberts *et al.*, 1991: 615). The authority attributed to the FWTAO's evidentiary record derived from the status of the academic women who had themselves successfully navigated their own male-oriented credentialing systems. The expert evidence that these academics produced came at a personal risk to themselves. The experts who participated risked being marginalized as feminist researchers in the academic community, thus losing opportunities for tenure, promotion, security, honor and money.

The authority of women advocates presenting the membership case came not only from their evidence, but also from 'the authenticity and self-regard with which they presented the case' (1991: 616). At the same time Eberts and Lennon observe that 'everything has a double edge when the issue is sex equality, and women and men in the courtroom are both actors and ground' (p. 616). In this context women advocates confronted the challenge of presenting the research on sex discrimination in a way which did not deafen male judges to the real issues of women's equality. In the membership case that meant that Eberts and Lennon, the only women lawyers involved, had not only to convince the judge of their interpretations of the facts and issues at hand, but they also had to 'negotiate all the pitfalls of gender bias in the courtroom in order to keep the judge listening' (p. 616). They confronted the dilemma of representing through their very presence the gist of the claim brought to the appeal by Ms Tomen, that women do not need to have membership in an all-women federation to achieve equality, while at the same time demonstrating women's disadvantaged status often as victims with no authority. The lesson for feminist policy analysis is that women must learn to manage to be 'treated as equals while arguing that women are unequal' (p. 616). The case I have presented in this chapter suggests that the tensions these challenges create can have a profound effect on the outcomes of judicial interventions in resolving the question of what to do about the problem of difference. Women's evidence is not always heard even when presented by women lawyers engaged in collective lawyering and supported by scholarly evidence. Basic issues of social justice and equality are raised in this silencing.

Reconstructing Political Theory as Feminist Advocacy for Equality

The discourse on equality which I have outlined in this chapter underlines the challenges which a feminist policy analysis confronts in reconstructing a political theory with a basic commitment to equality and social justice. The meaning of equality is central to this reconstruction. In their recent feminist critique Elizabeth Fraser and Nicola Lacey call for a reconstructed political theory based on a commitment to equality and the absence of oppression. They state 'by equality we mean not merely formal equality or even equality of material resources, but rather a commitment to the idea that substantial differences of power and well-being themselves raise central issues of social justice wherever their correction is within the ambit of collective effort of social policy' (1993: 191). Fraser and Lacey propose that a concept of 'oppression' should replace the 'distributive paradigm' which has constructed justice as a problem of unjust distribution as the central element of political theory of social justice. They support Marion Young's (1990) analysis call for a political theory based not primarily on distributional notions of social justice but on a sophisticated notion of oppression and domination, conceived in terms of: exploitation, marginalization, powerlessness, cultural imperialism and violence. Fraser and Lacey (1993) argue that taking into account institutional processes such as these which generate unjust outcomes could support an 'adequate theory of the ways in which power is enacted in practices and discourses found in law, in education and other domains'.

The crucial point to be taken from Fraser and Lacey is their emphasis on power as discursive practices, not only property, and the implication this holds for a feminist policy analysis incorporating examinations of how social policies have as both an effect and an object, created changes in power relations (p. 194). Fraser and Lacey comment:

> Although the operation or exercise of power inevitably reduces the freedom of some, where it generates within democratically endorsed and accountable practices to achieve ends or realize goods to which the polity or the relevant group has collectively subscribed, power is used in a substantial sense in the interests of all and hence constitutes 'power with' as opposed to merely 'power over.' On this conception, power can be thought of as a vital social resource whose creation, allocation, and management in the serve of the social good is the primary concern of democratic politics (1993: 195).

A view of power as inherent in practices and discourses suggests that every aspect of social life must be open to political critique, thus generates a broader conception of the political, which Fraser and Lacey believe must bring with it reconstructed political institutions. Policy analysis framed from this broadened political theory would examine the role of a range of institutions 'designed to facilitate directly or indirectly people's access to deliberation and decision-making about the organization of social life' (1993: 196). Fraser and Lacey argue that only when a political theory is framed in a broadened conception of the persuasiveness of power will it be able to cast light on pervasively unequal distributions of social goods, and the persistence of powerlessness and the marginalization of certain social groups.

Reconstructed political analysis able to account for the issues of equity in the lives of women teachers acknowledges that social positions, identities and the operations of power on individuals are largely determined not only by the actions of those individuals, but by social relations and locations. I have shown in this chapter that one important set of social relations is located in courts where judgments are made about women's claims for equality and social justice. That the gender politics in courtrooms are so powerful yet so invisible, simply affirms the need for an advocacy approach to feminist legal and policy analysis informed by theories of substantive equality which help to institutionalize women's voices not their echoes in all domains of social life. The imperative for feminist policy analysts is clear: they must reinvent their methods and theories as if women mattered.

Notes

1 For a discussion of the political organization of collective educational rights in Canada, and in Ontario specifically see Mawhinney (1993).
2 See Mawhinney & LaRocque (1995) for a study of leadership of women teachers who are also trustee chairpersons of school boards in Canada.
3 Catharine MacKinnon is prominent in feminist legal scholarship in the United States and Canada.
4 Until 1974 Ontarion elementary teachers could obtain teaching diplomas from Teachers Colleges. However over 86 per cent of teachers in the province now hold at least one degree.
5 An Ontario Appeal Court will hear in November, 1996, the appeal of the FWTAO to a decision upholding the invalidation of compulsory membership to the federation made by the Ontario Human Rights Commission.

References

ACKER, S. (1989) *Teachers, Gender and Careers*, Basingstoke, Falmer Press.
ARNOT, M. and WEILER, K. (1993) *Feminism and Social Justice in Education: International Perspectives*, London, Falmer Press.
BAUM, D.J. (1994) *Board of Inquiry Final Decision*, Ontario Human Rights Commission.
BELL, C. and CHASE, S. (1993) 'The underrepresentation of women in school leadership', in MARSHALL, C. (Ed) *The New Politics of Race and Gender: The 1992 Yearbook of the Politics of Education Association*, London, Falmer Press, pp. 141–54.
BLACKMORE, J. and KENWAY, J. (1993) *Gender Matters in Educational Administration and Policy*, London, Falmer Press.
CHEVIGNY, B.G. (1984) 'Daughters writing: Toward a theory of women's biography', in ASCHER, C., DeSALVO, L. and RUDDICK, S. (Eds) *Between Women*, Boston, Beacon Press, pp. 357–81.
DALY, R. (1994, April 2) 'All-female union suffers setback from rights body', *The Toronto Star*, p. A9.
DUERST-LAHTI, G. and KELLY, R.M. (1995) *Gender Power, Leadership and Governance*, Ann Arbor, MI, The University of Michigan Press.
EBERTS, M., HENDERSON, F.I., LAHEY, K.A., MacKINNON, C., McINTYRE, S. and SHILTON, E.J. (1991) *The Case for Women's Equality: The Federation of Women Teachers' Associations of Ontario and the Canadian Charter of Rights and Freedoms*, Toronto, FWTAO.
FRAZER, E. and LACEY, N. (1993) *The Politics of Community: A Feminist Critique of the Liberal-communitarian Debate*, Toronto, University of Toronto Press.
GASKELL, J., McLAREN, A. and NOVOGRODSKY, M. (1989) *Claiming and Education: Feminism and Canadian Schools*, Toronto, Our Schools/Our Selves.
HAWKESWORTH, M. (1994) 'Policy studies within a feminist frame', *Policy Sciences*, **27**, pp. 97–118.

LABATT, M. (1993) *Always a Journey*, Toronto, FWTAO.

MARSHALL, C. (1993) *The New Politics of Race and Gender*, London, Falmer Press.

MARSHALL, C. and ANDERSON, G.L. (1995) 'Rethinking the public and private spheres: Feminist and cultural studies perspectives on the politics of education', in SCRIBNER, J.D. and LAYTON, D.H. (Eds) *The Study of Educational Politics*, London, Falmer Press, pp. 169–82.

MAWHINNEY, H.B. (1993) 'An advocacy coalition approach to change in Canadian education', in SABATIER, P.A. and JENKINS-SMITH, H.C. (Eds) *Policy Change and Learning: An Advocacy Coalition Approach*, Boulder, CO, Westview, pp. 59–82.

MAWHINNEY, H.B. and LaROCQUE, L. (1995) 'Women educators as school board chairpersons: Problematizing the public/private dimensions of leadership', in REYNOLDS, C. and YOUNG, B. (Eds) *Women and Leadership in Canadian Education*, Calgary, Detselig, pp. 225–41.

ONTARIO HUMAN RIGHTS CODE R.S.O. (1990) c.H. 19.

ONTARIO DIVISIONAL COURT (1995, March 27–31) File No. 271/94, 273/94.

REYNOLDS, C. and YOUNG, B. (1995) *Women and Leadership in Canadian Education*, Calgary, Deselig.

TEACHING PROFESSION ACT (1944) R.S.O. 1990, c.T-2.

VICKERS, J., RANKIN, P. and APPELLE, C. (1993) *Politics as if Women Mattered: A Political Analysis of the National Action Committee on the Status of Women*, Toronto, University of Toronto Press.

VICTOR, S. (1995) '"I felt like we were rats or something": the problem of imposition in participatory research', in JIPSON, J., MUNRO, P., VICTOR, S., FROUDE JONES, K. and FREED-ROWLAND, G. (Eds) *Repositioning Feminism and Education: Perspectives on Educating for Social Change*, Westport, CT, Bergin & Garvey, pp. 173–85.

WEILER, K. (1993) 'Feminism and the struggle for a democratic education: A view from the United States', in ARNOT, M. and WEILER, K. (Eds) *Feminism and Social Justice in Education: International Perspectives*, London, Falmer Press, pp. 210–25.

YOUNG, I.M. (1990) *Justice and the Politics of Difference*, Princeton, NJ, University Press.

Chapter 13

Improving Girls' Educational Outcomes*

Joanna Wyn and Bruce Wilson

Introduction

What kind of policy approach is most likely to improve significantly the outcomes of all girls? This has been a fundamental concern of feminist educators for many years. An important priority has been to investigate the reasons for discrimination against and differential achievement by girls and women in educational settings, their experiences in those settings, and strategies likely to bring about change. Since the 1970s the complexities of the situation have become more apparent (see Kenway, 1990). Women have learned much about what they share and what can be gained through collaborating with each other in the struggle for social change. At the same time, early assumptions about objectives and strategies have been undermined by the persistence of occupational segregation and the apparent determination by many girls and women to place a continuing priority on relationships and domestic concerns (Wilson and Wyn, 1987). Furthermore, it is now recognized that the experience of particular groups of girls and women is deeply influenced by their differing material and cultural circumstances; that to look at gender alone is insufficient and inadequate. The significant influence of other forms of social division (class and racial conflict, for example) in shaping the educational and social outcomes achieved by girls and women has been widely researched and clearly demonstrated. Educational policy has been increasingly influenced by the efforts of feminist teachers, policymakers and parents. The result of this influence and policy is evident in the feminist practices of many schools. These included, among much else, the use of single-sex classes, counter-sexist resources and support groups, and the development of particular classroom methods. However, despite all this laudable effort, it is not at all clear that it is achieving its desired effects. One of the reasons for this, in our view, is that policymakers and practitioners have failed to conceptualize their intentions adequately; more specifically, they have failed to clarify and identify the specific outcomes toward which they are working. Rather, intentions are couched in very vague generalities.

A focus on outcomes is important because it helps to draw attention to the vision of society that is implicit in particular policies or programme strategies. Too

---

* First published in Blackmore, J. and Kenway, J. (Eds) (1993) *Gender Matters in Educational Administration and Policy*, London, Falmer Press.

often, government policies have been framed in terms of only one perspective on an issue or problem, obscuring important dimensions of the process of bringing about social change. A discussion of outcomes raises questions about the legitimacy and the kind of contribution expected from particular groups in a society. In educational terms, the attempt to specify desirable common outcomes is vital because it offers a framework for analyzing the characteristics of personal and social life considered to be essential for all people to participate fully in their society. Even though the phrase *full participation* has been widely used in statements of policy objectives, there have been very few efforts to indicate what is meant in practical terms. We suggest that it is worthwhile exploring the concept of common outcomes; distinguishing the material from the cultural. This approach is explored in the latter stages of this chapter, but first, we shall take a look at major government policy on the education of girls.

A National Policy

In 1987 the Commonwealth Schools Commission released its *National Policy for the Education of Girls in Australian Schools* (NPEG). As it is this document which has continued to inform subsequent policies on girls' education in the various states of Australia, it is worth returning to it in order to assess its underlying attitude on the matter of outcomes. This policy drew on the experiences and reflections of teachers and policymakers in the decade after the publication of *Girls, Schools and Society*, Schools Commission (1975) – the document which began the national policy imperative to improve the education of girls. While drawing attention to the gains that have been made during that time, the report also identified continuing shortcomings in the education system.

The National Policy was a comprehensive and in many senses far-sighted document directed towards guiding the direction of change and the coordination of effort across states and across the public and private sectors. This document suggested that the main issue at stake was the provision of more equitable education for girls, which would encourage girls and women to participate more fully in all aspects of public life. In this document the Commission has consolidated Commonwealth policies, referring to 'full participation in society' as the aim of equal outcomes from schooling. However, the argument continues to reflect considerable inconsistency in its understanding of the concept of *equality*. Johnston (1983) identified four basic, different and to some extent contradictory logics of equality which have recurred in various ways in education policy documents subsequent to the Karmel Report (1973). All four logics of equality are represented in the NPEG's Shared Values and Principles and Shared Objectives to guide the development of programmes (Commonwealth Schools Commission, 1987). They are:

- a compensatory logic – defining the problem in terms of producing optimum mobility in a competitive, individualistic, market society.

In the NPEG, improving outcomes for girls is seen as necessary because of the continued relative inequities in girls' post-school opportunities, in terms of post-secondary education and access to employment, despite improving school retention rates;
- an equality of respect logic – stressing a notion of valuing people equally, based on their common humanity.

One of the shared values and principles of the NPEG is that girls and boys should be valued equally in all aspects of schooling. A shared objective is 'to provide a supportive and challenging school environment for learning in which girls and boys are equally valued and their needs equitably catered for' (1987: 34);
- a mainstreaming logic – subcultures require the resources and skills to be able to compete effectively in mainstream schooling.

The NPEG Report makes one of its shared objectives 'to ensure that boys and girls have equal access to and participation in a school curriculum which contributes to full and equal participation in economic and social life' (1987: 33). A further objective is: 'to ensure that school resource allocation policies and practices operate in ways which are consistent with principles of equity and relative need' (1987: 34); and
- power over circumstances – participating with others to change the circumstances that block the aspirations and hopes of identifiable social groups, whether the group identity be based on class, ethnicity or gender.

A shared value and principle of the NPEG is that 'schooling should reflect the entitlement of all women, in their own right, to personal respect, to economic security and to participation in and influence over decisions which affect their lives' (1987: 28).

The use of all four logics may not reflect confused thinking on the part of the Commission as much as an attempt to incorporate the approaches which have influenced policy to date. Each of the logics of equality has an important contribution to make to an understanding of these issues. However, the inherent confusion (and contradiction) among them makes it difficult to provide guidance for schools. The 'framework for action' provided by the NPEG Report is an attempt to translate the broad principles of social equity and good educational practice into practical suggestions about what can be done in schools to implement the policy.

The range of strategies that are suggested as a means for achieving the objectives cover all aspects of schooling, from the resources used in classrooms to the administrative structure itself. The National Policy suggested that fundamental curriculum review would have to take place if its objectives were to be implemented. A number of specific reforms are suggested, including changes to gender-stereotyped areas of the curriculum, change in particular curriculum areas to enhance girls' participation and achievement, and the development of a new curriculum to include significant areas of knowledge of particular significance to girls which are presently omitted. The document also suggested specific ways in which the school environment could become more supportive for girls, in terms of teaching practice and classroom management, school organization and practice, and the social, cultural and physical environment. Changes such as these would make schools a more comfortable ('girl-friendly') environment for girls and young women. What is not evident, however, is how and if these changes would affect outcomes from schooling.

The suggestions for change derive from a critique of schooling, and the Commission is relatively clear about what is not desirable. However, a vision of the outcomes that would be wanted is missing. Some clues are provided through the use of the terms 'equity' and 'equality', and in the aim to encourage girls and women to participate fully in all aspects of society. These ideas do not provide a coherent framework for action, however, and in this policy document simply serve to provide an umbrella which obscures the tensions between the four logics of equality. Because of this there are a number of issues which are taken for granted throughout.

Issues

The Commission aims to provide a national policy that would benefit all girls and women. What is meant by 'all girls and women'? This question can be answered by exploring three dimensions.

Are All Girls the Same?

In a number of places the NPEG acknowledges that girls and women bring with them a range of perspectives based not only on gender but also on class, ethnicity and race, which affect their experience of schooling. There is a tendency for cultural and language differences to be seen as something to be valued, rather more than something that can also provide the basis for disadvantage, liability and racism. The specific needs of particular groups of girls are largely seen to be catered for through affirmations of various sorts.

Although seen as a worthwhile goal, the aim of affirming cultural differences is barely supported. It is suggested that cultural differences may be affirmed through the teaching of community languages, by having regular and consistent contact between home and school, and by providing a framework for improving schooling that derives from 'a variety of cultural perspectives'. However, these ideas are contradicted in the Report's treatment of two further issues.

Individual or Group Goals?

The idea of affirming cultural differences supports the view that all girls and women are not the same. However, in some important respects the National Policy underestimates the existence of cultural and social groupings. Instead, the ideal of improving girls' self-esteem, self-confidence and identity is given prominence, leaving the onus for change with individuals. This may be helpful to some girls and women under certain circumstances, and it is an attractive strategy for dealing with the day-to-day issues of the classroom. The weakness of this approach is that it sidesteps the question of why it is that particular groups are systematically marginalized and exist in a less powerful relation to other groups. Furthermore, the reference to raising girls' self-esteem, self-confidence and identity has the effect of treating girls as a single category, all of whom it is assumed received the same 'treatment' (see Kenway and Willis, 1990).

Unless strategies for change consider the social and cultural context in which girls and women live, they may undermine the position of those who the policies are intended to help. For example, it is often assumed that young women who live in non-English-speaking households are subject to particularly sexist practices in the home. While this may be so in terms of feminist perspectives, there are strengths in the vision of womanhood to which these young women adhere and on which they rely. Such a strategy may also suggest a negative view of their cultures, to themselves and to others. It requires an especially sensitive approach to draw attention to the negative aspects of particular cultural practices while still maintaining their strengths. This means that rather than focusing on the individual student, it is necessary to help all students to develop an awareness of the ways in which social division in our society affects different groups.

A Deficit Approach

Recognizing diversity is also compromised if the problem to be solved is regarded as a deficiency in the experience, knowledge or skills of girls and women. This approach has been especially popular in discussions of the 'problem of girls and maths', (see articles by Bannister, 1993; and Kenway, 1993). Only relatively recently have some begun to question the current outcomes of mathematics teaching and to argue that the process of mathematics teaching and the mathematics curriculum itself should be substantially revised.

The Commission believes that special measures are needed to ensure that those programmes especially designed to combat educational disadvantages relating to poverty and to cultural differences or other factors such as geographical isolation and intellectual disabilities serve the needs of girls as well as boys (1987: 16).

This approach locates the blame for lack of educational achievement with individuals or 'disadvantaged groups' rather than with schooling practices. While it is important that schools have the resources they need to develop worthwhile programmes, the receiving of funding on the basis of disadvantaged groups should not result in a deficit view of these groups. This approach easily slides into a rationale for providing particular groups with special help, while leaving the mainstream curriculum untouched. This approach, too, avoids exploring the underlying power relationships between groups which create and maintain inequalities. It is in terms of this relationship that the question of outcomes should be framed.

Joanna Wyn and Bruce Wilson

Policy which consolidates the assumptions written into past documents does not go far enough in providing a sound basis for developing the future education of all girls and women. Because of their cultural perspectives, groups of girls and women continue to place a priority on concerns and relationships that are easily undermined and marginalized by schooling. Strategies are required which recognize the diversity of groups from which girls and women come while clearly delineating the future outcomes from schooling for all girls and women.

Outcomes

What is meant by 'educational and social outcomes' in this context? In the Australian debate the concept was drawn initially from the work of Halsey, who had attempted to clarify the concern with equality in the following terms:

> the goal should not be the liberal one of equality of access but equality of outcome for the median member of each identifiable non-educationally defined group, i.e., the average woman or negro or proletarian or rural dweller should have the same level of educational attainment as the average male, white, white-collar suburbanite (Halsey, 1972: 8; quoted in Karmel, 1973).

After its decade of experience with various types of programmes, the Commonwealth Schools Commission reiterated its commitment to the concept of equality of outcomes in *In the National Interest* (1985). This was an important contribution, as the rhetoric of 'equity' in the PEP programme had served to muddy the waters considerably. Did 'equity' mean fairness in terms of individual treatment, fairness to groups, did it imply a focus on access to a range of opportunities, or did it retain the determination to achieve more equal outcomes? The Commission reasserted the view that the concept of equality of outcomes

> emphasized the idea of distributing success more equally in schools, and not just seeking to impose social equality through schooling . . . public authorities should not merely ensure a necessary minimum of provisions, or even equality of provision, but should, where necessary, allocate resources and effort to reduce inequalities in achievements and in the social distribution of outcomes. The idea of inclusiveness and co-operation thus came to the fore (Schools Commission, 1987: 30).

In other words, 'equality of outcomes' was an approach which emphasized the valuing of all students and their backgrounds and encouraged learning strategies in which all students could participate equally and from which the outcomes would be equally worthwhile. The Commission tackled the criticisms that this approach implied a 'levelling down' and that individual differences were being ignored. They argued that these criticisms reflected a very narrow perception of the purposes of

244

education and suggested that all students were capable of excellent performance in their own terms. All children should be encouraged to have a vision of what is potentially achievable and should recognize that excellence can be displayed in many domains of life, not only through academic work.

What does this mean for girls? Girls' experience of schooling has shifted significantly in that their retention rates at least until the end of year 12 are now higher than for boys. The problem, to some significant extent, is that their representation in post-school course and training options and in specific fields of employment is significantly different from that of boys. Overcoming these patterns is not just a matter of educational reform; it requires a challenge to the nature of social division which affects society as a whole, specifically those structures and processes which render as marginal the experience and perspectives of girls and women, leaving them vulnerable both materially and culturally.

Common Outcomes

At the very least a statement of common outcomes should give priority to recognition of the social and cultural concerns valued by women. What follows is an attempt to signal a more comprehensive outline of the common outcomes that might be expected for all students, encompassing the priorities not only of girls but also other groups whose social and educational accomplishments are marginalized at present. It is assumed that the existence of significant material and cultural division in society would imply different curricula in order to ensure that the common outcomes were achieved.

Material Outcomes

This dimension of outcomes is concerned with the immediate and tangible evidence about what happens to young people when they leave school to enter adult life. The following categories reflect different kinds of interests and require further discussion to determine an appropriate order of priority. These are starting-points for such a discussion.

- *Retention rates, credentials, further education*
  At the present time there is a relatively clear and hierarchical kind of streaming built into the credentials with which young people leave school and the types of options which they subsequently have. It goes something like this:
    tertiary professional course
    tertiary course
    full-time, potentially stable employment
    trade training
    full-time employment

technical and further education (TAFE) course
traineeship (or similar)
part-time work
short-term training (public or private)
unemployment.

Within each of these levels, there is a further hierarchy, part of which is determined by the predominance of males or females in that particular type of course, profession or trade. If this approach is generally applicable, a number of questions arise:

a) What is the cut off point (in other words, which of these options are unacceptable)?

b) Are social characteristics such as gender, ethnicity or class significant in shaping the choices which young people themselves would make between these various options?

c) Would parents and students tend to agree/disagree with teachers on which were the preferred options?

d) What records do the schools have about which of these options are achieved by their students, at what point of time?

e) What kinds of specific assistance are provided by the schools in relation to each of these options?

- *Specific knowledge, skills (academic, legal, health, and so on)*
These outcomes are perhaps best related to the content of school curricula. They concern the kinds of knowledge included in the curriculum and their accessibility to all students, together with any information collected about student performance in demonstrating their particular capacities.

a) One strategy for examining this topic would be to look for records of performance in specific subjects such as women's studies, parenting, health and human relations, legal studies, work education, community studies, or similar subjects (where the intention is to address directly aspects of the students' present social circumstances and needs).

b) It may be that particular learning strategies such as action–research projects, cross-age tutoring or media projects provide a context where students can develop and acquire knowledge which relates directly to their own experience yet also provide a basis for critical examination of broader social structures and the possibilities of change. Indications of student involvement in these kinds of activities and the products subsequently produced might provide an avenue for assessing progress in these areas.

c) Another approach may emerge through home group or pastoral care sessions, where teachers can deal more informally with whatever matters seem to be important at the time, as well as providing a more systematic coverage of knowledge appropriate to adult practices. Teachers themselves would have to develop appropriate criteria for recording the kinds of learning undertaken by their students.

d) In some schools, of course, there are also specific staff whose responsibility is to deal with the immediate problems or crises that students may have; in some cases these can be developed as learning situations and records kept of the strategies adopted by students to improve their approach to handling specific situations.

- *Occupational record*
  This kind of information is presumably available in few, if any, schools. It is difficult to collect, and to be of use needs to be based on data obtained at least 18 months after the students have left (because of 'natural' unemployment and the early job-changing that many students do). However, ultimately the kind of occupation that a young person obtains and his or her commitment to the work are two of the best indicators that are available in order to assess whether the schools have had some distinct effect in improving the outcomes which their students might otherwise have expected to obtain. It would be particularly important to seek sufficient detail on the kinds of domestic commitments which young women have and how it affects their entry to the labor market.

- *Adequate housing*
  This aspect of student outcomes raises similar difficulties to those encountered in compiling occupational records. Nevertheless, given the significance of youth homelessness, it may be another useful means of assessing the outcomes achieved by young people as they become adult members of their society. Having adequate housing is closely related to income level but it also provides a tangible indicator of what young people have learned about their rights and their resourcefulness (and cooperativeness).

Cultural Outcomes

Cultural outcomes represent a much more difficult area when it comes to trying to develop appropriate criteria for assessing what has been achieved. These are the outcomes of schooling which reflect 'power over circumstances' (power over circumstances means participating with others to change the circumstances that block the aspirations and hopes of identifiable social groups, whether the group identity be based on class, ethnicity or gender (quoted earlier from Johnston, 1983: 26)).

- *Personal dignity*
  This reflects the priority of wanting young people to have a strong sense of themselves as individuals in a social context. It involves the twin components of self-esteem and confidence on the one hand, and articulateness and the capacity to express oneself in a thoughtful, honest and unthreatened way within a group. By the time that students reach high school much will already have happened to affect their sense of dignity; there is a great deal

of evidence which demonstrates the particular relevance of these issues for girls. Opportunities for expressing their opinions and undertaking activities which examine the circumstances of girls can contribute to enabling them to establish a new perspective on themselves. Observation of their participation in various decision-making or small-group situations can provide feedback on their growth in this regard.

- *Social legitimacy (sense of belonging)*
  Effective participation in social activities depends not only on the presence of personal dignity but also on the development of the sense of legitimacy that comes from feeling that one belongs to a group; that as a member of the group, or of society, a person has the right to exercise influence over its shape and over the important decisions which are to be made. While women and girls place a priority on relationships and cooperative activities, their identification with belonging to a group does not seem to extend to exercising the right to demand change. This kind of energy is channelled much more into coping than it is into changing the circumstances which oppress them.

- *Exercise personal and social power*
  The nature of the cultural outcomes achieved is most likely to be demonstrated in the action taken by young people to influence, as much as they can, the situations in which they find themselves and to provide constructive solutions to problems which they may encounter. Examples may be found well before they leave school:
  - dealing with personal relationships
  - choice about jobs or further education
  - negotiation with family
  - negotiation with employers
  - negotiation with landlords
  - join a political party or movement
  - involved in community activities
  - take action on own behalf with police, etc.
  - critical assessment of media (etc.) messages.

This discussion of outcomes and how they might be specified in order to provide more concrete directions for policy and programme development is inevitably tentative. However, this task should be seen as a high priority if policy development is to provide clearer guidelines for school-based action. The rhetoric of full participation in society simply does not help either to outline a vision of the kind of society that is desired or to suggest the scope of practical curriculum or organizational change.

If we are to develop and administer policy that improves the outcomes for all girls and women, it needs to be recognized that the common outcomes for which we aim affirm the strengths of girls and women from different class and cultural backgrounds. Given the existence of social division and the significance of people's own cultural perspectives, unless these differences are not only recognized but valued, particular categories of students will continue to be marginalized.

References

BANNISTER, H. (1993) 'Truths about assessment and the learning of girls: From gender difference to the production of gendered attainment', in BLACKMORE, J. and KENWAY, J. (Eds) *Gender Matters in Educational Administration and Policy*, London, Falmer Press.

COMMONWEALTH SCHOOLS COMMISSION (1985) *In the National Interest*, Canberra, Australian Government Publishing Service.

COMMONWEALTH SCHOOLS COMMISSION (1987) *National Policy for the Education of Girls in Australian Schools*, Canberra, Australian Government Publishing Service.

HALSEY, A.H. (Ed) (1972) *Educational Priority, Volume 1: EPA Problems and Policies*, London, HMSO.

JOHNSTON, K. (1983) 'A discourse for all seasons? An ideological analysis of the Schools Commission Reports, 1973–1981', *Australian Journal of Education*, 27, 1, pp. 17–32.

KARMEL, P.H. (Chairman) (1973) *Schools in Australia*, Canberra, Australian Government Publishing Service.

KENWAY, J. (1990) *Gender and Education Policy: A Call For New Directions*, Geelong, Deakin University Press.

KENWAY, J. (1993) 'Non-traditional Pathways: Are they the way to the future?', in BLACKMORE, J. and KENWAY, J. (Eds) *Gender Matters in Educational Administration and Policy*, London, Falmer Press.

KENWAY, J. and WILLIS, S. (Eds) (1990) *Hearts and Minds: Self-Esteem and the Schooling of Girls*, London, Falmer Press.

SCHOOLS COMMISSION (1975) P. KARMEL (Chair) *Girls, School and Society*, Canberra, Australian Government Printing Service.

WILSON, B. and WYN, J. (1987) *Shaping Futures: Youth Action for Livelihood*, Sydney, Allen and Unwin.

Notes on Contributors

Natalie Adams is an Assistant Professor in the Department of Curriculum, Foundations and Research at Georgia Southern University. She is the author of several articles related to female adolescents, feminist qualitative research and multicultural education. She is currently coauthoring a book entitled *Learning to Teach: A Critical Look at Field Experiences* which is an attempt to translate feminist, critical and postmodern perspectives into concrete practice in preservice teacher education. The chapter she has written for this book stems from her on-going journey (hence now her research interest) in trying to make sense of the code of femininity she was taught as a young woman growing up in the Deep South.

Madeleine Arnot is a University Lecturer in the Department of Education at the University of Cambridge. She has been working on the interrelations of gender, class and race in education for the last 20 years. Her publications range from sociological perspectives on educational inequalities (see *Schooling and Society; Education and the State; Voicing Concerns: Sociological Perspectives on Contemporary Educational Reforms*) as well as specifically on gender (see *Race and Gender: Equal Opportunities Policies in Education*; and with G. Weiner, *Gender and the Politics of Schooling: Gender Under Scrutiny; Women's Education in Europe*). Her main theoretical contributions are the concept of *gender codes* in the processes of social and cultural reproduction and the development of the concept of male hegemony in relation to family, schooling and the state. More recently she has used her international work with Spain, Greece, Portugal, Argentina, amongst others, to interpret the conditions for development of national equal opportunities policies.

Miriam David is Professor of Social Sciences and Director of the Social Sciences Research Centre at South Bank University, London. She has published extensively in books and journals on issues concerning the family and education. She is Executive Editor of *British Journal of the Sociology of Education* and Co-editor of *The Journal of Social Policy*.

Sandra (Sam) Hollingsworth is the Division Head for Teacher Education at San Jose State University, San Jose, California, and a former historian and classroom teacher. She has conducted longitudinal research on the impact of teacher education coursework on beginning teachers' professional needs in urban schools. She has been involved in professional development school arrangements, both at an urban site in Michigan and in multiple sites at international schools across Asia. Dr

Hollingsworth has designed and taught coursework in the areas of women's studies, curriculum theory, interdisciplinary social studies and critical literacy. Using the inquiry process of action research as a unifying theme across these areas, she has published two books, coauthored many articles with teachers, spoken extensively and organized national and international conferences.

Julie Laible is an Assistant Professor of Administration and Educational Leadership at The University of Alabama. Her areas of interest include minority student school success, educational policy, qualitative research, collaborative inquiry, gender issues, and white racism. As a secondary Spanish teacher, community organizer, research assistant, professor, daughter, sister, and friend, Laible has experienced and recognized, in several cultures, how policy and everyday micropractices/social norms serve to oppress women and people of color and devalue their ways of knowing and being. In an effort to assist marginalized groups, including women, to gain more voice, Laible's current research focuses on what works educationally for Mexican-American females in Texas/Mexico border schools and for African-American females in Southern rural schools. Additionally, Laible is exploring the experiences of female assistant professors in traditional southern universities. Overall, Laible's research and culturally relevant theories promote the values of social justice, equity, and radical inclusiveness in diverse educational settings.

Catherine Marshall is Professor of Educational Policy and Leadership at the University of North Carolina, Chapel Hill, North Carolina, having started her career as a public school teacher. Her areas of expertise are displayed in titles of some of her publications, such as *Designing Qualitative Research, Culture and Educational Policy in the American States, The Assistant Principal, The New Politics of Race and Gender*, and *The Administrative Career*. Her observervations at all levels of education are the motivators for this book, providing a link between hers and others' observations of: seeing women's history and feminist theory placed at the margins in schooling; watching gender equity policy slippage; watching 'caring' professions being devalued; puzzling over her field's resistance to women in leadership, and increasingly seeing the connection to policy analysis. She is currently analyzing special education policy implementation and also writing up her observations of the cultural origins for the differences between gender equity policy in the US and Australia.

Hanne B. Mawhinney is Associate Professor in the Faculty of Education, University of Ottawa, Canada, responsible for a graduate professional development program. Her interest in women leaders at the margins of power in education emerged from her encounters with exceptional women teachers who have sustained and supported the professional growth of teachers by their own efforts, and from her own experiences as a classroom teacher. As a young teacher fresh from teaching in the hotbed of innovation in Vancouver, British Columbia in the 1970s, she first encountered the FWTAO women whom she writes about in this chapter while teaching in an isolated Northern Ontario community. The visit to her classroom of the President of the FWTAO one frigid January day stands out as the only time in her two years in the community where her efforts to infuse west coast innovations were recognized. That small act made a large difference in her view of who she was and what she could do. Years later, her career as an academic studying collaborative processes brought her to the Banff Short Course on Leadership as an instructor. Among those attending were women leaders of federations from across the country. The group of women from the FWTAO who decided that the course needed to model collaboration reminded her of the power of collective action. Her chapter is dedicated to the Hannrahan Sisters who challenged gender bias in education at the highest level with such panache.

Lesley Parker is an Associate Professor in the Teaching Learning Group at Curtin University of Technology in Western Australia. She is also the Assistant Director of Australia's National Key Centre for Teaching and Research in School Science and Mathematics. She has dedicated much of her research and professional practice to the enhancement of gender equity at all levels of education. She has published widely in the areas of curriculum and assessment reform, professional development of educators, critical issues in higher education, and policy and practice in the area of gender equity. She has played a major role in several major committees of enquiry into education at both state and national levels in Australia, alerting policymakers and practitioners to the need for system-wide change to address current inequities in education systems.

Wanda S. Pillow is an Assistant Professor of Educational Leadership and Cultural Foundations at the University of North Carolina at Greensboro, NC, where she teaches organizational theory, qualitative inquiry, feminist theory and policy courses. For the past four years she has been involved in research on teen pregnancy policies and programs and is committed to continuing to explore, analyze and voice how attention to and avoidance of gender impacts policy theory and development.

Parlo Singh lectures in the Sociology of Education at the Mt. Gravatt Campus of Griffith University. Her current Australian Research Council funded project examines the construction of identities through language and literacy practices in schools, communities and workplaces for Australian-Taiwanese and Australian-Samoan secondary school students.

Nelly P. Stromquist is a professor in the School of Education and a Faculty Affiliate in the Center for Feminist Reserch at the University of Southern California. She received her PhD in Education from Stanford University and specializes in gender issues, including education for empowerment, adult literacy, and government policies and practices in girls' and women's education. Her main geographical areas are Latin America and West Africa. She has published widely, both in the US and internationally. Recent publicatons include: *Literacy for Citizenship: Gender and Grassroots Dynamics in Brazil*, and *Gender Dimensions in Education in Latin America*. She is also the editor of *Encyclopedia of Third World Women*, a collection of about 80 articles on various issues of gender and development.

Gaby Weiner is professor of educational research at South Bank University, London, UK. Involved with feminist issues since the late 1960s, she has tried to bridge the personal and political sides of her life by writing about feminist issues in education. She has published widely on equal opportunities and gender, writing and editing a number of books and research reports. She is currently co-editor (with Lyn Yates and Kathleen Weiler) of the Open University Press series Feminist Educational Thinking. Her most recent publications are: *Feminisms in Education: An Introduction*, *Equal Opportunities in Colleges and Universities* and *Educational Reform and Gender Equality in Schools*.

Lois Weis is Professor of Sociology of Education at State University of New York, Buffalo. She is the author, editor or co-author of numerous books and articles, including *Working Class Without Work* (Routledge), *Beyond Silenced Voices: Class, Race and Gender in US Books* (SUNY Press), and the forthcoming *Off White* (Routledge). Most currently she is working on a Spencer Foundation project with Michelle Fine in which they capture the narrations of poor and working-class African America, Latino/Latina, and white young adults as they make their way through the American contradiction in the late twentieth century. Michelle and Lois are currently writing up the result of this study for Beacon Press.

Bruce Wilson is Director of the Union Research Centre on Organisation and Technology, Royal Melbourne Institute of Technology, Australia. His current research interests are focused on participative design approaches to organization and change and the implications for managers and workers. He is co-author *of Confronting School and Work, Shaping Futures, For Their Own Good* and *Pink Collar Clues: Gender, Technology and Work.*

Johanna Wyn is an Associate Professor in Education at the University of Melbourne, and Director of the Youth Research Centre. Her research interests are focused on the social and economic processes that affect young people's lives, particularly in relation to the social divisions of gender and social class. She is co-author of *Shaping Futures* and *Rethinking Youth*, as well as numerous monographs and articles.

Lyn Yates is an Associate Professor of Education and Director of Women's Studies at La Trobe University in Melbourne, Australia. She has written widely on inequality, feminist theory, curriculum and Australian education policy and practice and is the author of *Theory/Practice Dilemmas: Knowledge, Gender and Education* (Deakin University, 1991) and *The Education of Girls: Policy, Research and the Question of Gender* (Acer) and the edited collection, *Feminism and Education* (La Trobe University Press).

Index